# 2024

# BARRON'S

### THE TRUSTED NAME IN TEST PREP

# AP

# Computer
# Science A

## PREMIUM

Roselyn Teukolsky, M.S.

AP® is a registered trademark of the College Board, which is not affiliated with
Barron's and was not involved in the production of, and does not endorse, this product.

## Acknowledgments

Many people helped in the creation of this book.

I would like to thank my incredible editor, Samantha Karasik, for her expertise and assurance in taking the reins of the project. Thanks also to Megan Buckman, Christine Ricketts, Jeff Batzli, Alison Maresca, Jalisa Valladares, Mandy Luk, and all the other members of the Kaplan staff who worked on the production of the book and online tests.

I am most grateful to my former editors, Linda Turner and Annie Bernberg, for their friendly guidance and moral support over the years.

A very special thank you to Sage Miller for her careful reading of the manuscript and her valuable suggestions. Thanks also to Judy Hromcik and Richard Kick for their contributions over the years.

My husband, Saul, continues to be my partner in this project—typesetting the manuscript, producing the figures, and giving advice and moral support.

Thank you to the computer science teachers who taught AP Computer Science during the pandemic under very difficult circumstances. This book is dedicated to you.

Published by Kaplan North America, LLC, d/b/a Barron's Educational Series
1515 W. Cypress Creek Road
Fort Lauderdale, FL 33309
**www.barronseduc.com**

ISBN: 978-1-5062-8791-1

10 9 8 7 6 5 4 3 2 1

Kaplan North America, LLC, d/b/a Barron's Educational Series print books are available at special quantity discounts to use for sales promotions, employee premiums, or educational purposes. For more information or to purchase books, please call the Simon & Schuster special sales department at 866-506-1949.

# About the Author

**Roselyn Teukolsky** has an M.S. degree from Cornell University, and has been teaching programming and computer science since 1980. She has published articles in *The Mathematics Teacher* and in the National Council of Teachers of Mathematics Yearbook, and is the author of Barron's *ACT Math and Science Workbook* and co-author of Barron's *SAT 1600: Aiming for the Perfect Score*. The awards she has received include the Edyth May Sliffe Award for Distinguished Mathematics Teaching and the Alfred Kalfus Distinguished Coach Award from the New York State Math League (NYSML). For several years, Ms. Teukolsky served as a Reader for AP Computer Science.

Ms. Teukolsky started teaching AP Computer Science when the programming language was Pascal, the first language used for the exam. By the time she wrote this book (in 1997), software development was moving toward object-oriented programming and the language of the AP exam had switched to C++. In 2004 the language of the exam changed yet again, to Java. For more than 20 years, Ms. Teukolsky has kept this book—in its many incarnations—up to date.

# Table of Contents

# How to Use This Book

## Introduction

The introduction to this book provides an overview of the format and content of the AP Computer Science A exam.

## Diagnostic Test

The full-length practice test at the start of this book serves as a diagnostic test. It is accompanied by a diagnostic chart that identifies the topic related to each multiple-choice question and the page in the review chapters that discusses that topic. Detailed answer explanations are provided for all multiple-choice questions, and complete solutions and scoring rubrics are supplied for the free-response questions. You can also use this test as a practice test once you have completed your review.

## Review and Practice

Chapter 1 features tips and advice for tackling the multiple-choice and free-response questions on the exam.

Chapters 2 through 9 each contain a comprehensive review of a topic, multiple-choice practice questions that test your understanding of that topic, and detailed answer explanations for all questions. These questions are designed to help you review parts of the Java subset you should know for test day. A few questions are not typical AP exam questions—for example, questions that test low-level details of syntax. Most of these practice questions, however, and all the multiple-choice questions in the diagnostic and practice tests are representative of actual exam questions. Note that several groups of these practice questions are preceded by a single piece of code to which the questions refer. Be aware that the AP exam will usually restrict the number of questions per code example to two.

In both the text and questions/explanations, a special code font is used for parts of the text that are Java code.

```
//This is an example of code font
```
A different font is used for pseudocode.

< *Here is pseudocode font.* >

All features of Java that are likely to be tested on the AP exam are covered in this book, including arrays, two-dimensional arrays, strings, list processing, and inheritance in object-oriented programming. A small number of optional topics that are not part of the AP Java subset are included because they are useful for the free-response questions. Sections in the review text and multiple-choice questions that are optional topics are clearly marked as such.

## Practice Tests

This book concludes with two full-length practice tests that mirror the actual exam in format and content. Each test is followed by an answer key and detailed explanations for the multiple-choice questions and complete solutions and scoring rubrics for the free-response questions.

Once you complete a test, you may wish to calculate your approximate AP score. Use the scoring worksheet provided on the back of the answer sheet.

## Online Practice

There are three additional full-length practice tests online. You may take these tests in practice (untimed) mode or in timed mode. All multiple-choice questions are accompanied by detailed answer explanations, and there are complete solutions and scoring rubrics for the free-response questions.

## For Students

This book is designed to prepare you for the AP Computer Science A exam. It would typically be used upon completion of an AP course. However, since it contains a complete summary of all exam topics, you can use it for self-study throughout the school year, along with a suitable textbook. You can also use this book as a supplement to a first-semester college course where Java is the programming language.

Before the AP exam, study the tips in Chapter 1 and attempt as many of the practice tests as you can. Be sure to check out the appendix at the end of the book, which provides a glossary of useful computer terms that occasionally appear on the exam. One final hint: try the questions before you peek at the answers. Best of luck on exam day!

## For Teachers

This book covers the course and exam format outlined in the latest AP Computer Science A Course and Exam Description. It provides a review of object-oriented programming, algorithm analysis, and data structures. You can use this book as a resource in a high school class or an introductory college course, or you can assign practice questions as homework or test material.

# BARRON'S ESSENTIAL 5

As you review the content in this book to work toward earning that **5** on your AP COMPUTER SCIENCE A exam, here are five things that you **MUST** know above everything else:

**Learn the basics.** These are presented in Chapter 2. Every AP exam question uses these features. On the exam, free-response Question 1 will likely focus on control structures. Be familiar with:

- Identifiers: Rules for naming variables and methods
- Types: Primitive or built-in types versus reference types
- Operators: Arithmetic, relational, logical, assignment, and increment and decrement
- Control structures: conditionals with `if` and `if...else`, `for` loops, enhanced `for` loops, `while` loops, and nested loops

**Understand strings.** The `String` class is featured near the beginning of Chapter 5. You must be able to manipulate strings, which are sprinkled throughout the multiple-choice section of the AP exam, and will be featured in at least one free-response question. Be familiar with:

- Constructing `String` objects
- Concatenation of strings using the + operator
- Comparison of strings
- `String` methods `length`, `substring(start)`, `substring(start, end)`, `indexOf(str)`

**Study objects, classes, and inheritance.** These are discussed in Chapters 3 and 4. On the exam, free-response Question 2 will involve classes. You may have to write your own class or subclass. Be familiar with:

- Methods: Constructors, accessors, mutators, and overloaded methods
- Superclasses and subclasses: Inheritance
- Polymorphism: Dynamic binding, overridden methods, and the keyword `super`

**Know lists and arrays.** These are found in Chapter 7. This chapter, which features one-dimensional arrays, two-dimensional arrays, and `ArrayLists`, is crucial for the AP exam. You must learn to manipulate a list: search for a given item, delete an item, insert an item. On the exam, free-response Question 3 will involve an array or `ArrayList`. Free-response Question 4 will involve a 2D array. Be familiar with:

- One-dimensional arrays
- `ArrayList`, and the methods `size`, `add`, `get`, `set`, and `remove`
- Two-dimensional arrays. You must learn to access the elements using

    - Row-column traversal
    - Standard and enhanced `for` loops
    - Traversal of major and minor diagonals
    - Row-by-row array processing

---

**Understand sorting and searching.** The required sorting and searching algorithms are discussed in detail in Chapter 9. Without memorizing code, you must know how these algorithms work. Questions about sorting and searching often come up in the multiple-choice section of the AP exam, and may be featured in free-response questions. Be familiar with:

- Selection sort
- Insertion sort
- Merge sort
- Sequential search
- Binary search

# Introduction

*Computer Science: The boring art
of coping with a large number of trivialities.*
—*Stan Kelly-Bootle,* The Devil's DP Dictionary *(1981)*

The AP Computer Science A exam is a three-hour written exam. No books, calculators, or computers are allowed! The exam consists of two parts that have equal weight:

- Section I: 40 multiple-choice questions in 1 hour and 30 minutes

- Section II: 4 free-response questions in 1 hour and 30 minutes

Section I is scored by machine—you will bubble your answers with a pencil on a mark-sense sheet. Each question correctly answered is worth 1 point. There are no deductions for incorrect answers, and a question left blank is ignored.

Section II is scored by human readers—you will write your answers in a booklet provided. Free-response questions typically involve writing methods in Java to solve a given problem. Sometimes there are questions analyzing algorithms or designing and modifying data structures. You may be asked to write or design an entire class. To ensure consistency in the grading, each grader follows the same rubric, and each of your four answers may be examined by more than one reader. Each question is worth 9 points, with partial credit awarded where applicable. Your name and school are hidden from the readers.

Your raw score for both sections is converted to an integer score from 1 to 5, where 1 represents "Not at all qualified" and 5 represents "Extremely well qualified." Be aware that the awarding of AP credit varies enormously from college to college. The exam covers roughly a one-semester introductory college course.

The language of the AP exam is Java. Only a subset of the Java language will be tested on the exam. In writing your solutions to the free-response questions, however, you may use any Java features, including those that are not in the AP subset. For a complete description of this subset, visit the College Board website. **Every language topic in this review book is part of the AP Java subset unless explicitly stated otherwise. Note that the entire subset is covered in the book.**

For both the multiple-choice and free-response sections of the exam, there will be a Quick Reference in the appendix. You can look at this ahead of time by consulting the "AP Computer Science A Java Quick Reference" document on the College Board website.

> There is no penalty for wrong answers on the multiple-choice section.

# Diagnostic Test

The test that follows has the same format as that used on the actual AP exam. There are two ways you may use it:

1. As a diagnostic test before you start reviewing. A diagnostic chart that relates each question to sections that you should review follows the answer key.
2. As a practice test when you have completed your review.

Complete explanations are provided for each solution for both the multiple-choice and free-response questions.

## Section I

1. Ⓐ Ⓑ Ⓒ Ⓓ Ⓔ
2. Ⓐ Ⓑ Ⓒ Ⓓ Ⓔ
3. Ⓐ Ⓑ Ⓒ Ⓓ Ⓔ
4. Ⓐ Ⓑ Ⓒ Ⓓ Ⓔ
5. Ⓐ Ⓑ Ⓒ Ⓓ Ⓔ
6. Ⓐ Ⓑ Ⓒ Ⓓ Ⓔ
7. Ⓐ Ⓑ Ⓒ Ⓓ Ⓔ
8. Ⓐ Ⓑ Ⓒ Ⓓ Ⓔ
9. Ⓐ Ⓑ Ⓒ Ⓓ Ⓔ
10. Ⓐ Ⓑ Ⓒ Ⓓ Ⓔ
11. Ⓐ Ⓑ Ⓒ Ⓓ Ⓔ
12. Ⓐ Ⓑ Ⓒ Ⓓ Ⓔ
13. Ⓐ Ⓑ Ⓒ Ⓓ Ⓔ
14. Ⓐ Ⓑ Ⓒ Ⓓ Ⓔ

15. Ⓐ Ⓑ Ⓒ Ⓓ Ⓔ
16. Ⓐ Ⓑ Ⓒ Ⓓ Ⓔ
17. Ⓐ Ⓑ Ⓒ Ⓓ Ⓔ
18. Ⓐ Ⓑ Ⓒ Ⓓ Ⓔ
19. Ⓐ Ⓑ Ⓒ Ⓓ Ⓔ
20. Ⓐ Ⓑ Ⓒ Ⓓ Ⓔ
21. Ⓐ Ⓑ Ⓒ Ⓓ Ⓔ
22. Ⓐ Ⓑ Ⓒ Ⓓ Ⓔ
23. Ⓐ Ⓑ Ⓒ Ⓓ Ⓔ
24. Ⓐ Ⓑ Ⓒ Ⓓ Ⓔ
25. Ⓐ Ⓑ Ⓒ Ⓓ Ⓔ
26. Ⓐ Ⓑ Ⓒ Ⓓ Ⓔ
27. Ⓐ Ⓑ Ⓒ Ⓓ Ⓔ
28. Ⓐ Ⓑ Ⓒ Ⓓ Ⓔ

29. Ⓐ Ⓑ Ⓒ Ⓓ Ⓔ
30. Ⓐ Ⓑ Ⓒ Ⓓ Ⓔ
31. Ⓐ Ⓑ Ⓒ Ⓓ Ⓔ
32. Ⓐ Ⓑ Ⓒ Ⓓ Ⓔ
33. Ⓐ Ⓑ Ⓒ Ⓓ Ⓔ
34. Ⓐ Ⓑ Ⓒ Ⓓ Ⓔ
35. Ⓐ Ⓑ Ⓒ Ⓓ Ⓔ
36. Ⓐ Ⓑ Ⓒ Ⓓ Ⓔ
37. Ⓐ Ⓑ Ⓒ Ⓓ Ⓔ
38. Ⓐ Ⓑ Ⓒ Ⓓ Ⓔ
39. Ⓐ Ⓑ Ⓒ Ⓓ Ⓔ
40. Ⓐ Ⓑ Ⓒ Ⓓ Ⓔ

## How to Calculate Your (Approximate) AP Computer Science A Score

**Multiple-Choice**

Number correct (out of 40)   =   _____   ⟸   Multiple-Choice Score

**Free-Response**

Question 1   _____
(out of 9)

Question 2   _____
(out of 9)

Question 3   _____
(out of 9)

Question 4   _____
(out of 9)

Total   _____   ×   1.11   =   _____   ⟸   Free-Response Score
(Do not round.)

**Final Score**

_____   +   _____   =   _____

| Multiple- | Free- | Final Score |
| Choice | Response | (Round to nearest |
| Score | Score | whole number.) |

### Chart to Convert to AP Grade
### Computer Science A

| Final Score Range | AP Grade[a] |
| --- | --- |
| 62–80 | 5 |
| 47–61 | 4 |
| 37–46 | 3 |
| 29–36 | 2 |
| 0–28 | 1 |

[a]The score range corresponding to each grade varies from exam to exam and is approximate.

# Diagnostic Test

## COMPUTER SCIENCE A
## SECTION I

**Time—1 hour and 30 minutes**
**40 Questions**

**DIRECTIONS:** Determine the answer to each of the following questions or incomplete statements, using the available space for any necessary scratchwork. Then decide which is the best of the choices given and fill in the corresponding oval on the answer sheet. Do not spend too much time on any one problem.

**NOTES:**

- Assume that the classes in the Quick Reference have been imported where needed.
- Assume that variables and methods are declared within the context of an enclosing class.
- Assume that method calls that have no object or class name prefixed, and that are not shown within a complete class definition, appear within the context of an enclosing class.
- Assume that parameters in method calls are not `null` unless otherwise stated.

1. Consider this inheritance hierarchy, in which Novel and Textbook are subclasses of Book.

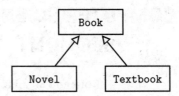

Which of the following is a false statement about the classes shown?

(A) The Textbook class can have private instance variables that are in neither Book nor Novel.

(B) Each of the classes—Book, Novel, and Textbook—can have a method computeShelfLife, whose code in Book and Novel is identical, but different from the code in Textbook.

(C) If the Book class has private instance variables title and author, then Novel and Textbook cannot directly access them.

(D) Both Novel and Textbook inherit the constructors in Book.

(E) If the Book class has a private method called readFile, this method may not be accessed in either the Novel or Textbook classes.

2. A programmer is designing a program to catalog all books in a library. She plans to have a `Book` class that stores features of each book: `author`, `title`, `isOnShelf`, and so on, with operations like `getAuthor`, `getTitle`, `getShelfInfo`, and `setShelfInfo`. Another class, `LibraryList`, will store an array of `Book` objects. The `LibraryList` class will include operations such as `listAllBooks`, `addBook`, `removeBook`, and `searchForBook`. What is the relationship between the `LibraryList` and `Book` classes?

   (A) Composition
   (B) Inheritance
   (C) Independent classes
   (D) Polymorphism
   (E) `ArrayList`

3. Consider the following code segment, which is intended to add zero to the end of `list` every time a certain condition is met. You may assume that `list` is an `ArrayList<Integer>` that contains at least one element.

```
for (Integer num : list)
{
    if (< condition >)
        list.add(0);
}
```

   Which of the following errors is most likely to occur?

   (A) `ArrayIndexOutOfBoundsException`
   (B) `IndexOutOfBoundsException`
   (C) `NullPointerException`
   (D) `ConcurrentModificationException`
   (E) `ArithmeticException`

Questions 4 and 5 refer to the Card and Deck classes shown below.

```java
public class Card
{
    private String suit;
    private int value;      //0 to 12

    public Card(String cardSuit, int cardValue)
    { /* implementation */ }

    public String getSuit()
    { return suit; }

    public int getValue()
    { return value; }

    public String toString()
    {
        String faceValue = "";
        if (value == 11)
            faceValue = "J";
        else if (value == 12)
            faceValue = "Q";
        else if (value == 0)
            faceValue = "K";
        else if (value == 1)
            faceValue = "A";
        if (value >= 2 && value <= 10)
            return value + " of " + suit;
        else
            return faceValue + " of " + suit;
    }
}

public class Deck
{
    private Card[] deck;
    public final static int NUMCARDS = 52;

    public Deck()
    { ...

    /** Simulate shuffling the deck. */
    public void shuffle()
    { ...

    //Other methods are not shown.
}
```

4. Which of the following represents correct /* *implementation* */ code for the constructor in the Card class?

(A) ```
suit = cardSuit;
value = cardValue;
```

(B) ```
cardSuit = suit;
cardValue = value;
```

(C) ```
Card = new Card(suit, value);
```

(D) ```
Card = new Card(cardSuit, cardValue);
```

(E) ```
suit = getSuit();
value = getValue();
```

5. Consider the implementation of a writeDeck method that is added to the Deck class.

```
/** Write the cards in deck, one per line. */
public void writeDeck()
{
    /* implementation code */
}
```

Which of the following is correct /* *implementation code* */?

I. ```
System.out.println(deck);
```

II. ```
for (Card card : deck)
        System.out.println(card);
```

III. ```
for (Card card : deck)
        System.out.println((String) card);
```

(A) I only
(B) II only
(C) III only
(D) I and III only
(E) II and III only

GO ON TO THE NEXT PAGE

6.  Refer to the following method that finds the smallest value in an array.

```
/** Precondition: arr is an array of nonzero length
 *                and is initialized with int values.
 *  @param arr the array to be processed
 *  @return the smallest value in arr
 */
public static int findMin(int[] arr)
{
    int min = /* some value */;
    int index = 0;
    while (index < arr.length)
    {
        if (arr[index] < min)
            min = arr[index];
        index++;
    }
    return min;
}
```

Which replacement(s) for /* *some value* */ will always result in correct execution of the findMin method?

I. Integer.MIN_VALUE

II. Integer.MAX_VALUE

III. arr[0]

(A) I only
(B) II only
(C) III only
(D) I and III only
(E) II and III only

7. Consider the following loop, where n is some positive integer.

```
for (int i = 0; i < n; i += 2)
{
    if (/* test */)
        /* perform some action */
}
```

In terms of n, which Java expression represents the maximum number of times that /* *perform some action* */ could be executed?

(A) n / 2
(B) (n + 1) / 2
(C) n
(D) n - 1
(E) (n - 1) / 2

8. A method is to be written to search an array for a value that is larger than a given item and return its index. The problem specification does not indicate what should be returned if there are several such values in the array. Which of the following actions would be best?

(A) The method should be written on the assumption that there is only one value in the array that is larger than the given item.
(B) The method should be written so as to return the index of every occurrence of a larger value.
(C) The specification should be modified to indicate what should be done if there is more than one index of larger values.
(D) The method should be written to output a message if more than one larger value is found.
(E) The method should be written to delete all subsequent larger items after a suitable index is returned.

9. When will method `whatIsIt` cause a stack overflow (i.e., cause computer memory to be exhausted)?

```
public static int whatIsIt(int x, int y)
{
    if (x > y)
        return x * y;
    else
        return whatIsIt(x - 1, y);
}
```

(A) Only when x < y

(B) Only when x ≤ y

(C) Only when x > y

(D) For all values of x and y

(E) The method will never cause a stack overflow.

10. The boolean expression `a[i] == max || !(max != a[i])` can be simplified to

(A) `a[i] == max`

(B) `a[i] != max`

(C) `a[i] < max || a[i] > max`

(D) `true`

(E) `false`

11. Consider the following code segment.

```
int[][] mat = {{3,4,5},
               {6,7,8}};

int sum = 0;
for (int[] arr: mat)
{
    for (int n = 0; n < mat.length; n++)
        sum += arr[n];
}
```

What is the value of `sum` as a result of executing the code segment?

(A) 9

(B) 11

(C) 13

(D) 20

(E) 33

12. Consider a `Clown` class that has a no-argument constructor.    Suppose a list `ArrayList<Clown>` list is initialized.    Which of the following will not cause an `IndexOutOfBoundsException` to be thrown?

    (A)   `for (int i = 0; i <= list.size(); i++)`
             `list.set(i, new Clown());`

    (B)   `list.add(list.size(), new Clown());`

    (C)   `Clown c = list.get(list.size());`

    (D)   `Clown c = list.remove(list.size());`

    (E)   `list.add(-1, new Clown());`

**GO ON TO THE NEXT PAGE**

Refer to the following class for Questions 13 and 14.

```
public class Tester
{
    private int[] testArray;

    public Tester()
    {
        testArray = new int[3];
        testArray[0] = 3;
        testArray[1] = 4;
        testArray[2] = 5;
    }

    /** @param n an int to be incremented by 1 */
    public void increment (int n)
    { n++; }

    public void firstTestMethod()
    {
        for (int i = 0; i < testArray.length; i++)
        {
            increment(testArray[i]);
            System.out.print(testArray[i] + " ");
        }
    }

    public void secondTestMethod()
    {
        for (int element : testArray)
        {
            increment(element);
            System.out.print(element + " ");
        }
    }
}
```

13. What output will be produced by invoking firstTestMethod for a Tester object?

    (A)  3 4 5
    (B)  4 5 6
    (C)  5 6 7
    (D)  0 0 0
    (E)  No output will be produced. An ArrayIndexOutOfBoundsException will be thrown.

14. What output will be produced by invoking secondTestMethod for a Tester object, assuming that testArray contains 3,4,5?

    (A)  3 4 5
    (B)  4 5 6
    (C)  5 6 7
    (D)  0 0 0
    (E)  No output will be produced. An ArrayIndexOutOfBoundsException will be thrown.

GO ON TO THE NEXT PAGE

Questions 15–17 refer to the following Point, Quadrilateral, and Rectangle classes.

```
public class Point
{
    private int xCoord;
    private int yCoord;

    //constructor
    public Point(int x, int y)
    {
        ...
    }

    //accessors

    public int get_x()
    {
        ...
    }

    public int get_y()
    {
        ...
    }

    //Other methods are not shown.
}

public class Quadrilateral
{
    private String labels;     //e.g., "ABCD"

    //constructor
    public Quadrilateral(String quadLabels)
    { labels = quadLabels; }

    public String getLabels()
    { return labels; }

    public int perimeter()
    { return 0; }

    public int area()
    { return 0; }
}
```

```
public class Rectangle extends Quadrilateral
{
    private Point topLeft;    //coords of top left corner
    private Point botRight;   //coords of bottom right corner

    //constructor
    public Rectangle(String theLabels, Point theTopLeft, Point theBotRight)
    { /* implementation code */ }

    public int perimeter()
    { /* implementation not shown */ }

    public int area()
    { /* implementation not shown */ }

    //Other methods are not shown.
}
```

15. Which of the following statements about the Point, Quadrilateral, and Rectangle classes are false?

    I. Point is a subclass of Quadrilateral.

    II. Point is a subclass of Rectangle.

    III. The Rectangle class inherits the constructor of Quadrilateral.

    (A) I only
    (B) II only
    (C) III only
    (D) I and II only
    (E) I, II, and III

16. Which represents correct /* *implementation code* */ for the Rectangle constructor?

    I. super(theLabels);

    II. super(theLabels, theTopLeft, theBotRight);

    III. super(theLabels);
         topLeft = theTopLeft;
         botRight = theBotRight;

    (A) I only
    (B) II only
    (C) III only
    (D) I and II only
    (E) II and III only

**GO ON TO THE NEXT PAGE**

17. Refer to the `Parallelogram` and `Square` classes below.

```
public class Parallelogram extends Quadrilateral
{
    //Private instance variables and constructor are not shown.
        ...

    public int perimeter()
    { /* implementation not shown */ }

    public int area()
    { /* implementation not shown */ }
}

public class Square extends Rectangle
{
    //Private instance variables and constructor are not shown.
        ...

    public int perimeter()
    { /* implementation not shown */ }

    public int area()
    { /* implementation not shown */ }
}
```

Consider an `ArrayList<Quadrilateral> quadList` whose elements are of type `Rectangle`, `Parallelogram`, or `Square`.

Refer to the following method, `writeAreas`:

```
/** Precondition: quadList contains Rectangle, Parallelogram, or
 *                 Square objects in an unspecified order.
 */
public static void writeAreas(ArrayList<Quadrilateral> quadList)
{
    for (Quadrilateral quad : quadList)
        System.out.println("Area of " + quad.getLabels()
            + " is " + quad.area());
}
```

What is the effect of executing this method?

(A) The area of each `Quadrilateral` in `quadList` will be printed.

(B) A value of 0 will be printed for each element of `quadList`.

(C) A compile-time error will occur, stating that there is no `getLabels` method in classes `Rectangle`, `Parallelogram`, or `Square`.

(D) A `NullPointerException` will be thrown.

(E) A `ConcurrentModificationException` will occur.

18. Refer to the doSomething method below.

```
// postcondition
public static void doSomething(ArrayList<SomeType> list, int i, int j)
{
    SomeType temp = list.get(i);
    list.set(i, list.get(j));
    list.set(j, temp);
}
```

Which best describes the **postcondition** for doSomething?

(A) Removes from list the objects indexed at i and j

(B) Replaces in list the object indexed at i with the object indexed at j

(C) Replaces in list the object indexed at j with the object indexed at i

(D) Replaces in list the objects indexed at i and j with temp

(E) Interchanges in list the objects indexed at i and j

19. Consider the `NegativeReal` class below, which defines a negative real number object.

```
public class NegativeReal
{
    private Double negReal;

    /** Constructor. Creates a NegativeReal object whose value is num.
     *  @param num  a negative real number
     */
    public NegativeReal(double num)
    { /* implementation not shown */ }

    /** @return the value of this NegativeReal */
    public double getValue()
    { /* implementation not shown */ }

    /** @return this NegativeReal rounded to the nearest integer */
    public int getRounded()
    { /* implementation */ }
}
```

Here are some rounding examples:

| Negative real number | Rounded to nearest integer |
|:---:|:---:|
| −3.5 | −4 |
| −8.97 | −9 |
| −5.0 | −5 |
| −2.487 | −2 |
| −0.2 | 0 |

Which /* *implementation* */ of getRounded produces the desired postcondition?

(A) `return (int) (getValue() - 0.5);`

(B) `return (int) (getValue() + 0.5);`

(C) `return (int) getValue();`

(D) `return (double) (getValue() - 0.5);`

(E) `return (double) getValue();`

20. Consider the following method.

```
public static void whatsIt(int n)
{
    if (n > 10)
        whatsIt(n / 10);
    System.out.print(n % 10);
}
```

What will be output as a result of the method call whatsIt(347)?
(A) 74
(B) 47
(C) 734
(D) 743
(E) 347

21. A large list of numbers is to be sorted into ascending order. Assuming that a "data movement" is a swap or reassignment of an element, which of the following is a true statement?
(A) If the array is initially sorted in descending order, then insertion sort will be more efficient than selection sort.
(B) The number of comparisons for selection sort is independent of the initial arrangement of elements.
(C) The number of comparisons for insertion sort is independent of the initial arrangement of elements.
(D) The number of data movements in selection sort depends on the initial arrangement of elements.
(E) The number of data movements in insertion sort is independent of the initial arrangement of elements.

GO ON TO THE NEXT PAGE

22. Refer to the definitions of `ClassOne` and `ClassTwo` below.

```
public class ClassOne
{
    public void methodOne()
    {
        ...
    }

    //Other methods are not shown.
}

public class ClassTwo extends ClassOne
{
    public void methodTwo()
    {
        ...
    }

    //Other methods are not shown.
}
```

Consider the following declarations in a client class. You may assume that `ClassOne` and `ClassTwo` have no-argument constructors.

```
ClassOne c1 = new ClassOne();
ClassOne c2 = new ClassTwo();
```

Which of the following method calls will cause an error?

   I.  `c1.methodTwo();`

  II.  `c2.methodTwo();`

 III.  `c2.methodOne();`

(A) None
(B) I only
(C) II only
(D) III only
(E) I and II only

23. Consider the code segment

```
if (n == 1)
    k++;
else if (n == 4)
    k += 4;
```

Suppose that the given segment is rewritten in the form

```
if (/* condition */)
    /* assignment statement */;
```

Given that n and k are integers and that the rewritten code performs the same task as the original code, which of the following could be used as

(1)  */* condition */*    and    (2)  */* assignment statement */*?

(A)  (1)  `n == 1 && n == 4`        (2)  `k += n`

(B)  (1)  `n == 1 && n == 4`        (2)  `k += 4`

(C)  (1)  `n == 1 || n == 4`        (2)  `k += 4`

(D)  (1)  `n == 1 || n == 4`        (2)  `k += n`

(E)  (1)  `n == 1 || n == 4`        (2)  `k = n - k`

24. Which of the following will execute *without* throwing an exception?

```
    I. String s = null;
       String t = "";
       if (s.equals(t))
           System.out.println("empty strings?");

   II. String s = "holy";
       String t = "moly";
       if (s.equals(t))
           System.out.println("holy moly!");

  III. String s = "holy";
       String t = s.substring(4);
       System.out.println(s + t);
```

(A)  I only
(B)  II only
(C)  III only
(D)  I and II only
(E)  II and III only

25. Three numbers *a*, *b*, and *c* are said to be a *Pythagorean Triple* if and only if the sum of the squares of two of the numbers equals the square of the third. A programmer writes a method isPythTriple to test if its three parameters form a Pythagorean Triple:

```
//Returns true if a * a + b * b == c * c; otherwise returns false.
public static boolean isPythTriple(double a, double b, double c)
{
    double d = Math.sqrt(a * a + b * b);
    return d == c;
}
```

When the method was tested with known Pythagorean Triples, isPythTriple sometimes erroneously returned false. What was the most likely cause of the error?

(A) Round-off error was caused by calculations with floating-point numbers.

(B) Type boolean was not recognized by an obsolete version of Java.

(C) An overflow error was caused by entering numbers that were too large.

(D) c and d should have been cast to integers before testing for equality.

(E) Bad test data were selected.

26. Refer to the following class containing the mystery method.

```
public class SomeClass
{
    private int[] arr;

    /** Constructor. Initializes arr to contain nonnegative
     *  integers k such that 0 <= k <= 9.
     */
    public SomeClass()
    { /* implementation not shown */ }

    public int mystery()
    {
        int value = arr[0];
        for (int i = 1; i < arr.length; i++)
            value = value * 10 + arr[i];
        return value;
    }
}
```

Which best describes what the mystery method does?

(A) It sums the elements of arr.

(B) It sums the products 10*arr[0] + 10*arr[1] + ⋯ + 10*arr[arr.length-1].

(C) It builds an integer of the form $d_1 d_2 d_3 \ldots d_n$, where $d_1 = $ arr[0], $d_2 = $ arr[1], …, $d_n = $ arr[arr.length-1].

(D) It builds an integer of the form $d_1 d_2 d_3 \ldots d_n$, where $d_1 = $ arr[arr.length-1], $d_2 = $ arr[arr.length-2], …, $d_n = $ arr[0].

(E) It converts the elements of arr to base-10.

**GO ON TO THE NEXT PAGE**

Questions 27 and 28 refer to the `search` method in the `Searcher` class below.

```
public class Searcher
{
    private int[] arr;

    /** Constructor. Initializes arr with integers. */
    public Searcher()
    { /* implementation not shown */ }

    /** Precondition:  arr[first]...arr[last] sorted in ascending order.
     *  Postcondition: Returns index of key in arr. If key not in arr,
     *                 returns -1.
     */
    public int search(int first, int last, int key)
    {
        int mid;
        while (first <= last)
        {
            mid = (first + last) / 2;
            if (arr[mid] == key)     //found key, exit search
                return mid;
            else if (arr[mid] < key) //key to right of arr[mid]
                first = mid + 1;
            else                     //key to left of arr[mid]
                last = mid - 1;
        }
        return -1;                   //key not in list
    }
}
```

27. Which assertion is true just before each execution of the `while` loop?
    (A) `arr[first]` < `key` < `arr[last]`
    (B) `arr[first]` ≤ `key` ≤ `arr[last]`
    (C) `arr[first]` < `key` < `arr[last]` or key is not in arr
    (D) `arr[first]` ≤ `key` ≤ `arr[last]` or key is not in arr
    (E) `key` ≤ `arr[first]` or key ≥ `arr[last]` or key is not in arr

28. Consider the array a with values

    4, 7, 19, 25, 36, 37, 50, 100, 101, 205, 220, 271, 306, 321

    where 4 is a[0] and 321 is a[13]. Suppose that the `search` method is called with `first` = 0 and `last` = 13 to locate the key 205. How many iterations of the `while` loop must be made in order to locate it?
    (A) 3
    (B) 4
    (C) 5
    (D) 10
    (E) 13

**GO ON TO THE NEXT PAGE**

29. Consider the following `RandomList` class.

```
public class RandomList
{
    private int[] ranList;

    public RandomList()
    { ranList = getList(); }

    /** @return array with random Integers from 0 to 100
     *     inclusive */
    public int[] getList()
    {
        System.out.println("How many integers? ");
        int listLength = ...;      //read user input
        int[] list = new int[listLength];
        for (int i = 0; i < listLength; i++)
        {
            /* code to add integer to list */
        }
        return list;
    }

    /** Print all elements of this list. */
    public void printList()
    { ... }
}
```

Which represents correct /* *code to add* integer *to* list */?

(A) `list[i] = (int) (Math.random() * 101);`

(B) `list.add((int) (Math.random() * 101));`

(C) `list[i] = (int) (Math.random() * 100);`

(D) `list.add(new Integer(Math.random() * 100))`

(E) `list[i] = (int) (Math.random() * 100) + 1;`

30. Refer to method `insert` described here. The `insert` method has two string parameters and one integer parameter. The method returns the string obtained by inserting the second string into the first starting at the position indicated by the integer parameter `pos`. For example, if `str1` contains `xy` and `str2` contains `cat`, then

```
insert(str1, str2, 0)   returns   catxy
insert(str1, str2, 1)   returns   xcaty
insert(str1, str2, 2)   returns   xycat
```

Method `insert` follows:

```
/** Precondition:    0 <= pos <= str1.length().
 *  Postcondition:   If str1 = a_0 a_1 ... a_{n-1} and str2 = b_0 b_1 ... b_{m-1},
                     returns a_0 a_1 ... a_{pos-1} b_0 b_1 ... b_{m-1} a_{pos} a_{pos+1} ... a_{n-1}
```

```java
public static String insert(String str1, String str2, int pos)
{
    String first, last;
        /* more code */
    return first + str2 + last;
}
```

Which of the following is a correct replacement for /* *more code* */?

(A)  `first = str1.substring(0, pos);`
     `last = str1.substring(pos);`

(B)  `first = str1.substring(0, pos - 1);`
     `last = str1.substring(pos);`

(C)  `first = str1.substring(0, pos + 1);`
     `last = str1.substring(pos + 1);`

(D)  `first = str1.substring(0, pos);`
     `last = str1.substring(pos + 1, str1.length());`

(E)  `first = str1.substring(0, pos);`
     `last = str1.substring(pos, str1.length() + 1);`

31. A matrix (two-dimensional array) is declared as

    ```
    int[][] mat = new int[2][3];
    ```

    Consider the following method.

    ```
    public static void changeMatrix(int[][] mat)
    {
        for (int r = 0; r < mat.length; r++)
            for (int c = 0; c < mat[r].length; c++)
                if (r == c)
                    mat[r][c] = Math.abs(mat[r][c]);
    }
    ```

    If mat is initialized to be

    ```
    -1 -2 -6
    -2 -4  5
    ```

    which matrix will be the result of a call to changeMatrix(mat)?

    (A)  1 -2 -6
        -2  4  5

    (B) -1  2 -6
         2 -4  5

    (C) -1 -2 -6
        -2 -4 -5

    (D)  1 2 -6
         2 4  5

    (E)  1 2 6
         2 4 5

Use the following program description for Questions 32–34.

A programmer plans to write a program that simulates a small bingo game (no more than six players). Each player will have a bingo card with 20 numbers from 0 to 90 (no duplicates). Someone will call out numbers one at a time, and each player will cross out a number on his card as it is called. The first player with all the numbers crossed out is the winner. In the simulation, as the game is in progress, each player's card is displayed on the screen.

The programmer envisions a short driver class whose `main` method has just two statements:

```
BingoGame b = new BingoGame();
b.playBingo();
```

The `BingoGame` class will have several objects: a `Display`, a `Caller`, and a `PlayerGroup`. The `PlayerGroup` will have a list of `Players`, and each `Player` will have a `BingoCard`.

32. The relationship between the `PlayerGroup` and `Player` classes is an example of
    (A) procedural abstraction.
    (B) data encapsulation.
    (C) composition.
    (D) inheritance.
    (E) independent classes.

33. Which is a reasonable data structure for a `BingoCard` object? Recall that there are 20 integers from 0 to 90 on a `BingoCard`, with no duplicates. There should also be mechanisms for crossing off numbers that are called, and for detecting a winning card (i.e., one where all the numbers have been crossed off).

```
 I. int[] bingoCard;     //will contain 20 integers
                         //bingoCard[k] is crossed off by setting it to -1.
    int numCrossedOff;   //player wins when numCrossedOff reaches 20.

II. boolean[] bingoCard;  //will contain 91 boolean values, of which
                          //20 are true. All the other values are false.
                          //Thus, if bingoCard[k] is true, then k is
                          //on the card, 0 <= k <= 90. A number k is
                          //crossed off by changing the value of
                          //bingoCard[k] to false.
    int numCrossedOff;    //player wins when numCrossedOff reaches 20.

III. ArrayList<Integer> bingoCard;  //will contain 20 integers.
        //A number is crossed off by removing it from the ArrayList.
        //Player wins when bingoCard.size() == 0.
```

    (A) I only
    (B) II only
    (C) III only
    (D) I and II only
    (E) I, II, and III

34. The programmer decides to use an `ArrayList<Integer>` to store the numbers to be called by the `Caller`, but there is an error in the code.

```java
public class Caller
{
    private ArrayList<Integer> numbers;

    public Caller()
    {
        numbers = getList();
        shuffleNumbers();
    }

    /** Returns the numbers 0...90 in order. */
    private ArrayList<Integer> getList()
    { /* implementation not shown */ }

    /** Shuffle the numbers. */
    private void shuffleNumbers()
    { /* implementation not shown */ }
}
```

When the programmer tests the constructor of the `Caller` class, she gets a `NullPointerException`. Which could be the cause of this error?

(A) The `Caller` object in the driver class was not created with `new`.

(B) The programmer forgot the `return` statement in `getList` that returns the list of `Integers`.

(C) The declaration of `numbers` is incorrect. It needed to be

    private ArrayList<Integer> numbers = null;

(D) In the `getList` method, an attempt was made to add an `Integer` to an `ArrayList` that had not been created with `new`.

(E) The `shuffleNumbers` algorithm went out of range, causing a `null` `Integer` to be shuffled into the `ArrayList`.

35. Consider method findSomething below.

```
/** Precondition:  a.length is equal to b.length. */
public static boolean findSomething(int[] a, int[] b)
{
    for (int aValue: a)
    {
        boolean found = false;
        for (int bValue: b)
        {
            if (bValue == aValue)
                found = true;
        }
        if (!found)
            return false;
    }
    return true;
}
```

Which best describes what method findSomething does?  Method findSomething returns true only if

(A) arrays a and b contain identical elements in the same order.

(B) arrays a and b contain identical elements in reverse order.

(C) arrays a and b are permutations of each other.

(D) array a contains at least one element that is also in b.

(E) every element of array a is also in b.

36. Consider a program that has a two-dimensional array `mat` of `int` values. The program has several methods that change `mat` by reflecting elements of `mat` across a mirror placed symmetrically on the matrix. Here are five such methods:

| | | | | | | | | | | |
|---|---|---|---|---|---|---|---|---|---|---|
| | | | 2 | 4 | 6 | | | 2 | 4 | 2 |
| `mirrorVerticalLeftToRight` | transforms | | 1 | 3 | 5 | to | | 1 | 3 | 1 |
| | | | 8 | 9 | 0 | | | 8 | 9 | 8 |

| | | | | | | | | | | |
|---|---|---|---|---|---|---|---|---|---|---|
| | | | 2 | 4 | 6 | | | 6 | 4 | 6 |
| `mirrorVerticalRightToLeft` | transforms | | 1 | 3 | 5 | to | | 5 | 3 | 5 |
| | | | 8 | 9 | 0 | | | 0 | 9 | 0 |

| | | | | | | | | | | |
|---|---|---|---|---|---|---|---|---|---|---|
| | | | 2 | 4 | 6 | | | 2 | 4 | 6 |
| `mirrorHorizontalTopToBottom` | transforms | | 1 | 3 | 5 | to | | 1 | 3 | 5 |
| | | | 8 | 9 | 0 | | | 2 | 4 | 6 |

| | | | | | | | | | | |
|---|---|---|---|---|---|---|---|---|---|---|
| | | | 2 | 4 | 6 | | | 8 | 9 | 0 |
| `mirrorHorizontalBottomToTop` | transforms | | 1 | 3 | 5 | to | | 1 | 3 | 5 |
| | | | 8 | 9 | 0 | | | 8 | 9 | 0 |

| | | | | | | | | | | |
|---|---|---|---|---|---|---|---|---|---|---|
| | | | 2 | 4 | 6 | | | 2 | 4 | 6 |
| `mirrorDiagonalRightToLeft` | transforms | | 1 | 3 | 5 | to | | 4 | 3 | 5 |
| | | | 8 | 9 | 0 | | | 6 | 5 | 0 |

Consider the following method that transforms the matrix in one of the ways shown above.

```
public static void someMethod(int[][] mat)
{
    int height = mat.length;
    int numCols = mat[0].length;
    for (int col = 0; col < numCols; col++)
        for (int row = 0; row < height/2; row++)
            mat[height - row - 1][col] = mat[row][col];
}
```

Which method described above corresponds to `someMethod`?

(A) `mirrorVerticalLeftToRight`
(B) `mirrorVerticalRightToLeft`
(C) `mirrorHorizontalTopToBottom`
(D) `mirrorHorizontalBottomToTop`
(E) `mirrorDiagonalRightToLeft`

Refer to the following for Questions 37 and 38.

A word creation game uses a set of small letter tiles, all of which are initially in a tile bag. A partial implementation of a `TileBag` class is shown below.

```
public class TileBag
{
    //tiles contains all the tiles in the bag
    private ArrayList<Tile> tiles;
    //size is the number of not-yet-used tiles
    private int size;

    //Constructors and other methods are not shown.
}
```

Consider the following method in the `TileBag` class that allows a player to get a new tile from the `TileBag`.

```
public Tile getNewTile()
{
    if (size == 0)  //no tiles left
        return null;
    int index = (int) (Math.random() * size);
    size--;
    Tile temp = tiles.get(index);
    /* code to swap tile at position size with tile at position index */
    return temp;
}
```

37. Which /* *code to swap tile at position* size *with tile at position* index */ performs the swap correctly?

    (A) `tiles.set(size, temp);`
        `tiles.set(index, tiles.get(size));`

    (B) `tiles.set(index, tiles.get(size));`
        `tiles.set(size, temp);`

    (C) `tiles.swap(index, size);`

    (D) `tiles.get(size, temp);`
        `tiles.get(index, tiles.set(size));`

    (E) `tiles.get(index, tiles.set(size));`
        `tiles.get(size, temp);`

38. Which is true about the `getNewTile` algorithm?
    (A) The algorithm allows the program to keep track of both used and unused tiles.
    (B) The `tiles` list becomes one element shorter when `getNewTile` is executed.
    (C) The algorithm selects a random `Tile` from all tiles in the list.
    (D) The `tiles` list has used tiles in the beginning and unused tiles at the end.
    (E) The `tiles` list contains only tiles that have not been used.

**GO ON TO THE NEXT PAGE**

39.  Consider the following two classes.

```
public class Bird
{
    public void act()
    {
        System.out.print("fly ");
        makeNoise();
    }

    public void makeNoise()
    {
        System.out.print("chirp ");
    }
}


public class Dove extends Bird
{
    public void act()
    {
        super.act();
        System.out.print("waddle ");
    }

    public void makeNoise()
    {
        super.makeNoise();
        System.out.print("coo ");
    }
}
```

Suppose the following declaration appears in a class other than Bird or Dove.

```
Bird pigeon = new Dove();
```

What is printed as a result of the call pigeon.act()?

(A) fly
(B) fly chirp
(C) fly chirp waddle
(D) fly chirp waddle coo
(E) fly chirp coo waddle

40. Consider a method `partialProd` that returns an integer array `prod` such that for all `k`, `prod[k]` is equal to `arr[0] * arr[1] * ... arr[k]`. For example, if `arr` contains the values {2,5,3,4,10}, the array `prod` will contain the values {2,10,30,120,1200}.

```
public static int[] partialProd(int[] arr)
{
    int[] prod = new int[arr.length];
    for (int j = 0; j < arr.length; j++)
        prod[j] = 1;
    /* missing code */
    return prod;
}
```

Consider the following two implementations of /* *missing code* */.

**Implementation 1**

```
for (int j = 1; j < arr.length; j++)
{
    prod[j] = prod[j - 1] * arr[j];
}
```

**Implementation 2**

```
for (int j = 0; j < arr.length; j++)
    for (int k = 0; k <= j; k++)
    {
        prod[j] = prod[j] * arr[k];
    }
```

Which of the following statements is true?

(A) Both implementations work as intended but Implementation 1 is faster than Implementation 2.

(B) Both implementations work as intended but Implementation 2 is faster than Implementation 1.

(C) Both implementations work as intended and are equally fast.

(D) Implementation 1 doesn't work as intended because the elements of `prod` are incorrectly assigned.

(E) Implementation 2 doesn't work as intended because the elements of `prod` are incorrectly assigned.

**END OF SECTION I**

# COMPUTER SCIENCE A
# SECTION II

**Time—1 hour and 30 minutes**
**4 Questions**

**DIRECTIONS:** SHOW ALL YOUR WORK. REMEMBER THAT PROGRAM
SEGMENTS ARE TO BE WRITTEN IN JAVA.

Write your answers in the separate Free-Response booklet provided.

**NOTES:**

- Assume that the classes in the Quick Reference have been imported where appropriate.

- Unless otherwise noted in the question, assume that parameters in method calls are not null and that methods are called only when their preconditions are satisfied.

- In writing solutions for each question, you may use any of the accessible methods that are listed in classes defined in that question. Writing significant amounts of code that can be replaced by a call to one of these methods will not receive full credit.

1. This question uses a class, FourDigitInteger, to manipulate and report properties about a given 4-digit integer. The precondition for each FourDigitInteger object is that the value is positive and lies between 1000 and 9999, inclusive.

   You will write three methods of the FourDigitInteger class.

```
public class FourDigitInteger
{
    private int value;

    public FourDigitInteger (int aValue)
    { value = aValue; }

    /** Returns true if value is odd, false otherwise. */
    public boolean isOdd()
    { /* to be implemented in part (a) */ }

    /** Returns true if value is a palindrome number, as described
     *  in part (b). Returns false otherwise.
     */
    public boolean isPalindrome()
    { /* to be implemented in part (b) */ }

    /** Returns true if value is a perfect square, false otherwise. */
    public boolean isPerfectSquare()
    { /* to be implemented in part (c) */ }

    //There may be instance variables, constructors, and methods not shown.
}
```

   (a) Complete the isOdd method. This method returns true if the value of a FourDigitInteger is odd, false otherwise. For example, if the value is 2389, isOdd should return true; but for a value of 9998, isOdd should return false.

   Complete the isOdd method.

```
/** Returns true if value is odd, false otherwise. */
public boolean isOdd()
```

   (b) A 4-digit palindrome number is one whose first digit is the same as the fourth digit, and whose second and third digits are the same. Some examples of palindrome numbers are: 2772, 8888, 1001, 6556, and so on. Some examples of numbers that are not palindromes are: 1442, 9459, 1000, and so on.

   Complete the isPalindrome method.

```
/** Returns true if value is a palindrome number, as described
 *  in part (b). Returns false otherwise.
 */
public boolean isPalindrome()
```

(c) A number n is a perfect square if n equals $k^2$, where k is an integer. For example, 16 is a perfect square because it equals $4^2$. Also, 625 is a perfect square because it equals $25^2$. You are to write the isPerfectSquare method of the FourDigitInteger class, to test if its value is a perfect square. Here is a hint:

$$31^2 = 961, \qquad 100^2 = 10000$$

Complete the isPerfectSquare method.

```
/** Returns true if value is a perfect square, false otherwise. */
public boolean isPerfectSquare()
```

2. This question involves keeping track of details for a world cruise, using a Cruise class. A Cruise object is created with two parameters, the number of people currently signed up for the cruise, and the current price.

The Cruise class provides a constructor and the following methods.

- setPrice, which can change the price of the cruise.

- checkResponse, which increments the count of people if someone has requested the cruise using a phrase that includes the word "cruise". You may assume all lowercase letters.

- calculateRevenue, which returns the number of signups so far multiplied by the current price. Note that if more than 300 people have signed up for the cruise, everyone will receive a $500 discount off the current price. If between 200 and 300 (including 200) people have signed up, everyone will receive a $350 discount off the current price.

The following table contains sample code and corresponding results.

| Statements and Expressions | Comments |
|---|---|
| Cruise cr = newCruise(78, 4000); | There are 78 signups so far, and the cruise price is $4,000. |
| cr.setPrice(5000); | Changes the price to $5,000. |
| cr.checkResponse("world cruise"); | Increments signup number to 79. |
| cr.checkResponse("ship trip"); | Does not change number. It is still 78. |
| cr.calculateRevenue(); | With 79 signups and price $5,000, returns $79 \times 5000$. |
| Cruise cr1 = newCruise(200, 2000); | |
| cr1.calculateRevenue(); | Returns $200 \times 1650$. |
| Cruise cr2 = newCruise(397, 6000); | |
| cr2.calculateRevenue(); | Returns $397 \times 5500$. |

Write the complete Cruise class, including the constructor and any required instance variables and methods. Your implementation must meet all specifications and be consistent with the examples shown above.

**GO ON TO THE NEXT PAGE**

3. A text-editing program uses a `Sentence` class that manipulates a single sentence. A sentence contains letters, blanks, and punctuation. The first character in a sentence is a letter, and the last character is a punctuation mark. Any two words in the sentence are separated by a single blank. A partial implementation of the `Sentence` class is as follows.

```
public class Sentence
{
    /** The sentence to manipulate */
    private String sentence;

    /**  Returns an ArrayList of integer positions containing a
     *   blank in this sentence. If there are no blanks in the
     *   sentence, returns an empty list.
     */
    public ArrayList<Integer> getBlankPositions()
    { /* to be implemented in part (a) */ }


    /**  Returns the number of words in this sentence
     *   Precondition: Sentence contains at least one word.
     */
    public int countWords()
    { /* implementation not shown */ }


    /** Returns the array of words in this sentence.
     *   Precondition:
     *     - Any two words in the sentence are separated by one blank.
     *     - The sentence contains at least one word.
     *   Postcondition: String[] contains the words in this sentence.
     */
    public String[] getWords()
    { /* to be implemented in part (b) */ }


    //Constructor and other methods are not shown.
}
```

(a) Write the `Sentence` method `getBlankPositions`, which returns an `ArrayList` of integers that represent the positions in a sentence containing blanks. If there are no blanks in the sentence, `getBlankPositions` should return an empty list.

Some results of calling `getBlankPositions` are shown below.

| Sentence | Result of call to getBlankPositions |
|---|---|
| I love you! | [1, 6] |
| The cat sat on the mat. | [3, 7, 11, 14, 18] |
| Why? | [ ] |

Complete method `getBlankPositions`.

```
/**  Returns an ArrayList of integer positions containing a
 *   blank in this sentence. If there are no blanks in the
 *   sentence, returns an empty list.
 */
public ArrayList<Integer> getBlankPositions()
```

(b) Write the `Sentence` method `getWords`, which returns an array of words in the sentence. A word is defined as a string of letters and punctuation, and does not contain any blanks. You may assume that a sentence contains at least one word.

Some examples of calling `getWords` are shown below.

| Sentence | Result returned by `getWords` |
|---|---|
| The bird flew away. | {The, bird, flew, away.} |
| Wow! | {Wow!} |
| Hi!  How are you? | {Hi!, How, are, you?} |

In writing method `getWords`, you *must* use methods `getBlankPositions` and `countWords`.

Complete method `getWords`.

```
/** Returns the array of words in this sentence.
 *  Precondition:
 *   - Any two words in the sentence are separated by one blank.
 *   - The sentence contains at least one word.
 *  Postcondition: String[] contains the words in this sentence.
 */
public String[] getWords()
```

4. This question manipulates a two-dimensional array. In parts (a) and (b) you will write two methods of a `Matrix` class.

In doing so, you will use the `reverseArray` method shown in the class below.

```
public class ArrayUtil
{
    /** Reverses elements of array arr.
     *  Precondition:  arr.length > 0.
     *  Postcondition: The elements of arr have been reversed.
     */
    public static void reverseArray(int[] arr)
    { /* implementation not shown */ }

    //Other methods are not shown.

}
```

Consider the following incomplete `Matrix` class, which represents a two-dimensional matrix of integers. Assume that the matrix contains at least one integer.

```
public class Matrix
{
    private int[][] mat;

    /** Constructs a matrix of integers. */
    public Matrix (int[][] m)
    {  mat = m; }

    /** Reverses the elements in each row of mat.
     *  Postcondition: The elements in each row have been reversed.
     */
    public void reverseAllRows()
    { /* to be implemented in part (a) */ }

    /** Reverses the elements of mat, as described in part (b).
     */
    public void reverseMatrix()
    { /* to be implemented in part (b) */ }

    //Other instance variables, constructors and methods are not shown.

}
```

(a) Write the `Matrix` method `reverseAllRows`. This method reverses the elements of each row. For example, if `mat1` refers to a `Matrix` object, then the call `mat1.reverseAllRows()` will change the matrix as shown below.

**Before call**

|   | 0 | 1 | 2 | 3 |
|---|---|---|---|---|
| 0 | 1 | 2 | 3 | 4 |
| 1 | 5 | 6 | 7 | 8 |
| 2 | 9 | 10 | 11 | 12 |

**After call**

|   | 0 | 1 | 2 | 3 |
|---|---|---|---|---|
| 0 | 4 | 3 | 2 | 1 |
| 1 | 8 | 7 | 6 | 5 |
| 2 | 12 | 11 | 10 | 9 |

In writing `reverseAllRows`, you *must* call the `reverseArray` method in the `ArrayUtil` class.

Complete method `reverseAllRows`.

```
/** Reverses the elements in each row of mat.
 *  Postcondition: The elements in each row have been reversed.
 */
public void reverseAllRows()
```

(b) Write the `Matrix` method `reverseMatrix`. This method reverses the elements of a matrix such that the final elements of the matrix, when read in row-major order, are the same as the original elements when read from the bottom corner, right to left, going upward. Again let `mat1` be a reference to a `Matrix` object. The call `mat1.reverseMatrix()` will change the matrix as shown below.

|   | **Before call** |   |   |   | **After call** |   |
|---|---|---|---|---|---|---|
|   | 0 | 1 |   |   | 0 | 1 |
| 0 | 1 | 2 |   | 0 | 6 | 5 |
| 1 | 3 | 4 |   | 1 | 4 | 3 |
| 2 | 5 | 6 |   | 2 | 2 | 1 |

In writing `reverseMatrix`, you *must* call the `reverseAllRows` method in part (a). Assume that `reverseAllRows` works correctly regardless of what you wrote in part (a).

Complete method `reverseMatrix`.

```
/** Reverses the elements of mat, as described in part (b).
 */
public void reverseMatrix()
```

**STOP**

**END OF EXAM**

# ANSWER KEY
## Diagnostic Test

### Section I

| | | | | | |
|---|---|---|---|---|---|
| 1. | **D** | 15. | **E** | 29. | **A** |
| 2. | **A** | 16. | **C** | 30. | **A** |
| 3. | **D** | 17. | **A** | 31. | **A** |
| 4. | **A** | 18. | **E** | 32. | **C** |
| 5. | **B** | 19. | **A** | 33. | **E** |
| 6. | **E** | 20. | **E** | 34. | **D** |
| 7. | **B** | 21. | **B** | 35. | **E** |
| 8. | **C** | 22. | **E** | 36. | **C** |
| 9. | **B** | 23. | **D** | 37. | **B** |
| 10. | **A** | 24. | **E** | 38. | **A** |
| 11. | **D** | 25. | **A** | 39. | **E** |
| 12. | **B** | 26. | **C** | 40. | **D** |
| 13. | **A** | 27. | **D** | | |
| 14. | **A** | 28. | **B** | | |

## Diagnostic Chart

Each multiple-choice question has a complete explanation (p. 44).

The following table relates each question to sections that you should review. For any given question, the topic(s) in the chart represent the concept(s) tested in the question. These topics are explained on the corresponding page(s) in the chart and should provide further insight into answering that question.

DIAGNOSTIC TEST

| Question | Topic | Page |
|:---:|:---|:---:|
| 1 | Inheritance | 142 |
| 2 | Relationship between classes | 216 |
| 3 | `ConcurrentModificationException` | 254 |
| 4 | Constructors | 102 |
| 5 | The `toString` method | 173 |
| 6 | `Integer.MIN_VALUE` and `Integer.MAX_VALUE` | 67 |
| 7 | `for` loop | 76 |
| 8 | Program specification | 213 |
| 9 | Recursion | 310 |
| 10 | Boolean expressions | 70 |
| 11 | 2D arrays | 257 |
| 12 | `IndexOutOfBoundsException` for `ArrayList` | 250 |
| 13 | Passing parameters | 243 |
| 14 | Passing parameters | 243 |
| 15 | Subclasses | 139 |
| 16 | Subclass constructors and `super` keyword | 143 |
| 17 | Polymorphism | 146 |
| 18 | `swap` method | 244 |
| 19 | Rounding real numbers | 66 |
| 20 | Recursion | 313 |
| 21 | Selection and insertion sort | 343 |
| 22 | Subclass method calls | 151 |
| 23 | Compound boolean expressions | 70 |
| 24 | `String` class `equals` method | 175 |
|  | `String` class `substring` method | 176 |
| 25 | Round-off error | 67 |
| 26 | Array processing | 241 |
| 27 | Assertions about algorithms | 225 |
|  | Binary search | 348 |
| 28 | Binary search | 348 |
| 29 | Random integers | 184 |
| 30 | `String` class `substring` method | 176 |
| 31 | Two-dimensional arrays | 257 |
| 32 | Relationships between classes | 221 |
| 33 | Array of objects | 247 |
|  | `ArrayList` | 249 |
| 34 | `NullPointerException` | 110 |
| 35 | Traversing an array | 241 |
|  | The `if` statement | 74 |
| 36 | Processing a 2D array | 259 |
|  | Mirror images | 263 |
| 37 | Using `ArrayList` | 251 |
| 38 | Using `ArrayList` | 251 |
| 39 | Using `super` in a subclass | 149 |
| 40 | One-dimensional arrays | 239 |

# Answer Explanations

## Section I

1. **(D)** Constructors are never inherited. If a subclass has no constructor, the default constructor is generated, which calls the no-argument superclass constructor. If the superclass does not have a no-argument constructor, a compile-time error will occur.

2. **(A)** The relationship between LibraryList and Book is: A LibraryList *has-a* Book. (It has a list of books.) The *has-a* relationship is a composition relationship. Choice B is wrong: An inheritance relationship is the *is-a* relationship between a subclass and superclass. A Book is not a LibraryList. Choice C is wrong: LibraryList and Book are not independent, since a LibraryBook has a list of Book objects. Choice D is wrong: Polymorphism is not a relationship between classes. It's a mechanism for selecting which subclass method to implement during run time of a program. Choice E is wrong: ArrayList is not a relationship between classes. It is a data structure that contains a list of object references.

3. **(D)** Changing the size of an ArrayList while traversing it with an enhanced for loop can result in a ConcurrentModificationException being thrown. Therefore, you should not add or remove elements during traversal of an ArrayList with an enhanced for loop. Choices A and B are wrong because you are not using indexes in the traversal. Choice C, a NullPointerException, would only be thrown if the list object had not been initialized. Choice E, an ArithmeticException, occurs most commonly when an attempt is made to divide by zero. There's no information in the question that suggests this is the case.

4. **(A)** In the constructor, the private instance variables suit and value must be initialized to the appropriate parameter values. Choice A is the only choice that does this.

5. **(B)** Implementation II invokes the toString method of the Card class. Implementation I fails because the default toString method for an array won't print individual elements of the array, just classname@hashcode. Implementation III will cause an error because you cannot cast a Card to a String.

6. **(E)** Since the values in arr cannot be greater than Integer.MAX_VALUE, the test in the while loop will be true at least once and will lead to the smallest element being stored in min. (If *all* the elements of the array are Integer.MAX_VALUE, the code still works.) Similarly, initializing min to arr[0], the first element in the array, ensures that all elements in arr will be examined and the smallest will be found. Choice I, Integer.MIN_VALUE, fails because the test in the loop will always be false! There is no array element that will be less than the smallest possible integer. The method will (incorrectly) return Integer.MIN_VALUE.

7. **(B)** The maximum number will be achieved if /* *test* */ is true in each pass through the loop. So the question boils down to: How many times is the loop executed? Try one odd and one even value of n:

$$\text{If } n = 7, \quad i = 0,2,4,6 \quad \text{Ans} = 4$$
$$\text{If } n = 8, \quad i = 0,2,4,6 \quad \text{Ans} = 4$$

Notice that choice B is the only expression that works for both n = 7 and n = 8.

8. **(C)** Here is one of the golden rules of programming: Don't start planning the program until every aspect of the specification is crystal clear. A programmer should never make unilateral decisions about ambiguities in a specification.

9. **(B)** When x ≤ y, a recursive call is made to whatIsIt(x-1, y). If x decreases at every recursive call, there is no way to reach a successful base case. Thus, the method never terminates and eventually exhausts all available memory.

10. **(A)** The expression !(max != a[i]) is equivalent to max == a[i], so the given expression is equivalent to a[i] == max || max == a[i], which is equivalent to a[i] == max.

11. **(D)** In this problem, mat.length equals 2, the number of rows in the matrix. Each row is an array of int. Note that arr.length, which isn't used in the code, is 3. Here's what the code does: For each array arr in mat, add arr[0] and arr[1] to the sum. Note that when n is 2, the inner for loop terminates, so arr[2], the elements of the third column, are not included in the sum, which equals 3 + 4 + 6 + 7 = 20.

12. **(B)** The index range for ArrayList is 0 ≤ index ≤ size()-1. Thus, for methods get, remove, and set, the last in-bounds index is size()-1. The one exception is the add method—to add an element to the end of the list takes an index parameter list.size().

13. **(A)** The array will not be changed by the increment method. Here are the memory slots:

The same analysis applies to the method calls increment(4) and increment(5).

14. **(A)** As in the previous question, the array will not be changed by the increment method. Nor will the local variable element! What *will* be changed by increment is the copy of the parameter n during each pass through the loop.

15. **(E)** Statements I and II are false because Point is neither a Quadrilateral nor is it a Rectangle. (Notice that the Point class does not have the extends keyword.) Statement III is false because subclasses never inherit the constructors of their superclass. The code for a subclass constructor must be explicitly written; otherwise, the compiler slots in code for the default constructor, which calls the no-argument constructor of the superclass.

16. **(C)** Segment I starts correctly but fails to initialize the additional private variables of the Rectangle class. Segment II is wrong because by using super with theTopLeft and theBotRight, it implies that these values are used in the Quadrilateral superclass. This is false—there isn't even a constructor with three arguments in the superclass.

17. **(A)** During execution the appropriate `area` method for each `quad` in `quadList` will be determined (polymorphism or dynamic binding). Choice B is wrong because the over-ridden method in the appropriate subclass is selected at run time—not the superclass method. Choice C is wrong because each of those subclasses inherit the `getLabels` method of `Quadrilateral`. Choice D would occur if `quadList` had a `null` value; but the precondition states that `quadList` is initialized. Choice E would occur if an attempt were made to alter `quadList` by adding or removing elements in the enhanced `for` loop.

18. **(E)** The algorithm has three steps:

    1. Store the object at `i` in `temp`.
    2. Place at location `i` the object at `j`.
    3. Place `temp` at location `j`.

    This has the effect of swapping the objects at `i` and `j`. Notice that choices B and C, while incomplete, are not incorrect. The question, however, asks for the *best* description of the postcondition, which is found in choice E.

19. **(A)** Subtracting 0.5 from a negative real number and then truncating it produces the number correctly rounded to the nearest integer. Note that casting to an `int` truncates a real number. The expression in choice B is correct for rounding a *positive* real number. Choice C won't round correctly. For example, −3.7 will be rounded to −3 instead of −4. Choices D and E don't make sense. Why cast to `double` if you're rounding to the nearest integer?

20. **(E)** The method call `whatsIt(347)` puts on the stack `System.out.print(7)`.
    The method call `whatsIt(34)` puts on the stack `System.out.print(4)`.
    The method call `whatsIt(3)` is a base case and writes out 3.
    Now the stack is popped from the top, and the 3 that was printed is followed by 4, then 7. The result is 347.

21. **(B)** Recall that insertion sort takes each element in turn and (a) finds its insertion point and (b) moves elements to insert that element in its correct place. Thus, if the array is in reverse sorted order, the insertion point will always be at the front of the array, leading to the maximum number of comparisons and data moves—very inefficient. Therefore choices A, C, and E are false.

    Selection sort finds the smallest element in the array and swaps it with `a[0]` and then finds the smallest element in the rest of the array and swaps it with `a[1]`, and so on. Thus, the same number of comparisons and moves will occur, irrespective of the original arrangement of elements in the array. So choice B is true, and choice D is false.

22. **(E)** Method call I fails because `ClassOne` does not have access to the methods of its subclass. Method call II fails because `c2` needs to be cast to `ClassTwo` to be able to access `methodTwo`. Thus, the following would be OK:

    ```
    ((ClassTwo) c2).methodTwo();
    ```

    Method call III works because `ClassTwo` inherits `methodOne` from its superclass, `ClassOne`.

23. **(D)** Notice that in the original code, if `n` is 1, `k` is incremented by 1, and if `n` is 4, `k` is incremented by 4. This is equivalent to saying "if `n` is 1 or 4, `k` is incremented by `n`."

24. **(E)** Segment I will throw a `NullPointerException` when `s.equals...` is invoked, because `s` is a null reference. Segment III looks suspect, but when the `startIndex` parameter of the `substring` method equals `s.length()`, the value returned is the empty string. If, however, `startIndex > s.length()`, a `StringIndexOutOfBoundsException` is thrown.

25. **(A)** Since results of calculations with floating-point numbers are not always represented exactly (round-off error), direct tests for equality are not reliable. Instead of the boolean expression `d == c`, a test should be done to check whether the difference of `d` and `c` is within some acceptable tolerance interval (see the Box on comparing floating-point numbers, p. 70).

26. **(C)** If `arr` has elements 2, 3, 5, the values of `value` are

```
2                    //after initialization
2*10 + 3 = 23        //when i = 1
23*10 + 5 = 235      //when i = 2
```

27. **(D)** The point of the binary search algorithm is that the interval containing `key` is repeatedly narrowed down by splitting it in half. For each iteration of the `while` loop, if `key` is in the list, `arr[first] ≤ key ≤ arr[last]`. Note that (i) the endpoints of the interval must be included, and (ii) `key` is not necessarily in the list.

28. **(B)**

|  | first | last | mid | a[mid] |
|---|---|---|---|---|
| After first iteration | 0 | 13 | 6 | 50 |
| After second iteration | 7 | 13 | 10 | 220 |
| After third iteration | 7 | 9 | 8 | 101 |
| After fourth iteration | 9 | 9 | 9 | 205 |

29. **(A)** The data structure is an array, not an `ArrayList`, so you cannot use the `add` method for inserting elements into the list. This eliminates choices B and D. Choice C gets integers from 0 to 99. The expression to return a random integer from 0 to `k-1` inclusive is

```
(int) (Math.random() * k)
```

Thus, to get integers from 0 to 100 requires `k` to be 101, which eliminates choice C. Choice E fails because it gets integers from 1 to 100.

30. **(A)** Suppose `str1` is `strawberry` and `str2` is `cat`. Then `insert(str1, str2, 5)` will return the following pieces, concatenated:

```
straw + cat + berry
```

Recall that `s.substring(k, m)` (a method of `String`) returns a substring of `s` starting at position `k` and ending at position `m-1`. String `str1` must be split into two parts, `first` and `last`. Then `str2` will be inserted between them. Since `str2` is inserted starting at position 5 (the `"b"`), `first = straw`, namely `str1.substring(0,pos)`. (Start at 0 and take all the characters up to and including location `pos-1`, which is 4.) Notice that `last`, the second substring of `str1`, must start at the index for `"b"`, which is `pos`, the index at which `str2` was inserted. The expression `str1.substring(pos)` returns the substring of `str1` that starts at `pos` and continues to the end of the string, which was required. Note that you don't need any "special case" tests. In the cases where `str2` is inserted at the front of `str1` (i.e., `pos` is 0) or the back of `str1` (i.e., `pos` is `str1.length()`), the code for the general case works.

31. **(A)** Method `changeMatrix` examines each element and changes it to its absolute value if its row number equals its column number. The only two elements that satisfy the condition `r == c` are `mat[0][0]` and `mat[1][1]`. Thus, –1 is changed to 1 and –4 is changed to 4, resulting in the matrix in choice A.

32. **(C)** Composition is the *has-a* relationship. A `PlayerGroup` *has-a* `Player` (several of them, in fact). Inheritance (choice D) is the *is-a* relationship, which doesn't apply here. None of the choices A, B, or E apply in this example: Procedural abstraction is the use of separate methods to encapsulate each task (see p. 218); data encapsulation is combining the data and methods of an object in a class so that the data can be hidden (see p. 100); and `PlayerGroup` and `Player` are clearly dependent on each other since `PlayerGroup` contains several `Player` objects (see p. 217).

33. **(E)** All of these data structures are reasonable. They all represent 20 bingo numbers in a convenient way and provide easy mechanisms for crossing off numbers and recognizing a winning card. Notice that data structure II provides a very quick way of searching for a number on the card. For example, if 48 is called, `bingoCard[48]` is inspected. If it is `true`, then it was one of the 20 original numbers on the card and gets crossed out. If `false`, 48 was not on that player's card. Data structures I and II require a linear search to find any given number that is called. (Note: There is no assumption that the array is sorted, which would allow a more efficient binary search.)

34. **(D)** A `NullPointerException` is thrown whenever an attempt is made to invoke a method with an object that hasn't been created with `new`. Choice A doesn't make sense: To test the `Caller` constructor requires a statement of the form

```
Caller c = new Caller();
```

Choice B is wrong: A missing `return` statement in a method triggers a compile-time error. Choice C doesn't make sense: In the declaration of `numbers`, its default initialization is to `null`. Choice E is bizarre. Hopefully you eliminated it immediately! An algorithm that goes out of range causes some kind of out of range exception, not a `NullPointerException`.

35. **(E)** For each element in `a`, `found` is switched to `true` if that element is found anywhere in `b`. Notice that for any element in `a`, if it is not found in `b`, the method returns `false`. Thus, to return `true`, every element in `a` must also be in `b`. Notice that this doesn't necessarily mean that `a` and `b` are permutations of each other. For example, consider the counterexample of `a=[1,1,2,3]` and `b=[1,2,2,3]`. Also, not every element in `b` needs to be in `a`. For example, if `a=[3,3,5]` and `b=[3,5,6]`, the method will return `true`.

36. **(C)** In the example given, `height = 3`, `height/2 = 1`, and `numCols = 3`. Notice that in each pass through the loop, `row` has value 0, while `col` goes from 0 through 2. So here are the assignments:

```
mat[2][0] = mat[0][0]
mat[2][1] = mat[0][1]
mat[2][2] = mat[0][2]
```

From this you should see that row 2 is being replaced by row 0.

37. **(B)** Eliminate choices D and E immediately, since assignment of new values in an `ArrayList` is done with the `set` method, not `get`. Eliminate choice C since you do not know that the `TileBag` class has a swap method. Choice A fails because it replaces the element at position `size` before storing it. Choice B works because the element at position `index` has been saved in `temp`.

38. **(A)** The `size` variable stores the number of unused tiles, which are in the `tiles` list from position 0 to position `size`. A random `int` is selected in this range, giving the index of the `Tile` that will be swapped to the end of the unused part of the `tiles` list. Note that the length of the `tiles` `ArrayList` stays constant. Each execution of `getNewTile` decreases the "unused tiles" part of the list and increases the "already used" part at the end of the list. In this way, both used and unused tiles are stored.

39. **(E)** When `pigeon.act()` is called, the `act` method of `Dove` is called (since `Pigeon` refers to a `Dove` object). This is an example of polymorphism. The `act` method of `Dove` starts with `super.act()`, which goes to the `act` method of `Bird`, the superclass. This prints `fly`, then calls `makeNoise()`. Using polymorphism, the `makeNoise` method in `Dove` is called, which starts with `super.makeNoise()`, which prints `chirp`. Completing the `makeNoise` method in `Dove` prints `coo`. Thus, so far we've printed `fly chirp coo`. But we haven't completed `Dove`'s `act` method, which ends with printing out `waddle`! The rule of thumb is: When `super` is used, find the method in the superclass. But if that method calls a method that's been overridden in the subclass, go back there for the overridden method. You also mustn't forget to check that you've executed any pending lines of code in that superclass method!

40. **(D)** In Implementation 1, the first element assigned is `prod[1]`, and it multiplies `arr[1]` by `prod[0]`, which was initialized to 1. To fix this implementation, you need a statement preceding the loop, which correctly assigns `prod[0]`: `prod[0]=arr[0];`.

## Section II

1. (a)
```
public boolean isOdd()
{
    return value % 2 == 1;
}
```

Alternative solution:

```
public boolean isOdd()
{
    if (value % 2 == 1)
        return true;
        else return false;
}
```

(b)
```
public boolean isPalindrome()
{
    int digit1 = value / 1000;
    int digit2 = value / 100 % 10;
    int digit3 = value / 10 % 10;
    int digit4 = value % 10;
    return (digit1 == digit4) && (digit2 == digit3);
}
```

(c)
```
public boolean isPerfectSquare()
{
    for (int n = 32; n < 100; n++)
    {
        if (n * n == value)
            return true;
    }
    return false;
}
```

### Note

- Here's what the solution to part (a) means: When you divide value by 2, if the remainder is 1 then value is odd, and otherwise it's even, so you return false.
- For part (b), you need to separate out the digits. For example, if value is 4629, a way to get digit2 is to start with 4629/100, which is 46. Now 46 % 10 is 6. Note that / and % have equal precedence, so calculate the expressions from left to right.
- For part (b), the last line of the solution does not need the parentheses, because == has a higher precedence than && (AND), so those equality tests will be done before the boolean expression is evaluated.
- For part (c), loop through all the possible perfect squares that are 4-digit integers, and compare them with value. The hint tells you that the largest perfect square less than 1000 is $31^2$ and the smallest perfect square greater than 9999 is $100^2$. Therefore, looping from 32 to 99 lets you generate all possible squares that are 4-digit integers.
- For part (c), the algorithm will return true only if you find a perfect square equal to value. If you're still in the method when you exit the loop, a perfect square

wasn't found and the method returns `false`. Note that it's important not to put an `else` in the `for` loop. This will have the unfortunate effect of returning `false` for the method the first time a non-perfect square is encountered.

## Scoring Rubric: FourDigitInteger

| Part (a) | isOdd | 1 point |
|---|---|---|
| +1 | using `value % 2 == 1` | |

| Part (b) | isPalindrome | 4 points |
|---|---|---|
| +1 | separating value into 4 digits | |
| +1 | using operators / and % correctly | |
| +1 | use of && | |
| +1 | digit 1 == digit 4, digit 2 == digit 3 | |

| Part (c) | isPerfectSquare | 4 points |
|---|---|---|
| +1 | for loop | |
| +1 | looping from `n == 32` to `n == 99` | |
| +1 | `if (n * n == value)` | |
| +1 | correct return value | |

2.
```java
public class Cruise
{
    private int numPassengers;
    private double price;

    public Cruise(int num, double thePrice)
    {
        numPassengers = num;
        price = thePrice;
    }

    public void setPrice (double newPrice)
    { price = newPrice;}

    public void checkResponse(String response)
    {
        if (response.indexOf("cruise") != -1)
            numPassengers++;
    }

    public double calculateRevenue()
    {
        if (numPassengers >= 300)
            return numPassengers * (price - 500);
        else if (numPassengers >= 200)
            return numPassengers * (price - 350);
        else return numPassengers * price;
    }
}
```

## Scoring Rubric: Cruise

| | class Cruise | 9 points |
|---|---|---|
| +1 | private instance variables | |
| +1 | constructor | |
| +1 | setPrice | |
| +1 | checkResponse | |
| +1 | indexOf | |
| +1 | numPassengers++ | |
| +1 | calculateRevenue | |
| +1 | correct if...else statements | |
| +1 | correct return values | |

3. (a)
```java
public ArrayList<Integer> getBlankPositions()
{
    ArrayList<Integer> posList = new ArrayList<Integer>();
    for (int i = 0; i < sentence.length(); i++)
    {
        if (sentence.substring(i, i + 1).equals(" "))
            posList.add(i);
    }
    return posList;
}
```

(b)
```java
public String[] getWords()
{
    ArrayList<Integer> posList = getBlankPositions();
    int numWords = countWords();
    String[] wordArr = new String[numWords];
    for (int i = 0; i < numWords; i++)
    {
        if (i == 0)
        {
            if (posList.size() != 0)
                wordArr[i] = sentence.substring(0, posList.get(0));
            else
                wordArr[i] = sentence;
        }
        else if (i == posList.size())
            wordArr[i] = sentence.substring(posList.get(i - 1) + 1);
        else
            wordArr[i] = sentence.substring(posList.get(i - 1) + 1,
                    posList.get(i));
    }
    return wordArr;
}
```

**Note**

- In part (a), it would also work to have the test

  ```
  i < sentence.length() - 1;
  ```

  in the for loop. But you don't need the –1 because the last character is a punctuation mark, not a blank.
- In part (b), you have to be careful when you get the first word. If there's only one word in the sentence, there are no blanks, which means posList is empty, and you can't use posList.get(0) (because that will throw an IndexOutOfBoundsException!).
- Also in part (b), the second test deals with getting the last word in the sentence. You have to distinguish between the cases of more than one word in the sentence and exactly one word in the sentence. Note that adding 1 to the start index of substring extracts the last word without the blank that precedes it.

## Scoring Rubric: Sentence Manipulation

| Part (a) | getBlankPositions | 4 points |
|---|---|---|
| +1 | create temporary ArrayList | |
| +1 | traverse sentence | |
| +1 | test a character for a blank | |
| +1 | update and return posList | |

| Part (b) | getWords | 5 points |
|---|---|---|
| +1 | get list of blank positions and word count | |
| +1 | get the first word of sentence | |
| +1 | get a middle word of sentence | |
| +1 | get the last word of sentence | |
| +1 | declaration and return of wordArr | |

4. (a)
```
public void reverseAllRows()
{
    for (int[] row: mat)
        ArrayUtil.reverseArray (row);
}
```

(b)
```
public void reverseMatrix()
{
    reverseAllRows();
    int mid = mat.length/2;
    for (int i = 0; i < mid; i++)
    {
        for (int col = 0; col < mat[0].length; col++)
        {
            int temp = mat[i][col];
            mat[i][col] = mat[mat.length - i - 1][col];
            mat[mat.length - i - 1][col] = temp;
        }
    }
}
```

Alternative solution:

```
public void reverseMatrix()
{
    reverseAllRows();
    int mid = mat.length/2;
    for (int i = 0; i < mid; i++)
    {
        int[] temp = mat[i];
        mat[i] = mat[mat.length - i - 1];
        mat[mat.length - i - 1] = temp;
    }
}
```

### Note

- The alternative solution in part (b) swaps the first and last elements, then the second and second last, etc., moving toward the middle. In this case, each element is a row. If there is an odd number of rows, the middle row does not move.
- In the first solution of part (b), start by reversing all rows. Then for each column, swap the elements in the first and last rows, then the second and second last, and so on, moving toward the middle.
- The alternative solution in part (b) is more elegant. It is not, however, part of the AP subset to replace one row of a matrix with a different array.

## Scoring Rubric: Reverse Matrix

| Part (a) | reverseAllRows | 3 points |
|---|---|---|
| +1 | traverse mat | |
| +1 | call to reverseArray | |
| +1 | correct parameter for reverseArray | |

| Part (b) | reverseMatrix | 6 points |
|---|---|---|
| +1 | call to reverseAllRows | |
| +1 | assign mid (or equivalent) | |
| +1 | outer for loop | |
| +1 | inner for loop | |
| +2 | swap matrix elements | |

# 1

# Tips for Taking the Exam

*Take time to deliberate, but when the time for action comes,*
*stop thinking and go in.*
*—Napoléon Bonaparte*

## Learning Objectives

In this chapter, you will learn:

→ Tips for the Multiple-Choice Section
→ Tips for the Free-Response Section

## Tips for the Multiple-Choice Section

### What Is Tested?

The questions in the multiple-choice section, Section I, span the entire AP Java subset, and the types of questions are classified according to the type of content. The table below shows the weighting of various topics on the multiple-choice section, as described in the College Board's latest AP Computer Science A Course and Exam Description. Note that categories can overlap in a given question (for example, a question can compare a recursive algorithm with a fundamental loop implementation), so the percentage total is greater than 100%.

| Topic | Exam Weighting |
|---|---|
| Primitive Types | 2.5–5% |
| Using Objects | 5–7.5% |
| Boolean Expressions and `if` Statements | 15–17.5% |
| Iteration | 17.5–22.5% |
| Writing Classes | 5–7.5% |
| Array | 10–15% |
| `ArrayList` | 2.5–7.5% |
| 2D Array | 7.5–10% |
| Inheritance | 5–10% |
| Recursion | 5–7.5% |

### Time Management

You have 90 minutes for 40 questions, which means a little more than 2 minutes per question. There are, however, several complicated questions that need to be hand traced, which may take longer than 2 minutes. The bottom line is that you don't have time to waste.

Don't let yourself become bogged down on a question. You know how it goes: You're so close to getting the answer, and you've already put in the time to trace the code, and maybe you made an error in your trace and should do it again ... meanwhile the clock is ticking. If a given question stymies you, circle it and move on. You can always come back to it if you have time at the end.

## Guessing

There's no penalty for guessing. If you don't know the answer to a question and are ready to move on, eliminate the answer choices that are clearly wrong, and guess one of the remaining choices.

When time is almost up, bubble in an answer for each of your unanswered questions. Remember, you should make random guesses rather than leaving blanks.

## The Java Quick Reference

You will have access to the Java Quick Reference for both the multiple-choice and free-response sections of the AP exam. You should familiarize yourself with it ahead of time (see p. xvii on how to find it), so that you don't waste time searching for something that isn't in it.

The Quick Reference contains specifications for methods and constants from the Java library for the `Object`, `Integer`, `Double`, `String`, `Math`, and `ArrayList` classes. Each of the methods provided may appear in multiple-choice questions on the AP exam.

## An Active Pencil

You will not be given scratch paper but you may write on the exam booklet. Don't trace tricky algorithms in your head. Here are some active-pencil tips:

- For each iteration of a loop, write down the values of the loop variables and other key variables. Often, just a few values on the page will reveal a pattern and clarify what an algorithm is doing.

- When you trace an algorithm that has a method with parameters, draw memory slots to visualize what's happening to the values. Remember, when a method is called, copies are made of the actual parameters. It's not possible to alter actual values, unless the parameters are references. (See p. 111.)

- To find a value returned by a recursive algorithm, write down the multiple method calls to keep track. (See, e.g., Question 5 on p. 327.)

- In a complicated question about inheritance, sketch a quick UML (inheritance) diagram to reinforce the relationships between classes. (See p. 217.)

- In the multiple-choice section, questions like the following occur frequently:

  - What does this algorithm do?
  - Which could be a postcondition for ...?
  - Which array will result from ...?
  - Which string will be returned?

The key to solving these easily is to think *small*. Give yourself a 3-element array, or a 2 × 2 matrix, or a 3-character string, and hand execute the code on your manageable little data structure. Write down values. Keep track of the loop variables. And the answer will be revealed.

### Troubleshooting—What's Wrong with This Code?

Some multiple-choice questions tell you that the code doesn't work as intended. You are to identify the incorrect replacement for /* more code */, or simply find the error. Here are some quick details you can check:

- If it's a recursive algorithm, does it have a base case?

- Does the base case in a recursive algorithm actually lead to termination?

- In an array algorithm, can the index equal `arr.length`? If so, it is out of bounds.

- Does the algorithm contain `arr[i]` and `arr[i + 1]`? Often `arr[i + 1]` goes out of bounds.

- In a string algorithm that has `str.substring[start]`, is `start` greater than `str.length()`? If so, it is out of bounds.

- In a string algorithm that has `str.substring[start, end]`, is `start` greater than or equal to `end`? If so, it will cause an error. Is `end` greater than `str.length()`? If so, it is out of bounds.

- In an `ArrayList` method other than `add`, is the index value greater than or equal to `list.size()`? If so, it is out of bounds.

- Is a client program of `SomeClass` trying to directly access the private instance variables or private methods of `SomeClass`? It will cause an error.

- Is the keyword `super` being used in a constructor? If so, it had better be in the first line of code; otherwise, it will cause a compile-time error.

- If a value is being inserted into a sorted list, is there a range check to make sure that the algorithm doesn't sail off the end of the list?

## Loop Tracing

Here are some tips:

- There are several questions that will ask how many times a loop is executed. This can be phrased in different ways: How many times will a word or phrase be printed? How many times will a method in the loop body be executed? If the numbers are small, write down all of the values of the loop variable for which the loop will be executed, and count them! That's the answer.

- If the answer to a question with a loop depends on a parameter *n*, try setting *n* to 2 or 3 to see the pattern.

- Be sure to pay attention to whether the loop test uses < or <= (or > or >=).

- Watch out for how the loop variable is being changed. It is not always `i++` (increment by 1) or `i--` (decrement by 1).

## Java Exceptions

Occasionally, one of the answer choices is the following:

The code throws `<some kind of run-time exception>`.

Run your eye down the algorithm and check for:

- An array, `ArrayList`, or `String` going out of bounds. Each situation will throw the corresponding exception: `ArrayIndexOutOfBoundsException`, `IndexOutOfBoundsException`, or `StringIndexOutOfBoundsException`. If you find it, you can move on without even glancing at the other answer choices.

- Integer division by zero. If division by zero occurs in the first part of a compound test, an `ArithmeticException` will always be thrown. If the division is in the second part of the test, you won't get the exception if the value of the whole test is already known (short-circuit evaluation). (See p. 71.)

## Matrix Manipulation

Suppose you are given a matrix and an algorithm that changes the matrix in some way. These algorithms are often hard to trace, and, to complicate the problem, you don't have much time.

Assume that `row` and `col` are loop variables in the algorithm. For a quick solution, try looking at the element that corresponds to the first `row` value and first `col` value of the loop. Often this is the element in the top left-hand corner. Does it change? Can you eliminate some of the answer choices, based on this one element? Repeat the process for the final `row` and `col` values. Often this is the element in the bottom right-hand corner. Can you eliminate other answer choices?

In other words, you don't always need to trace all of the values to find the answer.

## Comparing Algorithms

Several questions may ask you to compare two algorithms that supposedly implement the same algorithm. They may ask you which algorithm is more efficient. Factors that affect efficiency are the number of comparisons and the number of data moves. Check out the body of each loop. Count the comparisons and data movements. Multiply the total by the number of iterations of the loop. The algorithm with the lower answer is the more efficient algorithm.

You may be asked to compare data structures. These are the questions to ask yourself:

- Which involves the least number of comparisons to locate a given element?

- Which involves the least number of data moves to insert or remove an element?

- Does the structure store the entire state of the object?

## Mechanics of Answering Multiple-Choice Questions

Here are three final tips:

- Take care that you bubble in the answer that corresponds to the number of the question you just solved!

- Since the mark-sense sheet is scored by machine, make sure that you erase completely if you change an answer.

- Take a moment at the end to check that you have provided an answer for every question.

## Tips for the Free-Response Section

### What Is the Format?

- You will have 90 minutes for four free-response questions in Section II of the exam.

- Each question is worth 9 points. Note that the free-response and multiple-choice sections carry equal weight in determining your AP score.

- The code that you write must be in Java.

- Write your solutions to the questions on the answer booklet provided. Bubble the question number at the top of each answer page.

- You should use a No. 2 pencil for your solutions.

> Be aware that the separate answer booklet for the free-response questions will be blank.

### What Is Tested?

In theory, the entire AP Java subset is fair game for free-response questions. But you should pay special attention to each of the following:

- List manipulation using both arrays and `ArrayLists`

- String manipulation

- Two-dimensional arrays

- Classes and subclasses

### What Types of Questions Might Be Asked?

You may be asked to do each of the following:

- Write the body of a specified method

- Write the bodies of methods using code from previous parts of the question

- Write an overloaded method (p. 106)

- Write a constructor (p. 143)

- Provide an overridden method in a subclass (p. 143)

- Write a complete class or subclass

### Skill Focus in Free-Response Questions

As in past exams, all of the questions will test your ability to use expressions, conditional statements, and loops, according to various specifications.

Additionally, each free-response question will have a particular skill focus.

**QUESTION 1: METHODS AND CONTROL STRUCTURES**  This tests your ability to call methods, write code for methods, and write code to create objects of a class.

The question may include String manipulation, or expressions that use div (/) and mod (%), or sequences of `if...else` statements.

**QUESTION 2: CLASS WRITING**  This tests your ability to write code for a class or subclass according to various specifications.

Brush up on writing constructors, use of `super`, and overridden and inherited methods.

**QUESTION 3: ARRAY AND ARRAYLIST MANIPULATION**   This tests your ability to create, traverse, and manipulate elements in a 1D array or `ArrayList` of objects.

Review the rules for using enhanced `for` loops in traversals, and the specific methods of `ArrayList` for manipulating lists of objects.

**QUESTION 4: 2D ARRAY MANIPULATION**   This tests your ability to create, traverse, and manipulate elements in a 2D array of objects.

Brush up on row-by-row traversals, using the fact that a 2D array is an array of 1D arrays. Review the rules for using enhanced `for` loops in 2D array traversals.

## The Java Quick Reference

You will continue to have access to the Java Quick Reference for the free-response section of the AP exam. Here are tips for using it in the code you write:

- When you use a library method from the `ArrayList` interface, or from the `Object`, `String`, or `Math` classes, a glance at the Quick Reference will confirm that you're using the correct method name and also the correct format and ordering of parameters.

- The correct format of the constants for the smallest and largest `Integer` values (`Integer.MIN_VALUE` and `Integer.MAX_VALUE`) are shown.

- Again, use the Quick Reference throughout the year. Do not study it for the first time during the AP exam!

- When you write code that uses methods of the `String` class, the Quick Reference will help ensure that you use the correct type and order of parameters.

## Time Management

Here are some tips for managing your time:

- Just 90 minutes for four questions means fewer than 23 minutes per question. Since many of the questions involve up to two pages of reading, you don't have much time. Nevertheless, you should take a minute to read through the whole section so that you can start with a question you feel confident about. It gives you a psychological boost to have a solid question in the bag.

- When you tackle a free-response question, underline key words in the problem as well as return types and parameters. This kind of close reading will help you to process the question quickly without inadvertently missing important information.

- Take a minute to circle the methods that you are given to implement other methods. If you write code that reimplements those given methods, you won't get full credit.

- Work steadily through the questions. If you get stuck on a question, move on. If you can answer only one part of a question, do it and leave the other parts blank. You can return to them if there's time at the end.

- Don't waste time writing comments: the graders generally ignore them. The occasional comment that clarifies a segment of code is OK. I know this because I graded AP Computer Science exams for many years.

## Grading the Free-Response Questions

Be aware that this section is graded by humans. It's in your interest to have graders understand your solutions. With this in mind:

- Use a sharp pencil, write legibly, space your answers, and indent correctly.

- Use self-documenting names for variables, methods, and so on.

- Use the identifiers that are used in the question.

- Write clear, readable code. Avoid obscure, convoluted code.

The graders have a rubric that allocates each of the 9 points for solving the various parts of a problem. If your solution works, you will get full credit. This is irrespective of whether your code is efficient or elegant. You should never, ever take time to rewrite a working piece of code more elegantly.

You will be awarded partial credit if you used the right approach for a question, but didn't quite nail the solution. Each valid piece of your code that is included in the rubric will earn you some credit.

There are certain errors that are not penalized. For example, the graders will look the other way if you omit semicolons, or misspell identifiers, or use keywords as identifiers, or confuse `length` with `length()`, or use = instead of ==, or use the wrong kind of brackets for an array element.

They will, however, deduct points for each of the following types of errors:

- Including output statements in methods that don't require it.

- Including an output statement in a method, instead of returning a value. (Are you clear on this? No `System.out.print()` or `System.out.println()` statements in methods that didn't ask for output!).

- Using local variables that aren't declared.

- Returning the wrong type of value in a method, or returning a value in a `void` method, or having a constructor return a value.

- Using incorrect syntax for traversing and processing arrays and `ArrayLists`.

Take heart: On any given question, you won't receive a negative score!

## Writing Code

Here are important reminders for the code that you write:

- It's worth repeating: You must use Java for your solutions. No pseudocode, or C++, or any other programming language.

- If the statement of the question provides an algorithm, you should say "thank you" and use it. Don't waste time trying to reinvent the wheel.

- Don't omit a question just because you can't come up with a complete solution. Remember, partial credit is awarded. Also, don't omit part (b) of a question just because you couldn't do part (a)—the various parts of a question are graded independently.

- In writing solutions to a question, you must use the public methods of classes provided in that question wherever possible. If you write a significant chunk of code that can be replaced by a call to one of those methods, you will probably not receive full credit for the question.

■ If you're writing a subclass of a given superclass, don't rewrite the public methods of that class unless you are overriding them. All public methods are inherited.

■ It is fine to use methods from the Java library that are not in the AP Java subset. You will receive full credit if you use those methods correctly. If your usage, however, is incorrect, your solution will be penalized. Note that there is always a solution that uses the subset, and you should try to find it.

■ It is fine to write a helper method for your solution. But be aware that usually you can solve the question using methods that are already provided.

## Maximizing Your Score

Here are some final general tips for maximizing your free-response score:

■ At the start of the free-response section, clear the decks! The multiple-choice section is over, and whether you did great or not, it is past history. Take a deep breath and psych yourself up for the code-writing part of the exam. Now is the time to strut your stuff.

■ Don't ever erase a solution. Cross it out. You want to avoid a situation in which you erased some code, but don't have time to write the replacement code.

■ If you can't see a solution to a question, but have some understanding of what is required to solve it, write something down. Just showing that you understand that you must loop through all of the elements in a list, for example, may earn you a point from the rubric.

■ Don't provide more than one solution for a given part. The exam readers are instructed to grade the first attempt only, and to ignore all subsequent ones. Not even the most warm-hearted among us will go wading through the marshes of your various solutions, searching for the one that solves the problem correctly. This means that you must choose one solution and cross out the others with firm, legible lines.

■ One final reminder: Use clear, readable code from the AP Java subset. Avoid obscure, opaque brilliancies. The AP exam is not the place to show the world you're a genius.

Good luck!

# 2

# Introductory Java Language Features

*Fifty loops shalt thou make...*
—Exodus 26:5

## Learning Objectives

In this chapter, you will learn:

- → Packages and classes
- → Types and identifiers
- → Operators
- → Input/output
- → Control structures
- → Errors and exceptions

The AP Computer Science course includes algorithm analysis, data structures, and the techniques and methods of modern programming—specifically, object-oriented programming. A high-level programming language is used to explore these concepts. Java is the language currently in use on the AP exam.

Java was developed by James Gosling and a team at Sun Microsystems in California; it continues to evolve. The AP exam covers a clearly defined subset of Java language features that are presented throughout this book. A complete listing of this subset can be found on the College Board website.

Java provides basic control structures such as the `if-else` statement, `for` loop, enhanced `for` loop, and `while` loop, as well as fundamental built-in data types. But the power of the language lies in the manipulation of user-defined types called *objects*, many of which can interact in a single program.

## Packages and Classes

A typical Java program has user-defined classes whose objects interact with those from Java class libraries. In Java, related classes are grouped into *packages*, many of which are provided with the compiler. For example, the package `java.util` contains the collections classes. Note that you can put your own classes into a package—this facilitates their use in other programs.

The package `java.lang`, which contains many commonly used classes, is automatically provided to all Java programs. To use any other package in a program, an `import` statement must be used. To import all of the classes in a package called `packagename`, use the form

```
import packagename.*;
```

Note that the package name is all lowercase letters. To import a single class called `ClassName` from the package, use

```
import packagename.ClassName;
```

Java has a hierarchy of packages and subpackages. Subpackages are selected using multiple dots:

```
import packagename.subpackagename.ClassName;
```

For example,

```
import java.util.ArrayList;
```

The `import` statement allows the programmer to use the objects and methods defined in the designated package. You will not be expected to write any `import` statements.

A Java program must have at least one class, the one that contains the *main method.* The Java files that comprise your program are called *source files.*

A *compiler* converts source code into machine-readable form called *bytecode.*

Here is a typical source file for a Java program:

```
/* Program FirstProg.java
   Start with a comment, giving the program name and a brief
   description of what the program does.
 */
import package1.*;
import package2.subpackage.ClassName;

public class FirstProg  //note that the file name is FirstProg.java
{
    public static type1 method1(parameter list)
    {
        < code for method 1 >
    }
    public static type2 method2(parameter list)
    {
        < code for method 2 >
    }
        ...

    public static void main(String[] args)
    {
        < your code >
    }
}
```

## Note

1. All Java methods must be contained in a class.
2. The words `class`, `public`, `static`, and `void` are *reserved words*, also called *keywords.* (This means they have specific uses in Java and may not be used as identifiers.)
3. The keyword `public` signals that the class or method is usable outside of the class, whereas `private` data members or methods (see Chapter 3) are not.
4. The keyword `static` is used for methods that will not access any objects of a class, such as the methods in the `FirstProg` class in the example above. This is typically true for all methods in a source file that contains no *instance variables* (see Chapter 3). Most methods in Java do operate on objects and are not static. The `main` method, however, must always be static.
5. The program shown above is a Java *application.*

6. There are three different types of comment delimiters in Java:

   - /* ... */, which is the one used in the program shown, to enclose a block of comments. The block can extend over one or more lines.

   - //, which generates a comment on one line.

   - /** ... */, which generates Javadoc comments. These are used to create API documentation of Java library software.

## Javadoc Comments

The Javadoc comments @param and @return are no longer part of the AP Java subset.

## Types and Identifiers

### Identifiers

An *identifier* is a name for a variable, parameter, constant, user-defined method, or user-defined class. In Java, an identifier is any sequence of letters, digits, and the underscore character. Identifiers may not begin with a digit. Identifiers are case-sensitive, which means that age and Age are different. Wherever possible, identifiers should be concise and self-documenting. A variable called area is more illuminating than one called a.

By convention, identifiers for variables and methods are lowercase. Uppercase letters are used to separate these into multiple words, for example, getName, findSurfaceArea, preTaxTotal, and so on. Note that a class name starts with a capital letter. Reserved words are entirely lowercase and may not be used as identifiers.

### Built-in Types

Every identifier in a Java program has a type associated with it. The *primitive* or *built-in* types that are included in the AP Java subset are

| | |
|---|---|
| int | An integer. For example, 2, -26, 3000 |
| boolean | A boolean. Just two values, true or false |
| double | A double precision floating-point number. For example, 2.718, -367189.41, 1.6e4 |

(Note that primitive type char is not included in the AP Java subset.)

Integer values are stored exactly. Because there's a fixed amount of memory set aside for their storage, however, integers are bounded. If you try to store a value whose magnitude is too big in an int variable, you'll get an *overflow error*. (Java gives you no warning. You just get a wrong result!)

An identifier—for example, a *variable*—is introduced into a Java program with a *declaration* that specifies its type. A variable is often initialized in its declaration. Some examples follow:

```
int x;
double y,z;
boolean found;
int count = 1;               //count initialized to 1
double p = 2.3, q = 4.1;     //p and q initialized to 2.3 and 4.1
```

One type can be cast to another compatible type if appropriate. For example,

```
int total, n;
double average;
   ...
average = (double) total/n;    //total cast to double to ensure
                               //real division is used
```

Alternatively,

```
average = total/(double) n;
```

Assigning an int to a double automatically casts the int to double. For example,

```
int num = 5;
double realNum = num;    //num is cast to double
```

Assigning a double to an int without a cast, however, causes a compile-time error. For example,

```
double x = 6.79;
int intNum = x;        //Error. Need an explicit cast to int
```

Note that casting a floating-point (real) number to an integer simply truncates the number. For example,

```
double cost = 10.95;
int numDollars = (int) cost;    //sets numDollars to 10
```

If your intent was to round cost to the nearest dollar, you needed to write

```
int numDollars = (int) (cost + 0.5);  //numDollars has value 11
```

To round a negative number to the nearest integer:

```
double negAmount = -4.8;
int roundNeg = (int) (negAmount - 0.5);   //roundNeg has value -5
```

The strategy of adding or subtracting 0.5 before casting correctly rounds in all cases.

## Storage of Numbers

The details of storage are not tested on the AP exam. They are, however, useful for understanding the differences between types int and double.

### Integers

Integer values in Java are stored exactly, as a string of bits (binary digits). One of the bits stores the sign of the integer: 0 for positive, 1 for negative.

The Java built-in integral type, byte, uses one byte (eight bits) of storage.

| 0 | 1 | 1 | 1 | 1 | 1 | 1 | 1 |

The picture represents the largest positive integer that can be stored using type byte: $2^7 - 1$.

Type int in Java uses four bytes (32 bits). Taking one bit for a sign, the largest possible integer stored is $2^{31} - 1$. In general, an $n$-bit integer uses $n/8$ bytes of storage, and stores integers from $-2^{n-1}$ to $2^{n-1} - 1$. (Note that the extra value on the negative side comes from not having to store $-0$.) There are two Java constants that you should know. Integer.MAX_VALUE holds the maximum value an int can hold, $2^{31} - 1$. Integer.MIN_VALUE holds the minimum value an int can hold, $-2^{31}$.

Built-in integer types in Java are byte (one byte), short (two bytes), int (four bytes), and long (eight bytes). Of these, only int is in the AP Java subset.

### Floating-Point Numbers

There are two built-in types in Java that store real numbers: float, which uses four bytes, and double, which uses eight bytes. A *floating-point number* is stored in two parts: a *mantissa*, which specifies the digits of the number, and an exponent. The JVM (Java Virtual Machine) represents the number using scientific notation:

$$sign * mantissa * 2^{exponent}$$

In this expression, 2 is the *base* or *radix* of the number. In type double, 11 bits are allocated for the exponent, and (typically) 52 bits for the mantissa. One bit is allocated for the sign. This is a *double-precision* number. Type float, which is *single-precision*, is not in the AP Java subset.

When floating-point numbers are converted to binary, most cannot be represented exactly, leading to *round-off error*. These errors are compounded by arithmetic operations. For example,

$$0.1*26 \neq 0.1+0.1+\cdots+0.1 \quad (26 \text{ terms})$$

In Java, no exceptions are thrown for floating-point operations. There are two situations you should be aware of:

- When an operation is performed that gives an undefined result, Java expresses this result as NaN, "not a number." Examples of operations that produce NaN are: taking the square root of a negative number, and 0.0 divided by 0.0.

- An operation that gives an infinitely large or infinitely small number, like division by zero, produces a result of Infinity or -Infinity in Java.

### Hexadecimal and Octal Numbers

Base 2, base 8, and base 16 are no longer part of the AP Java subset. Only base 10 will be used on the AP exam.

### Final Variables

A *final variable* or *user-defined constant*, identified by the keyword final, is a quantity whose value will not change. Here are some examples of final declarations:

```
final double TAX_RATE = 0.08;
final int CLASS_SIZE = 35;
```

**Note**

1. Constant identifiers are, by convention, capitalized.
2. A `final` variable can be declared without initializing it immediately. For example,

```
final double TAX_RATE;
if (< some condition >)
    TAX_RATE = 0.08;
else
    TAX_RATE = 0.0;
// TAX_RATE can be given a value just once: its value is final!
```

3. A common use for a constant is as an array bound. For example,

```
final int MAXSTUDENTS = 25;
int[] classList = new int[MAXSTUDENTS];
```

4. Using constants makes it easier to revise code. Just a single change in the `final` declaration need be made, rather than having to change every occurrence of a value.


## Operators

### Arithmetic Operators

| Operator | Meaning | Example |
|---|---|---|
| + | addition | 3 + x |
| - | subtraction | p - q |
| * | multiplication | 6 * i |
| / | division | 10 / 4  //returns 2, not 2.5! |
| % | mod (remainder) | 11 % 8  //returns 3 |

**Note**

1. These operators can be applied to types `int` and `double`, even if both types occur in the same expression. For an operation involving a `double` and an `int`, the `int` is promoted to `double`, and the result is a `double`.
2. The mod operator `%`, as in the expression `a % b`, gives the remainder when `a` is divided by `b`. Thus `10 % 3` evaluates to `1`, whereas `4.2 % 2.0` evaluates to `0.2`.
3. Integer division `a/b` where both `a` and `b` are of type `int` returns the integer quotient only (i.e., the answer is truncated). Thus, `22/6` gives `3`, and `3/4` gives `0`. If at least one of the operands is of type `double`, then the operation becomes regular floating-point division, and there is no truncation. You can control the kind of division that is carried out by explicitly casting (one or both of) the operands from `int` to `double` and vice versa. Thus

```
3.0 / 4          →    0.75
3 / 4.0          →    0.75
(int) 3.0 / 4    →    0
(double) 3 / 4   →    0.75
```

You must, however, be careful:

$$(\text{double}) \ (3 \ / \ 4) \quad \rightarrow \quad 0.0$$

since the integer division 3/4 is computed first, before casting to `double`.

4. The arithmetic operators follow the normal precedence rules (order of operations):

      (1)    parentheses, from the inner ones out (highest precedence)

      (2)    `*`, `/`, `%`

      (3)    `+`, `-` (lowest precedence)

Here operators on the same line have the same precedence, and, in the absence of parentheses, are invoked from left to right. Thus, the expression `19 % 5 * 3 + 14 / 5` evaluates to `4 * 3 + 2` = 14. Note that casting has precedence over all of these operators. Thus, in the expression `(double) 3/4`, 3 will be cast to `double` before the division is done.

## Relational Operators

| Operator | Meaning | Example |
|---|---|---|
| `==` | equal to | `if (x == 100)` |
| `!=` | not equal to | `if (age != 21)` |
| `>` | greater than | `if (salary > 30000)` |
| `<` | less than | `if (grade < 65)` |
| `>=` | greater than or equal to | `if (age >= 16)` |
| `<=` | less than or equal to | `if (height <= 6)` |

### Note

1. Relational operators are used in *boolean expressions* that evaluate to `true` or `false`.

```
boolean x = (a != b);      //initializes x to true if a != b,
                           // false otherwise
return p == q;   //returns true if p equals q, false otherwise
```

2. If the operands are an `int` and a `double`, the `int` is promoted to a `double` as for arithmetic operators.

3. Relational operators should generally be used only in the comparison of primitive types (i.e., `int`, `double`, or `boolean`). Strings are compared using the `equals` and `compareTo` methods (see p. 175).

4. Be careful when comparing floating-point values! Since floating-point numbers cannot always be represented exactly in the computer memory, a round-off error could be introduced, leading to an incorrect result when `==` is used to test for equality.

**Do not routinely use `==` to test for equality of floating-point numbers.**

### Comparing Floating-Point Numbers

Because of round-off errors in floating-point numbers, you can't rely on using the == or != operators to compare two double values for equality. They may differ in their last significant digit or two because of round-off error. Instead, you should test that the magnitude of the difference between the numbers is less than some number about the size of the machine precision. The machine precision is usually denoted $\epsilon$ and is typically about $10^{-16}$ for double precision (i.e., about 16 decimal digits). So you would like to test something like $|x - y| \leq \epsilon$. But this is no good if $x$ and $y$ are very large. For example, suppose $x = 1234567890.123456$ and $y = 1234567890.123457$. These numbers are essentially equal to machine precision, since they differ only in the 16th significant digit. But $|x - y| = 10^{-6}$, not $10^{-16}$. So in general you should check the *relative* difference:

$$\frac{|x - y|}{\max(|x|, |y|)} \leq \epsilon$$

To avoid problems with dividing by zero, code this as

$$|x - y| \leq \epsilon \max(|x|, |y|)$$

## Logical Operators

A *logical operator* (sometimes called a *boolean operator*) is one that returns a boolean result that is based on the boolean result(s) of one or two other boolean expressions. The three logical operators are shown in the table below.

| Operator | Meaning | Example |
|----------|---------|---------|
| ! | NOT | if (!found) |
| && | AND | if (x < 3 && y > 4) |
| \|\| | OR | if (age < 2 \|\| height < 4) |

### Note

1. Logical operators are applied to boolean expressions to form *compound boolean expressions* that evaluate to true or false.
2. Values of true or false are assigned according to the truth tables for the logical operators.

| && | T | F |
|----|---|---|
| T | T | F |
| F | F | F |

| \|\| | T | F |
|------|---|---|
| T | T | T |
| F | T | F |

| ! | |
|---|---|
| T | F |
| F | T |

For example, F && T evaluates to F, while T || F evaluates to T.

3. *Short-circuit evaluation.* The subexpressions in a compound boolean expression are evaluated from left to right, and evaluation automatically stops as soon as the value of the entire expression is known. For example, consider a boolean OR expression of the form A || B, where A and B are some boolean expressions. If A is true, then the expression is true irrespective of the value of B. Similarly, if A is false, then A && B evaluates to false irrespective of the second operand. So in each case the second operand is not evaluated. For example,

```
if (numScores != 0 && scoreTotal/numScores > 90)
```

will not cause a run-time ArithmeticException (division-by-zero error) if the value of numScores is 0. This is because numScores != 0 will evaluate to false, causing the entire boolean expression to evaluate to false without having to evaluate the second expression containing the division.

## Assignment Operators

| Operator | Example | Meaning |
|---|---|---|
| = | x = 2 | simple assignment |
| += | x += 4 | x = x + 4 |
| -= | y -= 6 | y = y - 6 |
| *= | p *= 5 | p = p * 5 |
| /= | n /= 10 | n = n / 10 |
| %= | n %= 10 | n = n % 10 |

## Note

1. All these operators, with the exception of simple assignment, are called *compound assignment operators.*
2. *Chaining* of assignment statements is allowed, with evaluation from right to left. (This is not tested on the AP exam.)

```
int next, prev, sum;
next = prev = sum = 0;  //initializes sum to 0, then prev to 0
                        //then next to 0
```

## Increment and Decrement Operators

| Operator | Example | Meaning |
|---|---|---|
| ++ | i++ or ++i | i is incremented by 1 |
| -- | k-- or --k | k is decremented by 1 |

Note that i++ (postfix) and ++i (prefix) both have the net effect of incrementing i by 1, but they are not equivalent. For example, if i currently has the value 5, then System.out.println(i++) will print 5 and then increment i to 6, whereas System.out.println(++i) will first increment i to 6 and then print 6. It's easy to remember: If the ++ is first, you first increment. A similar distinction occurs between k-- and --k. (Note: You do not need to know these distinctions for the AP exam.)

## Operator Precedence

| highest precedence | → | (1) | !, ++, -- |
|---|---|---|---|
| | | (2) | *, /, % |
| | | (3) | +, - |
| | | (4) | <, >, <=, >= |
| | | (5) | ==, != |
| | | (6) | && |
| | | (7) | \|\| |
| lowest precedence | → | (8) | =, +=, -=, *=, /=, %= |

Here operators on the same line have equal precedence. The evaluation of the operators with equal precedence is from left to right, except for rows (1) and (8) where the order is right to left. It is easy to remember: The only "backward" order is for the unary operators (row 1) and for the various assignment operators (row 8).

### ▷ Example

What will be output by the following statement?

```
System.out.println(5 + 3 < 6 - 1);
```

### ✓ Solution

Since + and - have precedence over <, 5 + 3 and 6 - 1 will be evaluated before evaluating the boolean expression. Since the value of the expression is false, the statement will output `false`.

## Input/Output

### Input

Since there are so many ways to provide input to a program, user input is not a part of the AP Java subset. If reading input is a necessary part of a question on the AP exam, it will be indicated something like this:

```
double x = call to a method that reads a floating-point number
```

or

```
double x = ...;    //read user input
```

### Note

The `Scanner` class simplifies both console and file input. It will not, however, be tested on the AP exam.

### Output

Testing of output will be restricted to `System.out.print` and `System.out.println`. Formatted output will not be tested.

   `System.out` is an object in the `System` class that allows output to be displayed on the screen. The `println` method outputs an item and then goes to a new line. The `print` method outputs an item without going to a new line afterward. An item to be printed can be a string, or a number, or the value of a boolean expression (`true` or `false`). Here are some examples:

```
System.out.print("Hot");
System.out.println("dog");
```
} prints `Hotdog`

```
System.out.println("Hot");
System.out.println("dog");
```
prints
`Hot`
`dog`

```
System.out.println(7 + 3);
```
} prints `10`

```
System.out.println(7 == 2 + 5);
```
} prints `true`

```
int x = 27;
System.out.println(x);
```
} prints `27`

```
System.out.println("Value of x is " + x);
```
prints `Value of x is 27`

In the last example, the value of `x`, 27, is converted to the string `"27"`, which is then concatenated to the string `"Value of x is "`.

To print the "values" of user-defined objects, the `toString()` method is invoked (see p. 171).

## Escape Sequences

An *escape sequence* is a backslash followed by a single character. It is used to print special characters. The three escape sequences that you should know for the AP exam are

| Escape Sequence | Meaning |
|---|---|
| \n | newline |
| \" | double quote |
| \\ | backslash |

Here are some examples:

```
System.out.println("Welcome to\na new line");
```

prints

```
Welcome to
a new line
```

The statement

```
System.out.println("He is known as \"Hothead Harry\".");
```

prints

```
He is known as "Hothead Harry".
```

The statement

```
System.out.println("The file path is d:\\myFiles\\..");
```

prints

```
The file path is d:\myFiles\..
```

## Control Structures

Control structures are the mechanism by which you make the statements of a program run in a nonsequential order. There are two general types: decision-making and iteration.

### Decision-Making Control Structures

These include the `if`, `if...else`, and `switch` statements. They are all selection control structures that introduce a decision-making ability into a program. Based on the truth value of a boolean expression, the computer will decide which path to follow. The `switch` statement is not part of the AP Java subset.

### The `if` Statement

```
if (boolean expression)
{
    statements
}
```

Here the *statements* will be executed only if the ***boolean expression*** is `true`. If it is `false`, control passes immediately to the first statement following the `if` statement.

### The `if...else` Statement

```
if (boolean expression)
{
    statements
}
else
{
    statements
}
```

Here, if the ***boolean expression*** is `true`, only the *statements* immediately following the test will be executed. If the ***boolean expression*** is `false`, only the *statements* following the `else` will be executed.

### Nested `if` Statement

If the statement in an `if` statement is itself an `if` statement, the result is a *nested `if` statement*.

> **Example 1**

```
if (boolean expr1)
    if (boolean expr2)
        statement;
```

This is equivalent to

```
if (boolean expr1 && boolean expr2)
    statement;
```

## > Example 2

Beware the dangling `else`! Suppose you want to read in an integer and print it if it's positive and even. Will the following code do the job?

```
int n = ...;           //read user input
if (n > 0)
    if (n % 2 == 0)
        System.out.println(n);
else
    System.out.println(n + " is not positive");
```

A user enters 7 and is surprised to see the output

```
7 is not positive
```

The reason is that `else` always gets matched with the *nearest* unpaired `if`, not the first `if` as the indenting would suggest.

There are two ways to fix the preceding code. The first is to use {} delimiters to group the statements correctly.

```
int n = ...;           //read user input
if (n > 0)
{
    if (n % 2 == 0)
        System.out.println(n);
}
else
    System.out.println(n + " is not positive");
```

The second way of fixing the code is to rearrange the statements.

```
int n = ...;           //read user input
if (n <= 0)
    System.out.println(n + " is not positive");
else
    if (n % 2 == 0)
        System.out.println(n);
```

### Extended `if` Statement

For example,

```
String grade = ...;          //read user input
if (grade.equals("A"))
    System.out.println("Excellent!");
else if (grade.equals("B"))
    System.out.println("Good");
else if (grade.equals("C") || grade.equals("D"))
    System.out.println("Poor");
else if (grade.equals("F"))
    System.out.println("Egregious!");
else
    System.out.println("Invalid grade");
```

If any of A, B, C, D, or F are entered, an appropriate message will be written, and control will go to the statement immediately following the extended if statement. If any other string is entered, the final else is invoked, and the message Invalid grade will be written.

## Iteration

Java has three different control structures that allow the computer to perform iterative tasks: the for loop, while loop, and do...while loop. The do...while loop is not in the AP Java subset.

### The for Loop

The general form of the for loop is

```
for (initialization; termination condition; update statement)
{
    statements          //body of loop
}
```

The termination condition is tested at the top of the loop; the update statement is performed at the bottom.

### > Example 1

```
//outputs 1 2 3 4
for (i = 1; i < 5; i++)
    System.out.print(i + " ");
```

Here's how it works. The *loop variable* i is initialized to 1, and the termination condition i < 5 is evaluated. If it is true, the body of the loop is executed, and then the loop variable i is incremented according to the update statement. As soon as the termination condition is false (i.e., i >= 5), control passes to the first statement following the loop.

### > Example 2

```
//outputs 20 19 18 17 16 15
for (k = 20; k >= 15; k--)
    System.out.print(k + " ");
```

### > Example 3

```
//outputs 2 4 6 8 10
for (j = 2; j <= 10; j += 2)
    System.out.print(j + " ");
```

## Note

1. The loop variable should not have its value changed inside the loop body.
2. The initializing and update statements can use any valid constants, variables, or expressions.
3. The scope (see p. 106) of the loop variable can be restricted to the loop body by combining the loop variable declaration with the initialization. For example,

```
for (int i = 0; i < 3; i++)
{
    ...
}
```

4.  The following loop is syntactically valid:

```
for (int i = 1; i <= 0; i++)
{
    ...
}
```

The loop body will not be executed at all, since the exiting condition is true before the first execution.

### Enhanced `for` loop (for-each Loop)

This is used to iterate over an array or collection. The general form of the loop is

```
for (SomeType element : collection)
{
    statements
}
```

(Read the top line as "For each `element` of type `SomeType` in `collection` ...")

### ▷ Example

```
//Outputs all elements of arr, one per line.
for (int element : arr)
    System.out.println(element);
```

### Note

1.  The enhanced `for` loop should be used for accessing elements in the data structure, not for replacing or removing elements as you traverse.
2.  The loop hides the index variable that is used with arrays.

### The `while` Loop

The general form of the `while` loop is

```
while (boolean test)
{
    statements          //loop body
}
```

The *boolean test* is performed at the beginning of the loop. If `true`, the loop body is executed. Otherwise, control passes to the first statement following the loop. After execution of the loop body, the test is performed again. If `true`, the loop is executed again, and so on.

## > Example 1

```
int i = 1, mult3 = 3;
while (mult3 < 20)
{
    System.out.print(mult3 + " ");
    i++;
    mult3 *= i;
}                      //outputs 3 6 18
```

The body of a `while` loop must contain a statement that leads to termination.

### Note

1. It is possible for the body of a `while` loop never to be executed. This will happen if the test evaluates to `false` the first time.

2. Disaster will strike in the form of an infinite loop if the test can never be false. Don't forget to change the loop variable in the body of the loop in a way that leads to termination!

3. When the loop finishes executing, the value of the loop variable `mult3` is 72, causing the test `mult3 < 20` to fail. Notice that `i` is also updated and its final value is 4.

## > Example 2

```
int power2 = 1;
while (power2 != 20)
{
    System.out.println(power2);
    power2 *= 2;
}
```

Since `power2` will never exactly equal 20, the loop will grind merrily along eventually causing an integer overflow.

## > Example 3

```
/* Screen out bad data.
 * The loop won't allow execution to continue until a valid
 * integer is entered.
 */
System.out.println("Enter a positive integer from 1 to 100");
int num = ...;          //read user input
while (num < 1 || num > 100)
{
    System.out.println("Number must be from 1 to 100.");
    System.out.println("Please reenter");
    num = ...;
}
```

> **Example 4**

```
/* Uses a sentinel to terminate data entered at the keyboard.
 * The sentinel is a value that cannot be part of the data.
 * It signals the end of the list.
 */
final int SENTINEL = -999;
System.out.println("Enter list of positive integers," +
    " end list with " + SENTINEL);
int value = ...;        //read user input
while (value != SENTINEL)
{
    process the value
    value = ...;        //read another value
}
```

## Nested Loops

You create a *nested loop* when a loop is a statement in the body of another loop.

> **Example 1**

```
for (int k = 1; k <= 3; k++)
{
    for (int i = 1; i <= 4; i++)
        System.out.print("*");
    System.out.println();
}
```

The table below shows what the algorithm is doing.

| k | i | Steps |
|---|---|-------|
| 1 | 1<br>2<br>3<br>4 | When k is 1,<br>print 4 stars,<br>go to next line |
| 2 | 1<br>2<br>3<br>4 | When k is 2,<br>do it again |
| 3 | 1<br>2<br>3<br>4 | And again,<br>when k is 3 |

Think:

```
for each of 3 rows
{
        print 4 stars
        go to next line
}
```

Here is the final output:

```
****
****
****
```

## > Example 2

This example has two loops nested in an outer loop.

```java
for (int i = 1; i <= 6; i++)
{
    for (int j = 1; j <= i; j++)
        System.out.print("+");
    for (int j = 1; j <= 6 - i; j++)
        System.out.print("*");
    System.out.println();
}
```

Output:

```
+*****
++****
+++***
++++**
+++++*
++++++
```

## Errors and Exceptions

An *exception* is an error condition that occurs during the execution of a Java program. For example, if you divide an integer by zero, an `ArithmeticException` will be thrown. If you use a negative array index, an `ArrayIndexOutOfBoundsException` will be thrown.

An *unchecked exception* is one that is automatically handled by Java's standard exception-handling methods, which terminate execution. It is thrown if an attempt is made to divide an integer by 0, or if an array index goes out of bounds, and so on. The exception tells you that you now need to fix your code!

A *checked exception* is one where you provide code to handle the exception, either a `try`/`catch`/`finally` statement, or an explicit `throw new...Exception` clause. These exceptions are not necessarily caused by an error in the code. For example, an unexpected end-of-file could be due to a broken network connection. Checked exceptions are not part of the AP Java subset.

The following unchecked exceptions are in the AP Java subset:

| Exception | Discussed on page |
|---|---|
| ArithmeticException | on the previous page |
| NullPointerException | 110 |
| ArrayIndexOutOfBoundsException | 239 |
| IndexOutOfBoundsException | 250 |
| StringIndexOutOfBoundsException | 176 |
| ConcurrentModificationException | 254 |

Java allows you to write code that throws a standard unchecked exception. Here is a typical example.

> **Example**

```
if (numScores == 0)
    throw new ArithmeticException("Cannot divide by zero");
else
    findAverageScore();
```

**Note**

1. `throw` and `new` are both reserved words. (The keywords `throw` and `throws` are not in the AP Java subset.)
2. The error message is optional: The line in this example could have read

   ```
   throw new ArithmeticException();
   ```

   The message, however, is useful, since it tells the person running the program what went wrong.


## Chapter Summary

Be sure that you understand the difference between primitive and user-defined types and between the following types of operators: arithmetic, relational, logical, and assignment. Know which conditions lead to what types of errors.

You should be able to work with numbers—know how to compare them and be aware of the conditions that can lead to round-off error.

You should know the `Integer` constants `Integer.MIN_VALUE` and `Integer.MAX_VALUE`.

Be familiar with each of the following control structures: conditional statements, `for` loops, `while` loops, and enhanced `for` loops.

Be aware of the AP exam expectations concerning input and output.

Learn the unchecked exceptions that are part of the AP Java subset.

## Multiple-Choice Questions on Introductory Java Language Features

1. Which of the following pairs of declarations will cause an error message?

   I. ```
      double x = 14.7;
      int y = x;
      ```

   II. ```
      double x = 14.7;
      int y = (int) x;
      ```

   III. ```
      int x = 14;
      double y = x;
      ```

   (A) None
   (B) I only
   (C) II only
   (D) III only
   (E) I and III only

2. What output will be produced by the following?

   ```
   System.out.print("\\* This is not\n a comment *\\");
   ```

   (A) ```
       * This is not a comment *
       ```

   (B) ```
       \* This is not a comment *\
       ```

   (C) ```
       * This is not
       a comment *
       ```

   (D) ```
       \\* This is not
       a comment *\\
       ```

   (E) ```
       \* This is not
       a comment *\
       ```

3. Consider the following code segment.

   ```
   if (n != 0 && x / n > 100)
       statement1;
   else
       statement2;
   ```

   If n is of type int and has a value of 0 when the segment is executed, what will happen?
   (A) An ArithmeticException will be thrown.
   (B) A syntax error will occur.
   (C) *statement1*, but not *statement2*, will be executed.
   (D) *statement2*, but not *statement1*, will be executed.
   (E) Neither *statement1* nor *statement2* will be executed; control will pass to the first statement following the if statement.

4. Refer to the following code fragment.

```
double answer = 13 / 5;
System.out.println("13 / 5 = " + answer);
```

The output is

```
13 / 5 = 2.0
```

The programmer intends the output to be

```
13 / 5 = 2.6
```

Which of the following replacements for the first line of code will not fix the problem?

(A) `double answer = (double) 13 / 5;`

(B) `double answer = 13 / (double) 5;`

(C) `double answer = 13.0 / 5;`

(D) `double answer = 13 / 5.0;`

(E) `double answer = (double) (13 / 5);`

5. What value is stored in `result` if

```
int result = 13 - 3 * 6 / 4 % 3;
```

(A) −5

(B) 0

(C) 13

(D) −1

(E) 12

6. Suppose that addition and subtraction had higher precedence than multiplication and division. Then the expression

```
2 + 3 * 12 / 7 - 4 + 8
```

would evaluate to which of the following?

(A) 11

(B) 12

(C) 5

(D) 9

(E) −4

7. Which is true of the following boolean expression, given that x is a variable of type double?

```
3.0 == x * (3.0 / x)
```

(A) It will always evaluate to false.

(B) It may evaluate to false for some values of x.

(C) It will evaluate to false only when x is zero.

(D) It will evaluate to false only when x is very large or very close to zero.

(E) It will always evaluate to true.

8. Let x be a variable of type `double` that is positive. A program contains the boolean expression (`Math.pow(x,0.5)` == `Math.sqrt(x)`). Even though $x^{1/2}$ is mathematically equivalent to $\sqrt{x}$, the above expression returns the value `false` in a student's program. Which of the following is the most likely reason?

    (A) `Math.pow` returns an `int`, while `Math.sqrt` returns a `double`.

    (B) x was imprecisely calculated in a previous program statement.

    (C) The computer stores floating-point numbers with 32-bit words.

    (D) There is round-off error in calculating the `pow` and `sqrt` functions.

    (E) There is overflow error in calculating the `pow` function.

9. What will the output be for the following poorly formatted program segment, if the input value for `num` is 22?

```
int num =  call to a method that reads an integer;
if (num > 0)
if (num % 5 == 0)
System.out.println(num);
else System.out.println(num + " is negative");
```

    (A) 22

    (B) 4

    (C) 2 is negative

    (D) 22 is negative

    (E) Nothing will be output.

10. What values are stored in x and y after execution of the following program segment?

```
int x = 30, y = 40;
if (x >= 0)
{
    if (x <= 100)
    {
        y = x * 3;
        if (y < 50)
            x /= 10;
    }
    else
        y = x * 2;
}
else
    y = -x;
```

    (A) x = 30 y = 90

    (B) x = 30 y = -30

    (C) x = 30 y = 60

    (D) x = 3  y = -3

    (E) x = 30 y = 40

11. Which of the following will evaluate to true only if boolean expressions `A`, `B`, and `C` are all false?

    (A) `!A && !(B && !C)`

    (B) `!A || !B || !C`

    (C) `!(A || B || C)`

    (D) `!(A && B && C)`

    (E) `!A || !(B || !C)`

12. Assume that `a` and `b` are integers. The boolean expression

    ```
    !(a <= b) && (a * b > 0)
    ```

    will always evaluate to `true` given that

    (A) `a = b`.

    (B) `a > b`.

    (C) `a < b`.

    (D) `a > b` and `b > 0`.

    (E) `a > b` and `b < 0`.

13. Given that `a`, `b`, and `c` are integers, consider the boolean expression

    ```
    (a < b) || !((c == a * b) && (c < a))
    ```

    Which of the following will guarantee that the expression is `true`?

    (A) `c < a` is false.

    (B) `c < a` is true.

    (C) `a < b` is false.

    (D) `c == a * b` is true.

    (E) `c == a * b` is true, and `c < a` is true.

14. In the following code segment, you may assume that `a`, `b`, and `n` are all type `int`.

    ```
    if (a != b && n / (a - b) > 90)
    {
        /* statement 1 */
    }
    else
    {
        /* statement 2 */
    }
    /* statement 3 */
    ```

    What will happen if `a == b` is false?

    (A) /* *statement 1* */ will be executed.

    (B) /* *statement 2* */ will be executed.

    (C) Either /* *statement 1* */ or /* *statement 2* */ will be executed.

    (D) A compile-time error will occur.

    (E) An exception will be thrown.

15. Given that n and count are both of type int, which statement is true about the following code segments?

```
I.  for (count = 1; count <= n; count++)
        System.out.println(count);

II. count = 1;
    while (count <= n)
    {
        System.out.println(count);
        count++;
    }
```

(A) I and II are exactly equivalent for all input values n.
(B) I and II are exactly equivalent for all input values n ≥ 1, but differ when n ≤ 0.
(C) I and II are exactly equivalent only when n = 0.
(D) I and II are exactly equivalent only when n is even.
(E) I and II are not equivalent for any input values of n.

16. The following fragment intends that a user will enter a list of positive integers at the keyboard and terminate the list with a sentinel.

```
int value = 0;
final int SENTINEL = -999;
while (value != SENTINEL)
{
    //code to process value
        . . .
    value = ...;        //read user input
}
```

The fragment is not correct. Which is a true statement?
(A) The sentinel gets processed.
(B) The last nonsentinel value entered in the list fails to get processed.
(C) A poor choice of SENTINEL value causes the loop to terminate before all values have been processed.
(D) The code will always process a value that is not on the list.
(E) Entering the SENTINEL value as the first value causes a run-time error.

17. Consider this code segment.

```java
int x = 10, y = 0;
while (x > 5)
{
    y = 3;
    while (y < x)
    {
        y *= 2;
        if (y % x == 1)
            y += x;
    }
    x -= 3;
}
System.out.println(x + " " + y);
```

What will be output after execution of this code segment?

(A) 1    6
(B) 7    12
(C) -3    12
(D) 4    12
(E) -3    6

Questions 18 and 19 refer to the following method, checkNumber, which checks the validity of its four-digit integer parameter.

```
/** Returns true if the 4-digit integer n is valid,
 *  false otherwise.
 */
boolean checkNumber(int n)
{
    int d1,d2,d3,checkDigit,nRemaining,rem;
    //strip off digits
    checkDigit = n % 10;
    nRemaining = n / 10;
    d3 = nRemaining % 10;
    nRemaining /= 10;
    d2 = nRemaining % 10;
    nRemaining /= 10;
    d1 = nRemaining % 10;
    //check validity
    rem = (d1 + d2 + d3) % 7;
    return rem == checkDigit;
}
```

A program invokes method checkNumber with the statement

```
boolean valid = checkNumber(num);
```

18. Which of the following values of num will result in valid having a value of true?
    (A) 6143
    (B) 6144
    (C) 6145
    (D) 6146
    (E) 6147

19. What is the purpose of the local variable nRemaining?
    (A) It is not possible to separate n into digits without the help of a temporary variable.
    (B) nRemaining prevents the parameter n from being altered.
    (C) nRemaining enhances the readability of the algorithm.
    (D) On exiting the method, the value of nRemaining may be reused.
    (E) nRemaining is needed as the left-hand side operand for integer division.

20. For ticket-selling purposes, there are three categories at a certain theater.

| Age | Category |
| --- | --- |
| 65 or above | Senior |
| From 18 to 64 inclusive | Adult |
| Below 18 | Child |

Which of the following code segments will assign the correct string to `category` for a given integer age?

```
 I. if (age >= 65)
        category = "Senior";
    if (age >= 18)
        category = "Adult";
    else
        category = "Child";
```

```
II. if (age >= 65)
        category = "Senior";
    if (18 <= age <= 64)
        category = "Adult";
    else
        category = "Child";
```

```
III. if (age >= 65)
        category = "Senior";
     else if (age >= 18)
        category = "Adult";
     else
        category = "Child";
```

(A) I only
(B) II only
(C) III only
(D) II and III only
(E) I, II, and III

21.  What output will be produced by this code segment? (Ignore spacing.)

```
for (int i = 5; i >= 1; i--)
{
    for (int j = i; j >= 1; j--)
        System.out.print(2 * j - 1);
    System.out.println();
}
```

(A)  9  7  5  3  1
     9  7  5  3
     9  7  5
     9  7
     9

(B)  9  7  5  3  1
     7  5  3  1
     5  3  1
     3  1
     1

(C)  9  7  5  3  1
     7  5  3  1 -1
     5  3  1 -1 -3
     3  1 -1 -3 -5
     1 -1 -3 -5 -7

(D)  1
     1  3
     1  3  5
     1  3  5  7
     1  3  5  7  9

(E)  1  3  5  7  9
     1  3  5  7
     1  3  5
     1  3
     1

22. Which of the following program fragments will produce this output? (Ignore spacing.)

```
2 - - - - -
- 4 - - - -
- - 6 - - -
- - - 8 - -
- - - - 10 -
- - - - - 12
```

I. 
```java
for (int i = 1; i <= 6; i++)
{
    for (int k = 1; k <= 6; k++)
        if (k == i)
            System.out.print(2 * k);
        else
            System.out.print("-");
    System.out.println();
}
```

II. 
```java
for (int i = 1; i <= 6; i++)
{
    for (int k = 1; k <= i - 1; k++)
        System.out.print("-");
    System.out.print(2 * i);
    for (int k = 1; k <= 6 - i; k++)
        System.out.print("-");
    System.out.println();
}
```

III. 
```java
for (int i = 1; i <= 6; i++)
{
    for (int k = 1; k <= i - 1; k++)
        System.out.print("-");
    System.out.print(2 * i);
    for (int k = i + 1; k <= 6; k++)
        System.out.print("-");
    System.out.println();
}
```

(A) I only
(B) II only
(C) III only
(D) I and II only
(E) I, II, and III

23. Consider this program segment.

```
int newNum = 0, temp;
int num = k;              //k is some predefined integer value ≥ 0
while (num > 10)
{
    temp = num % 10;
    num /= 10;
    newNum = newNum * 10 + temp;
}
System.out.print(newNum);
```

Which is a true statement about the segment?

I. If 100 ≤ num ≤ 1000 initially, the final value of newNum must be in the range 10 ≤ newNum ≤ 100.

II. There is no initial value of num that will cause an infinite while loop.

III. If num ≤ 10 initially, newNum will have a final value of 0.

(A) I only
(B) II only
(C) III only
(D) II and III only
(E) I, II, and III

24. Consider the method reverse.

```
/** Returns n with its digits reversed.
 *    - Example: If n = 234, method reverse returns 432.
 *  Precondition: n > 0.
 */
int reverse(int n)
{
    int rem, revNum = 0;

    /* code segment */

    return revNum;
}
```

Which of the following replacements for /* **code segment** */ would cause the method to work as intended?

```
I. for (int i = 0; i <= n; i++)
   {
       rem = n % 10;
       revNum = revNum * 10 + rem;
       n /= 10;
   }

II. while (n != 0)
    {
        rem = n % 10;
        revNum = revNum * 10 + rem;
        n /= 10;
    }

III. for (int i = n; i != 0; i /= 10)
     {
         rem = i % 10;
         revNum = revNum * 10 + rem;
     }
```

(A) I only
(B) II only
(C) I and II only
(D) II and III only
(E) I and III only

## Answer Key

| | | |
|---|---|---|
| 1. **B** | 9. **D** | 17. **D** |
| 2. **E** | 10. **A** | 18. **B** |
| 3. **D** | 11. **C** | 19. **C** |
| 4. **E** | 12. **D** | 20. **C** |
| 5. **E** | 13. **A** | 21. **B** |
| 6. **C** | 14. **C** | 22. **E** |
| 7. **B** | 15. **A** | 23. **D** |
| 8. **D** | 16. **D** | 24. **D** |

## Answer Explanations

1. **(B)** When x is converted to an integer, as in segment I, information is lost. Java requires that an explicit cast to an int be made, as in segment II. Note that segment II will cause x to be truncated: The value stored in y is 14. By requiring the explicit cast, Java doesn't let you do this accidentally. In segment III, y will contain the value 14.0. No explicit cast to a double is required since no information is lost.

2. **(E)** The string argument contains two escape sequences: '\\', which means print a backslash (\), and '\n', which means go to a new line. Choice E is the only choice that does both of these.

3. **(D)** Short-circuit evaluation of the boolean expression will occur. The expression (n != 0) will evaluate to false, which makes the entire boolean expression false. Therefore the expression (x / n > 100) will not be evaluated. Hence no division by zero will occur, which would have caused an ArithmeticException to be thrown. When the boolean expression has a value of false, only the else part of the statement, *statement2*, will be executed.

4. **(E)** For this choice, the integer division 13/5 will be evaluated to 2, which will then be cast to 2.0. The output will be 13/5 = 2.0. The compiler needs a way to recognize that real-valued division is required. All the other options provide a way.

5. **(E)** The operators *, /, and % have equal precedence, all higher than -, and must be performed first, from left to right.

```
    13 - 3 * 6 / 4 % 3
  = 13 - 18 / 4 % 3
  = 13 - 4 % 3
  = 13 - 1
  = 12
```

6. **(C)** The expression must be evaluated as if parenthesized like this:

```
    (2 + 3) * 12 / (7 - 4 + 8)
```

This becomes 5 * 12 / 11 = 60 / 11 = 5.

7. **(B)** Although the expression is always algebraically true for nonzero x, the expression may evaluate to false. This could occur because of round-off error in performing the division and multiplication operations. Whether the right-hand side of the expression evaluates to exactly 3.0 depends on the value of x. Note that if x is zero, the expression will be evaluated to `false` because the right-hand side will be assigned a value of `Infinity`.

8. **(D)** Any time arithmetic operations are done with floating-point numbers, round-off error may occur. The `Math` class methods (see p. 182) such as `pow` and `sqrt` use various approximations to generate their answers to the required accuracy. Since they do different internal arithmetic, however, the round-off will usually not result in exactly the same answers. Note that choice A is not correct because both `Math.pow` and `Math.sqrt` return type `double`. Choice B is wrong because no matter how x was previously calculated, the same x is input to `pow` and `sqrt`. Choice C is wrong since round-off error occurs no matter how many bits are used to represent numbers. Choice E is wrong because if x is representable on the machine (i.e., hasn't overflowed), then its square root, $x^{1/2}$, will not overflow.

9. **(D)** Each `else` gets paired with the nearest unpaired `if`. Thus when the test (22 % 5 == 0) fails, the `else` part indicating that 22 `is negative` will be executed. This is clearly not the intent of the fragment, which can be fixed using delimiters:

```
int num =  call to a method that reads an integer;
if (num > 0)
{
    if (num % 5 == 0)
        System.out.println(num);
}
else
    System.out.println(num + " is negative");
```

10. **(A)** Since the first test (x >= 0) is `true`, the matching `else` part, y = -x, will not be executed. Since (x <= 100) is `true`, the matching `else` part, y = x * 2, will not be executed. The variable y will be set to x * 3 (i.e., 90) and will now fail the test y < 50. Thus, x will never be altered in this algorithm. Final values are x = 30 and y = 90.

11. **(C)** In order for !(A || B || C) to be true, (A || B || C) must evaluate to false. This will happen only if A, B, and C are *all* false. Choice A evaluates to true when A and B are false and C is true. In choice B, if any *one* of A, B, or C is false, the boolean expression evaluates to true. In choice D, if any one of A, B, or C is false, the boolean expression evaluates to true since we have !(false). All that's required for choice E to evaluate to true is for A to be false. Since true||(any) evaluates to true, both B and C can be either true or false.

12. **(D)** To evaluate to `true`, the expression must reduce to `true && true`. We therefore need !(false) && true. Choice D is the only condition that guarantees this: a > b provides !(false) for the left-hand expression, and a > b and b > 0 implies both a and b positive, which leads to `true` for the right-hand expression. Choice E, for example, will provide true for the right-hand expression only if a < 0. You have no information about a and can't make assumptions about it.

13. **(A)** If (c < a) is false, ((c == a*b) && (c < a)) evaluates to false irrespective of the value of c == a*b. In this case, !(c == a*b && c < a) evaluates to true. Then (a < b) || true evaluates to true irrespective of the value of the test (a < b). In all the other choices, the given expression *may* be true. There is not enough information given to guarantee this, however.

14. **(C)** If a == b is false, then a != b is true. Thus, the second piece of the compound test must be evaluated before the value of the whole test is known. Since a == b is false, a - b is not equal to zero. Thus, there is no division by zero, and no exception will be thrown. Also, since the relative values of a, b, and n are unknown, the value of the test n / (a - b) > 90 is unknown, and there is insufficient information to determine whether the compound test is true or false. Thus, either */* statement 1 */* or */* statement 2 */* will be executed.

15. **(A)** If n ≥ 1, both segments will print out the integers from 1 through n. If n ≤ 0, both segments will fail the test immediately and do nothing.

16. **(D)** The (value != SENTINEL) test occurs before a value has been read from the list. This will cause 0 to be processed, which may cause an error. The code must be fixed by reading the first value before doing the test:

```
final int SENTINEL = -999;
int value = ...;        //read user input
while (value != SENTINEL)
{
    //code to process value
    value = ...;        //read user input
}
```

17. **(D)** Here is a trace of the values of x and y during execution. Note that the condition (y % x == 1) is never true in this example.

| x | 10 | | | | 7 | | | | 4 |
|---|----|--|--|--|---|--|--|--|---|
| y | | 3 | 6 | 12 | | 3 | 6 | 12 | |

The while loop terminates when x is 4 since the test while (x > 5) fails.

18. **(B)** The algorithm finds the remainder when the sum of the first three digits of n is divided by 7. If this remainder is equal to the fourth digit, checkDigit, the method returns true, otherwise false. Note that (6+1+4) % 7 equals 4. Thus, only choice B is a valid number.

19. **(C)** As n gets broken down into its digits, nRemaining is the part of n that remains after each digit is stripped off. Thus, nRemaining is a self-documenting name that helps describe what is happening. Choice A is false because every digit can be stripped off using some sequence of integer division and mod. Choice B is false because num is passed by value and therefore will not be altered when the method is exited (see p. 111). Eliminate choice D: When the method is exited, all local variables are destroyed. Choice E is nonsense.

20. **(C)** Segment III works because if you enter an age of 90, say, `category` will correctly be assigned `"Senior"`, and none of the other `else` pieces of code will be executed. Similarly, if you enter an age corresponding to an adult or a child, only the correct assignment is made. Segment I fails because if you enter an age of 90, `category` will be assigned `"Senior"`, but then will be changed to `"Adult"` when the age passes the second test. Segment II uses incorrect syntax. The segment will work if you change the second test to

```
if (age >= 18 && age <= 64)
```

21. **(B)** The outer loop produces five rows of output. Each pass through the inner loop goes from `i` down to 1. Thus five odd numbers starting at 9 are printed in the first row, four odd numbers starting at 7 in the second row, and so on. You can picture what is happening in a chart.

| i | j | Steps |
|---|---|---|
| 5 | 5 | |
| | 4 | Print 5 odd numbers |
| | 3 | starting at 9: |
| | 2 | 9 7 5 3 1 |
| | 1 | |
| 4 | 4 | Print 4 odd numbers |
| | 3 | starting at 7: |
| | 2 | 7 5 3 1 |
| | 1 | Stop here! Answer must be **B**! |
| 3 | 3 | |
| | ⋮ | |

22. **(E)** All three algorithms produce the given output. The outer `for (int i ...)` loop produces six rows, and the inner `for (int k ...)` loops produce the symbols in each row.

23. **(D)** Statement I is false, since if 100 ≤ num ≤ 109, the body of the `while` loop will be executed just once. (After this single pass through the loop, the value of `num` will be 10, and the test `if (num > 10)` will fail.) With just one pass, `newNum` will be a one-digit number, equal to `temp` (which was the original `num % 10`). Note that statement II is true: There cannot be an infinite loop since `num /= 10` guarantees termination of the loop. Statement III is true because if num ≤ 10, the loop will be skipped, and `newNum` will keep its original value of 0.

24. **(D)** The algorithm works by stripping off the rightmost digit of `n` (stored in `rem`), multiplying the current value of `revNum` by 10, and adding that rightmost digit. When `n` has been stripped down to no digits (i.e., `n == 0` is true), `revNum` is complete. Both segments II and III work. Segment I fails to produce the right output whenever the input value `n` has a first digit less than (number of digits − 1). For these cases, the output has the first digit of the original number missing from the end of the returned number.

# 3

# Classes and Objects

*Work is the curse of the drinking classes.*
*—Oscar Wilde*

## Learning Objectives

In this chapter, you will learn:

- → Objects
- → Classes
- → Public, Private, and Static
- → Methods
- → Scope
- → References

## Objects

Most programs that you write involve at least one thing that is being created or manipulated by the program. This thing, together with the operations that manipulate it, is called an *object*.

Consider, for example, a program that must test the validity of a four-digit code number for accessing a photocopy machine. Rules for validity are provided. The object is a four-digit code number. Some of the operations to manipulate the object could be `readNumber`, `getSeparateDigits`, `testValidity`, and `writeNumber`.

Any given program can have several different types of objects. For example, a program that maintains a database of all books in a library has at least two objects:

1. A `Book` object, with operations like `getTitle`, `getAuthor`, `isOnShelf`, `isFiction`, and `goOutOfPrint`.
2. A `ListOfBooks` object, with operations like `search`, `addBook`, `removeBook`, and `sortByAuthor`.

An object is characterized by its *state* (or *attributes*) and *behavior*. For example, a book has a state described by its title, author, whether it's on the shelf, and so on. It also has behavior, like going out of print.

Notice that an object is an idea, separate from the concrete details of a programming language. It corresponds to some real-world object that is being represented by the program.

All object-oriented programming languages have a way to represent an object as a variable in a program. In Java, a variable that represents an object is called an *object reference*.

## Classes

A *class* is a software blueprint for implementing objects of a given type. In object-oriented programming, an object is a single *instance* of the class.

The current state of a given object is maintained in its *data fields* or *instance variables*, provided by the class. The *methods* of the class provide both the behaviors exhibited by the object and the operations that manipulate the object. Combining an object's data and methods into a single unit called a class is known as *data encapsulation*.

Here is the framework for a simple bank account class:

```java
public class BankAccount
{
    private String password;
    private double balance;
    public static final double OVERDRAWN_PENALTY = 20.00;

  //constructors
    /** No-argument constructor.
     *  Constructs bank account with default values. */
    public BankAccount()
    { /* implementation code */ }

    /** Constructs bank account with specified password and balance. */
    public BankAccount(String acctPassword, double acctBalance)
    { /* implementation code */ }

  //accessor
    /** Returns balance of this account. */
    public double getBalance()
    { /* implementation code */ }

  //mutators
    /** Deposits amount in bank account with given password.
    */
    public void deposit(String acctPassword, double amount)
    { /* implementation code */ }

    /** Withdraws amount from bank account with given password.
     * Assesses penalty if balance is less than amount.
     */
    public void withdraw(String acctPassword, double amount)
    { /* implementation code */ }
}
```

## Public, Private, and Static

The keyword public preceding the class declaration signals that the class is usable by all *client programs*—namely, pieces of code that are outside the class and use that class. If a class is not public, it can be used only by classes in its own package. In the AP Java subset, all classes are public.

Similarly, *public methods* are accessible to all client programs. Clients, however, are not privy to the class implementation and may not access the private instance variables and private methods of the class. In Java, restriction of access is implemented by using the keyword private. *Private methods and variables in a class can be accessed only by methods of that class.* Even though Java allows public instance variables, in the AP Java subset all instance variables are private.

A *static variable* (class variable) contains a value that is shared by all instances of the class. "Static" means that memory allocation happens once.

Typical uses of a static variable are to

- keep track of statistics for objects of the class.
- accumulate a total.
- provide a new identity number for each new object of the class.

For example,

```
public class Employee
{
    private String name;
    private static int employeeCount = 0; //number of employees

    public Employee(< parameter list >)
    {
        < initialization of private instance variables >
        employeeCount++; //increment count of all employees
    }
    ...
}
```

Notice that the static variable was initialized outside the constructor and that its value can be changed.

*Static final variables* (constants) in a class cannot be changed. They are often declared public (see some examples of Math class constants on p. 182). The variable OVERDRAWN_PENALTY is an example in the BankAccount class. Since the variable is public, it can be used in any client method. The keyword static indicates that there is a single value of the variable that applies to the whole class, rather than a new instance for each object of the class. A client method would refer to the variable as BankAccount.OVERDRAWN_PENALTY. In its own class it is referred to as simply OVERDRAWN_PENALTY.

See p. 104 for static methods.

## Methods

### Headers

All method headers, with the exception of constructors (see the next page) and static methods (p. 104), look like this:

```
    public        void     withdraw    (String password, double amount)
```
access specifier   return type   method name          parameter list

### Note

1. The *access specifier* tells which other methods can call this method (see the "Public, Private, and Static" section on the previous page).
2. A *return type* of void signals that the method does not return a value.
3. Items in the *parameter list* are separated by commas, and each item needs a data type.

The implementation of the method directly follows the header, enclosed in a {} block.

## Types of Methods

### Constructors

A *constructor* creates an object of the class. You can recognize a constructor by its name—always the same as the class. Also, a constructor has no return type.

Having several constructors provides different ways of initializing class objects. For example, there are two constructors in the BankAccount class.

1. The *no-argument constructor*[1] has no parameters. It provides reasonable initial values for an object. Here is its implementation:

```
/** No-argument constructor.
 * Constructs a bank account with default values. */
public BankAccount()
{
    password = "";
    balance = 0.0;
}
```

In a client method, the declaration

```
BankAccount b = new BankAccount();
```

constructs a BankAccount object with a balance of zero and a password equal to the empty string. The new operator returns the address of this newly constructed object. The variable b is assigned the value of this address—we say "b is a *reference* to the object." Picture the setup like this:

2. The constructor with parameters sets the instance variables of a BankAccount object to the values of those parameters.

   Here is the implementation:

```
/** Constructor. Constructs a bank account with
 * specified password and balance. */
public BankAccount(String acctPassword, double acctBalance)
{
    password = acctPassword;
    balance = acctBalance;
}
```

---

[1] In Java, modern usage reserves the term "default constructor" to mean the constructor with no arguments that is automatically provided by the compiler for a class that has no constructors itself (see p. 143). The term "no-argument constructor" is used for a constructor with no arguments that is explicitly provided in a class. In other computer languages, both cases are typically called default constructors.

In a client program a declaration that uses this constructor needs to have matching parameters:

```
BankAccount c = new BankAccount("KevinC", 800.00);
```

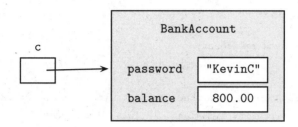

## Note

b and c are *object variables* that store the *addresses* of their respective BankAccount objects. They do not store the objects themselves (see "References" on p. 108).

## Accessors

An *accessor method* is a public method that accesses a class object without altering the object. An accessor returns some information about the object, and it allows other objects to get the value of a private instance variable.

The BankAccount class has a single accessor method, namely getBalance(). Here is its implementation:

```
/** Returns the balance of this account. */
public double getBalance()
{ return balance; }
```

A client program may use this method as follows:

```
BankAccount b1 = new BankAccount("MattW", 500.00);
BankAccount b2 = new BankAccount("DannyB", 650.50);
if (b1.getBalance() > b2.getBalance())
    ...
```

## Note

1. The . *operator* (dot operator) indicates that getBalance() is a method of the class to which b1 and b2 belong, namely the BankAccount class.
2. A non-void method returns a single value, whose type is specified in the header of the method.

## Mutators

A *mutator method* changes the state of an object by modifying at least one of its instance variables. It is often a void method (i.e., has no return type). A mutator can be a private helper method within its class, or a public method that allows other objects to change a private instance variable.

Here are the implementations of the deposit and withdraw methods, each of which alters the value of balance in the BankAccount class:

```
/** Deposits amount in a bank account with the given password.
 */
public void deposit(String acctPassword, double amount)
{
    if (!acctPassword.equals(password))
        /* throw an exception */
    else
        balance += amount;
}


/** Withdraws amount from bank account with given password.
 * Assesses penalty if balance is less than amount.
 */
public void withdraw(String acctPassword, double amount)
{
    if (!acctPassword.equals(password))
        /* throw an exception */
    else
    {
        balance -= amount;       //allows negative balance
        if (balance < 0)
            balance -= OVERDRAWN_PENALTY;
    }
}
```

A mutator method in a client program is invoked in the same way as an accessor: using an object variable with the dot operator. For example, assuming valid BankAccount declarations for b1 and b2:

```
b1.withdraw("MattW", 200.00);
b2.deposit("DannyB", 35.68);
```

## Static Methods

**STATIC METHODS VS. INSTANCE METHODS**   The methods that are discussed in the preceding sections—constructors, accessors, and mutators—all operate on individual objects of a class. They are called *instance methods*. A method that performs an operation for the entire class, not its individual objects, is called a *static method* (sometimes called a *class method*).

The implementation of a static method uses the keyword static in its header. There is no implied object in the code (as there is in an instance method). Thus, if the code tries to call an instance method or invoke a private instance variable for this nonexistent object, a syntax error will occur. A static method can, however, use a static variable in its code. For example, in the Employee example on p. 101, you could add a static method that returns the employeeCount:

```
public static int getEmployeeCount()
{ return employeeCount; }
```

Here's an example of a static method that might be used in the BankAccount class. Suppose the class has a static variable intRate, declared as follows:

```
private static double intRate;
```

The static method getInterestRate may be as follows:

```
public static double getInterestRate()
{
    System.out.println("Enter interest rate for bank account");
    System.out.println("Enter in decimal form:");
    intRate = ...;          // read user input
    return intRate;
}
```

Since the rate that's read in by this method applies to all bank accounts in the class, not to any particular BankAccount object, it's appropriate that the method should be static.

Recall that an instance method is invoked in a client program by using an object variable followed by the dot operator followed by the method name:

```
BankAccount b = new BankAccount();   //invokes the deposit method for
b.deposit(acctPassword, amount);     //BankAccount object b
```

A static method, by contrast, is invoked by using the *class name* with the dot operator:

```
double interestRate = BankAccount.getInterestRate();
```

**STATIC METHODS IN A DRIVER CLASS**   Often a class that contains the main() method is used as a driver program to test other classes. Usually such a class creates no objects of the class. So all the methods in the class must be static. Note that at the start of program execution, no objects exist yet. So the main() method must *always* be static.

For example, here is a program that tests a class for reading integers entered at the keyboard:

```
import java.util.*;
public class GetListTest
{
    /** Returns a list of integers from the keyboard. */
    public static ArrayList<Integer> getList()
    {
        ArrayList<Integer> a = new ArrayList<Integer>();
        < code to read integers into  a>
        return a;
    }

    /** Write contents of ArrayList a.
     */
    public static void writeList(ArrayList<Integer> a)
    {
        System.out.println("List is : " + a);
    }

    public static void main(String[] args)
    {
        ArrayList<Integer> list = getList();
        writeList(list);
    }
}
```

**Note**

1. The calls to `writeList(list)` and `getList()` do not need to be preceded by `GetListTest` plus a dot because `main` is not a client program: It is in the same class as `getList` and `writeList`.

2. If you omit the keyword `static` from the `getList` or `writeList` header, you get an error message like the following:

```
Can't make static reference to method getList()
in class GetListTest
```

The compiler has recognized that there was no object variable preceding the method call, which means that the methods were static and should have been declared as such.

## Method Overloading

*Overloaded methods* are two or more methods in the same class (or a subclass of that class) that have the same name but different parameter lists. For example,

```
public class DoOperations
{
    public int product(int n) { return n * n; }
    public double product(double x) { return x * x; }
    public double product(int x, int y) { return x * y; }
        ...
```

The compiler figures out which method to call by examining the method's *signature*. The signature of a method consists of the method's name and a list of the parameter types. Thus, the signatures of the overloaded `product` methods are

```
product(int)
product(double)
product(int, int)
```

Note that for overloading purposes, the return type of the method is irrelevant. You can't have two methods with identical signatures but different return types. The compiler will complain that the method call is ambiguous.

Having more than one constructor in the same class is an example of overloading. Overloaded constructors provide a choice of ways to initialize objects of the class.

## Scope

The *scope* of a variable or method is the region in which that variable or method is visible and can be accessed.

The instance variables, static variables, and methods of a class belong to that class's scope, which extends from the opening brace to the closing brace of the class definition. Within the class all instance variables and methods are accessible and can be referred to simply by name (no dot operator!).

A *local variable* is defined inside a method. It can even be defined inside a statement. Its scope extends from the point where it is declared to the end of the block in which its declaration occurs. A *block* is a piece of code enclosed in a {} pair. When a block is exited, the memory for a local variable is automatically recycled.

Local variables take precedence over instance variables with the same name. (Using the same name, however, creates ambiguity for the programmer, leading to errors. You should avoid the practice.)

## The this Keyword

An instance method is always called for a particular object. This object is an *implicit parameter* for the method and is referred to with the keyword this. You are expected to know this vocabulary for the exam.

In the implementation of instance methods, all instance variables can be written with the prefix this followed by the dot operator.

### ▷ Example 1

In the method call obj.doSomething("Mary",num), where obj is some class object and doSomething is a method of that class, "Mary" and num, the parameters in parentheses, are *explicit* parameters, whereas obj is an *implicit* parameter.

### ▷ Example 2

Here's an example where this is used as a parameter:

```
public class Person
{
    private String name;
    private int age;

    public Person(String aName, int anAge)
    {
        name = aName;
        age = anAge;
    }

    /** Returns the String form of this person. */
    public String toString()
    { return name + " " + age; }

    public void printPerson()
    { System.out.println(this); }

    //Other variables and methods are not shown.
}
```

Suppose a client class has these lines of code:

```
Person p = new Person("Dan", 10);
p.printPerson();
```

The statement

```
System.out.println(this);
```

in the printPerson method means "print the current Person object." The output should be Dan 10. Note that System.out.println invokes the toString method of the Person class.

> **Example 3**

The `deposit` method of the `BankAccount` class can refer to `balance` as follows:

```
public void deposit(String acctPassword, double amount)
{
    this.balance += amount;
}
```

The use of `this` is unnecessary in the above example.

> **Example 4**

Consider a rational number class called `Rational`, which has two private instance variables:

```
private int num;          //numerator
private int denom;        //denominator
```

Now consider a constructor for the `Rational` class:

```
public Rational(int num, int denom)
{
    this.num = num;
    this.denom = denom;
}
```

It is definitely *not* a good idea to use the same name for the explicit parameters and the private instance variables. But if you do, you can avoid errors by referring to `this.num` and `this.denom` for the current object that is being constructed. (This particular use of `this` will not be tested on the exam.)

## References

### Reference vs. Primitive Data Types

Simple built-in data types, like `double` and `int`, as well as types `char` and `boolean`, are *primitive* data types. All objects and arrays are *reference* data types, such as `String`, `Random`, `int []`, `String[] []`, `Cat` (assuming there is a `Cat` class in the program), and so on. The difference between primitive and reference data types lies in the way they are stored.

Consider the statements

```
int num1 = 3;
int num2 = num1;
```

The variables `num1` and `num2` can be thought of as memory slots, labeled `num1` and `num2`, respectively:

If either of the above variables is now changed, the other is not affected. Each has its own memory slot.

Contrast this with the declaration of a reference data type. Recall that an object is created using `new`:

```
Date d = new Date(2, 17, 1948);
```

This declaration creates a reference variable d that refers to a Date object. The value of d is the address in memory of that object:

Suppose the following declaration is now made:

```
Date birthday = d;
```

This statement creates the reference variable birthday, which contains the same address as d:

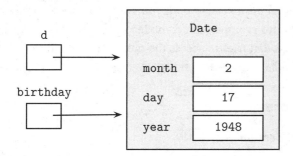

Having two references for the same object is known as *aliasing*. Aliasing can cause unintended problems for the programmer. The statement

```
d.changeDate();
```

will automatically change the object referred to by birthday as well.

What the programmer probably intended was to create a second object called birthday whose attributes exactly matched those of d. This cannot be accomplished without using new. For example,

```
Date birthday = new Date(d.getMonth(), d.getDay(), d.getYear());
```

The statement d.changeDate() will now leave the birthday object unchanged.

## The Null Reference

The declaration

```
BankAccount b;
```

defines a reference b that is uninitialized. (To construct the object that b refers to requires the new operator and a BankAccount constructor.) An uninitialized object variable is called a *null reference* or *null pointer*. You can test whether a variable refers to an object or is uninitialized by using the keyword null:

```
        if (b == null)
```

If a reference is not null, it can be set to null with the statement

```
    b = null;
```

An attempt to invoke an instance method with a null reference may cause your program to terminate with a `NullPointerException`. For example,

```
    public class PersonalFinances
    {
        BankAccount b;                      //b is a null reference
            ...
        b.withdraw(acctPassword, amt);      //throws a NullPointerException
            ...                             //if b not constructed with new
```

### Note

If you fail to initialize a local variable in a method before you use it, you will get a compile-time error. If you make the same mistake with an instance variable of a class, the compiler provides reasonable default values for primitive variables (0 for numbers, `false` for booleans), and the code may run without error. However, if you don't initialize *reference* instance variables in a class, as in the above example, the compiler will set them to `null`. Any method call for an object of the class that tries to access the null reference will cause a run-time error: The program will terminate with a `NullPointerException`.

> Do not make a method call with an object whose value is `null`.

## Method Parameters

### Formal vs. Actual Parameters

The header of a method defines the *parameters* of that method. For example, consider the `withdraw` method of the `BankAccount` class:

```
    public class BankAccount
    {  ...
        public void withdraw(String acctPassword, double amount)
            ...
```

This method has two explicit parameters, `acctPassword` and `amount`. These are *dummy* or *formal parameters*. Think of them as placeholders for the pair of *actual parameters* or *arguments* that will be supplied by a particular method call in a client program.

For example,

```
    BankAccount b = new BankAccount("TimB", 1000);
    b.withdraw("TimB", 250);
```

Here "TimB" and 250 are the actual parameters that match up with `acctPassword` and `amount` for the `withdraw` method.

### Note

1. The number of arguments in the method call must equal the number of parameters in the method header, and the type of each argument must be compatible with the type of each corresponding parameter.

2. In addition to its explicit parameters, the `withdraw` method has an implicit parameter, `this`, the `BankAccount` from which money will be withdrawn. In the method call

```
b.withdraw("TimB", 250);
```

the actual parameter that matches up with `this` is the object reference `b`.

## Passing Primitive Types as Parameters

Parameters are *passed by value*. For primitive types this means that when a method is called, a new memory slot is allocated for each parameter. The value of each argument is copied into the newly created memory slot corresponding to each parameter.

During execution of the method, the parameters are local to that method. *Any changes made to the parameters will not affect the values of the arguments in the calling program.* When the method is exited, the local memory slots for the parameters are erased.

Here's an example. What will the output be?

```java
public class ParamTest
{
    public static void foo(int x, double y)
    {
        x = 3;
        y = 2.5;
    }

    public static void main(String[] args)
    {
        int a = 7;
        double b = 6.5;
        foo(a, b);
        System.out.println(a + "   " + b);
    }
}
```

The output will be

```
7   6.5
```

The arguments `a` and `b` remain unchanged, despite the method call!

This can be understood by picturing the state of the memory slots during execution of the program.

Just before the `foo(a, b)` method call:

```
   a        b
  ┌───┐   ┌─────┐
  │ 7 │   │ 6.5 │
  └───┘   └─────┘
```

At the time of the `foo(a, b)` method call:

```
   a        b
  ┌───┐   ┌─────┐
  │ 7 │   │ 6.5 │
  └───┘   └─────┘

   x        y
  ┌───┐   ┌─────┐
  │ 7 │   │ 6.5 │
  └───┘   └─────┘
```

Just before exiting the method: (Note that the values of x and y have been changed.)

a        b

| 7 |   | 6.5 |

x        y

| 3 |   | 2.5 |

After exiting the method: (Note that the memory slots for x and y have been reclaimed. The values of a and b remain unchanged.)

a        b

| 7 |   | 6.5 |

## Passing Objects as Parameters

In Java both primitive types and object references are passed by value. When an object's reference is a parameter, the same mechanism of copying into local memory is used. The key difference is that the *address* (reference) is copied, not the values of the individual instance variables. As with primitive types, changes made to the parameters will not change the values of the matching arguments. What this means in practice is that it is not possible for a method to replace an object with another one—you can't change the reference that was passed. It is, however, possible to change the state of the object to which the parameter refers through methods that act on the object.

### ▷ Example 1

A method that changes the state of an object:

```
/** Subtracts fee from balance in b if current balance too low. */
public static void chargeFee(BankAccount b, String password,
        double fee)
{
    final double MIN_BALANCE = 10.00;
    if (b.getBalance() < MIN_BALANCE)
        b.withdraw(password, fee);
}

public static void main(String[] args)
{
    final double FEE = 5.00;
    BankAccount andysAccount = new BankAccount("AndyS", 7.00);
    chargeFee(andysAccount, "AndyS", FEE);
        ...
}
```

Here are the memory slots before the chargeFee method call:

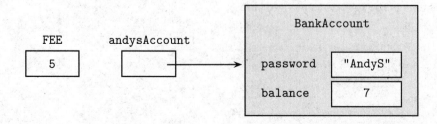

At the time of the `chargeFee` method call, copies of the matching parameters are made:

Just before exiting the method: (The `balance` field of the `BankAccount` object has been changed.)

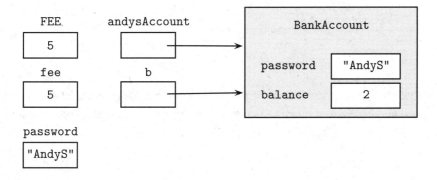

After exiting the method: (All parameter memory slots have been erased, but the object remains altered.)

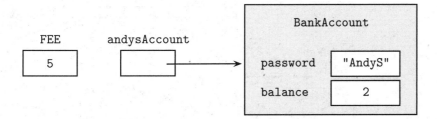

## Note

The `andysAccount` reference is unchanged throughout the program segment. The object to which it refers, however, has been changed. This is significant. Contrast this with Example 2 on the next page in which an attempt is made to replace the object itself.

> **Example 2**

A `chooseBestAccount` method attempts—erroneously—to set its `betterFund` parameter to the `BankAccount` with the higher balance:

```
public static void chooseBestAccount(BankAccount better,
        BankAccount b1, BankAccount b2)
{
    if (b1.getBalance() > b2.getBalance())
        better = b1;
    else
        better = b2;
}


public static void main(String[] args)
{
    BankAccount briansFund = new BankAccount("BrianL", 10000);
    BankAccount paulsFund = new BankAccount("PaulM", 90000);
    BankAccount betterFund = null;

    chooseBestAccount(betterFund, briansFund, paulsFund);
        ...
}
```

The intent is that `betterFund` will be a reference to the `paulsFund` object after execution of the `chooseBestAccount` statement. A look at the memory slots illustrates why this fails.

Before the `chooseBestAccount` method call:

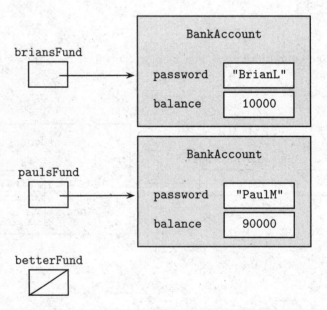

At the time of the `chooseBestAccount` method call, copies of the matching references are made:

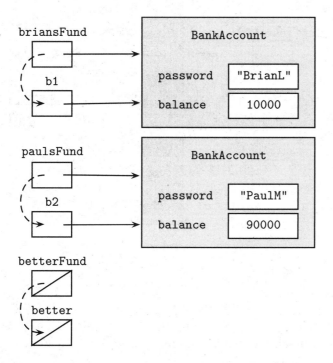

Just before exiting the method, the value of `better` has been changed; `betterFund`, however, remains unchanged:

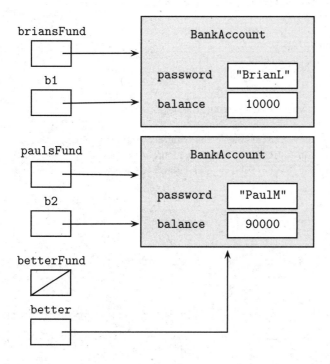

After exiting the method, all parameter slots have been erased:

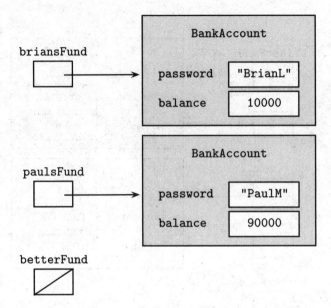

Note that the betterFund reference continues to be null, contrary to the programmer's intent.

The way to fix the problem is to modify the method so that it returns the better account. Returning an object from a method means that you are returning the address of the object.

```java
public static BankAccount chooseBestAccount(BankAccount b1,
        BankAccount b2)
{
    BankAccount better;
    if (b1.getBalance() > b2.getBalance())
        better = b1;
    else
        better = b2;
    return better;
}

public static void main(String[] args)
{
    BankAccount briansFund = new BankAccount("BrianL", 10000);
    BankAccount paulsFund = new BankAccount("PaulM", 90000);
    BankAccount betterFund = chooseBestAccount(briansFund, paulsFund);
        ...
}
```

**Note**

The effect of this is to create the betterFund reference, which refers to the same object as paulsFund:

What the method does *not* do is create a new object to which betterFund refers. To do that would require the keyword new and use of a BankAccount constructor. Assuming that a getPassword() accessor has been added to the BankAccount class, the code would look like this:

```
public static BankAccount chooseBestAccount(BankAccount b1,
        BankAccount b2)
{
    BankAccount better;
    if (b1.getBalance() > b2.getBalance())
        better = new BankAccount(b1.getPassword(), b1.getBalance());
    else
        better = new BankAccount(b2.getPassword(), b2.getBalance());
    return better;
}
```

Using this modified method with the same main() method above has the following effect:

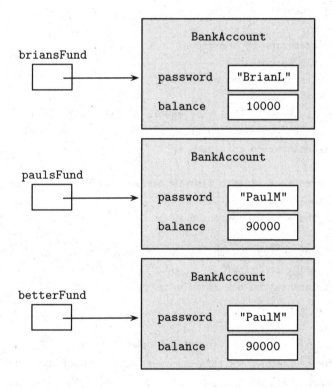

## Chapter Summary

By now you should be able to write code for any given object, with its private data fields and methods encapsulated in a class. Be sure that you know the various types of methods—static, instance, and overloaded. You should know how to include constructors, both a no-argument constructor and a constructor with parameters.

You should also understand the difference between storage of primitive types and the references used for objects.

## Multiple-Choice Questions on Classes and Objects

Questions 1–3 refer to the Time class declared below.

```java
public class Time
{
    private int hrs;
    private int mins;
    private int secs;

    public Time()
    { /* implementation not shown */ }

    public Time(int h, int m, int s)
    { /* implementation not shown */ }

    /** Resets time to hrs = h, mins = m, secs = s. */
    public void resetTime(int h, int m, int s)
    { /* implementation not shown */ }

    /** Advances time by one second. */
    public void increment()
    { /* implementation not shown */ }

    /** Returns true if this time equals t, false otherwise. */
    public boolean equals(Time t)
    { /* implementation not shown */ }

    /** Returns true if this time is earlier than t, false otherwise. */
    public boolean lessThan(Time t)
    { /* implementation not shown */ }

    /** Returns a String with the time in the form hrs:mins:secs. */
    public String toString()
    { /* implementation not shown */ }
}
```

1.  Which of the following is a false statement about the methods?
    (A) equals, lessThan, and toString are all accessor methods.
    (B) increment is a mutator method.
    (C) Time() is the no-argument constructor.
    (D) The Time class has three constructors.
    (E) There are no static methods in this class.

2. Which of the following represents correct *implementation code* for the constructor with parameters?

    (A)  `hrs = 0;`
          `mins = 0;`
          `secs = 0;`

    (B)  `hrs = h;`
          `mins = m;`
          `secs = s;`

    (C)  `resetTime(hrs, mins, secs);`

    (D)  `h = hrs;`
          `m = mins;`
          `s = secs;`

    (E)  `Time = new Time(h, m, s);`

3. A client class has a `display` method that writes the time represented by its parameter:

```
/** Outputs time t in the form hrs:mins:secs.
 */
public void display (Time t)
{
    /* method body */
}
```

Which of the following are correct replacements for /* *method body* */?

    I.  `Time T = new Time(h, m, s);`
       `System.out.println(T);`

    II.  `System.out.println(t.hrs + ":" + t.mins + ":" + t.secs);`

    III.  `System.out.println(t);`

    (A) I only
    (B) II only
    (C) III only
    (D) II and III only
    (E) I, II, and III

4. Which statement about parameters is false?
    (A) The scope of parameters is the method in which they are defined.
    (B) Static methods have no implicit parameter `this`.
    (C) Two overloaded methods in the same class must have parameters with different names.
    (D) All parameters in Java are passed by value.
    (E) Two different constructors in a given class can have the same number of parameters.

Questions 5–11 refer to the following `Date` class declaration.

```
public class Date
{
    private int day;
    private int month;
    private int year;

    public Date()                          //no-argument constructor
    {
        ...
    }

    public Date(int mo, int da, int yr)    //constructor
    {
        ...
    }

    public int month()      //returns month of Date
    {
        ...
    }

    public int day()        //returns day of Date
    {
        ...
    }

    public int year()       //returns year of Date
    {
        ...
    }

    //Returns String representation of Date as "m/d/y", e.g. 4/18/1985.
    public String toString()
    {
        ...
    }
}
```

5.  Which of the following correctly constructs a `Date` object in a client class?

    (A) `Date d = new (2, 13, 1947);`

    (B) `Date d = new Date(2, 13, 1947);`

    (C) `Date d;`
        `d = new (2, 13, 1947);`

    (D) `Date d;`
        `d = Date(2, 13, 1947);`

    (E) `Date d = Date(2, 13, 1947);`

6. Which of the following will cause an error message?

     I. ```Date d1 = new Date(8, 2, 1947);```
       ```Date d2 = d1;```

    II. ```Date d1 = null;```
      ```Date d2 = d1;```

   III. ```Date d = null;```
      ```int x = d.year();```

    (A) I only
    (B) II only
    (C) III only
    (D) II and III only
    (E) I, II, and III

7. A client program creates a `Date` object as follows.

```
Date d = new Date(1, 13, 2002);
```

Which of the following subsequent code segments will cause an error?

    (A) ```String s = d.toString();```
    (B) ```int x = d.day();```
    (C) ```Date e = d;```
    (D) ```Date e = new Date(1, 13, 2002);```
    (E) ```int y = d.year;```

8. Consider the implementation of a `write()` method that is added to the `Date` class.

```
/** Write the date in the form m/d/y, for example 2/17/1948. */
public void write()
{
    /* implementation code */
}
```

Which of the following could be used as /* *implementation code* */?

     I. ```System.out.println(month + "/" + day + "/" + year);```

    II. ```System.out.println(month() + "/" + day() + "/" + year());```

   III. ```System.out.println(this);```

    (A) I only
    (B) II only
    (C) III only
    (D) II and III only
    (E) I, II, and III
```

9. Here is a client program that uses Date objects:

```
public class BirthdayStuff
{
    public static Date findBirthdate()
    {
        /* code to get birthDate */
        return birthDate;
    }

    public static void main(String[] args)
    {
        Date d = findBirthdate();
        ...
    }
}
```

Which of the following is a correct replacement for
/* *code to get* birthDate */?

```
I.  System.out.println("Enter birthdate: mo, day, yr: ");
    int m = ...;                    //read user input
    int d = ...;                    //read user input
    int y = ...;                    //read user input
    Date birthDate = new Date(m, d, y);

II. System.out.println("Enter birthdate: mo, day, yr: ");
    int birthDate.month() = ...;        //read user input
    int birthDate.day() = ...;          //read user input
    int birthDate.year() = ...;         //read user input
    Date birthDate = new Date(birthDate.month(), birthDate.day(),
        birthDate.year());

III. System.out.println("Enter birthdate: mo, day, yr: ");
    int birthDate.month = ...;      //read user input
    int birthDate.day = ...;        //read user input
    int birthDate.year = ...;       //read user input
    Date birthDate = new Date(birthDate.month, birthDate.day,
        birthDate.year);
```

(A) I only
(B) II only
(C) III only
(D) I and II only
(E) I and III only

10. A method in a client program for the `Date` class has the following declaration.

    ```
    Date d1 = new Date(mo, da, yr);
    ```

    Here, `mo`, `da`, and `yr` are previously defined integer variables. The same method now creates a second `Date` object `d2` that is an exact copy of the object `d1` refers to. Which of the following code segments will not do this correctly?

    I. `Date d2 = d1;`

    II. `Date d2 = new Date(mo, da, yr);`

    III. `Date d2 = new Date(d1.month(), d1.day(), d1.year());`

    (A) I only
    (B) II only
    (C) III only
    (D) II and III only
    (E) I, II, and III

11. The `Date` class is modified by adding the following mutator method:

    ```
    public void addYears(int n)     //add n years to date
    ```

    Here is part of a poorly coded client program that uses the `Date` class:

    ```
    public static void addCentury(Date recent, Date old)
    {
        old.addYears(100);
        recent = old;
    }

    public static void main(String[] args)
    {
        Date oldDate = new Date(1, 13, 1900);
        Date recentDate = null;
        addCentury(recentDate, oldDate);
            . . .
    }
    ```

    Which will be true after executing this code?
    (A) A `NullPointerException` is thrown.
    (B) The `oldDate` object remains unchanged.
    (C) `recentDate` is a null reference.
    (D) `recentDate` refers to the same object as `oldDate`.
    (E) `recentDate` refers to a separate object whose contents are the same as those of `oldDate`.

12. Here are the private instance variables for a `Frog` object:

```
public class Frog
{
    private String species;
    private int age;
    private double weight;
    private Position position;      //position (x,y) in pond
    private boolean amAlive;
        ...
```

Which of the following methods in the `Frog` class is the best candidate for being a static method?

(A) swim                //frog swims to new position in pond

(B) getPondTemperature  //returns temperature of pond

(C) eat                 //frog eats and gains weight

(D) getWeight           //returns weight of frog

(E) die                 //frog dies with some probability based
                        //on frog's age and pond temperature

13. What output will be produced by this program?

```
public class Mystery
{
    public static void strangeMethod(int x, int y)
    {
        x += y;
        y *= x;
        System.out.println(x + " " + y);
    }

    public static void main(String[] args)
    {
        int a = 6, b = 3;
        strangeMethod(a, b);
        System.out.println(a + " " + b);
    }
}
```

(A) 36
    9

(B) 3 6
    9

(C) 9 27
    9 27

(D) 6 3
    9 27

(E) 9 27
    6 3

Questions 14–17 refer to the following definition of the `Rational` class.

```
public class Rational
{
    private int numerator;
    private int denominator;

    Rational()
    { /* implementation not shown */ }

    /** Constructs a Rational with numerator n and
     *  denominator 1. */
    Rational(int n)
    { /* implementation not shown */ }

    /** Constructs a Rational with specified numerator and
     *  denominator. */
    Rational(int numer, int denom)
    { /* implementation not shown */ }

    /** Returns numerator. */
    int numerator()
    { /* implementation not shown */ }

    /** Returns denominator. */
    int denominator()
    { /* implementation not shown */ }

    /** Returns (this + r). Leaves this unchanged.
     */
    public Rational plus(Rational r)
    { /* implementation not shown */ }

    //Similarly for times, minus, divide
            ...
    /** Ensures denominator > 0. */
    private void fixSigns()
    { /* implementation not shown */ }

    /** Ensures lowest terms. */
    private void reduce()
    { /* implementation not shown */ }
}
```

14. The method `reduce()` is not a public method because
    (A) methods whose return type is `void` cannot be public.
    (B) methods that change `this` cannot be public.
    (C) the `reduce()` method is not intended for use by objects outside the `Rational` class.
    (D) the `reduce()` method is intended for use only by objects outside the `Rational` class.
    (E) the `reduce()` method uses only the private data fields of the `Rational` class.

15. The constructors in the `Rational` class allow initialization of `Rational` objects in several different ways. Which of the following will cause an error?

    (A) `Rational r1 = new Rational();`

    (B) `Rational r2 = r1;`

    (C) `Rational r3 = new Rational(2,-3);`

    (D) `Rational r4 = new Rational(3.5);`

    (E) `Rational r5 = new Rational(10);`

16. Here is the implementation code for the `plus` method:

```
/** Returns (this + r). Leaves this unchanged.
 */
public Rational plus(Rational r)
{
    fixSigns();
    r.fixSigns();
    int denom = denominator * r.denominator;
    int numer = numerator * r.denominator
              + r.numerator * denominator;
    /* more code */
}
```

Which of the following is a correct replacement for /* *more code* */?

    (A)
```
Rational rat(numer, denom);
rat.reduce();
return rat;
```

    (B)
```
return new Rational(numer, denom);
```

    (C)
```
reduce();
Rational rat = new Rational(numer, denom);
return rat;
```

    (D)
```
Rational rat = new Rational(numer, denom);
Rational.reduce();
return rat;
```

    (E)
```
Rational rat = new Rational(numer, denom);
rat.reduce();
return rat;
```

17. Assume these declarations:

```
Rational a = new Rational();
Rational r = new Rational(numer, denom);
int n = value;
//numer, denom, and value are valid integer values
```

Which of the following will cause a compile-time error?

    (A) `r = a.plus(r);`

    (B) `a = r.plus(new Rational(n));`

    (C) `r = r.plus(r);`

    (D) `a = n.plus(r);`

    (E) `r = r.plus(new Rational(n));`

Questions 18–20 refer to the `Temperature` class shown below.

```
public class Temperature
{
    private String scale;   //valid values are "F" or "C"
    private double degrees;

    /** constructor with specified degrees and scale */
    public Temperature(double tempDegrees, String tempScale)
    { /* implementation not shown */ }

    /** Mutator. Converts this Temperature to degrees Fahrenheit.
     *  Returns this temperature in degrees Fahrenheit.
     *  Precondition:  Temperature is a valid temperature
     *                 in degrees Celsius.
     */
    public Temperature toFahrenheit()
    { /* implementation not shown */ }

    /** Mutator. Converts this Temperature to degrees Celsius.
     *  Returns this temperature in degrees Celsius.
     *  Precondition:  Temperature is a valid temperature
     *                 in degrees Fahrenheit.
     */
    public Temperature toCelsius()
    { /* implementation not shown */ }

    /** Mutator.
     *  Returns this temperature raised by amt degrees.
     */
    public Temperature raise(double amt)
    { /* implementation not shown */ }

    /** Mutator.
     *  Returns this temperature lowered by amt degrees.
     */
    public Temperature lower(double amt)
    { /* implementation not shown */ }

    /** Returns true if tempDegrees is a valid temperature
     *  in the given temperature scale, false otherwise.
     */
    public static boolean isValidTemp(double tempDegrees,
                                      String tempScale)
    { /* implementation not shown */ }

    //Other methods are not shown.
}
```

18. A client method contains this code segment:

```
Temperature t1 = new Temperature(40, "C");
Temperature t2 = t1;
Temperature t3 = t2.lower(20);
Temperature t4 = t1.toFahrenheit();
```

Which statement is true following execution of this segment?

(A) t1, t2, t3, and t4 all represent the identical temperature, in degrees Celsius.

(B) t1, t2, t3, and t4 all represent the identical temperature, in degrees Fahrenheit.

(C) t4 represents a Fahrenheit temperature, while t1, t2, and t3 all represent degrees Celsius.

(D) t1 and t2 refer to the same Temperature object; t3 refers to a Temperature object that is 20 degrees lower than t1 and t2, while t4 refers to an object that is t1 converted to Fahrenheit.

(E) A NullPointerException was thrown.

19. Consider the following code.

```
public class TempTest
{
    public static void main(String[] args)
    {
        System.out.println("Enter temperature scale: ");
        String tempScale = ...;     //read user input
        System.out.println("Enter number of degrees: ");
        double tempDegrees = ...;   //read user input
        /* code to construct a valid temperature from user input */
    }
}
```

Which is the best replacement for /* code to construct... */?

(A) Temperature t = new Temperature(tempDegrees, tempScale);

(B) Temperature t = new Temperature(tempDegrees, tempScale);
    if (Temperature.isNotValidTemp(tempDegrees, tempScale))
        /* error message and exit program */

(C) Temperature t = new Temperature(tempDegrees, tempScale);
    if (!t.isValidTemp(tempDegrees,tempScale))
        /* error message and exit program */

(D) if (isValidTemp(tempDegrees,tempScale))
        Temperature t = new Temperature(tempDegrees, tempScale);
    else
        /* error message and exit program */

(E) if (Temperature.isValidTemp(tempDegrees,tempScale))
        Temperature t = new Temperature(tempDegrees, tempScale);
    else
        /* error message and exit program */

20. The formula to convert degrees Celsius $C$ to Fahrenheit $F$ is

$$F = 1.8C + 32$$

For example, $30°\,C$ is equivalent to $86°\,F$.

An `inFahrenheit()` accessor method is added to the `Temperature` class. Here is its implementation:

```
/** Returns an equivalent temperature in degrees Fahrenheit.
 *  Precondition:  The temperature is a valid temperature
 *                    in degrees Celsius.
 *  Postcondition:
 *    - An equivalent temperature in degrees Fahrenheit has been
 *      returned.
 *    - Original temperature remains unchanged.
 */
public Temperature inFahrenheit()
{
    Temperature result;
    /* more code */
    return result;
}
```

Which of the following correctly replaces /* *more code* */ so that the postcondition is achieved?

```
  I. result = new Temperature(degrees * 1.8 + 32, "F");

 II. result = new Temperature(degrees * 1.8, "F");
     result = result.raise(32);

III. degrees *= 1.8;
     this = this.raise(32);
     result = new Temperature(degrees, "F");
```

(A) I only
(B) II only
(C) III only
(D) I and II only
(E) I, II, and III

21. Consider this program.

```
public class CountStuff
{
    public static void doSomething()
    {
        int count = 0;
            ...
        //code to do something - no screen output produced
        count++;
    }

    public static void main(String[] args)
    {
        int count = 0;
        System.out.println("How many iterations?");
        int n = ...;      //read user input
        for (int  i = 1; i <= n; i++)
        {
            doSomething();
            System.out.println(count);
        }
    }
}
```

If the input value for n is 3, what screen output will this program subsequently produce?

(A)  0
     0
     0

(B)  1
     2
     3

(C)  3
     3
     3

(D)  ?
     ?
     ?

where ? is some undefined value.

(E)  No output will be produced.

22. This question refers to the following class.

```
public class IntObject
{
    private int num;

    public IntObject()        //constructor
    { num = 0; }

    public IntObject(int n)  //constructor
    { num = n; }

    public void increment()  //increment by 1
    { num++; }
}
```

Here is a client program that uses this class:

```
public class IntObjectTest
{
    public static IntObject someMethod(IntObject obj)
    {
        IntObject ans = obj;
        ans.increment();
        return ans;
    }

    public static void main(String[] args)
    {
        IntObject x = new IntObject(2);
        IntObject y = new IntObject(7);
        IntObject a = y;
        x = someMethod(y);
        a = someMethod(x);
    }
}
```

Just before exiting this program, what are the object values of x, y, and a, respectively?

(A)  9, 9, 9
(B)  2, 9, 9
(C)  2, 8, 9
(D)  3, 8, 9
(E)  7, 8, 9

23. Consider the following program.

```
public class Tester
{
    public void someMethod(int a, int b)
    {
        int temp = a;
        a = b;
        b = temp;
    }
}

public class TesterMain
{
    public static void main(String[] args)
    {
        int x = 6, y = 8;
        Tester tester = new Tester();
        tester.someMethod(x, y);
    }
}
```

Just before the end of execution of this program, what are the values of x, y, and temp, respectively?

(A) 6, 8, 6

(B) 8, 6, 6

(C) 6, 8, ?, where ? means undefined

(D) 8, 6, ?, where ? means undefined

(E) 8, 6, 8

## Answer Key

| | | |
|---|---|---|
| 1. **D** | 9. **A** | 17. **D** |
| 2. **B** | 10. **A** | 18. **B** |
| 3. **C** | 11. **C** | 19. **E** |
| 4. **C** | 12. **B** | 20. **D** |
| 5. **B** | 13. **E** | 21. **A** |
| 6. **C** | 14. **C** | 22. **A** |
| 7. **E** | 15. **D** | 23. **C** |
| 8. **E** | 16. **E** | |

## Answer Explanations

1. **(D)** There are just two constructors. Constructors are recognizable by having the same name as the class, and no return type.

2. **(B)** Each of the private instance variables should be assigned the value of the matching parameter. Choice B is the only choice that does this. Choice D confuses the order of the assignment statements. Choice A gives the code for the *no-argument* constructor, ignoring the parameters. Choice C would be correct if it were `resetTime(h, m, s)`. As written, it doesn't assign the parameter values `h`, `m`, and `s` to `hrs`, `mins`, and `secs`. Choice E is wrong because the keyword `new` should be used to create a new object, not to implement the constructor!

3. **(C)** Replacement III will automatically print time `t` in the required form since a `toString` method was defined for the `Time` class. Replacement I is wrong because it doesn't refer to the parameter, `t`, of the method. Replacement II is wrong because a client program may not access private data of the class.

4. **(C)** The parameter names can be the same—the *signatures* must be different. For example,

```
public void print(int x)        //prints x
public void print(double x)     //prints x
```

The signatures (method name plus parameter types) here are `print(int)` and `print(double)`, respectively. The parameter name x is irrelevant. Choice A is true: All local variables and parameters go out of scope (are erased) when the method is exited. Choice B is true: Static methods apply to the whole class. Only instance methods have an implicit `this` parameter. Choice D is true even for object parameters: Their references are passed by value. Note that choice E is true because it's possible to have two different constructors with different signatures but the same number of parameters (e.g., one for an `int` argument and one for a `double`).

5. **(B)** Constructing an object requires the keyword `new` and a constructor of the `Date` class. Eliminate choices D and E since they omit `new`. The class name `Date` should appear on the right-hand side of the assignment statement, immediately following the keyword `new`. This eliminates choices A and C.

6. **(C)** Segment III will cause a `NullPointerException` to be thrown since `d` is a null reference. You cannot invoke a method for a null reference. Segment II has the effect of assigning `null` to both `d1` and `d2`—obscure but not incorrect. Segment I creates the object reference `d1` and then declares a second reference `d2` that refers to the same object as `d1`.

7. **(E)** A client program cannot access a private instance variable.

8. **(E)** All are correct. Since `write()` is a `Date` instance method, it is OK to use the private data members in its implementation code. Segment III prints `this`, the current `Date` object. This usage is correct since `write()` is part of the `Date` class. The `toString()` method guarantees that the date will be printed in the required format (see p. 171).

9. **(A)** The idea here is to read in three separate variables for month, day, and year and then to construct the required date using `new` and the `Date` class constructor with three parameters. Code segment II won't work because `month()`, `day()`, and `year()` are accessor methods that access existing values and may not be used to read new values into `bDate`. Segment III is wrong because it tries to access private instance variables from a client program.

10. **(A)** Segment I will not create a second object. It will simply cause `d2` to refer to the *same* object as `d1`, which is not what was required. The keyword `new` *must* be used to create a new object.

11. **(C)** When `recentDate` is declared in `main()`, its value is null. Recall that a method is not able to replace an object reference, so `recentDate` remains null. Note that the intent of the program is to change `recentDate` to refer to the updated `oldDate` object. The code, however, doesn't do this. Choice A is false: No methods are invoked with a null reference. Choice B is false because `addYears()` is a mutator method. Even though a method doesn't change the address of its object parameter, it can change the contents of the object, which is what happens here. Choices D and E are wrong because the `addCentury()` method cannot change the value of its `recentDate` argument.

12. **(B)** The method `getPondTemperature` is the only method that applies to more than one frog. It should therefore be static. All of the other methods relate directly to one particular `Frog` object. So `f.swim()`, `f.die()`, `f.getWeight()`, and `f.eat()` are all reasonable methods for a single instance `f` of a `Frog`. On the other hand, it doesn't make sense to say `f.getPondTemperature()`. It makes more sense to say `Frog.getPondTemperature()`, since the same value will apply to all frogs in the class.

13. **(E)** Here are the memory slots at the start of `strangeMethod(a, b)`:

|  a  |  b  |
|:---:|:---:|
|  6  |  3  |

|  x  |  y  |
|:---:|:---:|
|  6  |  3  |

Before exiting `strangeMethod(a, b)`:

|  a  |  b  |
|:---:|:---:|
|  6  |  3  |

|  x  |  y  |
|:---:|:---:|
|  9  |  27 |

Note that 9  27 is output before exiting. After exiting `strangeMethod(a, b)`, the memory slots are

The next step outputs 6  3.

14. **(C)** The `reduce()` method will be used only in the implementation of the instance methods of the `Rational` class. It's a private helper method.

15. **(D)** None of the constructors in the `Rational` class takes a real-valued parameter. Thus, the real-valued parameter in choice D will need to be converted to an integer. Since in general truncating a real value to an integer involves a loss of precision, it is not done automatically—you have to do it explicitly with a cast. Omitting the cast causes a compile-time error.

16. **(E)** A new `Rational` object must be created using the newly calculated `numer` and `denom`. Then it must be reduced before being returned. Choice A is wrong because it doesn't correctly create the new object. Choice B returns a correctly constructed object, but one that has not been reduced. Choice C reduces the current object, `this`, instead of the new object, `rat`. Choice D is wrong because it invokes `reduce()` for the `Rational` class instead of the specific `rat` object.

17. **(D)** The `plus` method of the `Rational` class can only be invoked by `Rational` objects. Since `n` is an `int`, the statement in choice D will cause an error.

18. **(B)** This is an example of *aliasing*. The keyword `new` is used just once, which means that just one object is constructed. Here are the memory slots after each declaration:

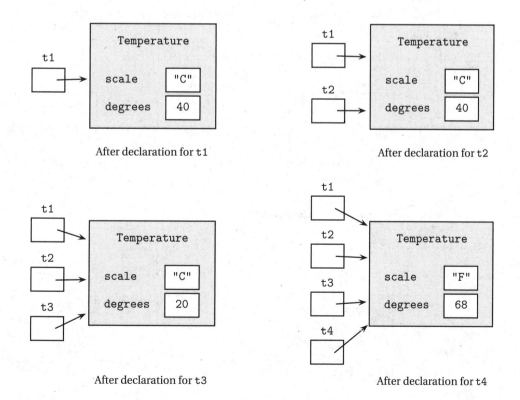

After declaration for t1

After declaration for t2

After declaration for t3

After declaration for t4

19. **(E)** Notice that `isValidTemp` is a static method for the `Temperature` class, which means that it should be invoked with the class name, `Temperature`, as in choice E. The method

should not be invoked with `t`, a `Temperature` object, as is done in choice C. (Even though `t.isValidTemp` may work, its use is discouraged. A good compiler will give you a warning.) Choice A is not a good choice because it is not robust: It allows the program to proceed with data that may be invalid. Choice B fails because it uses `isNotValidTemp`, a method that is not in the program. Choice D fails because `isValidTemp` is not a method of the `TempTest` class.

20. **(D)**  A new `Temperature` object must be constructed to prevent the current `Temperature` from being changed. Segment I, which applies the conversion formula directly to `degrees`, is the best way to do this. Segment II, while not the best algorithm, does work. The statement

    ```
    result = result.raise(32);
    ```

    has the effect of raising the `result` temperature by 32 degrees, and completing the conversion. Segment III fails because

    ```
    degrees *= 1.8;
    ```

    alters the `degrees` instance variable of the current object, as does

    ```
    this = this.raise(32);
    ```

    To be correct, these operations must be applied to the `result` object.

21. **(A)** This is a question about the scope of variables. The scope of the `count` variable that is declared in `main()` extends up to the closing brace of `main()`. In `doSomething()`, `count` is a local variable. After the method call in the `for` loop, the local variable `count` goes out of scope, and the value that's being printed is the value of the `count` in `main()`, which is unchanged from 0.

22. **(A)** Here are the memory slots before the first `someMethod` call:

Just before exiting `x = someMethod(y)`:

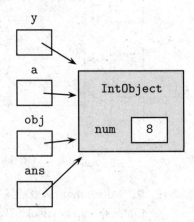

After exiting

```
x = someMethod(y);
```

x has been reassigned, so the object with `num` = 2 has been recycled:

After exiting `a = someMethod(x)`:

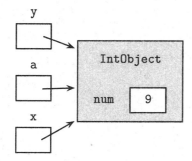

23. **(C)** Recall that when primitive types are passed as parameters, copies are made of the actual arguments. All manipulations in the method are performed on the copies, and the arguments remain unchanged. Thus x and y retain their values of 6 and 8. The local variable `temp` goes out of scope as soon as `someMethod` is exited and is therefore undefined just before the end of execution of the program.

# 4

# Inheritance and Polymorphism

*Say not you know another entirely,*
*till you have divided an inheritance with him.*
—*Johann Kaspar Lavater*, Aphorisms on Man

## Learning Objectives

In this chapter, you will learn:

→ Inheritance

→ Polymorphism

→ Type Compatibility

## Inheritance

### Superclass and Subclass

*Inheritance* defines a relationship between objects that share characteristics. Specifically it is the mechanism whereby a new class, called a *subclass*, is created from an existing class, called a *superclass*, by absorbing its state and behavior and augmenting these with features unique to the new class. We say that the subclass *inherits* characteristics of its superclass.

Don't get confused by the names: a subclass is bigger than a superclass—it contains more data and more methods!

Inheritance provides an effective mechanism for code reuse. Suppose the code for a superclass has been tested and debugged. Since a subclass object shares features of a superclass object, the only new code required is for the additional characteristics of the subclass.

### Inheritance Hierarchy

A subclass can itself be a superclass for another subclass, leading to an *inheritance hierarchy* of classes.

For example, consider the relationship between these classes: Person, Employee, Student, GradStudent, and UnderGrad.

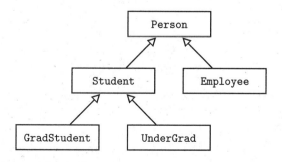

For any of these classes, an arrow points to its superclass. The arrow designates an inheritance relationship between classes, or, informally, an *is-a* relationship. Thus, an Employee *is-a* Person; a Student *is-a* Person; a GradStudent *is-a* Student; an UnderGrad *is-a* Student. Notice that the opposite is not necessarily true: A Person may not be a Student, nor is a Student necessarily an UnderGrad.

Note that the *is-a* relationship is transitive: If a GradStudent *is-a* Student and a Student *is-a* Person, then a GradStudent *is-a* Person.

Every subclass inherits the public or protected variables and methods of its superclass (see p. 142). Subclasses may have additional methods and instance variables that are not in the superclass. A subclass may redefine a method it inherits. For example, GradStudent and UnderGrad may use different algorithms for computing the course grade, and need to change a computeGrade method inherited from Student. This is called *method overriding*. If part of the original method implementation from the superclass is retained, we refer to the rewrite as *partial overriding* (see p. 143).

## Implementing Subclasses

### The extends Keyword

The inheritance relationship between a subclass and a superclass is specified in the declaration of the subclass, using the keyword extends. The general format looks like this:

```
public class Superclass
{
    //private instance variables
    //other data members
    //constructors
    //public methods
    //private methods
}


public class Subclass extends Superclass
{
    //additional private instance variables
    //additional data members
    //constructors  (Not inherited!)
    //additional public methods
    //inherited public methods whose implementation is overridden
    //additional private methods
}
```

For example, consider the following inheritance hierarchy:

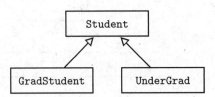

The implementation of the classes may look something like this (discussion follows the code):

```java
public class Student
{
    //data members
    public final static int NUM_TESTS = 3;
    private String name;
    private int[] tests;
    private String grade;

    //constructor
    public Student()
    {
        name = "";
        tests = new int[NUM_TESTS];
        grade = "";
    }


    //constructor
    public Student(String studName, int[] studTests, String studGrade)
    {
        name = studName;
        tests = studTests;
        grade = studGrade;
    }

    public String getName()
    { return name; }

    public String getGrade()
    { return grade; }

    public void setGrade(String newGrade)
    { grade = newGrade; }

    public void computeGrade()
    {
        if (name.equals(""))
            grade = "No grade";
        else if (getTestAverage() >= 65)
            grade = "Pass";
        else
            grade = "Fail";
    }

    public double getTestAverage()
    {
        double total = 0;
        for (int score : tests)
            total += score;
        return total/NUM_TESTS;
    }
}
```

```
public class UnderGrad extends Student
{
    public UnderGrad()    //constructor
    { super(); }

    //constructor
    public UnderGrad(String studName, int[] studTests, String studGrade)
    { super(studName, studTests, studGrade); }

    public void computeGrade()
    {
        if (getTestAverage() >= 70)
            setGrade("Pass");
        else
            setGrade("Fail");
    }
}

public class GradStudent extends Student
{
    private int gradID;

    public GradStudent()        //constructor
    {
        super();
        gradID = 0;
    }

    //constructor
    public GradStudent(String studName, int[] studTests,
            String studGrade, int gradStudID)
    {
        super(studName, studTests, studGrade);
        gradID = gradStudID;
    }

    public int getID()
    { return gradID; }

    public void computeGrade()
    {
        //invokes computeGrade in Student superclass
        super.computeGrade();
        if (getTestAverage() >= 90)
            setGrade("Pass with distinction");
    }
}
```

## Inheriting Instance Methods and Variables

A subclass inherits all the public and protected methods of its superclass. It does not, however, inherit the private instance variables or private methods of its parent class, and therefore does not have direct access to them. To access private instance variables, a subclass must use the accessor or mutator methods that it has inherited.

In the `Student` example, the `UnderGrad` and `GradStudent` subclasses inherit all of the methods of the `Student` superclass. Notice, however, that the `Student` instance variables `name`, `tests`, and `grade` are private and are therefore not inherited or directly accessible to the methods in the `UnderGrad` and `GradStudent` subclasses. A subclass can, however, directly invoke the public accessor and mutator methods of the superclass. Thus, both `UnderGrad` and `GradStudent` use `getTestAverage`. Additionally, both `UnderGrad` and `GradStudent` use `setGrade` to access indirectly—and modify—`grade`.

If, instead of `private`, the access specifier for the instance variables in `Student` were `public` or `protected`, then the subclasses could directly access these variables. The keyword `protected` is not part of the AP Java subset.

Classes on the same level in a hierarchy diagram do not inherit anything from each other (for example, `UnderGrad` and `GradStudent`). All they have in common is the identical code they inherit from their superclass.

## Method Overriding and the super Keyword

Any public method in a superclass can be overridden in a subclass by defining a method with the same return type and signature (name and parameter types). For example, the `computeGrade` method in the `UnderGrad` subclass overrides the `computeGrade` method in the `Student` superclass.

Sometimes the code for overriding a method includes a call to the superclass method. This is called *partial overriding*. Typically this occurs when the subclass method wants to do what the superclass does, plus something extra. This is achieved by using the keyword `super` in the implementation. The `computeGrade` method in the `GradStudent` subclass partially overrides the matching method in the `Student` class. The statement

```
super.computeGrade();
```

signals that the `computeGrade` method in the superclass should be invoked here. The additional test

```
if (getTestAverage() >= 90)
    ...
```

allows a `GradStudent` to have a grade `Pass with distinction`. Note that this option is open to GradStudents only.

## Note

Private methods cannot be overridden.

## Constructors and super

Constructors are never inherited! If no constructor is written for a subclass, a *default constructor* with no parameters is generated, which calls the no-argument constructor from the superclass. If the superclass does not have a no-argument constructor, but only a constructor with parameters, a compiler error will occur. If there is a no-argument constructor in the superclass, inherited data members will be initialized as for the superclass. Additional instance variables in the subclass will get a default initialization—0 for primitive types and `null` for reference types.

---

> A default constructor is a no-argument constructor generated by the compiler when a subclass doesn't have an explicit constructor.

---

A subclass constructor can be implemented with a call to the `super` method, which invokes the superclass constructor. For example, the no-argument constructor in the `UnderGrad` class is identical to that of the `Student` class. This is implemented with the statement

```
super();
```

The second constructor in the `UnderGrad` class is called with parameters that match those in the constructor of the `Student` superclass.

```
public UnderGrad(String studName, int[] studTests, String studGrade)
{ super(studName, studTests, studGrade); }
```

For each constructor, the call to `super` has the effect of initializing the instance variables `name`, `tests`, and `grade` exactly as they are initialized in the `Student` class.

Contrast this with the constructors in `GradStudent`. In each case, the instance variables `name`, `tests`, and `grade` are initialized as for the `Student` class. Then the new instance variable, `gradID`, must be explicitly initialized.

```
public GradStudent()
{
    super();
    gradID = 0;
}

public GradStudent(String studName, int[] studTests,
            String studGrade, int gradStudID)
{
    super(studName, studTests, studGrade);
    gradID = gradStudID;
}
```

## Note

1. If `super` is used in the implementation of a subclass constructor, it *must* be used in the first line of the constructor body.
2. If no constructor is provided in a subclass, the compiler provides the following default constructor:

```
public SubClass()
{
    super();       //calls no-argument constructor of superclass
}
```

**3.** If the superclass has at least one constructor with parameters, the code in Note 2 above will cause a compile-time error if the superclass does not also contain a no-argument constructor.

**Rules for Subclasses**

- A subclass can add new private instance variables.

- A subclass can add new public, private, or static methods.

- A subclass can override inherited methods.

- A subclass may not redefine a public method as private.

- A subclass may not override static methods of the superclass.

- A subclass should define its own constructors.

- A subclass cannot directly access the private members of its superclass. It must use accessor or mutator methods.

## Declaring Subclass Objects

When a superclass object is declared in a client program, that reference can refer not only to an object of the superclass, but also to objects of any of its subclasses. Thus, each of the following is legal:

```
Student s = new Student();
Student g = new GradStudent();
Student u = new UnderGrad();
```

This works because a `GradStudent` *is-a* `Student`, and an `UnderGrad` *is-a* `Student`.

Note that since a `Student` is not necessarily a `GradStudent` nor an `UnderGrad`, the following declarations are *not* valid:

```
GradStudent g = new Student();
UnderGrad u = new Student();
```

Consider these valid declarations:

```
Student s = new Student("Brian Lorenzen", new int[] {90,94,99},
        "none");
Student u = new UnderGrad("Tim Broder", new int[] {90,90,100},
        "none");
Student g = new GradStudent("Kevin Cristella",
        new int[] {85,70,90}, "none", 1234);
```

Suppose you make the method call

```
s.setGrade("Pass");
```

The appropriate method in `Student` is found and the new grade assigned. The method calls

```
        g.setGrade("Pass");
```

and

```
        u.setGrade("Pass");
```

achieve the same effect on g and u since GradStudent and UnderGrad both inherit the setGrade method from Student. The following method calls, however, won't work:

```
        int studentNum = s.getID();
        int underGradNum = u.getID();
```

These don't compile because Student does not contain getID.

Now consider the following valid method calls:

```
        s.computeGrade();
        g.computeGrade();
        u.computeGrade();
```

Since s, g, and u have all been declared to be of type Student, will the appropriate method be executed in each case? That is the topic of the next section, *polymorphism*.

### Note

The initializer list syntax used in constructing the array parameters—for example, new int[] {90,90,100}— will not be tested on the AP exam.

## Polymorphism

A method that has been overridden in at least one subclass is said to be *polymorphic*. An example is computeGrade, which is redefined for both GradStudent and UnderGrad.

   *Polymorphism* is the mechanism of selecting the appropriate method for a particular object in a class hierarchy. The correct method is chosen because, in Java, method calls are always determined by the type of the *actual object*, not the type of the object reference. For example, even though s, g, and u are all declared as type Student, s.computeGrade(), g.computeGrade(), and u.computeGrade() will all perform the correct operations for their particular instances. In Java, the selection of the correct method occurs *during the run of the program*.

   Here is a simple example.

```
public class Dog
{
    private String name;
    private String breed;

    public Dog (String aName, String aBreed)
    {
        name = aName;
        breed = aBreed;
    }
        ...
}
```

```
public class Poodle extends Dog
{
    private boolean needsGrooming;

    public Poodle (String aName, String aBreed, boolean grooming)
    {
        super(aName, aBreed);
        needsGrooming = grooming;
    }
        . . .
}
```

Now consider this hierarchy of classes, and the declarations that follow it:

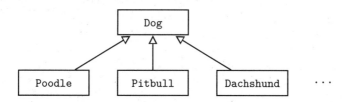

Suppose the `Dog` class has this method:

```
public void eat()
{ /* implementation not shown */ }
```

And each of the subclasses, `Poodle`, `PitBull`, `Dachshund`, etc., has a different, overridden `eat` method. Now suppose that `allDogs` is an `ArrayList<Dog>` where each `Dog` declared above has been added to the list. Each `Dog` in the list will be processed to eat by the following lines of code:

```
for (Dog d: allDogs)
    d.eat();
```

Polymorphism is the process of selecting the correct `eat` method, during run time, for each of the different dogs.

Recall that constructors are not inherited, and if you use the keyword `super` in writing a constructor for your subclass, the line containing it should precede any other code in the constructor.

Recall also that if the superclass does not have a no-argument constructor, then you must write an explicit constructor for the subclass. If you don't do this, later code that tries to create a subclass object will get a compile-time error. This is because the compiler will generate a default constructor for the subclass that tries to invoke the no-argument constructor of the superclass.

## Dynamic Binding (Late Binding)

Making a run-time decision about which instance method to call is known as *dynamic binding* or *late binding*. Contrast this with selecting the correct method when methods are *overloaded* (see p. 106) rather than overridden. The compiler selects the correct overloaded method at compile time by comparing the methods' signatures. This is known as *static binding*, or *early binding.* In polymorphism, the actual method that will be called is not determined by the compiler. Think of it this way: The compiler determines *if* a method can be called (i.e., does the method exist in the class of the reference?), while the run-time environment determines *how* it will be called (i.e., which overridden form should be used?).

> **Example 1**

```
Student s = null;
Student u = new UnderGrad("Tim Broder", new int[] {90,90,100},
        "none");
Student g = new GradStudent("Kevin Cristella",
        new int[] {85,70,90}, "none", 1234);
System.out.print("Enter student status: ");
System.out.println("Grad (G), Undergrad (U), Neither (N)");
String str = ...;        //read user input
if (str.equals("G"))
    s = g;
else if (str.equals("U"))
    s = u;
else
    s = new Student();
s.computeGrade();
```

When this code fragment is run, the `computeGrade` method used will depend on the type of the actual object s refers to, which in turn depends on the user input.

> **Example 2**

```
public class StudentTest
{
    public static void computeAllGrades(Student[] studentList)
    {
        for (Student s : studentList)
            if (s != null)
                s.computeGrade();
    }

    public static void main(String[] args)
    {
        Student[] stu = new Student[5];
        stu[0] = new Student("Brian Lorenzen",
                    new int[] {90,94,99}, "none");
        stu[1] = new UnderGrad("Tim Broder",
                    new int[] {90,90,100}, "none");
        stu[2] = new GradStudent("Kevin Cristella",
                    new int[] {85,70,90}, "none", 1234);
        computeAllGrades(stu);
    }
}
```

Polymorphism applies only to overridden methods in subclasses.

Here an array of five `Student` references is created, all initially null. Three of these references, `stu[0]`, `stu[1]`, and `stu[2]`, are then assigned to actual objects. The `computeAllGrades` method steps through the array invoking for each of the objects the appropriate computeGrade method, using dynamic binding in each case. The null test in computeAllGrades is necessary because some of the array references could be null.

## Using super in a Subclass

A subclass can call a method in its superclass by using super. Suppose that the superclass method then calls another method that has been overridden in the subclass. By polymorphism, the method that is executed is the one in the subclass. The computer keeps track and executes any pending statements in either method.

### ▷ Example

```
public class Dancer
{
    public void act()
    {
        System.out.print (" spin ");
        doTrick();
    }

    public void doTrick()
    {
        System.out.print (" float ");
    }
}


public class Acrobat extends Dancer
{
    public void act()
    {
        super.act();
        System.out.print (" flip ");
    }

    public void doTrick()
    {
        System.out.print (" somersault ");
    }
}
```

Suppose the following declaration appears in a class other than Dancer or Acrobat:

```
Dancer a = new Acrobat();
```

What is printed as a result of the call a.act()?

### ✓ Solution

When a.act() is called, the act method of Acrobat is executed. This is an example of polymorphism. The first line, super.act(), goes to the act method of Dancer, the superclass. This prints spin, then calls doTrick(). Again, using polymorphism, the doTrick method in Acrobat is called, printing somersault. Now, completing the act method of Acrobat, flip is printed. So the complete output is the following:

```
spin somersault flip
```

### Note

Even though there are no constructors in either the Dancer or Acrobat classes, the declaration

```
Dancer a = new Acrobat();
```

compiles without error. This is because Dancer, while not having an explicit superclass, has an implicit superclass, Object, and a default constructor is generated that calls super(), Object's no-argument constructor. Similarly the Acrobat class gets this constructor slotted into its code.

The statement Dancer a = new Acrobat(); will not compile, however, if the Dancer class has at least one constructor with parameters but does not have a no-argument constructor.

## Type Compatibility

### Downcasting

Consider the statements

```
Student s = new GradStudent();
GradStudent g = new GradStudent();
int x = s.getID();              //compile-time error
int y = g.getID();              //legal
```

Both s and g represent GradStudent objects, so why does s.getID() cause an error? The reason is that s is of type Student, and the Student class doesn't have a getID method. At compile time, only nonprivate methods of the Student class can appear to the right of the dot operator when applied to s. Don't confuse this with polymorphism: getID is not a polymorphic method. It occurs in just the GradStudent class and can therefore be called only by a GradStudent object.

The error shown above can be fixed by casting s to the correct type:

```
int x = ((GradStudent) s).getID();
```

Since s (of type Student) is actually representing a GradStudent object, such a cast can be carried out. Casting a superclass to a subclass type is called a *downcast*.

### Note

1. The outer parentheses are necessary, so

   ```
   int x = (GradStudent) s.getID();
   ```

   will still cause an error, despite the cast. This is because the dot operator has higher precedence than casting, so s.getID() is invoked before s is cast to GradStudent.

2. The statement

   ```
   int y = g.getID();
   ```

   compiles without problem because g is declared to be of type GradStudent, and this is the class that contains getID. No cast is required.

3. Class casts will not explicitly be tested on the AP exam. You should, however, understand why the following statement will cause a compile-time error:

```
int x = s.getID(); //No getID method in Student class
```

And the following statement will compile without error:

```
int y = g.getID(); //getID method is in GradStudent class
```

---

**Type Rules for Polymorphic Method Calls**

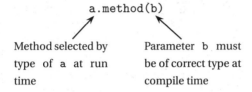

a.method(b)

Method selected by          Parameter b must
type of a at run            be of correct type at
time                        compile time

- For a declaration like

    ```
    Superclass a = new Subclass();
    ```

    the type of a at compile time is Superclass; at run time it is Subclass.

- At compile time, method must be found in the class of a, that is, in Superclass. (This is true whether the method is polymorphic or not.) If method cannot be found in the class of a, you need to do an explicit cast on a to its actual type.

- For a polymorphic method, at run time the actual type of a is determined—Subclass in this example—and method is selected from Subclass. This could be an inherited method if there is no overriding method.

- The type of parameter b is checked at compile time. It must pass the *is-a* test for the type in the method declaration. You may need to do an explicit cast to a subclass type to make this correct.

---

## Abstract Classes

Abstract classes are no longer part of the AP Java subset.

## Interfaces

Interfaces are no longer part of the AP Java subset.

## Chapter Summary

You should be able to write your own subclasses, given any superclass.

Be sure you understand the use of the keyword super, both in writing constructors and calling methods of the superclass.

You should understand what polymorphism is: Recall that it only operates when methods have been overridden in at least one subclass. You should also be able to explain the difference between the following concepts:

- An overloaded method and an overridden method

- Dynamic binding (late binding) and static binding (early binding)

- A default constructor and a no-argument constructor

# Multiple-Choice Questions on Inheritance and Polymorphism

Questions 1–9 refer to the BankAccount, SavingsAccount, and CheckingAccount classes defined below.

```
public class BankAccount
{
    private double balance;

    public BankAccount()
    { balance = 0; }

    public BankAccount(double acctBalance)
    { balance = acctBalance; }

    public void deposit(double amount)
    { balance += amount; }

    public void withdraw(double amount)
    { balance -= amount; }

    public double getBalance()
    { return balance; }
}

public class SavingsAccount extends BankAccount
{
    private double interestRate;

    public SavingsAccount()
    { /* implementation not shown */ }

    public SavingsAccount(double acctBalance, double rate)
    { /* implementation not shown */ }

    public void addInterest()     //Add interest to balance
    { /* implementation not shown */ }
}

public class CheckingAccount extends BankAccount
{
    private static final double FEE = 2.0;
    private static final double MIN_BALANCE = 50.0;

    public CheckingAccount(double acctBalance)
    { /* implementation not shown */ }

    /** FEE of $2 deducted if withdrawal leaves balance less
     *  than MIN_BALANCE. Allows for negative balance. */
    public void withdraw(double amount)
    { /* implementation not shown */ }
}
```

1. Of the methods shown, how many different nonconstructor methods can be invoked by a SavingsAccount object?
   (A) 1
   (B) 2
   (C) 3
   (D) 4
   (E) 5

2. Which of the following correctly implements the no-argument constructor of the SavingsAccount class?

   I. interestRate = 0;
      super();

   II. super();
       interestRate = 0;

   III. super();

   (A) II only
   (B) I and II only
   (C) II and III only
   (D) III only
   (E) I, II, and III

3. Which is a correct implementation of the constructor with parameters in the SavingsAccount class?

   (A) balance = acctBalance;
       interestRate = rate;

   (B) getBalance() =  acctBalance;
       interestRate = rate;

   (C) super();
       interestRate = rate;

   (D) super(acctBalance);
       interestRate = rate;

   (E) super(acctBalance, rate);

4. Which is a correct implementation of the CheckingAccount constructor?

   I. super(acctBalance);

   II. super();
       deposit(acctBalance);

   III. deposit(acctBalance);

   (A) I only
   (B) II only
   (C) III only
   (D) II and III only
   (E) I, II, and III

5. Which is correct implementation code for the `withdraw` method in the `CheckingAccount` class?

    (A) ```
        super.withdraw(amount);
            if (balance < MIN_BALANCE)
                super.withdraw(FEE);
        ```

    (B) ```
        withdraw(amount);
            if (balance < MIN_BALANCE)
                withdraw(FEE);
        ```

    (C) ```
        super.withdraw(amount);
            if (getBalance() < MIN_BALANCE)
                super.withdraw(FEE);
        ```

    (D) ```
        withdraw(amount);
            if (getBalance() < MIN_BALANCE)
                withdraw(FEE);
        ```

    (E) ```
        balance -= amount;
            if (balance < MIN_BALANCE)
                balance -= FEE;
        ```

6. Redefining the `withdraw` method in the `CheckingAccount` class is an example of
    (A) method overloading.
    (B) method overriding.
    (C) downcasting.
    (D) dynamic binding (late binding).
    (E) static binding (early binding).

Use the following for Questions 7 and 8.

A program to test the `BankAccount`, `SavingsAccount`, and `CheckingAccount` classes has these declarations:

```
BankAccount b = new BankAccount(1400);
BankAccount s = new SavingsAccount(1000, 0.04);
BankAccount c = new CheckingAccount(500);
```

7. Which method call will cause an error?
    (A) `b.deposit(200);`
    (B) `s.withdraw(500);`
    (C) `c.withdraw(500);`
    (D) `s.deposit(10000);`
    (E) `s.addInterest();`

8. In order to test polymorphism, which method must be used in the program?
    (A) Either a `SavingsAccount` constructor or a `CheckingAccount` constructor
    (B) `addInterest`
    (C) `deposit`
    (D) `withdraw`
    (E) `getBalance`
```

9. A new method is added to the BankAccount class.

```
/** Transfer amount from this BankAccount to another BankAccount.
 * Precondition: balance > amount
 * @param another a different BankAccount object
 * @param amount the amount to be transferred
 */
public void transfer(BankAccount another, double amount)
{
    withdraw(amount);
    another.deposit(amount);
}
```

A program has these declarations:

```
BankAccount b = new BankAccount(650);
SavingsAccount timsSavings = new SavingsAccount(1500, 0.03);
CheckingAccount daynasChecking = new CheckingAccount(2000);
```

Which of the following will transfer money from one account to another without error?

  I. `b.transfer(timsSavings, 50);`

 II. `timsSavings.transfer(daynasChecking, 30);`

III. `daynasChecking.transfer(b, 55);`

(A) I only
(B) II only
(C) III only
(D) I, II, and III
(E) None

10.  Consider these class declarations.

```
public class Person
{
    ...
}


public class Teacher extends Person
{
    ...
}
```

Which is a true statement?

I.  Teacher inherits the constructors of Person.
II.  Teacher can add new methods and private instance variables.
III.  Teacher can override existing private methods of Person.

(A)  I only
(B)  II only
(C)  III only
(D)  I and II only
(E)  II and III only

11.  Which statement about subclass methods is false?
(A)  Writing two subclass methods with the same name but different parameters is called method overriding.
(B)  A public method in a subclass that is not in its superclass is not accessible by the superclass.
(C)  A private method in a superclass is not inherited by its subclass.
(D)  Two different subclasses of the same superclass inherit the same methods of the superclass.
(E)  If Class1 is a superclass of Class2, and Class2 is a superclass of Class3, and Class2 has no overridden methods, Class3 inherits all the public methods of Class1.

12. Consider a program to manipulate digital images. The inheritance hierarchy is as follows.

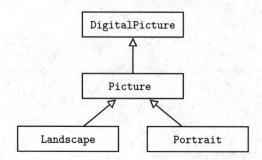

You may assume that DigitalPicture and Picture have no-argument constructors, but that Landscape and Portrait do not have any constructors. Which of the following declarations will compile?

   I. DigitalPicture p = new Portrait();

  II. Landscape p = new Picture();

 III. DigitalPicture p = new DigitalPicture();

(A) I only
(B) II only
(C) III only
(D) I and II only
(E) I and III only

13. Consider the following hierarchy of classes.

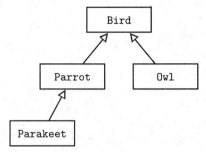

A program is written to print data about various birds:

```
public class BirdStuff
{
    public static void printName(Bird b)
    { /* implementation not shown */ }

    public static void printBirdCall(Parrot p)
    { /* implementation not shown */ }

    //several more Bird methods

    public static void main(String[] args)
    {
        Bird bird1 = new Bird();
        Bird bird2 = new Parrot();
        Parrot parrot1 = new Parrot();
        Parrot parrot2 = new Parakeet();
        /* more code */
    }
}
```

Assuming that all of the given classes have no-argument constructors, which of the following segments of /* *more code* */ will cause an error?

(A) printBirdCall(bird2);

(B) printName(parrot2);

(C) printName(bird2);

(D) printBirdCall(parrot2);

(E) printBirdCall(parrot1);

Refer to the classes below for Questions 14 and 15.

```
public class ClassA
{
    //no-argument constructor not shown ...

    public void method1()
    { /* implementation of method1 */ }

    public void method2()
    { /* implementation of method2 */ }
}

public class ClassB extends ClassA
{
    public void method1()
    { /* different implementation from method1 in ClassA*/ }

    public void method3()
    { /* implementation of method3 */ }
}
```

14.  The `method1` method in `ClassB` is an example of
    (A)  method overloading.
    (B)  method overriding.
    (C)  polymorphism.
    (D)  data encapsulation.
    (E)  procedural abstraction.

15.  Consider the following declarations in a client class.

```
ClassA ob1 = new ClassA();
ClassA ob2 = new ClassB();
ClassB ob3 = new ClassB();
```

Which of the following method calls will cause an error?

    I.  `ob1.method3();`

    II. `ob2.method3();`

    III. `ob3.method2();`

    (A)  I only
    (B)  II only
    (C)  III only
    (D)  I and II only
    (E)  I, II, and III

Use the declarations below for Questions 16 and 17.

```
public class Solid
{
    private String name;

    //constructor
    public Solid(String solidName)
    { name = solidName; }

    public String getName()
    { return name; }

    public double volume()
    { /* implementation not shown */ }
}

public class Sphere extends Solid
{
    private double radius;

    //constructor
    public Sphere(String sphereName, double sphereRadius)
    {
        super(sphereName);
        radius = sphereRadius;
    }

    public double volume()
    { return (4.0/3.0) * Math.PI * radius * radius * radius; }
}

public class RectangularPrism extends Solid
{
    private double length;
    private double width;
    private double height;

    //constructor
    public RectangularPrism(String prismName, double l, double w,
            double h)
    {
        super(prismName);
        length = l;
        width = w;
        height = h;
    }

    public double volume()
    { return length * width * height; }
}
```

16. A program that tests these classes has the following declarations and assignments:

```
Solid s1, s2, s3, s4;
s1 = new Solid("blob");
s2 = new Sphere("sphere", 3.8);
s3 = new RectangularPrism("box", 2, 4, 6.5);
s4 = null;
```

How many of the above lines of code are incorrect?

(A) 0

(B) 1

(C) 2

(D) 3

(E) 4

17. Here is a program that prints the volume of a solid:

```
public class SolidMain
{
    /** Output volume of Solid s. */
    public static void printVolume(Solid s)
    {
        System.out.println("Volume = " + s.volume() +
                " cubic units");
    }

    public static void main(String[] args)
    {
        Solid sol;
        Solid sph = new Sphere("sphere", 4);
        Solid rec = new RectangularPrism("box", 3, 6, 9);
        int flipCoin = (int) (Math.random() * 2);    //0 or 1
        if (flipCoin == 0)
            sol = sph;
        else
            sol = rec;
        printVolume(sol);
    }
}
```

Which is a true statement about this program?

(A) It will output the volume of the sphere or box, as intended.

(B) It will output the volume of the default Solid s, which is neither a sphere nor a box.

(C) It will randomly print the volume of a sphere or a box.

(D) A run-time error will occur because it is not specified whether s is a sphere or a box.

(E) A run-time error will occur because of parameter type mismatch in the method call printVolume(sol).

18. Consider these class declarations.

```
public class Player
{
    public Player()
    { /* implementation not shown */ }

    public int getMove()
    { /* implementation not shown */ }

    //Other constructors and methods not shown.
}

public class ExpertPlayer extends Player
{
    public int compareTo(ExpertPlayer expert)
    { /* implementation not shown */ }

    //Constructors and other methods not shown.
}
```

Which code segment in a client program will cause an error?

```
  I. Player p1 = new ExpertPlayer();
     int x1 = p1.getMove();

 II. int x;
     ExpertPlayer c1 = new ExpertPlayer();
     ExpertPlayer c2 = new ExpertPlayer();
     if (c1.compareTo(c2) < 0)
         x = c1.getMove();
     else
         x = c2.getMove();

III. int x;
     Player h1 = new ExpertPlayer();
     Player h2 = new ExpertPlayer();
     if (h1.compareTo(h2) < 0)
         x = h1.getMove();
     else
         x = h2.getMove();
```

(A) I only
(B) II only
(C) III only
(D) I and II only
(E) I, II, and III

19. Consider the following class definitions.

```
public class Animal
{
    private String type;

    public Animal(String theType)
    {
        type = theType;
    }

    public String getType()
    {
        return type;
    }
}

public class Dog extends Animal
{
    public Dog(String theType)
    {
        super(theType);
    }
}
```

The following code segment appears in a class other than Animal or Dog.

```
Animal d1 = new Animal("poodle");
Animal d2 = new Dog("schnauzer");
Dog d3 = new Dog("yorkie");

public static void display(Animal a)
{
    System.out.println("This dog is a " + a.getType();)
}
```

Which of the following method calls will compile without error?

  I. display(d1);

 II. display(d2);

III. display(d3);

(A) I only
(B) II only
(C) III only
(D) I and II only
(E) I, II, and III

20. Consider the following class definitions.

```
public class StrStuff1
{
    public void printSub(String str)
    {
        String s = str.substring(2);
        System.out.print(s);
    }
}


public class StrStuff2 extends StrStuff1
{
    public void printSub(String str)
    {
        String s = str.substring(1);
        super.printSub(s);
        System.out.print(s);
    }
}
```

The following code segment appears in a class other than StrStuff1 and StrStuff2.

```
StrStuff1 p = new StrStuff2();
p.printSub("crab");
```

What is printed as a result of executing the code segment?

(A) crabab

(B) brab

(C) rabb

(D) abb

(E) ab

21. Consider the following class definitions.

```
public class Class1
{
    public void doSomething(int n)
    {
        n -= 4;
        System.out.print(n);
    }
}

public class Class2 extends Class1
{
    public void doSomething(int n)
    {
        super.doSomething(n + 3);
        n *= 2;
        System.out.print(n);
    }
}
```

The following code segment appears in a class other than Class1 and Class2.

```
Class1 c = new Class2();
c.doSomething(8);
```

What is printed as a result of executing the code segment?

(A)  416

(B)  422

(C)  714

(D)  716

(E)  722

## Answer Key

| | | |
|---|---|---|
| 1. **D** | 8. **D** | 15. **D** |
| 2. **C** | 9. **D** | 16. **A** |
| 3. **D** | 10. **B** | 17. **A** |
| 4. **E** | 11. **A** | 18. **C** |
| 5. **C** | 12. **E** | 19. **E** |
| 6. **B** | 13. **A** | 20. **B** |
| 7. **E** | 14. **B** | 21. **D** |

## Answer Explanations

1. **(D)** The methods are `deposit`, `withdraw`, and `getBalance`, all inherited from the `BankAccount` class, plus `addInterest`, which was defined just for the class `SavingsAccount`.

2. **(C)** Implementation I fails because `super()` *must* be the first line of the implementation whenever it is used in a constructor. Implementation III may appear to be incorrect because it doesn't initialize `interestRate`. Since `interestRate`, however, is a primitive type—`double`—the compiler will provide a default initialization of 0, which was required.

3. **(D)** First, the statement `super(acctBalance)` initializes the inherited private variable `balance` as for the `BankAccount` superclass. Then the statement `interestRate = rate` initializes `interestRate`, which belongs uniquely to the `SavingsAccount` class. Choice E fails because `interestRate` does not belong to the `BankAccount` class and therefore cannot be initialized by a `super` method. Choice A is wrong because the `SavingsAccount` class cannot directly access the private instance variables of its superclass. Choice B assigns a value to an accessor method, which is meaningless. Choice C is incorrect because `super()` invokes the no-argument constructor of the superclass. This will cause `balance` of the `SavingsAccount` object to be initialized to 0, rather than `acctBalance`, the parameter value.

4. **(E)** The constructor must initialize the inherited instance variable `balance` to the value of the `acctBalance` parameter. All three segments achieve this. Implementation I does it by invoking `super(acctBalance)`, the constructor in the superclass. Implementation II first initializes `balance` to 0 by invoking the no-argument constructor of the superclass. Then it calls the inherited `deposit` method of the superclass to add `acctBalance` to the account. Implementation III works because `super()` is automatically called as the first line of the constructor code if there is no explicit call to `super`.

5. **(C)** First the `withdraw` method of the `BankAccount` superclass is used to withdraw `amount`. A prefix of `super` must be used to invoke this method, which eliminates choices B and D. Then the balance must be tested using the accessor method `getBalance`, which is inherited. You can't test `balance` directly since it is private to the `BankAccount` class. This eliminates choices A and E, and provides another reason for eliminating choice B.

6. **(B)** When a superclass method is redefined in a subclass, the process is called *method overriding*. Which method to call is determined at run time. This is called *dynamic binding* (p. 147). *Method overloading* is two or more methods with different signatures in the same class (p. 106). The compiler recognizes at compile time which method to call. This is *early binding*. The process of *downcasting* is unrelated to these principles (p. 150).

7. **(E)** The addInterest method is defined only in the SavingsAccount class. It therefore cannot be invoked by a BankAccount object. The error can be fixed by casting s to the correct type:

```
((SavingsAccount) s).addInterest();
```

The other method calls do not cause a problem because withdraw and deposit are both methods of the BankAccount class.

8. **(D)** The withdraw method is the only method that has one implementation in the superclass and a *different* implementation in a subclass. Polymorphism is the mechanism of selecting the correct method from the different possibilities in the class hierarchy. Notice that the deposit method, for example, is available to objects of all three bank account classes, but it's the *same* code in all three cases. So polymorphism isn't tested.

9. **(D)** It is OK to use timsSavings and daynasChecking as parameters since each of these *is-a* BankAccount object. It is also OK for timsSavings and daynasChecking to call the transfer method (statements II and III), since they inherit this method from the BankAccount superclass.

10. **(B)** Statement I is false: A subclass must specify its own constructors. Otherwise the compiler will generate a default constructor that calls the no-argument constructor of the superclass. Note that statement III is false: Private instance methods cannot be overridden.

11. **(A)** What is described in choice A is an example of overloaded methods. A key point is that one method is in the same class as the other method, and therefore cannot be an overridden method. An overridden method in a subclass has the same header as a method in its superclass, but different implementation.

12. **(E)** Declaration I works because a Portrait *is-a* DigitalPicture, and the compiler will generate a default constructor from Picture, its superclass. Declaration II fails because a Picture is *not* a Landscape. Declaration III works because DigitalPicture *is-a* DigitalPicture.

13. **(A)** There is a quick test you can do to find the answer to this question: Test the *is-a* relationship—namely, the parameter for printName *is-a* Bird? and the parameter for printBirdCall *is-a* Parrot? Note that to get the type of the actual parameter, you must look at its left-hand-side declaration. Choice A fails the test: bird2 *is-a* Parrot? The variable bird2 is declared a Bird, which is not necessarily a Parrot. Each other choice passes the test: Choice B: parrot2 *is-a* Bird. Choice C: bird2 *is-a* Bird. Choice D: parrot2 *is-a* Parrot. Choice E: parrot1 *is-a* Parrot.

14. **(B)** Method overriding occurs whenever a method in a superclass is redefined in a subclass. Method overloading is a method in the same class that has the same name but different parameter types. Polymorphism is when the correct overridden method is called for a particular subclass object during run time. Data encapsulation is when data and methods of an object are combined in a class so that the data can be hidden. Procedural abstraction is using separate methods to encapsulate each task in a class.

15. **(D)** Both method calls I and II will cause errors.
    I: An object of a superclass does not have access to a new method of its subclass.
    II: ob2 is declared to be of type ClassA, so a compile-time error will occur with a message indicating that there is no method2 in ClassA. Casting ob2 to ClassB would correct the problem. (Note: Class casting is no longer included in the AP Java subset.)
    III is correct because a subclass inherits all the public methods of its superclass.

16. **(A)** All are correct! They all pass the *is-a* test: (a Solid *is-a* Solid, a Sphere *is-a* Solid, a RectangularPrism *is-a* Solid); and the parameters all match the constructors. Note that the default value for s4 is null, so the assignment s4 = null is redundant (but correct).

17. **(A)** This is an example of polymorphism: The correct volume method is selected at run time. The parameter expected for printVolume is a Solid reference, which is what it gets in main(). The reference sol will refer either to a Sphere or a RectangularPrism object depending on the outcome of the coin flip. Since a Sphere is a Solid and a RectangularPrism is a Solid, there will be no type mismatch when these are the actual parameters in the printVolume method. (Note: The Math.random method is discussed in Chapter 5.)

18. **(C)** Segment III won't work because Player doesn't have a compareTo method. The method call h1.compareTo... will cause a compile-time error. Also, the compareTo method requires an ExpertPlayer parameter, but h2 is a Player, which isn't necessarily an ExpertPlayer. Segment II avoids both of these pitfalls. Segment I works because the Player class has a getMove method.

19. **(E)** All compile without error. For the method call display(arg), the compiler checks that the parameter arg *is-a* Animal, the type in the method's signature. Each of the objects d1, d2, and d3 passes the *is-a* test.

20. **(B)** Since the actual type of p is StrStuff2, the printSub method of StrStuff2, the subclass, will be called first. This is polymorphism, which calls the method of the actual object during run time. The String s is set equal to "rab", and the printSub method of the superclass, StrStuff1, will be called, namely printSub("rab"). This gets the substring of "rab" starting at position 2, which is "b". Then "b" is printed. At this point, only "b" has been printed. But recall that execution of the subclass method was halted for super.printSub(s), so this method must now be completed by executing System.out.print("rab").
    Whew!
    To recap, here is the order of execution of the statements:
    - Set local String s to "rab".
    - Call the superclass printSub("rab").
    - Set local s variable in superclass method to "b".
    - Print "b".
    - Print the value of s in the subclass method—namely, "rab".
    - So, the output is "brab".

21. **(D)** As in the previous question, the method in the subclass will be executed first. Here is the order of execution of the statements:

   - ■ `super.doSomething(11)`
   - ■ `n` is set equal to 7.
   - ■ Print 7.
   - ■ Go back to finish `doSomething` in `Class2`. (Note that the parameter in this method is 8.)
   - ■ `n` is set equal to 16.
   - ■ Print 16.

   Therefore, what gets printed is 716.

# 5

# Some Standard Classes

*Anyone who considers arithmetical methods of producing*
*random digits is, of course, in a state of sin.*
*—John von Neumann (1951)*

## Learning Objectives

In this chapter, you will learn:

→ The `Object` class

→ The `String` class

→ Wrapper classes

→ The `Math` class

## The `Object` Class

### The Universal Superclass

Think of `Object` as the superclass of the universe. Every class automatically extends `Object`, which means that `Object` is a direct or indirect superclass of every other class. In a class hierarchy tree, `Object` is at the top:

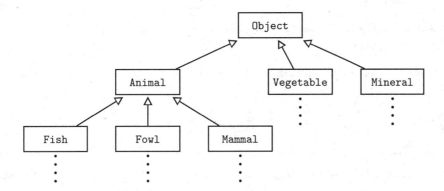

### Methods in `Object`

There are many methods in `Object`, all of them inherited by every other class. The expectation is that these methods will be overridden in any class where the default implementation is not suitable. The methods of `Object` in the AP Java subset are `toString` and `equals`.

### The `toString` Method

```
public String toString()
```

This method returns a version of your object in `String` form.

When you attempt to print an object, the inherited default `toString` method is invoked, and what you will see is the class name followed by an @ followed by a string of characters, which is not what you intended. For example,

```
SavingsAccount s = new SavingsAccount(500);
System.out.println(s);
```

produces something like

```
SavingsAccount@fea485c4
```

To have more meaningful output, you need to override the `toString` method for your own classes. Even if your final program doesn't need to output any objects, you should define a `toString` method for each class to help in debugging.

> **Example 1**

```
public class OrderedPair
{
    private double x;
    private double y;

    //constructors and other methods ...

    /** Returns this OrderedPair in String form. */
    public String toString()
    {
        return "(" + x + "," + y + ")";
    }
}
```

Now the statements

```
OrderedPair p = new OrderedPair(7,10);
System.out.println(p);
```

will invoke the overridden `toString` method and produce output that looks like an ordered pair:

```
(7,10)
```

> **Example 2**

For a `BankAccount` class the overridden `toString` method may look something like this:

```
/** Returns this BankAccount in String form. */
public String toString()
{
    return "Bank Account: balance = $" + balance;
}
```

The statements

```
BankAccount b = new BankAccount(600);
System.out.println(b);
```

will produce output that looks like this:

```
Bank Account: balance = $600
```

## Note

1. The + sign is a concatenation operator for strings (see p. 174).
2. Array objects are unusual in that they do not have a `toString` method. To print the elements of an array, the array must be traversed and each element must explicitly be printed.

### The `equals` Method

```
public boolean equals(Object other)
```

All classes inherit this method from the `Object` class. It returns `true` if this object and `other` are the same object, `false` otherwise. Being the same object means referencing the same memory slot. For example,

```
Date d1 = new Date("January", 14, 2001);
Date d2 = d1;
Date d3 = new Date("January", 14, 2001);
```

The test `if (d1.equals(d2))` returns `true`, but the test `if (d1==d3)` returns `false`, since `d1` and `d3` do not refer to the same object. Often, as in this example, you may want two objects to be considered equal if their *contents* are the same. In that case, you have to override the `equals` method in your class to achieve this. Some of the standard classes described later in this chapter have overridden `equals` in this way. You will not be required to write code that overrides `equals` on the AP exam.

> **Do not use == to test objects for equality. Use the `equals` method.**

## Note

1. The default implementation of `equals` is equivalent to the `==` relation for objects: In the `Date` example above, the test `if (d1 == d2)` returns `true`; the test `if (d1 == d3)` returns `false`.
2. The operators `<`, `>`, and so on are not used for objects (reference types) in Java. To compare objects, you must use either the `equals` method or define a `compareTo` method for the class.

# The `String` Class

## `String` Objects

An object of type `String` is a sequence of characters. All *string literals*, such as `"yikes!"`, are implemented as instances of this class. A string literal consists of zero or more characters, including escape sequences, surrounded by double quotes. (The quotes are not part of the `String` object.) Thus, each of the following is a valid string literal:

```
""                //empty string
"2468"
"I must\n go home"
```

`String` objects are *immutable*, which means that there are no methods to change them after they've been constructed. You can, however, always create a new `String` that is derived from an existing `String`.

## Constructing String Objects

A String object is unusual in that it can be initialized like a primitive type:

```
String s = "abc";
```

This is equivalent to

```
String s = new String("abc");
```

in the sense that in both cases s is a reference to a String object with contents "abc" (see Box on p. 176).

It is possible to reassign a String reference:

```
String s = "John";
s = "Harry";
```

This is equivalent to

```
String s = new String("John");
s = new String("Harry");
```

Notice that this is consistent with the immutable feature of String objects. "John" has not been changed; he has merely been discarded! The fickle reference s now refers to a new String, "Harry". It is also OK to reassign s as follows:

```
s = s + " Windsor";
```

s now refers to the object "Harry Windsor".

Here are other ways to initialize String objects:

```
String s1 = null;         //s1 is a null reference
String s2 = new String();   //s2 is an empty character sequence

String state = "Alaska";
String dessert = "baked " + state;  //dessert has value "baked Alaska"
```

## The Concatenation Operator

The dessert declaration above uses the *concatenation operator*, +, which operates on String objects. Given two String operands lhs and rhs, lhs + rhs produces a single String consisting of lhs followed by rhs. If either lhs or rhs is an object other than a String, the toString method of the object is invoked, and lhs and rhs are concatenated as before. If one of the operands is a String and the other is a primitive type, then the non-String operand is converted to a String, and concatenation occurs as before. If neither lhs nor rhs is a String object, an error occurs. Here are some examples:

```
int five = 5;
String state = "Hawaii-";
String tvShow = state + five + "-0";  //tvShow has value
                                       //"Hawaii-5-0"
int x = 3, y = 4;
String sum = x + y;        //error: can't assign int 7 to String
```

Suppose a Date class has a toString method that outputs dates that look like this: 2/17/1948.

```
Date d1 = new Date(8, 2, 1947);
Date d2 = new Date(2, 17, 1948);
String s = "My birthday is " + d2;  //s has value
                                    //"My birthday is 2/17/1948"
String s2 = d1 + d2;    //error: + not defined for objects
String s3 = d1.toString() + d2.toString();  //s3 has value
                                            //8/2/19472/17/1948
```

## Comparison of String Objects

There are two ways to compare String objects:

1. Use the equals method that is inherited from the Object class and overridden to do the correct thing:

   ```
   if (string1.equals(string2)) ...
   ```

   This returns true if string1 and string2 are identical strings, false otherwise.

2. Use the compareTo method. The String class has a compareTo method:

   ```
   int compareTo(String otherString)
   ```

   It compares strings in dictionary (lexicographical) order:

   - If string1.compareTo(string2) < 0, then string1 precedes string2 in the dictionary.
   - If string1.compareTo(string2) > 0, then string1 follows string2 in the dictionary.
   - If string1.compareTo(string2) == 0, then string1 and string2 are identical. (This test is an alternative to string1.equals(string2).)

Be aware that Java is case-sensitive. Thus, if s1 is "cat" and s2 is "Cat", s1.equals(s2) will return false.

Characters are compared according to their position in the ASCII chart. All you need to know is that all digits precede all capital letters, which precede all lowercase letters. Thus "5" comes before "R", which comes before "a". Two strings are compared as follows: Start at the left end of each string and do a character-by-character comparison until you reach the first character in which the strings differ, the $k$th character, say. If the $k$th character of s1 comes before the $k$th character of s2, then s1 will come before s2, and vice versa. If the strings have identical characters, except that s1 terminates before s2, then s1 comes before s2. Here are some examples:

```
String s1 = "HOT", s2 = "HOTEL", s3 = "dog";
if (s1.compareTo(s2) < 0))     //true, s1 terminates first
    ...
if (s1.compareTo(s3) > 0))     //false, "H" comes before "d"
```

### Don't Use == to Test Strings!

The expression if (string1 == string2) tests whether string1 and string2 are the same reference. It does not test the actual strings. Using == to compare strings may lead to unexpected results.

> **Example 1**

```
String s = "oh no!";
String t = "oh no!";
if (s == t) ...
```

The test returns true even though it appears that s and t are different references. The reason is that, for efficiency, Java makes only one String object for equivalent string literals. This is safe in that a String cannot be altered.

> **Example 2**

```
String s = "oh no!";
String t = new String("oh no!");
if (s == t) ...
```

The test returns false because use of new creates a new object, and s and t *are* different references in this example!

The moral of the story? Use equals not == to test strings. It always does the right thing.

## Other String Methods

The Java String class provides many methods, only a small number of which are in the AP Java subset. In addition to the constructors, comparison methods, and concatenation operator + discussed so far, you should know the following methods:

```
int length()
```

Returns the length of this string.

```
String substring(int startIndex)
```

Returns a new string that is a substring of this string. The substring starts with the character at startIndex and extends to the end of the string. The first character is at index zero. The method throws an IndexOutOfBoundsException if startIndex is negative or larger than the length of the string. Note that if you're using Java 7 or above, you will see the error StringIndexOutOfBoundsException. However, the AP Java subset lists only IndexOutOfBoundsException, which is what they will use on the AP exam.

```
String substring(int startIndex, int endIndex)
```

Returns a new string that is a substring of this string. The substring starts at index `startIndex` and extends to the character at `endIndex-1`. (Think of it this way: `startIndex` is the first character that you want; `endIndex` is the first character that you *don't* want.) The method throws a `StringIndexOutOfBoundsException` if `startIndex` is negative, or `endIndex` is larger than the length of the string, or `startIndex` is larger than `endIndex`.

```
int indexOf(String str)
```

Returns the index of the first occurrence of `str` within this string. If `str` is not a substring of this string, –1 is returned. The method throws a `NullPointerException` if `str` is null.

Here are some examples:

```
"unhappy".substring(2)          //returns "happy"
"cold".substring(4)             //returns "" (empty string)
"cold".substring(5)             //StringIndexOutOfBoundsException
"strawberry".substring(5,7)     //returns "be"
"crayfish".substring(4,8)       //returns "fish"
"crayfish".substring(4,9)       //StringIndexOutOfBoundsException
"crayfish".substring(5,4)       //StringIndexOutOfBoundsException
"crayfish".substring(4,"crayfish".length());  //returns "fish"
"crayfish".substring(4);        //returns "fish".
                                //This is a less error-prone form of the
                                // substring method if you want to start at
                                // an index and return the rest of the string.

String s = "funnyfarm";
int x = s.indexOf("farm");   //x has value 5
x = s.indexOf("farmer");     //x has value -1
int y = s.length();          //y has value 9
```

## Special Emphasis

The `String` methods `substring` and `indexOf` are used frequently on the AP exam. Be sure that you recall:

- The first index of a `String` is 0.
- The method call `s.substring(start, end)` returns the substring of `s` starting at index start but ending at index `end-1`.
- The method call `s.indexOf(sub)` returns the index of the first occurrence of substring `sub` in `s`.
- `s.indexOf(sub)` returns –1 if `sub` is not in `s`.

You should be nimble and well practiced in processing strings.

> **Example 1**

The following type of code can be used to look for multiple occurrences of a substring in a given string.

```
int pos = s.indexOf(someSubstring);
while (pos >= 0)                    //the substring was found
{
    doSomething();
    s = s.substring(pos + 1);  //throw away all characters of s
                               //up to and including someSubstring

    pos = s.indexOf(someSubstring);  //Is there another occurrence
                                     //of someSubstring?
}
```

A modified version of the above code, using some combination of a loop, `indexOf`, and `substring`, can be used to

- count number of occurrences of `substring` in `str`.
- replace all occurrences of `substring` in `str` with `replacementStr`.
- remove all occurrences of `substring` in `str`.

Often conditionals are used to search for keywords that will trigger different responses from a program. Using `if` and `if...else` should be second nature to you.

> **Example 2**

The user will enter a `sentence` and the program will produce a `Reply`.

```
if (sentence.indexOf ("love") != -1)
{
    if (sentence.indexOf ("you") != -1)
        Reply = "I'm in heaven!";
    else
        Reply = "But do you love me?";
}
else
    Reply = "My heart is in pieces on the floor.";
```

Here are some possible sentences that the user may enter, with the corresponding `Reply`:

| Sentence | Reply |
|---|---|
| I love chocolate cake. | But do you love me? |
| I love chocolate cake; do you? | I'm in heaven! |
| I hate fudge. | My heart is in pieces on the floor. |

If the substring `"love"` isn't in the sentence, the opening test will be `false`, and execution skips to the `else` outside the braces, producing the `Reply` `"My heart is in pieces on the floor"`. If sentence contains both `"love"` and `"you"`, the first test in the braces will be `true`, and the `Reply` will be `"I'm in heaven!"` The middle response `"But do you love me?"` will be triggered by a sentence that contains `"love"` but doesn't contain `"you"`, causing the first test in the braces to be `false`, and the `else` part in the braces to be executed.

# Wrapper Classes

A *wrapper class* takes either an existing object or a value of primitive type, "wraps" or "boxes" it in an object, and provides a new set of methods for that type. The point of a wrapper class is to provide extended capabilities for the boxed quantity:

- It can be used in generic Java methods that require objects as parameters.
- It can be used in Java container classes like `ArrayList` that require the items be objects.

In each case, the wrapper class allows:

1. Construction of an object from a single value (wrapping or boxing the primitive in a wrapper object).
2. Retrieval of the primitive value (unwrapping or unboxing from the wrapper object).

Java provides a wrapper class for each of its primitive types. The two that you should know for the AP exam are the `Integer` and `Double` classes.

## The `Integer` Class

The `Integer` class wraps a value of type `int` in an object. An object of type `Integer` contains just one instance variable whose type is `int`.

Here are the `Integer` methods and constants you should know for the AP exam. These are part of the Java Quick Reference.

```
Integer(int value)
```

Constructs an `Integer` object from an `int`. (Boxing)

```
int intValue()
```

Returns the value of this `Integer` as an `int`. (Unboxing)

```
Integer.MIN_VALUE
```

A constant equal to the minimum value represented by an `int` or `Integer`.

```
Integer.MAX_VALUE
```

A constant equal to the maximum value represented by an `int` or `Integer`.

## The `Double` Class

The `Double` class wraps a value of type `double` in an object. An object of type `Double` contains just one instance variable whose type is `double`.

The methods you should know for the AP exam are analogous to those for type `Integer`. These, too, are part of the Java Quick Reference.

```
Double(double value)
```

Constructs a `Double` object from a `double`. (Boxing)

```
double doubleValue()
```

Returns the value of this `Double` as a `double`. (Unboxing)

**Note**

1. The `compareTo` and `equals` methods for the `Integer` and `Double` classes are no longer part of the AP Java subset. This is probably because the later versions of Java make extensive use of autoboxing and auto-unboxing.
2. `Integer` and `Double` objects are immutable. This means there are no mutator methods in the classes.

## Autoboxing and Unboxing

This topic is part of the AP Java subset.

*Autoboxing* is the automatic conversion that the Java compiler makes between primitive types and their corresponding wrapper classes. This includes converting an `int` to an `Integer` and a `double` to a `Double`.

Autoboxing is applied when a primitive value is assigned to a variable of the corresponding wrapper class. For example,

```
Integer intOb = 3;    //3 is boxed

ArrayList<Integer> list = new ArrayList<Integer>();
list.add(4); //4 is boxed
```

Autoboxing also occurs when a primitive value is passed as a parameter to a method that expects an object of the corresponding wrapper class. For example,

```
public String stringMethod(Double d)
{ /* return string that has d embedded in it */ }

double realNum = 4.5;
String str = stringMethod(realNum);    //realNum is boxed
```

*Unboxing* is the automatic conversion that the Java compiler makes from the wrapper class to the primitive type. This includes converting an `Integer` to an `int` and a `Double` to a `double`.

Unboxing is applied when a wrapper class object is passed as a parameter to a method that expects a value of the corresponding primitive type. For example,

```
Integer intOb1 = 9;
Integer intOb2 = 8;

public static int sum (int num1, int num2)
{ return num1 + num2; }

System.out.println(sum(intOb1, intOb2)); //intOb1 and intOb2 are unboxed
```

Unboxing is also applied when a wrapper class object is assigned to a variable of the corresponding primitive type. For example,

```
int p = intOb1; //intOb1 is unboxed
```

## Comparison of Wrapper Class Objects

Unboxing is often used in the comparison of wrapper objects of the same type. But it's trickier than it sounds. Don't use `==` to test `Integer` objects! You may get surprising results. The expression `if (intOb1 == intOb2)` tests whether `intOb1` and `intOb2` are the same *reference*. It does not test the actual values.

## Example 1

```
Integer intOb1 = 4; //boxing
Integer intOb2 = 4; //boxing
if (intOb1 == intOb2)...
```

The test returns true, but not for the reason you might expect. The reason is that for efficiency Java creates only one Integer object if the int values are the same. So the references are the same. This is safe because an Integer cannot be altered. (It's immutable.)

## Example 2

```
Integer intOb1 = 4;              //boxing
Integer intOb2 = new Integer(4); //boxing
if (intOb1 == intOb2)...
```

This test returns false because use of new creates a new object. intOb1 and intOb2 are different references in this example. See the analogous situation for String objects in the Box on p. 176.

## Example 3

```
Integer intOb1 = 4;  //boxing
int n = 4;
if (intOb1 == n)...
```

This test returns true because if the comparison is between an Integer object and a primitive integer type, the object is automatically unboxed.

## Example 4

```
Integer intOb1 = 4;              //boxing
Integer intOb2 = new Integer(4); //boxing
if (intOb1.intValue() == intOb2.intValue())...
```

This test returns true because the values of the objects are being tested. This is the correct way to test Integer objects for equality.

The relational operators less than (<) and greater than (>) do what you may expect when testing Integer and Double objects.

## Example 5

```
Integer intOb1 = 4;   //boxing
Integer intOb2 = 8;   //boxing
if (intOb1 < intOb2)...
```

This test returns true because the compiler unboxes the objects as follows:

```
if (intOb1.intValue() < intOb2.intValue())
```

> **Example 6**

```
Integer intOb1 = 4; //boxing
int n = 8;
if (intOb1 < n)...
```

This test will return `true` because, again, if one of the operands is a primitive type, the object will be unboxed.

## The `Math` Class

This class implements standard mathematical functions such as absolute value, square root, trigonometric functions, the log function, the power function, and so on. It also contains mathematical constants such as $\pi$ and $e$.

Here are the functions you should know for the AP exam:

```
static int abs(int x)
```

Returns the absolute value of integer $x$.

```
static double abs(double x)
```

Returns the absolute value of real number $x$.

```
static double pow(double base, double exp)
```

Returns `base`$^{exp}$. Assumes base > 0, or base = 0 and exp > 0, or base < 0 and exp is an integer.

```
static double sqrt(double x)
```

Returns $\sqrt{x}$, $x \geq 0$.

```
static double random()
```

Returns a random number $r$, where $0.0 \leq r < 1.0$. (See the next section, "Random Numbers.")

All of the functions and constants are implemented as static methods and variables, which means that there are no instances of `Math` objects. The methods are invoked using the class name, `Math`, followed by the dot operator.

Here are some examples of mathematical formulas and the equivalent Java statements.

1. The relationship between the radius and area of a circle is

$$r = \sqrt{A/\pi}$$

In code:

```
radius = Math.sqrt(area / Math.PI);
```

2. The amount of money $A$ in an account after ten years, given an original deposit of $P$ and an interest rate of 5% compounded annually, is

$$A = P(1.05)^{10}$$

In code:

```
a = p * Math.pow(1.05, 10);
```

3. The distance $D$ between two points $P(x_P, y)$ and $Q(x_Q, y)$ on the same horizontal line is

$$D = |x_P - x_Q|$$

In code:

```
d = Math.abs(xp - xq);
```

## Note

The static import construct allows you to use the static members of a class without the class name prefix. For example, the statement

```
import static java.lang.Math.*;
```

allows use of all `Math` methods and constants without the `Math` prefix. Thus, the statement in formula 1 above could be written

```
radius = sqrt(area / PI);
```

Static imports are not part of the AP subset.

## Random Numbers

### Random Reals

The statement

```
double r = Math.random();
```

produces a random real number in the range 0.0 to 1.0, where 0.0 is included and 1.0 is not.

This range can be scaled and shifted. On the AP exam you will be expected to write algebraic expressions involving `Math.random()` that represent linear transformations of the original interval $0.0 \leq x < 1.0$.

### ▷ Example 1

Produce a random real value $x$ in the range $0.0 \leq x < 6.0$.

```
double x = 6 * Math.random();
```

### ▷ Example 2

Produce a random real value $x$ in the range $2.0 \leq x < 3.0$.

```
double x = Math.random() + 2;
```

### ▷ Example 3

Produce a random real value $x$ in the range $4.0 \leq x < 6.0$.

```
double x = 2 * Math.random() + 4;
```

In general, to produce a random real value in the range `lowValue` $\leq x <$ `highValue`:

```
double x = (highValue - lowValue) * Math.random() + lowValue;
```

### Random Integers

Using a cast to `int`, a scaling factor, and a shifting value, `Math.random()` can be used to produce random integers in any range.

### ▷ Example 1

Produce a random integer from 0 to 99.

```
int num = (int) (Math.random() * 100);
```

In general, the expression

```
(int) (Math.random() * k)
```

produces a random `int` in the range $0, 1, \ldots, k-1$, where $k$ is called the scaling factor. Note that the cast to `int` truncates the real number `Math.random() * k`.

### ▷ Example 2

Produce a random integer from 1 to 100.

```
int num = (int) (Math.random() * 100) + 1;
```

In general, if $k$ is a scaling factor, and $p$ is a shifting value, the statement

```
int n = (int) (Math.random() * k) + p;
```

produces a random integer $n$ in the range $p, p+1, \ldots, p+(k-1)$.

### ▷ Example 3

Produce a random integer from 5 to 24.

```
int num = (int) (Math.random() * 20) + 5;
```

Note that there are 20 possible integers from 5 to 24, inclusive.

## Chapter Summary

All students should know about overriding the `equals` and `toString` methods of the `Object` class and should be familiar with the `Integer` and `Double` wrapper classes.

Know the AP subset methods of the `Math` class, especially the use of `Math.random()` for generating random numbers. Learn the `String` methods `substring` and `indexOf`, including knowing where exceptions are thrown in the `String` methods.

# Multiple-Choice Questions on Some Standard Classes

1. Consider the following declarations in a program to find the quantity $base^{exp}$.

   ```
   double base = < a double value >
   double exp = < a double value >
   /* code to find power, which equals base^exp */
   ```

   Which is a correct replacement for
   /* *code to find* power, *which equals* $base^{exp}$ */?

   ```
    I. double power;
       Math m = new Math();
       power = m.pow(base, exp);

   II. double power;
       power = Math.pow(base, exp);

   III. int power;
        power = Math.pow(base, exp);
   ```

   (A) I only
   (B) II only
   (C) III only
   (D) I and II only
   (E) I and III only

2. Consider the squareRoot method defined below.

   ```
   /** Returns a Double whose value is the square root
    *  of the value represented by d.
    */
   public Double squareRoot(Double d)
   {
       /* implementation code */
   }
   ```

   Which /* *implementation code* */ satisfies the postcondition?

   ```
    I. double x = d;
       x = Math.sqrt(x);
       return x;

   II. return new Double(Math.sqrt(d.doubleValue()));

   III. return Double(Math.sqrt(d.doubleValue()));
   ```

   (A) I only
   (B) I and II only
   (C) I and III only
   (D) II and III only
   (E) I, II, and III

3. Here are some examples of negative numbers rounded to the nearest integer:

| Negative real number | Rounded to nearest integer |
|:---:|:---:|
| −3.5 | −4 |
| −8.97 | −9 |
| −5.0 | −5 |
| −2.487 | −2 |
| −0.2 | 0 |

Refer to the following declaration.

```
double d = -4.67;
```

Which of the following correctly rounds d to the nearest integer?

(A) `int rounded = Math.abs(d);`

(B) `int rounded = (int) (Math.random() * d);`

(C) `int rounded = (int) (d - 0.5);`

(D) `int rounded = (int) (d + 0.5);`

(E) `int rounded = Math.abs((int) (d - 0.5));`

4. A program is to simulate plant life under harsh conditions. In the program, plants die randomly according to some probability. Here is part of a `Plant` class defined in the program:

```
public class Plant
{
    /** Probability that plant dies is a real number between 0 and 1. */
    private double probDeath;

    public Plant(double plantProbDeath, < other parameters >)
    {
        probDeath = plantProbDeath;
        < initialization of other instance variables >
    }

    /** Plant lives or dies. */
    public void liveOrDie()
    {
        /* statement to generate random number */
        if (/* test to determine if plant dies */)
            < code to implement plant's death >
        else
            < code to make plant continue living >
    }

    //Other variables and methods are not shown.
}
```

Which of the following are correct replacements for
(1) /* *statement to generate random number* */ and
(2) /* *test to determine if plant dies* */?

(A)   (1) `double x = Math.random();`
      (2) `x == probDeath`

(B)   (1) `double x = (int) (Math.random());`
      (2) `x > probDeath`

(C)   (1) `double x = Math.random();`
      (2) `x < probDeath`

(D)   (1) `int x = (int) (Math.random() * 100);`
      (2) `x < (int) probDeath`

(E)   (1) `int x = (int) (Math.random() * 100) + 1;`
      (2) `x == (int) probDeath`

5. A program simulates 50 slips of paper, numbered 1 through 50, placed in a bowl for a raffle drawing. Which of the following statements stores in `winner` a random integer from 1 to 50?

    (A) `int winner = (int) (Math.random() * 50) + 1;`

    (B) `int winner = (int) (Math.random() * 50);`

    (C) `int winner = (int) (Math.random() * 51);`

    (D) `int winner = (int) (Math.random() * 51) + 1;`

    (E) `int winner = (int) (1 + Math.random() * 49);`

6. Consider the following code segment.

```
Integer i = new Integer(20);
/* more code */
```

Which of the following replacements for /* *more code* */ correctly sets i to have an Integer value of 25?

    I. `i = new Integer(25);`

    II. `i.intValue() = 25;`

    III. `Integer j = new Integer(25);`
        `i = j;`

    (A) I only

    (B) II only

    (C) III only

    (D) I and III only

    (E) II and III only

7. Refer to these declarations.

```
Integer k = new Integer(8);
Integer m = new Integer(4);
```

Which test(s) will generate a compile-time error?

    I. `if (k == m)...`

    II. `if (k.intValue() == m.intValue())...`

    III. `if ((k.intValue()).equals(m.intValue()))...`

    (A) I only

    (B) II only

    (C) III only

    (D) I and II only

    (E) II and III only

8. Consider the following code fragment.

```
Object intObj = new Integer(9);
System.out.println(intObj);
```

You may assume that the `Integer` class has a `toString` method. What will be output as a result of running the fragment?

(A) No output. A `StringIndexOutOfBoundsException` will be thrown.

(B) No output. An `ArithmeticException` will be thrown.

(C) 9

(D) "9"

(E) An address in memory of the reference `IntObj`

9. Consider these declarations.

```
String s1 = "crab";
String s2 = new String("crab");
String s3 = s1;
```

Which expression involving these strings evaluates to `true`?

I. `s1 == s2`

II. `s1.equals(s2)`

III. `s3.equals(s2)`

(A) I only

(B) II only

(C) II and III only

(D) I and II only

(E) I, II, and III

10. Suppose that `strA = "TOMATO"`, `strB = "tomato"`, and `strC = "tom"`. Given that `"A"` comes before `"a"` in dictionary order, which is true?

(A) `strA.compareTo(strB) < 0 && strB.compareTo(strC) < 0`

(B) `strB.compareTo(strA) < 0 || strC.compareTo(strA) < 0`

(C) `strC.compareTo(strA) < 0 && strA.compareTo(strB) < 0`

(D) `!(strA.equals(strB)) && strC.compareTo(strB) < 0`

(E) `!(strA.equals(strB)) && strC.compareTo(strA) < 0`

11. This question refers to the following declaration.

```
String line = "Some more silly stuff on strings!";
//the words are separated by a single space
```

What string will str refer to after execution of the following?

```
int x = line.indexOf("m");
String str = line.substring(10, 15) + line.substring(25, 25 + x);
```

(A) "sillyst"
(B) "sillystr"
(C) "silly st"
(D) "silly str"
(E) "sillystrin"

12. A program has a String variable fullName that stores a first name, followed by a space, followed by a last name. There are no spaces in either the first or last names. Here are some examples of fullName values: "Anthony Coppola", "Jimmy Carroll", and "Tom DeWire". Consider this code segment that extracts the last name from a fullName variable, and stores it in lastName with no surrounding blanks:

```
int k = fullName.indexOf(" ");    //find index of blank
String lastName = /* expression */
```

Which is a correct replacement for /* expression */?

```
  I. fullName.substring(k);

 II. fullName.substring(k + 1);

III. fullName.substring(k + 1, fullName.length());
```

(A) I only
(B) II only
(C) III only
(D) II and III only
(E) I and III only

13. One of the rules for converting English to Pig Latin states: If a word begins with a consonant, move the consonant to the end of the word and add "ay". Thus "dog" becomes "ogday," and "crisp" becomes "rispcay". Suppose s is a String containing an English word that begins with a consonant. Which of the following creates the correct corresponding word in Pig Latin? Assume the declarations

```
String ayString = "ay";
String pigString;
```

(A) pigString = s.substring(0, s.length()) + s.substring(0,1)
            + ayString;

(B) pigString = s.substring(1, s.length()) + s.substring(0,0)
            + ayString;

(C) pigString = s.substring(0, s.length()-1) + s.substring(0,1)
            + ayString;

(D) pigString = s.substring(1, s.length()-1) + s.substring(0,0)
            + ayString;

(E) pigString = s.substring(1, s.length()) + s.substring(0,1)
            + ayString;

14. This question refers to the getString method shown below.

```
public static String getString(String s1, String s2)
{
    int index = s1.indexOf(s2);
    return s1.substring(index, index + s2.length());
}
```

Which is true about getString? It may return a string that

   I. Is equal to s2.
  II. Has no characters in common with s2.
 III. Is equal to s1.

(A) I and III only
(B) II and III only
(C) I and II only
(D) I, II, and III
(E) None is true.

15. Consider this method.

```
public static String doSomething(String s)
{
    final String BLANK = " ";    //BLANK contains a single space
    String str = "";             //empty string
    String temp;
    for (int i = 0; i < s.length(); i++)
    {
        temp = s.substring(i, i + 1);
        if (!(temp.equals(BLANK)))
            str += temp;
    }
    return str;
}
```

Which of the following is the most precise description of what doSomething does?

(A) It returns s unchanged.

(B) It returns s with all its blanks removed.

(C) It returns a String that is equivalent to s with all its blanks removed.

(D) It returns a String that is an exact copy of s.

(E) It returns a String that contains s.length() blanks.

Questions 16 and 17 refer to the classes `Position` and `PositionTest` below.

```java
public class Position
{
    /** row and col are both >= 0 except in the no-argument
     *  constructor where they are initialized to -1.
     */
    private int row, col;

    public Position()          //constructor
    {
        row = -1;
        col = -1;
    }

    public Position(int r, int c)      //constructor
    {
        row = r;
        col = c;
    }

    /** Returns row of Position. */
    public int getRow()
    { return row; }

    /** Returns column of Position. */
    public int getCol()
    { return col; }

    /** Returns Position north of (up from) this position. */
    public Position north()
    { return new Position(row - 1, col); }

    //Similar methods south, east, and west
            ...

    /** Compares this Position to another Position object.
     *  Returns -1 (less than), 0 (equals), or 1 (greater than).
     */
    public int compareTo(Position p)
    {
        if (this.getRow() < p.getRow() || this.getRow() == p.getRow()
            && this.getCol() < p.getCol())
                return -1;
        if (this.getRow() > p.getRow() || this.getRow() == p.getRow()
            && this.getCol() > p.getCol())
                return 1;
        return 0;              //row and col both equal
    }

    /** Returns String form of Position. */
    public String toString()
    { return "(" + row + "," + col + ")"; }
}
```

```
public class PositionTest
{
    public static void main(String[] args)
    {
        Position p1 = new Position(2, 3);
        Position p2 = new Position(4, 1);
        Position p3 = new Position(2, 3);

        //tests to compare positions
            ...
    }
}
```

16. Which is true about the value of p1.compareTo(p2)?
    (A) It equals true.
    (B) It equals false.
    (C) It equals 0.
    (D) It equals 1.
    (E) It equals -1.

17. Which boolean expression about p1 and p3 is true?

    I.   p1 == p3

    II.  p1.equals(p3)

    III. p1.compareTo(p3) == 0

    (A) I only
    (B) II only
    (C) III only
    (D) II and III only
    (E) I, II, and III

Questions 18 and 19 deal with the problem of swapping two integer values. Three methods are proposed to solve the problem, using primitive int types, Integer objects, and IntPair objects, where IntPair is defined as follows.

```java
public class IntPair
{
    private int firstValue;
    private int secondValue;

    public IntPair(int first, int second)
    {
        firstValue = first;
        secondValue = second;
    }

    public int getFirst()
    { return firstValue; }

    public int getSecond()
    { return secondValue; }

    public void setFirst(int a)
    { firstValue = a; }

    public void setSecond(int b)
    { secondValue = b;}
}
```

18. Here are three different swap methods, each intended for use in a client program.

```
I.  public static void swap(int a, int b)
    {
        int temp = a;
        a = b;
        b = temp;
    }
```

```
II. public static void swap(Integer obj_a, Integer obj_b)
    {
        Integer temp = new Integer(obj_a.intValue());
        obj_a = obj_b;
        obj_b = temp;
    }
```

```
III. public static void swap(IntPair pair)
     {
         int temp = pair.getFirst();
         pair.setFirst(pair.getSecond());
         pair.setSecond(temp);
     }
```

When correctly used in a client program with appropriate parameters, which method will swap two integers, as intended?

(A) I only

(B) II only

(C) III only

(D) II and III only

(E) I, II, and III

19. Consider the following program that uses the `IntPair` class.

```java
public class TestSwap
{
    public static void swap(IntPair pair)
    {
        int temp = pair.getFirst();
        pair.setFirst(pair.getSecond());
        pair.setSecond(temp);
    }

    public static void main(String[] args)
    {
        int x = 8, y = 6;
        /* code to swap x and y */
    }
}
```

Which is a correct replacement for /* *code to swap* x *and* y */?

I.
```java
IntPair iPair = new IntPair(x, y);
swap(x, y);
x = iPair.getFirst();
y = iPair.getSecond();
```

II.
```java
IntPair iPair = new IntPair(x, y);
swap(iPair);
x = iPair.getFirst();
y = iPair.getSecond();
```

III.
```java
IntPair iPair = new IntPair(x, y);
swap(iPair);
x = iPair.setFirst();
y = iPair.setSecond();
```

(A) I only
(B) II only
(C) III only
(D) II and III only
(E) None is correct.

Refer to the Name class below for Questions 20 and 21.

```java
public class Name
{
    private String firstName;
    private String lastName;

    public Name(String first, String last)  //constructor
    {
        firstName = first;
        lastName = last;
    }

    public String toString()
    { return firstName + " " + lastName; }

    public boolean equals(Object obj)
    {
        Name n = (Name) obj;
        return n.firstName.equals(firstName) &&
                n.lastName.equals(lastName);
    }

    public int compareTo(Name n)
    {
        /* more code */
    }
}
```

20. The `compareTo` method implements the standard name-ordering algorithm where last names take precedence over first names. Lexicographic or dictionary ordering of `Strings` is used. For example, the name Scott Dentes comes before Nick Elser, and Adam Cooper comes before Sara Cooper.

    Which of the following is a correct replacement for /* *more code* */?

    ```
    I.  int lastComp = lastName.compareTo(n.lastName);
        if (lastComp != 0)
            return lastComp;
        else
            return firstName.compareTo(n.firstName);

    II. if (lastName.equals(n.lastName))
            return firstName.compareTo(n.firstName);
        else
            return 0;

    III. if (!(lastName.equals(n.lastName)))
             return firstName.compareTo(n.firstName);
         else
             return lastName.compareTo(n.lastName);
    ```

    (A) I only
    (B) II only
    (C) III only
    (D) I and II only
    (E) I, II, and III

21. Which statement about the `Name` class is false?
    (A) `Name` objects are immutable.
    (B) It is possible for the methods in `Name` to throw a `NullPointerException`.
    (C) If `n1` and `n2` are `Name` objects in a client class, then the expressions `n1.equals(n2)` and `n1.compareTo(n2) == 0` must have the same value.
    (D) The `compareTo` method throws a run-time exception if the parameter is null.
    (E) Since the `Name` class has a `compareTo` method, it *must* provide an implementation for an `equals` method.

22. What is the output of the following code segment?

```
String s = "How do you do?";
int index = s.indexOf("o");
while (index >= 0)
{
    System.out.print(index + " ");
    s = s.substring(index + 1);
    index = s.indexOf("o");
}
```

(A) 1 3 2 3
(B) 2 4 3 4
(C) 1 5 8 12
(D) 1 5 8 11
(E) No output because of an IndexOutOfBoundsException

23. Consider the following method `removeAll` that creates and returns a string that has stripped its input phrase of all occurrences of its single-character `String` parameter `ch`.

```
Line 1:  public static String removeAll(String phrase, String ch)
Line 2:  {
Line 3:       String str = "";
Line 4:       String newPhrase = phrase;
Line 5:       int pos = phrase.indexOf(ch);
Line 6:       if (pos == -1)
Line 7:           return phrase;
Line 8:       else
Line 9:       {
Line 10:          while (pos >= 0)
Line 11:          {
Line 12:              str = str + newPhrase.substring(0, pos - 1);
Line 13:              newPhrase = newPhrase.substring(pos + 1);
Line 14:              pos = newPhrase.indexOf(ch);
Line 15:              if (pos == -1)
Line 16:                  str = str + newPhrase;
Line 17:          }
Line 18:          return str;
Line 19:      }
Line 20: }
```

The method doesn't work as intended. Which of the following changes to the `removeAll` method will make it work as specified?

(A) Change Line 10 to
```
while (pos >= -1)
```
(B) Change Line 12 to
```
str = str + newPhrase.substring(0, pos);
```
(C) Change Line 13 to
```
newPhrase = newPhrase.substring(pos);
```
(D) Change Line 14 to
```
pos = phrase.indexOf(ch);
```
(E) Change Line 16 to
```
str = str + newPhrase.substring(pos + 1);
```

24. A programmer has written a program that "chats" to a human user based on statements that the human inputs. The program contains a method findKeyWord that searches an input statement for a given keyword. The findKeyWord method contains the following line of code.

```
pos = statement.indexOf(word);
```

Suppose pos has a value >= 0; that is, word was found. The programmer now wants to test that an actual word was found, not part of another word. For example, if "cat" is the keyword, the programmer needs to check that it's not part of "catch" or "category." Here is the code that tests if word is a stand-alone word. (You may assume that statement is all lowercase and contains only letters and blanks.)

```
pos = statement.indexOf(word);
//Check for first or last word
if (pos == 0 || pos + word.length() == statement.length())
{
    before = " ";
    after = " ";
}
else
{
    before = statement.substring(pos - 1, pos);
    after = statement.substring(pos + word.length(),
            pos + word.length() + 1);
    if (/* test */)
        //then a stand-alone word was found ...
    else
        //word was part of a larger word
}
```

Which replacement for /* test */ will give the desired result?
(A) (before < "a" || before > "z") && (after < "a" || after > "z")
(B) (before > "a" || before < "z") && (after > "a" || after < "z")
(C) (before.compareTo("a") < 0 && before.compareTo("z") > 0) ||
    (after.compareTo("a") > 0 && after.compareTo("z") < 0)
(D) (before.compareTo("a") > 0 && before.compareTo("z") < 0) &&
    (after.compareTo("a") > 0 && after.compareTo("z") < 0)
(E) (before.compareTo("a") < 0 || before.compareTo("z") > 0) &&
    (after.compareTo("a") < 0 || after.compareTo("z") > 0)

25. A program that simulates a conversation between a computer and a human user generates a random response to a user's comment. All possible responses that the computer can generate are stored in an array of `String` called `allResponses`. The method given below, `getResponse`, returns a random response string from the array.

```
/** Precondition:  array allResponses is initialized with strings.
 *  Postcondition: returns a random response from allResponses.
 */
public String getResponse();
{ /* implementation */ }
```

Which is a correct /* *implementation* */?

(A) `int i = (int) (Math.random() * allResponses.length);`
`return allResponses[i];`

(B) `return (String) (Math.random() * allResponses.length);`

(C) `int i = Math.random() * allResponses.length;`
`return allResponses[i];`

(D) `int i = (int) (Math.random() * (allResponses.length - 1));`
`return allResponses[i];`

(E) `return (int) (Math.random() * allResponses.length);`

Questions 26 and 27 refer to the following.

A word creation game uses letter tiles, where each tile has a letter and a point value for scoring purposes. A `Tile` class is used to represent a letter tile.

```
public class Tile
{
    private String letter;
    private int pointValue;

    //Constructors and other methods are not shown.
}
```

26. The `Tile` class contains a `toString` method that creates a `String` containing the letter and point value of a `Tile`. The string should be in the following format.

    Letter *letter* (point value = *pointValue*)

    For example,

    ```
    Letter A (point value = 1)
    Letter Z (point value = 10)
    ```

    Consider the `toString` method below.

    ```
    public String toString()
    {
        return /* code */
    }
    ```

    Which `/* code */` leads to correct output?
    (A) `Letter + "letter " + "(point value = " + pointValue + ")";`
    (B) `"Letter " + letter + ("point value = " + pointValue);`
    (C) `Letter + this.letter + " (point value = " + pointValue + ")";`
    (D) `"Letter " + letter + " (point value = " + (String) pointValue + ")";`
    (E) `"Letter " + letter + " (point value = " + pointValue + ")";`

27. Any two tiles in the word game that have the same letter also have the same point value, but the opposite is not necessarily true. For example, all the vowels have a point value of 1. Two tiles are said to match if they have the same letter. Consider the following `matches` method for the `Tile` class.

    ```
    /** Returns true if the letter on this tile equals the letter
     *  on otherTile. */
    public boolean matches(Tile otherTile)
    { return /* code */; }
    ```

    Which replacements for `/* code */` return the desired result? Note: You may not assume that the `Tile` class has its own `equals` method.

    I.   `letter == otherTile.letter`

    II.  `this.equals(otherTile)`

    III. `letter.equals(otherTile.letter)`

    (A) I only
    (B) II only
    (C) III only
    (D) II and III only
    (E) I and III only

## Answer Key

| | | |
|---|---|---|
| 1. **B** | 10. **D** | 19. **B** |
| 2. **B** | 11. **A** | 20. **A** |
| 3. **C** | 12. **D** | 21. **E** |
| 4. **C** | 13. **E** | 22. **A** |
| 5. **A** | 14. **A** | 23. **B** |
| 6. **D** | 15. **C** | 24. **E** |
| 7. **C** | 16. **E** | 25. **A** |
| 8. **C** | 17. **C** | 26. **E** |
| 9. **C** | 18. **C** | 27. **C** |

## Answer Explanations

1. **(B)** All the `Math` class methods are static methods, which means you can't use a `Math` object that calls the method. The method is invoked using the class name, `Math`, followed by the dot operator. Thus segment II is correct, and segment I is incorrect. Segment III will cause an error: Since the parameters of `pow` are of type `double`, the result should be stored in a `double`.

2. **(B)** The `Math.sqrt` method must be invoked on a primitive type `double`, but auto-unboxing takes care of that in the line

   ```
   double x = d;
   ```

   The return type of the method is `Double`, and autoboxing takes care of that in the statement

   ```
   return x;
   ```

   Segment III fails because you can't use the `Double` constructor to create a new object without using the keyword `new`.

3. **(C)** The value −4.67 must be rounded to −5. Subtracting 0.5 gives a value of −5.17. Casting to `int` truncates the number (chops off the decimal part) and leaves a value of −5. None of the other choices produces −5. Choice A gives the absolute value of d: 4.67. Choice B is an incorrect use of `Random`. The parameter for `nextInt` should be an integer $n$, $n \geq 2$. The method then returns a random `int` $k$, where $0 \leq k < n$. Choice D is the way to round a *positive* real number to the nearest integer. In the actual case it produces −4. Choice E gives the absolute value of −5—namely, 5.

4. **(C)** The statement `double x = Math.random();` generates a random `double` in the range $0 \leq x < 1$. Suppose `probDeath` is 0.67, or 67%. Assuming that random doubles are uniformly distributed in the interval, one can expect that 67% of the time x will be in the range $0 \leq x < 0.67$. You can therefore simulate the probability of death by testing if $x$ is between 0 and 0.67, that is, if $x < 0.67$. Thus, `x < probDeath` is the desired condition for plant death, eliminating choices A and B. Choices D and E fail because `(int) probDeath` truncates `probDeath` to 0. The test `x < 0` will always be false, and the test `x == 0` will only be true if the random number generator returned exactly 0, an extremely unlikely occurrence! Neither of these choices correctly simulates the probability of death.

5. **(A)** The expression

    ```
    (int) (Math.random() * 50);
    ```

    returns an int from 0 to 49. Therefore, adding 1 shifts the range to be 1 to 50, which was required.

6. **(D)** The Integer class has no methods that can change the contents of i. However, i can be reassigned so that it refers to another object. This happens in both segments I and III. Segment II is wrong because intValue is an *accessor*—it cannot be used to change the value of object i.

7. **(C)** Tests I and II both get past the compiler. Test I compiles because == tests the *references* for equality. To test the values, use intValue, which Test II does correctly. Test III fails because you can't invoke a method (in this case equals) with an int.

8. **(C)** The toString method of the Integer class is invoked, which returns a string representing the value of intObj:

    ```
    System.out.println(intObj.toString());    //outputs 9
    ```

9. **(C)** Here are the memory slots:

    Statements II and III are true because the contents of s1 and s2 are the same, and the contents of s3 and s2 are the same. Statement I is false because s1 and s2 are not the same reference. Note that the expression s1 == s3 would be true since s1 and s3 *are* the same reference.

10. **(D)** Note that "TOMATO" precedes both "tomato" and "tom", since "T" precedes "t". Also, "tom" precedes "tomato" since the length of "tom" is less than the length of "tomato". Therefore each of the following is true:

    ```
    strA.compareTo(strB) < 0
    strA.compareTo(strC) < 0
    strC.compareTo(strB) < 0
    ```

    So
    Choice A is T and F, which evaluates to F.
    Choice B is F or F, which evaluates to F.
    Choice C is F and T, which evaluates to F.
    Choice D is T and T, which evaluates to T.
    Choice E is T and F, which evaluates to F.

11. **(A)** x contains the index of the first occurrence of "m" in line—namely, 2. (Remember that "S" is at index 0.) The method call line.substring(10,15) returns "silly", the substring starting at index 10 and extending though index 14. The method call line.substring(25,27) returns "st" (don't include the character at index 27!). The concatenation operator, +, joins these.

12. **(D)** The first character of the last name starts at the first character after the space. Thus, `startIndex` for `substring` must be `k+1`. This eliminates expression I. Expression II takes all the characters from position `k+1` to the end of the `fullName` string, which is correct. Expression III takes all the characters from position `k+1` to position `fullName.length()-1`, which is also correct.

13. **(E)** Suppose `s` contains `"cat"`. You want `pigString = "at" + "c" + "ay"`. Now the string `"at"` is the substring of `s` starting at position 1 and ending at position `s.length()-1`. The correct substring call for this piece of the word is `s.substring(1,s.length())`, which eliminates choices A, C, and D. (Recall that the first parameter is the starting position, and the second parameter is one position past the last index of the substring.) The first letter of the word—`"c"` in the example—starts at position 0 and ends at position 0. The correct expression is `s.substring(0,1)`, which eliminates choice B.

14. **(A)** Statement I is true whenever `s2` occurs in `s1`. For example, if strings `s1 = "catastrophe"` and `s2 = "cat"`, then `getString` returns `"cat"`. Statement II will never happen. If `s2` is not contained in `s1`, the `indexOf` call will return `-1`. Using a negative integer as the first parameter of `substring` will cause a `StringIndexOutOfBoundsException`. Statement III will be true whenever `s1` equals `s2`.

15. **(C)** The `String temp` represents a single-character substring of `s`. The method examines each character in `s` and, if it is a nonblank, appends it to `str`, which is initially empty. Each assignment `str += temp` assigns a new reference to `str`. Thus, `str` ends up as a copy of `s` but without the blanks. A reference to the final `str` object is returned. Choice A is correct in that `s` is left unchanged, but it is not the *best* characterization of what the method does. Choice B is not precise because an object parameter is never modified: Changes, if any, are performed on a copy. Choices D and E are wrong because the method removes blanks.

16. **(E)** The `compareTo` method returns an `int`, so eliminate choices A and B. In the implementation of `compareTo`, the code segment that applies to the particular example is

```
if (this.getRow() < p.getRow() || ...
    return -1;
```

Since 2 < 4, the value -1 is returned.

17. **(C)** Expression III is true: The `compareTo` method is implemented to return 0 if two `Position` objects have the same row and column. Expression I is false because `object1 == object2` returns `true` only if `object1` and `object2` are the *same reference*. Expression II is tricky. You would like `p1` and `p3` to be equal since they have the same row and column values. This is not going to happen automatically, however. The `equals` method must explicitly be overridden for the `Position` class. If this hasn't been done, the default `equals` method, which is inherited from class `Object`, will return true only if `p1` and `p3` are the same reference, which is not true.

18. **(C)** Recall that primitive types and object references are passed by value. This means that copies are made of the actual arguments. Any changes that are made are made to the *copies*. The actual parameters remain unchanged. Thus, in methods I and II, the parameters will retain their original values and remain unswapped.

To illustrate, for example, why method II fails, consider the following piece of code that tests it:

```
public static void main(String[] args)
{
    int x = 8, y = 6;
    Integer xObject = new Integer(x);
    Integer yObject = new Integer(y);
    swap(xObject, yObject);
    x = xObject.intValue();    //surprise! still has value 8
    y = yObject.intValue();    //surprise! still has value 6
    ...
}
```

Here are the memory slots before swap is called:

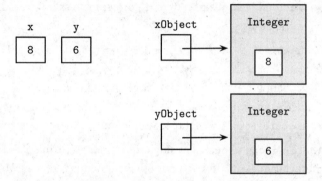

Here they are when swap is invoked:

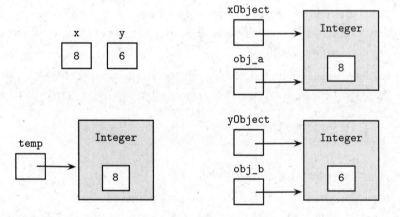

Just before exiting the swap method:

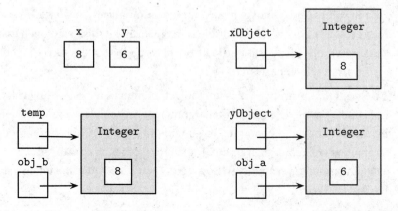

After exiting, xObject and yObject have retained their original values:

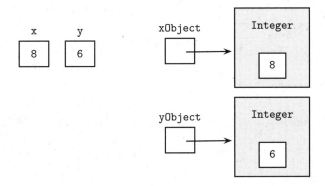

The reason method III works is that instead of the object references being changed, the object *contents* are changed. Thus, after exiting the method, the IntPair reference is as it was, but the first and second values have been interchanged. (See the explanation of the next question for diagrams of the memory slots.) In this question, IntPair is used as a wrapper class for a pair of integers whose values need to be swapped.

19. **(B)** The swap method has just a single IntPair parameter, which eliminates segment I. Segment III fails because setFirst and setSecond are used incorrectly. These are mutator methods that change an IntPair object. What is desired is to return the (newly swapped) first and second values of the pair: Accessor methods getFirst and getSecond do the trick. To see why the swap code in segment II works, look at the memory slots.

Before the swap method is called:

Just after the swap method is called:

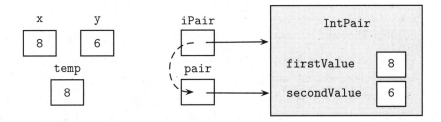

Just before exiting the swap method:

Just after exiting the swap method:

After the statements:

```
x = iPair.getFirst();
y = iPair.getSecond();
```

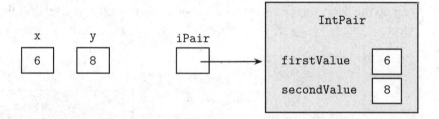

Notice that x and y have been swapped!

20. **(A)** The first statement of segment I compares last names. If these are different, the method returns the int value lastComp, which is negative if lastName precedes n.lastName, positive otherwise. If the last names are the same, the method returns the int result of comparing first names. Segments II and III use incorrect algorithms for comparing names. Segment II would be correct if the else part were

```
return lastName.compareTo(n.lastName);
```

Segment III would be correct if the two return statements were interchanged.

21. **(E)** It is *wise* to have an equals method that is compatible with the compareTo method; namely, n1.equals(n2) and n1.compareTo(n2)==0 have the same value if n1 and n2 are Name objects. However, nothing in the Java language *mandates* that if a class has a compareTo method, it must also have an equals method. Choice A is true. You know this because the Name class has no mutator methods. Thus, Name objects can never be changed. Choice B is true: If a Name is initialized with null references, each of the methods will throw a NullPointerException. Choice C is true: If n1.equals(n2) is true, then n1.compareTo(n2) == 0 is true, because both are conditions for equality of n1 and n2 and should therefore be consistent. Choice D is true: If the parameter is null, the compareTo method will throw a NullPointerException.

22. **(A)** The algorithm prints the current index of `"o"` in the string, and then creates a new substring containing all remaining characters following that `"o"`. Here is the series of substrings and the corresponding output for each (the symbol ␣ denotes a blank character):

```
How␣do␣you␣do?    1
w␣do␣you␣do?      3
␣you␣do?          2
u␣do?             3
```

23. **(B)** Here is a description of the algorithm:

Make a copy of `phrase` in `newPhrase`.
Find the first occurrence of `ch` in `newPhrase` (`pos` is the index).
If you found it, concatenate to `str` the characters in `newPhrase` from 0 to `pos-1`.
Change `newPhrase` to contain all characters from `ch` to the end, excluding `ch`.
Repeat the process until there are no more occurrences of `ch` in `newPhrase`.

So Line 12 is wrong because `newPhrase.substring(0,pos-1)` will not include the character at `pos-1`, which means that the string returned will lose a character that is *not* equal to `ch`.

24. **(E)** The program has found a stand-alone word if the characters `before` and `after` are both blank. Choice E tests that they are not letters between `"a"` and `"z"`; i.e., they must be blank. Choices A and B fail because you must use `compareTo` for inequality tests on strings. Choices C and D allow at least one of `before` and `after` to be a letter, which would mean that `word` was not a stand-alone word.

25. **(A)** The first line in choice A returns a random integer that lies between 0 and `allResponses.length-1`. This range corresponds to the range of the array indexes and so it is correct. Choice B is wrong—you cannot cast a real number to a string. Choice C fails because `Math.random()` is type `double` and you require an `int`; you must do the cast to `int` shown in choice A. Choice D fails because the element `allResponses[allResponses.length-1]` will never be returned: `i` will contain a random `int` from 0 to `allResponses.length-2`. Choice E returns an `int`, not a `String`.

26. **(E)** The actual letter and its point value must not be in quotes because their *values* must be printed. Everything else, including the parentheses, must be in quotes. (All text in quotes is printed literally, as is.) Choices A and C fail because they don't place the opening word, `Letter`, in quotes. Choice B doesn't have the parentheses in quotes. Choice D incorrectly tries to cast an `int` to a `String`.

27. **(C)** Segment I will only be true if an object and its parameter are the same reference, which is not necessarily true for two matching tiles. Segment II fails similarly if the `Tile` class doesn't have its own `equals` method. (The inherited method from `Object` compares references.)

# 6

# Program Design and Analysis

*Weeks of coding can save you hours of planning.*
*—Anonymous*

## Learning Objectives

In this chapter, you will learn:

→ Software development          → Program analysis

→ Object-oriented program design

Students of introductory computer science typically see themselves as programmers. They no sooner have a new programming project in their heads than they're at the computer, typing madly to get some code up and running. (Is this you?)

To succeed as a programmer, however, you have to combine the practical skills of a software engineer with the analytical mindset of a computer scientist. A software engineer oversees the life cycle of software development: initiation of the project, analysis of the specification, and design of the program, as well as implementation, testing, and maintenance of the final product. A computer scientist (among other things!) analyzes the implementation, correctness, and efficiency of algorithms. All these topics are tested on the AP exam.

## Software Development

### Program Specification

The *specification* is an explicit written description of the project. Typically it is based on a customer's (or a teacher's!) requirements. The first step in writing a program is to analyze the specification. Make sure you understand it, and clarify with the customer anything that is unclear.

### Program Design

Even for a small-scale program a good design can save programming time and enhance the reliability of the final program. The design is a fairly detailed plan for solving the problem outlined in the specification. It should include all objects that will be used in the solution, the data structures that will implement them, plus a detailed list of the tasks to be performed by the program.

A good design provides a fairly detailed overall plan at a glance, without including the minutiae of Java code.

## Program Implementation

Program implementation is the coding phase. Design and implementation are discussed in more detail on the next page.

## Testing and Debugging

### Test Data

Not every possible input value can be tested, so a programmer should be diligent in selecting a representative set of *test data*. Typical values in each part of a domain of the program should be selected, as well as endpoint values and out-of-range values. If only positive input is required, your test data should include a negative value just to check that your program handles it appropriately.

### ▷ Example

A program must be written to insert a value into its correct position in this sorted list:

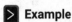
2    5    9

Test data should include:

- A value less than 2
- A value between 2 and 5
- A value between 5 and 9
- A value greater than 9
- 2, 5, and 9
- A negative value

### Types of Errors (Bugs)

- A *compile-time error* occurs during compilation of the program. The compiler is unable to translate the program into bytecode and prints an appropriate error message. A *syntax error* is a compile-time error caused by violating the rules of the programming language. Some examples are omitting semicolons or braces, using undeclared identifiers, using keywords inappropriately, having parameters that don't match in type and number, and invoking a method for an object whose class definition doesn't contain that method.

- A *run-time error* occurs during execution of the program. The Java run-time environment *throws an exception*, which means that it stops execution and prints an error message. Typical causes of run-time errors include attempting to divide an integer by zero, using an array index that is out of bounds, attempting to open a file that cannot be found, and so on. An error that causes a program to run forever ("infinite loop") can also be regarded as a run-time error. (See also "Errors and Exceptions," p. 80.)

- An *intent* or *logic error* is one that fails to carry out the specification of the program. The program compiles and runs but does not do the job. These are sometimes the hardest types of errors to fix.

## Robustness

Always assume that any user of your program is not as smart as you are. You must therefore aim to write a *robust* program—namely, one that:

- Won't give inaccurate answers for some input data.
- Won't crash if the input data are invalid.
- Won't allow execution to proceed if invalid data are entered.

Examples of bad input data include out-of-range numbers, characters instead of numerical data, and a response of "maybe" when "yes" or "no" was asked for.

Note that bad input data that invalidate a computation won't be detected by Java. Your program should include code that catches the error, allows the error to be fixed, and allows program execution to resume.

## Program Maintenance

Program maintenance involves upgrading the code as circumstances change. New features may be added. New programmers may come on board. To make their task easier, the original program must have clear and precise documentation.

# Object-Oriented Program Design

Object-oriented programming has been the dominant programming methodology since the mid 1990s.

Here are the steps in object-oriented design:

- Identify classes to be written.
- Identify behaviors (i.e., methods) for each class.
- Determine the relationships between classes.
- Write the public method headers for each class.
- Implement the methods.

## Identifying Classes

Identify the objects in the program by picking out the nouns in the program specification. Ignore pronouns and nouns that refer to the user. Select those nouns that seem suitable as classes, the "big-picture" nouns that describe the major objects in the application. Some of the other nouns may end up as attributes of the classes.

Many applications have similar object types: a low-level basic component; a collection of low-level components; a controlling object that puts everything together; and a display object that could be a GUI (graphical user interface) but doesn't have to be.

## > Example 1

Write a program that maintains an inventory of stock items for a small store.

Nouns to consider: inventory, item, store.

| | |
|---|---|
| Basic Object: | `StockItem` |
| Collection: | `Inventory` (a list of `StockItems`) |
| Controller: | `Store` (has an `Inventory`, uses a `StoreDisplay`) |
| Display: | `StoreDisplay` (could be a GUI) |

> **Example 2**

Write a program that simulates a game of bingo. There should be at least two players, each of whom has a bingo card, and a caller who calls the numbers.

Nouns to consider: game, players, bingo card, caller.

| | |
|---|---|
| Basic Objects: | BingoCard, Caller |
| Collection: | Players (each has a BingoCard) |
| Controller: | GameMaster (sets up the Players and Caller) |
| Display: | BingoDisplay (shows each player's card and displays winners, etc.) |

> **Example 3**

Bridge is a card game that has a regular deck of 52 cards that are dealt among 4 players so that each player has 13 cards. Write a program that creates random bridge deals and displays them in a specified format. (The specification defines a "deal" as consisting of four hands. It also describes a deck of cards, and shows how each card should be displayed.)

Nouns to consider: deal, hand, format, deck, card.

| | |
|---|---|
| Basic Object: | Card |
| Collection: | Deck (has an array of Cards) |
| | Hand (has an array of Cards) |
| | Deal (has an array of Hands) |
| | Dealer (has a Deck, or several Decks) |
| Controller: | Formatter (has a Deal and a TableDisplay) |
| Display: | TableDisplay (could be a GUI) |

## Identifying Behaviors

Find all verbs in the program description that help lead to the solution of the programming task. These are likely behaviors that will probably become the methods of the classes. Now decide which methods belong in which classes. Recall that the process of bundling methods and data fields into a class to enable its data to be hidden is called *data encapsulation*.

Think carefully about who should do what. Do not ask a basic object to perform operations for the group. For example, a StockItem should keep track of its own details (price, description, how many on the shelf, etc.) but should not be required to search for another item. A Card should know its value and suit but should not be responsible for keeping track of how many cards are left in a deck. A Caller in a bingo game should be responsible for keeping track of the numbers called so far and for producing the next number but not for checking whether a player has bingo: That is the job of an individual player (element of Players) and their BingoCard.

You will also need to decide which data fields each class will need and which data structures should store them. For example, if an object represents a list of items, consider an array or ArrayList as the data structure.

## Determining Relationships Between Classes

### Inheritance Relationships

Look for classes with common behaviors. This will help identify *inheritance relationships*. Recall the *is-a* relationship—if object1 *is-a* object2, then object2 is a candidate for a superclass.

## Composition Relationships

Composition relationships are defined by the *has-a* relationship. For example, a `Nurse` *has-a* `Uniform`. Typically, if two classes have a composition relationship, one of them contains an instance variable whose type is the other class.

Note that a wrapper class always implements a *has-a* relationship with any objects that it wraps.

## UML Diagrams

An excellent way to keep track of the relationships between classes and show the inheritance hierarchy in your programs is with a UML (Unified Modeling Language) diagram. This is a standard graphical scheme used by object-oriented programmers. Although it is not part of the AP subset, on the AP exam you may be expected to interpret simple UML diagrams and inheritance hierarchies.

Here is a simplified version of the UML rules:

- Represent classes with rectangles.

- Show the *is-a* relationship between classes with an open up-arrow.

- Show the *has-a* relationship with a down arrow or sideways arrow (indicates composition).

> ### Example

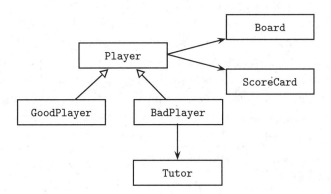

From this diagram you can see at a glance that `GoodPlayer` and `BadPlayer` are subclasses of a class `Player`, and that every `Player` has a `Board` and a `ScoreCard`, while only the `BadPlayer` has a `Tutor`.

## Implementing Classes

### Bottom-Up Development

For each method in a class, list all of the other classes needed to implement that particular method. These classes are called *collaborators*. A class that has no collaborators is *independent*.

To implement the classes, often an incremental, *bottom-up* approach is used. This means that independent classes are fully implemented and tested before being incorporated into the overall project. Typically, these are the basic objects of the program, like `StockItem`, `Card`, and `BingoCard`. Unrelated classes in a programming project can be implemented by different programmers.

Note that a class can be tested using a dummy `Tester` class that will be discarded when the methods of the class are working. Constructors, then methods, should be added, and tested, one at a time. A *driver class* that contains a `main` method can be used to test the program as you go. The purpose of the driver is to test the class fully before incorporating it as an object in a new class.

When each of the independent classes is working, classes that depend on just one other class are implemented and tested, and so on. This may lead to a working, bare bones version of the project. New features and enhancements can be added later.

Design flaws can be corrected at each stage of development. Remember, a design is never set in stone: It simply guides the implementation.

### Top-Down Development

In a top-down design, the programmer starts with an overview of the program, selecting the highest-level controlling object and the tasks needed. During development of the program, subsidiary classes may be added to simplify existing classes.

## Implementing Methods

### Procedural Abstraction

A good programmer avoids chunks of repeated code wherever possible. To this end, if several methods in a class require the same task, like a search or a swap, you should use *helper methods*. The `reduce` method in the `Rational` class on p. 125 is an example of such a method. Also, wherever possible you should enhance the readability of your code by using helper methods to break long methods into smaller tasks. The organization of code into different methods is known as *procedural abstraction*, which encapsulates each task in a class in a separate method of the class. Procedural abstraction is an example of top-down development within a class. The process of breaking a long method into a sequence of smaller tasks is sometimes called *stepwise refinement*.

### Data Encapsulation

Instance variables and helper methods are generally declared as `private`, which prevents client classes from accessing them. *Data encapsulation* is when the data and methods of an object are combined in a class so that the data can be hidden.

### Stub Method

Sometimes it makes more sense in the development of a class to test a calling method before testing a method it invokes. A *stub* is a dummy method that stands in for a method until the actual method has been written and tested. A stub typically has an output statement to show that it was called in the correct place, or it may return some reasonable values if necessary.

## Algorithm

An *algorithm* is a precise step-by-step procedure that solves a problem or achieves a goal. Don't write any code for an algorithm in a method until the steps are completely clear to you.

> **Example 1**

A program must test the validity of a four-digit code number that a person will enter to be able to use a photocopy machine. The number is valid if the fourth digit equals the remainder when the sum of the first three digits is divided by seven.

Classes in the program may include an `IDNumber`, the four-digit code; `Display`, which would handle input and output; and `IDMain`, the driver for the program. The data structure used to implement an `IDNumber` could be an instance variable of type `int`, or an instance variable of type `String`, or four instance variables of type `int`—one per digit, and so on.

A top-down design for the program that tests the validity of the number is reflected in the steps of the `main` method of `IDMain`:

Create `Display`
Read in `IDNumber`
Check validity
Print message

Each method in this design is tested before the next method is added to `main`. If the display will be handled in a GUI (graphical user interface), stepwise refinement of the design might look like this:

Create `Display`
    Construct a `Display`
    Create window panels
    Set up text fields
    Add panels and fields to window

Read in `IDNumber`
    Prompt and read

Check validity of `IDNumber`
    Check input
        Check characters
        Check range
    Separate into digits
    Check validity property

Print message
    Write number
    State if valid

## Note

1. The `IDNumber` class, which contains the four-digit code, is responsible for the following operations:

Split value into separate digits

Check condition for validity

The `Display` class, which contains objects to read and display, must also contain an `IDNumber` object. It is responsible for the following operations:

Set up display

Read in code number

Display validity message

Creating these two classes with their data fields (instance variables) and operations (methods) is an example of data encapsulation.

2. The `Display` method `readCodeNumber` needs private helper methods to check the input: `checkCharacters` and `checkRange`. This is an example of procedural abstraction (the use of separate methods to implement each task) and data encapsulation (making the data private within the class).

3. Initially the programmer had just an `IDNumber` class and a driver class. The `Display` class was added as a refinement, when it was realized that handling the input and message display was separate from checking the validity of the `IDNumber`. This is an example of top-down development (adding an auxiliary class to clarify the code).

4. The `IDNumber` class contains no data fields that are objects. It is therefore an independent class. The `Display` class, which contains an `IDNumber` data member, has a composition relationship with `IDNumber` (`Display` *has-a* `IDNumber`).

5. When testing the final program, the programmer should be sure to include each of the following as a user-entered code number: a valid four-digit number, an invalid four-digit number, an $n$-digit number, where $n \neq 4$, and a "number" that contains a nondigit character. A robust program should be able to deal with all these cases.

## ▷ Example 2

A program must create a teacher's grade book. The program should maintain a class list of students for any number of classes in the teacher's schedule. A menu should be provided that allows the teacher to:

- Create a new class of students.

- Enter a set of scores for any class.

- Correct any data that have been entered.

- Display the record of any student.

- Calculate the final average and grade for all students in a class.

- Print a class list, with or without grades.

- Add a student, delete a student, or transfer a student to another class.

- Save all the data in a file.

**Use nouns in the specification to identify possible classes.**

### Identifying Classes

Use the nouns in the specification as a starting point for identifying classes in the program. The nouns are: program, teacher, grade book, class list, class, student, schedule, menu, set of scores, data, record, average, grade, and file.

Eliminate each of the following:

program     (Always eliminate "program" when used in this context.)

teacher     (Eliminate, because he or she is the user.)

schedule    (This will be reflected in the name of the external file for each class, e.g., `apcs_period3.dat`.)

data, record    (These are synonymous with student name, scores, grades, etc., and will be covered by these features.)

class       (This is synonymous with class list.)

The following seem to be excellent candidates for classes: `GradeBook`, `ClassList`, `Student`, and `FileHandler`. Other possibilities are `Menu`, `ScoreList`, and a `GUI_Display`.

On further thought: Basic independent objects are `Student`, `Menu`, `Score`, and `FileHandler`. Group objects are `ClassList` (collection of students), `ScoreList` (collection of scores), and `AllClasses` (collection of `ClassLists`). The controlling class is the `GradeBook`. A `Display` class is essential for many of the grade book operations, like showing a class list or displaying information for a single student.

## Relationships Between Classes

There are no inheritance relationships. There are many composition relationships between objects, however. The `GradeBook` *has-a* `Menu`, the `ClassList` *has-a* `Student` (several, in fact!), a `Student` *has-a* `name`, `average`, `grade`, `list_of_scores`, etc. The programmer must decide whether to code these attributes as classes or data fields.

## Identifying Behaviors

Use the verbs in the specification to identify required operations in the program. The verbs are: maintain <list>, provide <menu>, allow <user>, create <list>, enter <scores>, correct <data>, display <record>, calculate <average>, calculate <grade>, print <list>, add <student>, delete <student>, transfer <student>, and save <data>.

> Use verbs in the specification to identify possible methods.

You must make some design decisions about which class is responsible for which behavior. For example, will a `ClassList` display the record of a single `Student`, or will a `Student` display his or her own record? Who will enter scores—the `GradeBook`, a `ClassList`, or a `Student`? Is it desirable for a `Student` to enter scores of other `Students`? Probably not!

## Decisions

Here are some preliminary decisions. The `GradeBook` will `provideMenu`. The menu selection will send execution to the relevant object.

The `ClassList` will maintain an updated list of each class. It will have these public methods: `addStudent`, `deleteStudent`, `transferStudent`, `createNewClass`, `printClassList`, `printScores`, and `updateList`. A good candidate for a helper method in this class is `search` for a given student.

Each `Student` will have complete personal and grade information. Public methods will include `setName`, `getName`, `enterScore`, `correctData`, `findAverage`, `getAverage`, `getGrade`, and `displayRecord`.

Saving and retrieving information is crucial to this program. The `FileHandler` will take care of `openFileForReading`, `openFileForWriting`, `closeFiles`, `loadClass`, and `saveClass`. The `FileHandler` class should be written and tested right at the beginning, using a small dummy class list.

Score, ScoreList, and Student are easy classes to implement. When these are working, the programmer can go on to ClassList. Finally, the Display GUI class, which will have the GradeBook, can be developed. This is an example of bottom-up development.

> **Example 3**

A program simulates a game of Battleships, which is a game between two players, each of whom has a grid where ships are placed. Each player has five ships:

```
battleship  o  o  o  o  o
cruiser     o  o  o  o
submarine   o  o  o
destroyer   o  o
frigate     o
```

The grids of the players' fleets may look like this. Any two adjacent squares that are taken must belong to the same ship; i.e., different ships shouldn't "touch."

Player 1                    Player 2

Each player's grid is hidden from the other player. Players alternate "shooting" at each other's ships by calling out a position, a row and column number. A player must make an honest response, "hit" or "miss." If it's a hit, a player gets another turn. If the whole ship has been hit, the owner must say something like, "You sank my cruiser." Each player must keep track of hits and misses. The first player to sink his opponent's fleet is the winner.

**Identifying Classes**

The nouns in the specification are program, game, players, grid, ship, battleship, cruiser, submarine, destroyer, frigate, square, position, opponent, row, column, turn, hits, misses, fleet, winner.

Eliminate each of the following:

| | |
|---|---|
| program | Always eliminate. |
| row, col | These are parts of a given position or square, more suitable as instance variables for a position or square object. |
| hits, misses | These are simply marked positions and probably don't need their own class. |
| turn | Taking a turn is an action and will be described by a method rather than a class. |
| opponent | This is another word for player. |

The following seem to be good candidates for classes: `Player`, `Grid`, `Position`, `Ship`, `Battleship`, `Cruiser`, `Submarine`, `Destroyer`, and `Frigate`. Additionally, it seems there should be a `GameManager` and `Display`.

## Relationships Between Classes

This program provides two examples of inheritance relationships. Each of the five ships *is-a* `Ship`, and shares common features, like `isHit`, `isSunk`, and array of positions. However, each has a unique name, length, and position in the grid. This means that `Ship` is a good candidate for an abstract class with abstract methods like `getLength`, `getName`, and `getPositions`, which depend on the kind of ship.

The second inheritance relationship is between the grids. There are two types of grids for each player: his own `FleetGrid` (the current state of his own ships) and his opponent's `HitGrid`, which keeps track of his hits and misses. Each of these grids *is-a* `Grid`. A grid is a candidate for an interface, with a list of methods like `getAdjacentNeighbors`, `getRightNeighbor`, etc. Each of `FleetGrid` and `HitGrid` would implement `Grid`.

There are several composition relationships in this program. A `Player` *has-a* `HitGrid` and a `FleetGrid` and also has five ships. The `GameManager` has each of the two `Player` objects and also *has-a* `Display`. The `Display` has each of the grids.

## Identifying Behaviors

Use the verbs to identify key methods in the program: simulate <game>, place <ships>, shoot <at position>, call out <position>, respond <hit or miss>, sink <ship>, inform that <ship was sunk>, keep track of <hits or misses>, sink <opponent's fleet>, win <game>.

You need to decide who will do what. There's no definitive way of implementing the program, but it seems clear that the `GameManager` should run the game and declare the winner. Should the `GameManager` also be in charge of announcing if a ship is sunk? It makes sense because the game manager can see both players' grids. Each player should keep track of his calls, so that he can make an intelligent next call and also respond "hit" or "miss." Will each player have a display? Or will the `Display` have both players? You have to set it up so that a player can't see his opponent's `FleetGrid`, but he can see his own and also a grid showing the state of the calls he has made. Should each player have a list of his ships, so he can keep track of the state of his fleet? And what about each ship in the fleet? Should a ship have a list of its positions, and should it keep track of if it's hit or sunk?

Saving and retrieving updated information is crucial to this program. It seems a bit overwhelming. Where should you start? The `Ship` classes are low-level classes, independent of the players and grids. Start with these and test that you can get accurate information about each ship. In your driver program create an `ArrayList<Ship>`. Have a loop that prints information about each ship. Polymorphism will take care of getting the correct information about each ship.

Now try the `Grid` classes. This is a complicated program where each small piece should be coded and tested with simple output. For example, a `Grid` can be displayed with a two-dimensional array of 0's and 1's to show the positions of ships. Other symbols can be used to show what's been hit and what's been sunk.

When everything is working with the grids, you could add a `Display` class that has `Grid` variables and a `display` method.

Try a `Player`. Give him a list of ships, two grids, and a `Display`.

Then create a `GameManager`. Give her two `Player` variables and be sure she has a `playGame` method.

The program development shown above is an example of bottom-up development.

## Vocabulary Summary

Know these terms for the AP exam:

| Vocabulary | Meaning |
| --- | --- |
| software development | Writing a program |
| object-oriented program | Uses interacting objects |
| program specification | Description of a task |
| program design | A written plan, an overview of the solution |
| program implementation | The code |
| test data | Input to test the program |
| program maintenance | Keeping the program working and up to date |
| top-down development | Implement main classes first, subsidiary classes later |
| independent class | Doesn't use other classes of the program in its code |
| bottom-up development | Implement lowest level, independent classes first |
| driver class | Used to test other classes; contains `main` method |
| inheritance relationship | *is-a* relationship between classes |
| composition relationship | *has-a* relationship between classes |
| inheritance hierarchy | Inheritance relationship shown in a tree-like diagram |
| UML diagram | Tree-like representation of relationship between classes |
| data structure | Java construct for storing a data field (e.g., array) |
| data encapsulation | Hiding data fields and methods in a class |
| stepwise refinement | Breaking methods into smaller methods |
| procedural abstraction | Using separate methods to encapsulate each task |
| algorithm | Step-by-step process that solves a problem |
| stub method | Dummy method called by another method being tested |
| debugging | Fixing errors |
| robust program | Screens out bad input |
| compile-time error | Usually a syntax error; prevents program from compiling |
| syntax error | Bad language usage (e.g., missing brace) |
| run-time error | Occurs during execution (e.g., `int` division by 0) |
| exception | Run-time error thrown by Java method |
| logic error | Program runs but does the wrong thing |

# Program Analysis

## Program Correctness

Testing that a program works does not prove that the program is correct. After all, you can hardly expect to test programs for every conceivable set of input data. Computer scientists have developed mathematical techniques to prove correctness in certain cases, but these are beyond the scope of the AP course. Nevertheless, you are expected to be able to make assertions about the state of a program at various points during its execution.

## Assertions

An *assertion* is a precise statement about a program at any given point. The idea is that if an assertion is proved to be true, then the program is working correctly at that point.

An informal step on the way to writing correct algorithms is to be able to make different kinds of assertions about your code.

### Precondition

The *precondition* for any piece of code, whether it is a method, loop, or block, is a statement of what is true immediately before execution of that code.

### Postcondition

The *postcondition* for a piece of code is a statement of what is true immediately after execution of that code.

## Efficiency

An efficient algorithm is one that is economical in the use of:

- CPU time. This refers to the number of machine operations required to carry out the algorithm (arithmetic operations, comparisons, data movements, etc.).
- Memory. This refers to the number and complexity of the variables used.

Some factors that affect run-time efficiency include unnecessary tests, excessive movement of data elements, and redundant computations, especially in loops.

Always aim for early detection of output conditions: Your sorting algorithm should halt when the list is sorted; your search should stop if the key element has been found.

In discussing efficiency of an algorithm, we refer to the *best case*, *worst case*, and *average case*. The best case is a configuration of the data that causes the algorithm to run in the least possible amount of time. The worst case is a configuration that leads to the greatest possible run time. Typical configurations (i.e., not specially chosen data) give the average case. It is possible that best, worst, and average cases don't differ much in their run times.

For example, suppose that a list of distinct random numbers must be searched for a given key value. The algorithm used is a sequential search starting at the beginning of the list. In the best case, the key will be found in the first position examined. In the worst case, it will be in the last position or not in the list at all. On average, the key will be somewhere in the middle of the list.

## Chapter Summary

There's a lot of vocabulary that you are expected to know in this chapter. Learn the words!

Never make assumptions about a program specification, and always write a design before starting to write code. Even if you don't do this for your own programs, these are the answers you will be expected to give on the AP exam. You are certain to get questions about program design. Know the procedures and terminology involved in developing an object-oriented program.

Be sure you understand what is meant by best case, worst case, and average case for an algorithm. There will be questions about efficiency on the AP exam.

By now you should know what a precondition and postcondition are.

# Multiple-Choice Questions on Program Design and Analysis

1. A program that reads in a five-digit identification number is to be written. The specification does not state whether zero can be entered as a first digit. The programmer should
   (A) write the code to accept zero as a first digit since zero is a valid digit.
   (B) write the code to reject zero as a first digit since five-digit integers do not start with zero.
   (C) eliminate zero as a possibility for any of the digits.
   (D) treat the identification number as a four-digit number if the user enters a number starting with zero.
   (E) check with the writer of the specification whether zero is acceptable as a first digit.

2. Refer to the following three program descriptions.

   I. Test whether there exists at least one three-digit integer whose value equals the sum of the squares of its digits.
   II. Read in a three-digit code number and check if it is valid according to some given formula.
   III. Passwords consist of three digits and three capital letters in any order. Read in a password, and check if there are any repeated characters.

   For which of the preceding program descriptions would a `ThreeDigitNumber` class be suitable?
   (A) I only
   (B) II only
   (C) III only
   (D) I and II only
   (E) I, II, and III

3. Top-down programming is illustrated by which of the following?
   (A) Writing a program from top to bottom in Java
   (B) Writing an essay describing how the program will work, without including any Java code
   (C) Using driver programs to test all methods in the order that they're called in the program
   (D) Writing and testing the lowest level methods first and then combining them to form appropriate abstract operations
   (E) Writing the program in terms of the operations to be performed and then refining these operations by adding more detail

4. Which of the following should influence your choice of a particular algorithm?

    I. The run time of the algorithm
    II. The memory requirements of the algorithm
    III. The ease with which the logic of the algorithm can be understood

    (A) I only
    (B) III only
    (C) I and III only
    (D) I and II only
    (E) I, II, and III

5. A list of numbers is stored in a sorted array. It is required that the list be maintained in sorted order. This requirement leads to inefficient execution for which of the following processes?

    I. Summing the five smallest numbers in the list
    II. Finding the maximum value in the list
    III. Inserting and deleting numbers

    (A) I only
    (B) III only
    (C) II and III only
    (D) I and III only
    (E) I, II, and III

6. Which of the following is not necessarily a feature of a robust program?
    (A) Does not allow execution to proceed with invalid data
    (B) Uses algorithms that give correct answers for extreme data values
    (C) Will run on any computer without modification
    (D) Will not allow division by zero
    (E) Will anticipate the types of errors that users of the program may make

7. A certain freight company charges its customers for shipping overseas according to this scale.

    $80 per ton for a weight of 10 tons or less
    $40 per ton for each additional ton over 10 tons but
        not exceeding 25 tons
    $30 per ton for each additional ton over 25 tons

For example, to ship a weight of 12 tons will cost 10(80) + 2(40) = $880. To ship 26 tons will cost 10(80) + 15(40) + 1(30) = $1430.

    A method takes as parameter an integer that represents a valid shipping weight and outputs the charge for the shipment. Which of the following is the smallest set of input values for shipping weights that will adequately test this method?
    (A) 10, 25
    (B) 5, 15, 30
    (C) 5, 10, 15, 25, 30
    (D) 0, 5, 10, 15, 25, 30
    (E) 5, 10, 15, 20, 25, 30

8. A code segment calculates the mean of values stored in integers n1, n2, n3, and n4 and stores the result in average, which is of type double. What kind of error is caused with this statement?

```
double average = n1 + n2 + n3 + n4 / (double) 4;
```

(A) Logic
(B) Run-time
(C) Overflow
(D) Syntax
(E) Type mismatch

9. A program evaluates binary arithmetic expressions that are read from an input file. All of the operands are integers, and the only operators are +, -, *, and /. In writing the program, the programmer forgot to include a test that checks whether the right-hand operand in a division expression equals zero. When will this oversight be detected by the computer?

(A) At compile time
(B) While editing the program
(C) As soon as the data from the input file is read
(D) During evaluation of the expressions
(E) When at least one incorrect value for the expressions is output

10. A programmer plans to write a program that simulates various games. In the program, there is a Player class that has a getMove method. Method getMove returns an int value to simulate a move in a game.

Which of the games described below are suitable candidates for using the getMove method as specified above?

I. High-Low Guessing Game: The computer thinks of a number and the player who guesses it with the least number of guesses wins. After each guess, the computer tells whether its number is higher or lower than the player's guess.

II. Chips: Start with a pile of chips. Each player, in turn, removes some number of chips, but not all of them. The winner is the one who removes the final chip.

III. Tic-Tac-Toe: Two players alternate placing "X" or "O" on a 3 × 3 grid. The first player to get three in a row, where a row can be horizontal, vertical, or diagonal, wins.

(A) I only
(B) II only
(C) III only
(D) I and II only
(E) I, II, and III

11. Which best describes the precondition of a method? It is an assertion that
    (A) describes precisely the conditions that must be true at the time the method is
        called.
    (B) initializes the parameters of the method.
    (C) describes the effect of the method on its postcondition.
    (D) explains what the method does.
    (E) states what the initial values of the local variables in the method must be.

12. Consider the following code fragment.

```
/** Precondition: a1, a2, a3 contain 3 distinct integers.
 *  Postcondition: max contains the largest of a1, a2, a3.
 */
//first set max equal to larger of a1 and a2
if (a1 > a2)
    max = a1;
else
    max = a2;
//set max equal to larger of max and a3
if (max < a3)
    max = a3;
```

For this algorithm, which of the following initial setups for a1, a2, and a3 will cause
    (1) the least number of computer operations (best case) and
    (2) the greatest number of computer operations (worst case)?

    (A)  (1) largest value in a1 or a2     (2) largest value in a3
    (B)  (1) largest value in a2 or a3     (2) largest value in a1
    (C)  (1) smallest value in a1          (2) largest value in a2
    (D)  (1) largest value in a2           (2) smallest value in a3
    (E)  (1) smallest value in a1 or a2    (2) largest value in a3

13. Refer to the following code segment.

```
/** Compute the mean of integers 1 ... N.
 *  N is an integer >= 1 and has been initialized.
 */
int k = 1;
double mean, sum = 1.0;
while (k < N)
{
    /* loop body */
}
mean = sum / N;
```

What is the precondition for the while loop?
    (A) $k \geq N$,  sum = 1.0
    (B) sum = 1 + 2 + 3 + ... + k
    (C) $k < N$,  sum = 1.0
    (D) $N \geq 1$,  k = 1,  sum = 1.0
    (E) mean = sum / N

14. The sequence of Fibonacci numbers is 1, 1, 2, 3, 5, 8, 13, 21, .... The first two Fibonacci numbers are each 1. Each subsequent number is obtained by adding the previous two. Consider this method.

```
/** Precondition: n >= 1.
 *  Postcondition: The nth Fibonacci number has been returned.
 */
public static int fib(int n)
{
    int prev = 1, next = 1, sum = 1;
    for (int i = 3; i <= n; i++)
    {
        /* assertion */
        sum = next + prev;
        prev = next;
        next = sum;
    }
    return sum;
}
```

Which of the following is a correct /* *assertion* */ about the loop variable i?

(A) $1 \le i \le n$

(B) $0 \le i \le n$

(C) $3 \le i \le n$

(D) $3 < i \le n$

(E) $3 < i < n+1$

15. Refer to the following method.

```
/** Precondition: a and b are initialized integers.
 */
public static int mystery(int a, int b)
{
    int total = 0, count = 1;
    while (count <= b)
    {
        total += a;
        count++;
    }
    return total;
}
```

What is the postcondition for method mystery?

(A) $total = a + b$

(B) $total = a^b$

(C) $total = b^a$

(D) $total = a * b$

(E) $total = a/b$

16. A program is to be written that prints an invoice for a small store. A copy of the invoice will be given to the customer and will display:

   - A list of items purchased.
   - The quantity, unit price, and total price for each item.
   - The amount due.

   Three candidate classes for this program are `Invoice`, `Item`, and `ItemList`, where an `Item` is a single item purchased and `ItemList` is the list of all items purchased. Which class is a reasonable choice to be responsible for the `amountDue` method, which returns the amount the customer must pay?

   I. `Item`

   II. `ItemList`

   III. `Invoice`

   (A) I only
   (B) III only
   (C) I and II only
   (D) II and III only
   (E) I, II, and III

17. Which is a false statement about classes in object-oriented program design?
   (A) If a class `C1` has an instance variable whose type is another class, `C2`, then `C1` *has-a* `C2`.
   (B) If a class `C1` is associated with another class, `C2`, then `C1` depends on `C2` for its implementation.
   (C) If classes `C1` and `C2` are related such that `C1` *is-a* `C2`, then `C2` *has-a* `C1`.
   (D) If class `C1` is independent, then none of its methods will have parameters that are objects of other classes.
   (E) Classes that have common methods do not necessarily define an inheritance relationship.

18. A Java program maintains a large database of vehicles and parts for a car dealership. Some of the classes in the program are Vehicle, Car, Truck, Tire, Circle, SteeringWheel, and AirBag. The declarations below show the relationships between classes. Which is a poor choice?

    (A) ```
        public class Vehicle
        {   ...
            private Tire[] tires;
            private SteeringWheel sw;
            ...
        }
        ```

    (B) ```
        public class Tire extends Circle
        {   ...
            //inherits methods that compute circumference
            //and center point
        }
        ```

    (C) ```
        public class Car extends Vehicle
        {   ...
            //inherits private Tire[] tires from Vehicle class
            //inherits private SteeringWheel sw from Vehicle class
            ...
        }
        ```

    (D) ```
        public class Tire
        {   ...
            private String rating;      //speed rating of tire
            private Circle boundary;
        }
        ```

    (E) ```
        public class SteeringWheel
        {   ...
            private AirBag ab;   //AirBag is stored in SteeringWheel
            private Circle boundary;
        }
        ```

19. A Java programmer has completed a preliminary design for a large program. The programmer has developed a list of classes, determined the methods for each class, established the relationships between classes, and written an outline for each class. Which class(es) should be implemented first?

    (A) Any superclasses
    (B) Any subclasses
    (C) All collaborator classes (classes that will be used to implement other classes)
    (D) The class that represents the dominant object in the program
    (E) All independent classes (classes that have no references to other classes)
        ```

Use the program description below for Questions 20–22.

A program is to be written that simulates bumper cars in a video game. The cars move on a square grid and are located on grid points $(x, y)$, where $x$ and $y$ are integers between $-20$ and 20. A bumper car moves in a random direction, either left, right, up, or down. If it reaches a boundary (i.e., $x$ or $y$ is $\pm 20$), then it reverses direction. If it is about to collide with another bumper car, it reverses direction. Your program should be able to add bumper cars and run the simulation. One step of the simulation allows each car in the grid to move. After a bumper car has reversed direction twice, its turn is over and the next car gets to move.

20. To identify classes in the program, the nouns in the specification are listed:

> program, bumper car, grid, grid point, integer, direction, boundary, simulation

How many nouns in the list should immediately be discarded because they are unsuitable as classes for the program?

(A) 0
(B) 1
(C) 2
(D) 3
(E) 4

A programmer decides to include the following classes in the program. Refer to them for Questions 21 and 22.

- `Simulation` will run the simulation.

- `Display` will show the state of the game.

- `BumperCar` will know its identification number, position in the grid, and current direction when moving.

- `GridPoint` will be a position in the grid. It will be represented by two integer fields, `x_coord` and `y_coord`.

- `Grid` will keep track of all bumper cars in the game, the number of cars, and their positions in the grid. It will update the grid each time a car moves. It will be implemented with a two-dimensional array of `BumperCar`.

21. Which operation should not be the responsibility of the `GridPoint` class?

    (A)   `isEmpty`     returns false if the grid point contains a `BumperCar`, true otherwise

    (B)   `atBoundary`   returns true if $x$ or $y$ coordinate $= \pm20$, false otherwise

    (C)   `left`     if not at left boundary, change the grid point to 1 unit left of current point

    (D)   `up`     if not at top of grid, change the grid point to 1 unit above current point

    (E)   `get_x`     return $x$-coordinate of this point

22. Which method is not suitable for the `BumperCar` class?

    (A) `public boolean atBoundary()`
        `//Returns true if BumperCar at boundary, false otherwise.`

    (B) `public void selectRandomDirection()`
        `//Select random direction (up, down, left, or right)`
        `// at start of turn.`

    (C) `public void reverseDirection()`
        `//Move to grid position that is in direction opposite to`
        `// current direction.`

    (D) `public void move()`
        `//Take turn to move. Stop move after two changes`
        `// of direction.`

    (E) `public void update()`
        `//Modify Grid to reflect new position after each stage`
        `// of move.`

## Answer Key

| | | |
|---|---|---|
| 1. **E** | 9. **D** | 17. **C** |
| 2. **D** | 10. **D** | 18. **B** |
| 3. **E** | 11. **A** | 19. **E** |
| 4. **E** | 12. **A** | 20. **C** |
| 5. **B** | 13. **D** | 21. **A** |
| 6. **C** | 14. **C** | 22. **E** |
| 7. **C** | 15. **D** | |
| 8. **A** | 16. **D** | |

## Answer Explanations

1. **(E)** A programmer should never make unilateral decisions about a program specification. When in doubt, check with the person who wrote the specification.

2. **(D)** In I and II a three-digit number is the object being manipulated. For III, however, the object is a six-character string, suggesting a class other than a `ThreeDigitNumber`.

3. **(E)** Top-down programming consists of listing the methods for the main object and then using stepwise refinement to break each method into a list of subtasks. Eliminate choices A, C, and D: Top-down programming refers to the design and planning stage and does not involve any actual writing of code. Choice B is closer to the mark, but "top-down" implies a list of operations, not an essay describing the methods.

4. **(E)** All three considerations are valid when choosing an algorithm. III is especially important if your code will be part of a larger project created by several programmers. Yet even if you are the sole writer of a piece of software, be aware that your code may one day need to be modified by others.

5. **(B)** A process that causes excessive data movement is inefficient. Inserting an element into its correct (sorted) position involves moving elements to create a slot for this element. In the worst case, the new element must be inserted into the first slot, which involves moving every element up one slot. Similarly, deleting an element involves moving elements down a slot to close the "gap." In the worst case, where the first element is deleted, all elements in the array will need to be moved. Summing the five smallest elements in the list means summing the first five elements. This requires no testing of elements and no excessive data movement, so it is efficient. Finding the maximum value in a sorted list is very fast—just select the element at the appropriate end of the list.

6. **(C)** "Robustness" implies the ability to handle all data input by the user and to give correct answers even for extreme values of data. A program that is not robust may well run on another computer without modification, and a robust program may need modification before it can run on another computer.

7. **(C)** Eliminate choice D because 0 is an invalid weight, and you may infer from the method description that invalid data have already been screened out. Eliminate choice E because it tests two values in the range 10–25. (This is not wrong, but choice C is better.) Eliminate choice A since it tests only the endpoint values. Eliminate B because it tests *no* endpoint values.

8. **(A)** The statement is syntactically correct, but as written it will not find the mean of the integers. The bug is therefore an intent or logic error. To execute as intended, the statement needs parentheses:

```
double average = (n1 + n2 + n3 + n4) / (double) 4;
```

9. **(D)** The error that occurs is a run-time error caused by an attempt to divide by zero (`ArithmeticException`). Don't be fooled by choice C. Simply reading an expression 8/0 from the input file won't cause the error. Note that if the operands were of type `double`, the correct answer would be E. In this case, dividing by zero does not cause an exception; it gives an answer of `Infinity`. Only on inspecting the output would it be clear that something was wrong.

10. **(D)** Games I and II are perfect games for using an integer value to describe the next move. For the High-Low Guessing Game, `getMove()` will return the next guess, and for Chips, `getMove()` will return the number of chips removed at the player's turn. Game III, Tic-Tac-Toe, requires a location on a 3 × 3 grid as a player's next move: a simple integer value isn't a suitable return type for the `getMove` method.

11. **(A)** A precondition does not concern itself with the action of the method, the local variables, the algorithm, or the postcondition. Nor does it initialize the parameters. It simply asserts what must be true directly before execution of the method.

12. **(A)** The best case causes the fewest computer operations, and the worst case leads to the maximum number of operations. In the given algorithm, the initial test `if (a1 > a2)` and the assignment to `max` will occur irrespective of which value is the largest. The second test, `if (max < a3)`, will also always occur. The final statement, `max = a3`, will occur only if the largest value is in `a3`; thus, this represents the worst case. So the best case must have the biggest value in `a1` or `a2`.

13. **(D)** The precondition is an assertion about the variables in the loop just before the loop is executed. Variables `N`, `k`, and `sum` have all been initialized to the values shown in choice D. Choice C is wrong because `k` may equal `N`. Choice A is wrong because `k` may be less than `N`. Choice E is wrong because `mean` is not defined until the loop has been exited. Choice B is wrong because it omits the assertions about `N` and `k`.

14. **(C)** Eliminate choices A and B, since `i` is initialized to 3 in the `for` loop. Choices D and E are wrong because `i` is equal to 3 the first time through the loop.

15. **(D)** The quantity `a` is being added to `total` `b` times, which means that at the end of execution `total = a*b`.

16. **(D)** It makes sense for an `Item` to be responsible for its name, unit price, quantity, and total price. It is *not* reasonable for it to be responsible for other `Items`. Since an `ItemList`, however, will contain information for all the `Items` purchased, it is reasonable to have it also compute the total `amountDue`. It makes just as much sense to give an `Invoice` the responsibility for displaying information for the items purchased, as well as providing a final total, `amountDue`.

17. **(C)** The *is-a* relationship defines inheritance, while the *has-a* relationship defines association. These types of relationships are mutually exclusive. For example, a graduate student *is-a* student. It doesn't make sense to say a student *has-a* graduate student!

18. **(B)** Even though it's convenient for a `Tire` object to inherit `Circle` methods, an inheritance relationship between a `Tire` and a `Circle` is incorrect: It is false to say that a `Tire` *is-a* `Circle`. A `Tire` is a car part, while a `Circle` is a geometric shape. Notice that there is an *association* relationship between a `Tire` and a `Circle`: A `Tire` *has-a* `Circle` as its boundary.

19. **(E)** Independent classes do not have relationships with other classes and can therefore be more easily coded and tested.

20. **(C)** The word "program" is never included when it's used in this context. The word "integer" describes the type of coordinates $x$ and $y$ and has no further use in the specification. While words like "direction," "boundary," and "simulation" may later be removed from consideration as classes, it is not unreasonable to keep them as candidates while you ponder the design.

21. **(A)** A `GridPoint` object knows only its $x$ and $y$ coordinates. It has no information about whether a `BumperCar` is at that point. Notice that operations in all of the other choices depend on the $x$ and $y$ coordinates of a `GridPoint` object. An `isEmpty` method should be the responsibility of the `Grid` class that keeps track of the status of each position in the grid.

22. **(E)** A `BumperCar` is responsible for itself—keeping track of its own position, selecting an initial direction, making a move, and reversing direction. It is not, however, responsible for maintaining and updating the grid. That should be done by the `Grid` class.

# 7

# Arrays and Array Lists

*Should array indices start at 0 or 1?*
*My compromise of 0.5 was rejected,*
*without, I thought, proper consideration.*
—*S. Kelly-Bootle*

## Learning Objectives

In this chapter, you will learn:

→ One-dimensional arrays
→ Array lists
→ Two-dimensional arrays

## One-Dimensional Arrays

A one-dimensional array is a data structure used to implement a list object, where the elements in the list are of the same type; for example, a class list of 25 test scores, a membership list of 100 names, or a store inventory of 500 items.

For an array of $N$ elements in Java, index values ("subscripts") go from 0 to $N - 1$. Individual elements are accessed as follows: If `arr` is the name of the array, the elements are `arr[0]`, `arr[1]`, ..., `arr[N-1]`. If a negative subscript is used, or a subscript $k$ where $k \geq N$, an `ArrayIndexOutOfBoundsException` is thrown.

### Initialization

In Java, an array is an object; therefore, the keyword `new` must be used in its creation. The one exception is an initializer list (discussed on the next page). The size of an array remains fixed once it has been created. As with `String` objects, however, an array reference may be reassigned to a new array of a different size.

> **Example**

All of the following are equivalent. Each creates an array of 25 `double` values and assigns the reference `data` to this array.

1. `double[] data = new double[25];`

2. `double data[] = new double[25];`

3. `double[] data;`
   `data = new double[25];`

A subsequent statement like

```
data = new double[40];
```

reassigns `data` to a new array of length 40. The memory allocated for the previous `data` array is recycled by Java's automatic garbage collection system.

When arrays are declared, the elements are automatically initialized to zero for the primitive numeric data types (`int` and `double`), to `false` for boolean variables, or to `null` for object references.

It is possible to declare several arrays in a single statement. For example,

```
int[] intList1, intList2;    //declares intList1 and intList2 to
                             //contain int values
int[] arr1 = new int[15], arr2 = new int[30];  //reserves 15 slots
                                               //for arr1, 30 for arr2
```

## Initializer List

Small arrays whose values are known can be conveniently declared with an *initializer list*. For example, instead of writing

```
int[] coins = new int[4];
coins[0] = 1;
coins[1] = 5;
coins[2] = 10;
coins[3] = 25;
```

you can write

```
int[] coins = {1, 5, 10, 25};
```

This construction is the one case where `new` is not required to create an array.

## Length of Array

A one-dimensional array in Java has a final public instance variable (i.e., a constant), `length`, which can be accessed when you need the number of elements in the array. For example,

```
String[] names = new String[25];
< code to initialize names >

//loop to process all names in array
for (int i = 0; i < names.length; i++)
    < process names >
```

## Note

1. The array subscripts go from 0 to `names.length-1`; therefore, the test on `i` in the `for` loop must be strictly less than `names.length`.
2. `length` is not a method and therefore is not followed by parentheses. Contrast this with `String` objects, where `length` *is* a method and *must* be followed by parentheses. For example,

```
String s = "Confusing syntax!";
int size = s.length();    //assigns 17 to size
```

## Traversing a One-Dimensional Array

Use an enhanced `for` loop whenever you need access to every element in an array without replacing or removing any elements, and without needing the position of any element. Use a `for` loop in all other cases: to access the index of any element, to replace or remove elements, or to access just some of the elements.

> **Do not use an enhanced `for` loop to remove or replace elements of an array.**

Note that if you have an array of objects (not primitive types), you can use the enhanced `for` loop and mutator methods of the object to modify the fields of any instance (see the `shuffleAll` method on p. 247).

### ▷ Example 1

```
/** Returns the number of even integers in array arr of integers. */
public static int countEven(int[] arr)
{
    int count = 0;
    for (int num : arr)
        if ( num % 2 == 0)    //num is even
            count++;
    return count;
}
```

### ▷ Example 2

```
/** Change each even-indexed element in array arr to 0.
 * Precondition:  arr contains integers.
 * Postcondition: arr[0], arr[2], arr[4], ... have value 0.
 */
public static void changeEven(int[] arr)
{
    for (int i = 0; i < arr.length; i += 2)
        arr[i] = 0;
}
```

## Arrays as Parameters

Since arrays are treated as objects, passing an array as a parameter means passing its object reference. No copy is made of the array. *Thus, the elements of the actual array can be accessed—and modified.*

> **Example 1**

Array elements accessed but not modified:

```java
/** Returns index of smallest element in array arr of integers. */
public static int findMin (int[] arr)
{
    int min = arr[0];
    int minIndex = 0;
    for (int i = 1; i < arr.length; i++)
        if (arr[i] < min)    //found a smaller element
        {
            min = arr[i];
            minIndex = i;
        }
    return minIndex;
}
```

To call this method (in the same class that it's defined):

```java
int[] array;
< code to initialize array >
int min = findMin(array);
```

> **Example 2**

Array elements modified:

```java
/** Add 3 to each element of array b. */
public static void changeArray(int[] b)
{
    for (int i = 0; i < b.length; i++)
        b[i] += 3;
}
```

To call this method (in the same class):

```java
int[] list = {1, 2, 3, 4};
changeArray(list);
System.out.print("The changed list is ");
for (int num : list)
    System.out.print(num + " ");
```

> When an array is passed as a parameter, it is possible to alter the contents of the array.

The output produced is

```
The changed list is 4 5 6 7
```

Look at the memory slots to see how this happens:

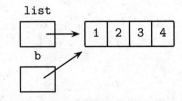

Before the method call:                        At the start of the method call:

Just before exiting the method:

After exiting the method:

> **Example 3**

Contrast the `changeArray` method with the following attempt to modify one array element:

```
/** Add 3 to an element. */
public static void changeElement(int n)
{ n += 3; }
```

Here is some code that invokes this method:

```
int[] list = {1, 2, 3, 4};
System.out.print("Original array: ");
for (int num : list)
    System.out.print(num + " ");
changeElement(list[0]);
System.out.print("\nModified array: ");
for (int num : list)
    System.out.print(num + " ");
```

Contrary to the programmer's expectation, the output is

```
Original array: 1 2 3 4
Modified array: 1 2 3 4
```

A look at the memory slots shows why the list remains unchanged.

Before the method call:

At the start of the method call:

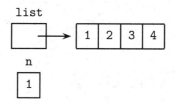

Just before exiting the method:

After exiting the method:

The point of this is that primitive types—including single array elements of type `int` or `double`—are passed by value. A copy is made of the actual parameter, and the copy is erased on exiting the method.

> **Example 4**

```java
/** Swap arr[i] and arr[j] in array arr. */
public static void swap(int[] arr, int i, int j)
{
    int temp = arr[i];
    arr[i] = arr[j];
    arr[j] = temp;
}
```

To call the swap method:

```java
int[] list = {1, 2, 3, 4};
swap(list, 0, 3);
System.out.print("The changed list is: ");
for (int num : list)
    System.out.print(num + " ");
```

The output shows that the program worked as intended:

```
The changed list is: 4 2 3 1
```

A look at the memory slots shows why the list changes.

Before the method call

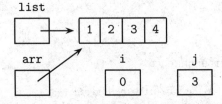

At the start of the method call

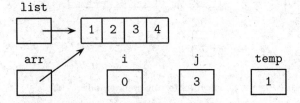

After the statement
`int temp = arr[i];`

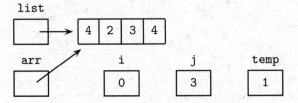

After the statement
`arr[i] = arr[j];`

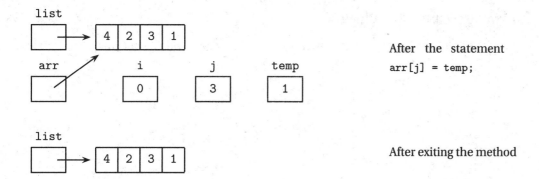

After the statement
`arr[j] = temp;`

After exiting the method

## > Example 5

```
/** Returns array containing NUM_ELEMENTS integers read from the keyboard.
 *  Precondition:  Array undefined.
 *  Postcondition: Array contains NUM_ELEMENTS integers read from
 *                 the keyboard.
 */
public int[] getIntegers()
{
    int[] arr = new int[NUM_ELEMENTS];
    for (int i = 0; i < arr.length; i++)
    {
        System.out.println("Enter integer: ");
        arr[i] = ...;          //read user input
    }
    return arr;
}
```

To call this method:

```
int[] list = getIntegers();
```

## Shuffling

Several different algorithms are discussed for shuffling an array of elements. A key ingredient of a good shuffle is generation of random integers.

## > Example 6

To shuffle a deck of 52 cards in an array may require a random `int` from 0 to 51:

```
int cardNum = (int) (Math.random() * 52);
```

(Recall that the multiplier in parentheses is the number of possible random integers.)

The following code for shuffling an array of `Type` elements is used often:

```
for (int k = arr.length - 1; k > 0; k--)
{
    //Pick a random index in the array from 0 to k
    int index = (int) (Math.random() * (k + 1));
    //Swap randomly selected element with element at position k
    Type temp = arr[k];
    arr[k] = arr[index];
    arr[index] = temp;
}
```

## Array Variables in a Class

Consider a simple Deck class in which a deck of cards is represented by the integers 0 to 51.

```java
public class Deck
{
    private int[] deck;
    public static final int NUMCARDS = 52;

    /** constructor */
    public Deck()
    {
        deck = new int[NUMCARDS];
        for (int i = 0; i < NUMCARDS; i++)
            deck[i] = i;
    }

    /** Write contents of Deck. */
    public void writeDeck()
    {
        for (int card : deck)
            System.out.print(card + " ");
        System.out.println();
        System.out.println();
    }

    /** Swap arr[i] and arr[j] in array arr. */
    private void swap(int[] arr, int i, int j)
    {
        int temp = arr[i];
        arr[i] = arr[j];
        arr[j] = temp;
    }

    /** Shuffle Deck: Generate a random permutation by picking a
     *    random card from those remaining and putting it in the
     *    next slot, starting from the right.
     */
    public void shuffle()
    {
        int index;
        for (int i = NUMCARDS - 1; i > 0; i--)
        {
            //generate an int from 0 to i
            index = (int) (Math.random() * (i + 1));
            swap(deck, i, index);
        }
    }
}
```

Here is a simple driver class that tests the Deck class:

```
public class DeckMain
{
    public static void main(String args[])
    {
        Deck d = new Deck();
        d.shuffle();
        d.writeDeck();
    }
}
```

## Note

There is no evidence of the array that holds the deck of cards—deck is a private instance variable and is therefore invisible to clients of the Deck class.

## Array of Class Objects

Suppose a large card tournament needs to keep track of many decks. The code to do this could be implemented with an array of Deck:

```
public class ManyDecks
{
    private Deck[] allDecks;
    public static final int NUMDECKS = 500;

    /** constructor */
    public ManyDecks()
    {
        allDecks = new Deck[NUMDECKS];
        for (int i = 0; i < NUMDECKS; i++)
            allDecks[i] = new Deck();
    }

    /** Shuffle the Decks. */
    public void shuffleAll()
    {
        for (Deck d : allDecks)
            d.shuffle();
    }

    /** Write contents of all the Decks. */
    public void printDecks()
    {
        for (Deck d : allDecks)
            d.writeDeck();
    }
}
```

## Note

1. The statement

    ```
    allDecks = new Deck[NUMDECKS];
    ```

    creates an array, allDecks, of 500 Deck objects. The default initialization for these Deck objects is null. In order to initialize them with actual decks, the Deck constructor must be called for each array element. This is achieved with the `for` loop of the `ManyDecks` constructor.

2. In the `shuffleAll` method, it's OK to use an enhanced `for` loop to modify each deck in the array with the mutator method `shuffle`.

## Analyzing Array Algorithms

### ▷ Example 1

Discuss the efficiency of the `countNegs` method below. What are the best and worst case configurations of the data?

```
/** Returns the number of negative values in arr.
 *  Precondition:   arr[0],...,arr[arr.length-1] contain integers.
 */
public static int countNegs(int[] arr)
{
    int count = 0;
    for (int num : arr)
        if (num < 0)
            count++;
    return count;
}
```

### ✓ Solution

This algorithm sequentially examines each element in the array. In the best case, there are no negative elements, and `count++` is never executed. In the worst case, all the elements are negative, and `count++` is executed in each pass of the `for` loop.

### ▷ Example 2

The code fragment below inserts a value, `num`, into its correct position in a sorted array of integers. Discuss the efficiency of the algorithm.

```
/** Precondition:
 *   - arr[0],...,arr[n-1] contain integers sorted in increasing order.
 *   - n < arr.length.
 *  Postcondition: num has been inserted in its correct position.
 */
{
    //find insertion point
    int i = 0;
    while (i < n && num > arr[i])
        i++;
    //if necessary, move elements arr[i]...arr[n-1] up 1 slot
    for (int j = n; j >= i + 1; j--)
        arr[j] = arr[j-1];
    //insert num in i-th slot and update n
    arr[i] = num;
    n++;
}
```

✓ **Solution**

In the best case, num is greater than all the elements in the array: Because it gets inserted at the end of the list, no elements must be moved to create a slot for it. The worst case has num less than all the elements in the array. In this case, num must be inserted in the first slot, arr[0], and every element in the array must be moved up one position to create a slot.

This algorithm illustrates a disadvantage of arrays: Insertion and deletion of an element in an ordered list is inefficient, since, in the worst case, it may involve moving all the elements in the list.

## Array Lists

An ArrayList provides an alternative way of storing a list of objects and has the following advantages over an array:

- An ArrayList shrinks and grows as needed in a program, whereas an array has a fixed length that is set when the array is created.

- In an ArrayList list, the last slot is always list.size()-1, whereas in a partially filled array, you, the programmer, must keep track of the last slot currently in use.

- For an ArrayList, you can do insertion or deletion with just a single statement. Any shifting of elements is handled automatically. In an array, however, insertion or deletion requires you to write the code that shifts the elements.

- It is easier to print the elements of an ArrayList than those of an array. For an ArrayList list and an array arr, the statement

```
System.out.print(list);
```

will output the elements of list, nicely formatted in square brackets, with the elements separated by commas. However, to print the elements of arr, an explicit piece of code that accesses and prints each element is needed. The statement

```
System.out.print(arr);
```

will produce weird output that includes an @ symbol—not the elements of the array.

## The ArrayList Class

The ArrayList class is part of the java.util package. An import statement makes this class available in a program. Java allows the generic type ArrayList<E>, where E is the type of the elements in the ArrayList. When a generic class is declared, the type parameter is replaced by an actual object type. For example,

```
private ArrayList<Clown> clowns;
```

## Note

The clowns list must contain only Clown objects. An attempt to add an Acrobat to the list, for example, will cause a compile-time error.

## The Methods of `ArrayList<E>`

Here are the methods you should know:

`ArrayList()`

Constructor constructs an empty list.

`int size()`

Returns the number of elements in the list.

`boolean add(E obj)`

Appends `obj` to the end of the list. Always returns `true`. If the specified element is not of type E, throws a run-time exception.

`void add(int index, E element)`

Inserts `element` at specified `index`. Elements from position `index` and higher have 1 added to their indices. Size of list is incremented by 1.

`E get(int index)`

Returns the element at the specified `index` in the list.

`E set(int index, E element)`

Replaces item at specified `index` in the list with specified `element`. Returns the element that was previously at `index`. If the specified element is not of type E, throws a run-time exception.

`E remove(int index)`

Removes and returns the element at the specified `index`. Elements to the right of position `index` have 1 subtracted from their indices. Size of list is decreased by 1.

### Note

Each of these methods that has an `index` parameter—add, get, remove, and set—throws an `IndexOutOfBoundsException` if index is out of range. For get, remove, and set, index is out of range if

```
index < 0 || index >= size()
```

For add, however, it is OK to add an element at the end of the list. Therefore index is out of range if

```
index < 0 || index > size()
```

## Autoboxing and Unboxing

An `ArrayList` cannot contain a primitive type like `double` or `int`: It must only contain *objects*. (It actually contains the references to those objects.) Numbers must therefore be boxed—placed in wrapper classes like `Integer` and `Double`—before insertion into an `ArrayList`.

*Autoboxing* is the automatic wrapping of primitive types in their wrapper classes (see p. 180).

To retrieve the numerical value of an `Integer` (or `Double`) stored in an `ArrayList`, the `intValue()` (or `doubleValue()`) method must be invoked (unwrapping). *Unboxing* is the automatic conversion of a wrapper class to its corresponding primitive type. This means that you don't need to explicitly call the `intValue()` or `doubleValue()` methods. Be aware that if a program tries to auto-unbox `null`, the method will throw a `NullPointerException`.

Note that while autoboxing and unboxing cut down on code clutter, these operations must still be performed behind the scenes, leading to decreased run-time efficiency. It is much more efficient to assign and access primitive types in an array than an `ArrayList`. You should therefore consider using an array for a program that manipulates sequences of numbers and does not need to use objects.

**Note**
1. Autoboxing and unboxing are part of the AP Java subset.
2. The `List<E>` interface and the methods of `List<E>` are no longer part of the AP Java subset.

## Using `ArrayList<E>`

> **Example 1**

```
//Create an ArrayList containing 0 1 4 9.
ArrayList<Integer> list = new ArrayList<Integer>();
for (int i = 0; i < 4; i++)
    list.add(i * i);  //example of autoboxing
                      //i*i wrapped in an Integer before insertion

Integer intOb = list.get(2); //assigns Integer with value 4 to intOb.
                             //Leaves list unchanged.

int n = list.get(3);  //example of auto-unboxing
                      //Integer is retrieved and converted to int
                      //n contains 9

Integer x = list.set(3, 5);  //list is 0 1 4 5
                             //x contains Integer with value 9

x = list.remove(2);          //list is 0 1 5
                             //x contains Integer with value 4

list.add(1, 7);              //list is 0 7 1 5

list.add(2, 8);              //list is 0 7 8 1 5
```

> **Example 2**

```
/** Swap two values in list, indexed at i and j. */
public static void swap(ArrayList<E> list, int i, int j)
{
    E temp = list.get(i);
    list.set(i, list.get(j));
    list.set(j, temp);
}
```

> **Example 3**

```
/** Returns an ArrayList of random integers from 0 to 100. */
public static ArrayList<Integer> getRandomIntList()
{
    ArrayList<Integer> list = new ArrayList<Integer>();
    System.out.print("How many integers? ");
    int length = ...;      //read user input
    for (int i = 0; i < length; i++)
    {
        int newNum = (int) (Math.random() * 101);
        list.add(newNum);   //autoboxing
    }
    return list;
}
```

## Traversing an `ArrayList`

To traverse an `ArrayList` means to access all of the elements of the list using an iteration statement (`for` loop, `while` loop, or enhanced `for` loop).

Here are several examples to illustrate different types of traversals.

For simple accessing—for example, printing each element or adding each element to a running total, etc.—an enhanced `for` loop is a convenient method of traversal.

> **Example 4**

```
/** Print all negatives in list.
 * Precondition: list contains Integer values.
 */
public static void printNegs(ArrayList<Integer> list)
{
    System.out.println("The negative values in the list are: ");
    for (Integer i : list)
        if (i < 0)              //auto-unboxing
            System.out.println(i);
}
```

## Note

Here's how to think of this algorithm: For each `Integer i` in `ArrayList list`, create a local copy of the element, test if it's negative, and print it if negative.

To access an element with a specific index—for example, to replace the element at that index, or insert an element at that index—use an index traversal. Since the indices for an `ArrayList` start at 0 and end at `list.size()-1`, trying to access an element with an index value outside of this range will cause an `IndexOutOfBoundsException` to be thrown.

### > Example 5

```
/** Precondition:  ArrayList list contains Integer values sorted in increasing order.
 *  Postcondition: value inserted in its correct position in list.
 */
public static void insert(ArrayList<Integer> list, Integer value)
{
    int index = 0;
    //find insertion point
    while (index < list.size() &&
            value > list.get(index)        //unboxing
        index++;
    //insert value
    list.add(index, value);
}
```

### Note

Suppose `value` is larger than all the elements in `list`. Then the `insert` method will throw an `IndexOutOfBoundsException` if the first part of the test is omitted, that is, `index < list.size()`.

### > Example 6

```
/** Change every even-indexed element of strList to the empty string.
 *  Precondition:  strList contains String values.
 */
public static void changeEvenToEmpty(ArrayList<String> strList)
{
    boolean even = true;
    int index = 0;
    while (index < strList.size())
    {
        if (even)
            strList.set(index, "");
        index++;
        even = !even;
    }
}
```

### Note

Deleting elements during the traversal of an `ArrayList` requires special care to avoid skipping elements.

> **Example 7**

```
/* Remove all occurrences of value from list. */
public static void removeAll(ArrayList<Integer> list, int value)
{
    int index = 0;
    while (index < list.size())
    {
        if (list.get(index) == value)
            list.remove(index);
        else
            index++;
    }
}
```

**Note**

1. The statement

   ```
   list.remove(index);
   ```

   causes the elements to the right of the removed element to be shifted left to fill the "hole." In this case, if `index` is incremented, the current element will be skipped, and if two consecutive elements are equal to `value`, one will be missed and (mistakenly) remain in the list.

2. Trying to add or delete an element during a traversal with an enhanced `for` loop may result in a `ConcurrentModificationException` being thrown. Therefore, if you want to add or delete elements, don't use an enhanced `for` loop to traverse the `ArrayList`.

> **Example 8**

```
ArrayList<Integer> list = new ArrayList<Integer>();
< code to initialize list >

for (Integer num : list)
{
    if (num < 0)
        list.add(0);        //WRONG!
}
```

**Note**

This code segment throws a `ConcurrentModificationException`.

It is okay, however, to use an enhanced `for` loop to *modify* objects that have a mutator method in their class definition.

> **Example 9**

Consider a `Clown` class that has a `changeAct` method, and an `ArrayList<Clown>` that has been initialized with `Clown` objects. The following code is fine.

```
for (Clown c : clownList)
{
    if ( < some condition on Clown c > )
        clownList.changeAct();
}
```

## Random Element Selection

You should know how to return a random element from an array or `ArrayList`.

> **Example 10**

Suppose `responses` is an `ArrayList<String>` of surprised responses the computer may make to a user's crazy input. If the contents of `responses` are currently

| 0 | 1 | 2 | 3 | 4 | 5 |
|---|---|---|---|---|---|
| Oh my! | Say what? | No! | Heavens! | You're kidding me. | Jumping Jellybeans! |

you should be able to randomly return one of these responses. The key is to select a random index from 0 to 5, inclusive, and then return the string in the `responses` list that is at that index.

Recall that the expression `(int)(Math.random()*howMany)` generates a random `int` in the range 0...howMany-1. In the given example, `howMany` is 6, the number of elements in the array. The piece of code that returns a random response is:

```
int randIndex = (int) (Math.random() * 6);
String response = responses.get(randIndex);
```

## Simultaneous Traversal of an `ArrayList` and an Array

In the traversal of a list, if it's important to keep track of indices (positions) in the list, you must use an index traversal. Sometimes an algorithm requires the simultaneous traversal of an array and an `ArrayList`. Try your hand at writing code for the following problems.

> **Example 11**

Consider an `ArrayList<Integer>` list, and an array `arr` of `int` that have both been initialized. A method `getProductSum` returns the sum of products of the values of corresponding elements. Thus, `prodArr[0]` will be the product of `arr[0]` and the first `Integer` value in `list`; `prodArr[1]` will be the product of `arr[1]` and the second `Integer` value in `list`; and so on. The algorithm stops when the end of the shorter list is reached.

Here are some examples:

| list | arr | getProductSum |
|---|---|---|
| [2,1,4] | {5,0,3} | 22 |
| [1,3,5,7,9] | {2,4} | 14 |
| [7,6,5] | {1,2,3,4,5} | 34 |
| [] | {2,3,7} | 0 |

The method `getProductSum`, whose header is given below, returns the sum of products as described above. Write code for the method.

```
public static int getProductSum(ArrayList<Integer> list, int[] arr)
```

✓ **Solution**

```
public static int getProductSum(ArrayList<Integer> list, int[] arr)
{
    int sum = 0;
    int index = 0;

    //Traverse both arr and list, until the end of
    //one of the lists is reached.
    while(index < arr.length && index < list.size())
    {
        sum += arr[index] * list.get(index);      //auto-unboxing;
        index++;
    }
    return sum;
}
```

**Note**

Beware of going off the end of either list!

▷ **Example 12**

Here is a trickier example.

Consider an `ArrayList<Integer>` list and an array arr of int that have both been initialized. An array called productArr is to be created that contains the products of the values of corresponding elements. Thus, prodArr[0] will be the product of arr[0] and the first Integer value in list; prodArr[1] will be the product of arr[1] and the second Integer value in list; and so on. When the end of the shorter list is reached, the algorithm should copy the remaining elements of the longer list into productArr.

Here are some examples:

| list | arr | productArr |
|------|-----|------------|
| [2,1,4] | {5,0,3} | {10, 0, 12} |
| [1,3,5,7,9] | {2,4} | {2,12,5,7,9} |
| [7,6,5] | {1,2,3,4,5} | {7,12,15,4,5} |
| [] | {2,3,7} | {2,3,7} |

The method getProducts, whose header is given below, returns an array of products as described above. Write code for the method.

```
public static int[] getProducts(ArrayList<Integer> list, int[] arr)
```

☑ **Solution**

```
public static int[] getProducts(ArrayList<Integer> list, int[] arr)
{
    int prodArrSize, smallerCount;
    boolean arrayIsLonger;
    //Determine length of prodArray.
    if (list.size() < arr.length)
    {
        prodArrSize = arr.length;
        smallerCount = list.size();
        arrayIsLonger = true;
    }
    else
    {
        prodArrSize = list.size();
        smallerCount = arr.length;
        arrayIsLonger = false;
    }
    int [] prodArray = new int[prodArrSize];
    //Place all products in prodArray.
    for (int i = 0; i < smallerCount; i++)
        prodArray[i] = arr[i] * list.get(i);
    //How many elements must be transferred to prodArray?
    int numExtra = Math.abs(arr.length - list.size());
    //Transfer those final elements to prodArray.
    for (int i = 0; i <= numExtra - 1; i++)
    {
        if (arrayIsLonger)
            prodArray[prodArrSize - numExtra + i] =
                    arr[prodArrSize - numExtra + i];
        else
            prodArray[prodArrSize - numExtra + i] =
                    list.get(prodArrSize - numExtra + i);
    }
    return prodArray;
}
```

**Note**

1. Use Math.abs to get a positive value for the number of extra elements to be copied.
2. prodArray already has slots for the leftover elements that must be copied. But you must be careful in the indexes for these elements that are taken from the end of the longer list and placed in the end slots of the prodArray.

## Two-Dimensional Arrays

A two-dimensional array (matrix) is often the data structure of choice for objects like board games, tables of values, theater seats, and mazes.

Look at the following 3 × 4 matrix:

```
2  6  8  7
1  5  4  0
9  3  2  8
```

If `mat` is the matrix variable, the row subscripts go from 0 to 2 and the column sub-scripts go from 0 to 3. The element `mat[1][2]` is 4, whereas `mat[0][2]` and `mat[2][3]` are both 8. As with one-dimensional arrays, if the subscripts are out of range, an `ArrayIndexOutOfBoundsException` is thrown.

## Declarations

Each of the following declares a two-dimensional array:

```
int[][] table;        //table can reference a 2D array of integers
                      //table is currently a null reference
double[][] matrix = new double[3][4];  //matrix references a 3 × 4
                                       //array of real numbers.
                                       //Each element has value 0.0
String[][] strs = new String[2][5]; //strs references a 2 × 5
                                    //array of String objects.
                                    //Each element is null
```

An *initializer list* can be used to specify a two-dimensional array:

```
int[][] mat = { {3, 4, 5},        //row 0
                {6, 7, 8} };      //row 1
```

This defines a 2 × 3 *rectangular* array (i.e., one in which each row has the same number of elements). All two-dimensional arrays on the AP exam are rectangular.

The initializer list is a list of lists in which each inside list represents a row of the matrix.

## Matrix as Array of Row Arrays

A matrix is implemented as an array of rows, where each row is a one-dimensional array of elements. Suppose `mat` is the 3 × 4 matrix

```
2 6 8 7
1 5 4 0
9 3 2 8
```

Then `mat` is an array of three arrays:

```
mat[0]    contains    {2, 6, 8, 7}
mat[1]    contains    {1, 5, 4, 0}
mat[2]    contains    {9, 3, 2, 8}
```

The quantity `mat.length` represents the number of rows. In this case it equals 3 because there are three row arrays in `mat`. For any given row k, where 0 ≤ k < `mat.length`, the quan-tity `mat[k].length` represents the number of elements in that row—namely, the number of columns. (Java allows a variable number of elements in each row. Since these "jagged arrays" are not part of the AP Java subset, you can assume that `mat[k].length` is the same for all rows k of the matrix, i.e., that the matrix is rectangular.)

## Processing a Two-Dimensional Array

There are three common ways to traverse a two-dimensional array:

- row-column (for accessing elements, modifying elements that are class objects, or replacing elements)

- enhanced `for` loop (for accessing elements or modifying elements that are class objects, but no replacement)

- row-by-row array processing (for accessing, modifying, or replacement of elements)

### Note

A row-by-row traversal, starting in the top, leftmost corner and going from left to right is called a *row-major traversal*:

```
for (row = 0; row < mat.length; row++)
    for (col = 0; col < mat[0].length; col++)
        processElements();
```

A column-by-column traversal, starting in the top, leftmost corner and going from top to bottom is less common and is called a *column-major traversal*:

```
for (col = 0; col < mat[0].length; col++)
    for (row = 0; row < mat.length; row++)
        processElements();
```

### > Example 1

Find the sum of all elements in a matrix `mat`.

### ✓ Solution

Here is a row-column traversal:

```
/** Precondition: mat is initialized with integer values. */
int sum = 0;
for (int r = 0; r < mat.length; r++)
    for (int c = 0; c < mat[r].length; c++)
        sum += mat[r][c];
```

### Note

1. `mat[r][c]` represents the `r`th row and the `c`th column.
2. Rows are numbered from `0` to `mat.length-1`, and columns are numbered from `0` to `mat[r].length-1`. Any index that is outside these bounds will generate an `ArrayIndexOutOfBoundsException`.

Since elements are not being replaced, nested enhanced `for` loops can be used instead:

```
for (int[] row : mat)        //for each row array in mat
    for (int element : row)  //for each element in this row
        sum += element;
```

## Note

You also need to know how to process a matrix as shown below, using a third type of traversal, row-by-row array processing. This traversal

- assumes access to a method that processes an array;
- passes a one-dimensional array reference as a parameter to a method that processes each row;
- traverses the rows using either a regular loop or an enhanced `for` loop.

So, continuing with the example to find the sum of all elements in mat: In the class where mat is defined, suppose you have the method sumArray.

```
/** Returns the sum of integers in arr. */
public int sumArray(int[] arr)
{ /* implementation not shown */ }
```

You could use this method to sum all the elements in mat as follows:

```
int sum = 0;
for (int row = 0; row < mat.length; row++) //for each row in mat,
    sum += sumArray(mat[row]);                //add that row's total to sum
```

Note how, since mat[row] is an array of int for $0 \le row < mat.length$, you can use the sumArray method for each row in mat. Alternatively, you can use an enhanced `for` loop traversal:

```
for (int [] rowArr: mat)       //for each row array in mat
    sum += sumArray(rowArr);   //add that row's total to sum
```

### ▷ Example 2

Add 10 to each element in row 2 of matrix mat.

### ✓ Solution

```
for (int c = 0; c < mat[2].length; c++)
    mat[2][c] += 10;
```

## Note

1. In the `for` loop, you can use `c < mat[k].length`, where $0 \le k < mat.length$, since each row has the same number of elements.
2. You should not use an enhanced `for` loop here because elements are being replaced.
3. You can, however, use row-by-row array processing. Suppose you have method addTen shown below.

    ```
    /** Add 10 to each int in arr */
    public void addTen(int[] arr)
    {
        for (int i = 0; i < arr.length; i++)
            arr[i] += 10;
    }
    ```

    You could add 10 to each element in row 2 with the single statement,

```
addTen(mat[2]);
```

You could also add 10 to every element in mat:

```
for (int row = 0; row < mat.length; row++)
    addTen(mat[row]);
```

## > Example 3

Suppose Card objects have a mutator method changeValue:

```
public void changeValue(int newValue)
{ value = newValue; }
```

Now consider the following declaration.

```
Card[][] cardMatrix;
```

Suppose cardMatrix is initialized with Card objects. A piece of code that traverses the cardMatrix and changes the value of each Card to v is

```
for (Card[] row : cardMatrix)  //for each row array in cardMatrix,
    for (Card c : row)         //for each Card in that row,
        c.changeValue(v);      //change the value of that card
```

Alternatively:

```
for (int row = 0; row < cardMatrix.length; row++)
    for (int col = 0; col < cardMatrix[0].length; col++)
        cardMatrix[row][col].changeValue(v);
```

## Note

The use of the nested enhanced for loop is OK. Modifying the objects in the matrix with a mutator method is fine. What you shouldn't do is *replace* the Card objects with new Cards.

## > Example 4

The major and minor diagonals of a square matrix are shown below:

**Major diagonal**          **Minor diagonal**

You can process the diagonals as follows:

```
int[][] mat = new int[SIZE][SIZE];  //SIZE is a constant int value
for (int i = 0; i < SIZE; i++)
    Process mat[i][i];              //major diagonal
        OR
    Process mat[i][SIZE - i - 1];   //minor diagonal
```

## Two-Dimensional Array as Parameter

### ▷ Example 1

Here is a method that counts the number of negative values in a matrix:

```
/** Returns count of negative values in mat.
 *  Precondition: mat is initialized with integers.
 */
public static int countNegs (int[][] mat)
{
    int count = 0;
    for (int[] row : mat)
        for (int num : row)
            if (num < 0)
                count++;
    return count;
}
```

A method in the same class can invoke this method with a statement such as

```
int negs = countNegs(matrix);
```

### ▷ Example 2

Reading elements into a matrix:

```
/** Returns matrix containing rows × cols integers
 *  read from the keyboard.
 *  Precondition: Number of rows and columns known.
 */
public static int[][] getMatrix(int rows, int cols)
{
    int[][] mat = new int[rows][cols];   //initialize slots
    System.out.println("Enter matrix, one row per line:");
    System.out.println();

    //read user input and fill slots
    for (int r = 0; r < rows; r++)
        for (int c = 0; c < cols; c++)
            mat[r][c] = ...;   //read user input
    return mat;
}
```

To call this method:

```
//prompt for number of rows and columns
int rows = ...;      //read user input
int cols = ...;      //read user input
int[][] mat = getMatrix(rows, cols);
```

### Note

You should not use an enhanced `for` loop in `getMatrix` because elements in `mat` are being replaced. (Their current value is the initialized value of 0. The new value is the input value from the keyboard.)

### Mirror Images

A tricky multiple-choice question on two-dimensional arrays may involve an algorithm that creates some kind of mirror image of a matrix. The code could reflect a matrix across mirrors placed somewhere in the center of the matrix, horizontally, vertically, or diagonally.

Note that if a vertical mirror is placed down the center of a matrix, so that all elements to the left of the mirror are reflected across it, the element `mat[row][col]` reflects across to element `mat[row][numCols-col-1]`.

You should teach yourself to trace the following type of code:

```
public static void matrixMethod(int[][] mat)
{
    int height = mat.length;
    int numCols = mat[0].length;
    for (int col = 0; col < numCols; col++)
        for (int row = 0; row < height/2; row++)
            mat[height - row - 1][col] = mat[row][col];
}
```

What does it do? How does it transform the matrix below?

```
2 3 4
5 6 7
8 9 0
1 1 1
```

The answer is that the algorithm reflects the matrix from top to bottom across a horizontal mirror placed at its center.

```
height = 4, numCols = 3
col takes on values 0, 1, and 2
row takes on values 0 and 1
```

Here are the replacements that are made:

```
col = 0, row = 0: mat[3][0] = mat[0][0]
        row = 1: mat[2][0] = mat[1][0]


col = 1, row = 0: mat[3][1] = mat[0][1]
        row = 1: mat[2][1] = mat[1][1]


col = 2, row = 0: mat[3][2] = mat[0][2]
        row = 1: mat[2][2] = mat[1][2]
```

This transforms the matrix into:

```
2 3 4
5 6 7
5 6 7
2 3 4
```

Note that an enhanced `for` loop was not used in the traversal, because elements in the matrix are being replaced.

## Chapter Summary

Manipulation of one-dimensional arrays, two-dimensional arrays, and array lists should be second nature to you by now. Know the Java subset methods for the `ArrayList<E>` class. You must also know when these methods throw an `IndexOutOfBoundsException` and when an `ArrayIndexOutOfBoundsException` can occur.

When traversing an `ArrayList`:

■ Use an enhanced `for` loop to access each element without changing it, or to modify each object in the list using a mutator method.

■ Take special care with indices when removing multiple elements from an `ArrayList`.

A two-dimensional array is an array of row arrays. The number of rows is `mat.length`. The number of columns is `mat[0].length`.

When traversing a two-dimensional array:

■ Use a row-column traversal to access, modify, or replace elements. Know the difference between row-major order and column-major order.

■ Use a nested `for` loop to access or modify elements, but not replace them.

■ Know how to do row-by-row array processing if you have an appropriate method that takes an array parameter.

# Multiple-Choice Questions on Arrays and Array Lists

1. Which of the following correctly initializes an array `arr` to contain four elements each with value 0?

    I. `int[] arr = {0, 0, 0, 0};`

    II. `int[] arr = new int[4];`

    III. 
    ```
    int[] arr = new int[4];
    for (int i = 0; i < arr.length; i++)
        arr[i] = 0;
    ```

    (A) I only
    (B) III only
    (C) I and III only
    (D) II and III only
    (E) I, II, and III

2. The following program segment is intended to find the index of the first negative integer in `arr[0] ... arr[N-1]`, where `arr` is an array of N integers.

    ```
    int i = 0;
    while (arr[i] >= 0)
    {
        i++;
    }
    location = i;
    ```

    This segment will work as intended
    (A) always.
    (B) never.
    (C) whenever `arr` contains at least one negative integer.
    (D) whenever `arr` contains at least one nonnegative integer.
    (E) whenever `arr` contains no negative integers.

3. Refer to the following code segment. You may assume that `arr` is an array of `int` values.

```
int sum = arr[0], i = 0;
while (i < arr.length)
{
    i++;
    sum += arr[i];
}
```

Which of the following will be the result of executing the segment?

(A) Sum of `arr[0]`, `arr[1]`, ..., `arr[arr.length-1]` will be stored in `sum`.

(B) Sum of `arr[1]`, `arr[2]`, ..., `arr[arr.length-1]` will be stored in `sum`.

(C) Sum of `arr[0]`, `arr[1]`, ..., `arr[arr.length]` will be stored in `sum`.

(D) An infinite loop will occur.

(E) A run-time error will occur.

4. Refer to the following code segment. You may assume that array `arr1` contains elements `arr1[0]`, `arr1[1]`, ..., `arr1[N-1]`, where N = `arr1.length`.

```
int count = 0;
for (int i = 0; i < N; i++)
    if (arr1[i] != 0)
    {
        arr1[count] = arr1[i];
        count++;
    }
int[] arr2 = new int[count];
for (int i = 0; i < count; i++)
    arr2[i] = arr1[i];
```

If array `arr1` initially contains the elements 0, 6, 0, 4, 0, 0, 2 in this order, what will `arr2` contain after execution of the code segment?

(A) 6, 4, 2

(B) 0, 0, 0, 0, 6, 4, 2

(C) 6, 4, 2, 4, 0, 0, 2

(D) 0, 6, 0, 4, 0, 0, 2

(E) 6, 4, 2, 0, 0, 0, 0

5. Consider this program segment.

```
for (int i = 2; i <= k; i++)
    if (arr[i] < someValue)
        System.out.print("SMALL");
```

What is the maximum number of times that SMALL can be printed?
   (A) 0
   (B) 1
   (C) k - 1
   (D) k - 2
   (E) k

6. What will be output from the following code segment, assuming it is in the same class as the doSomething method?

```
int[] arr = {1, 2, 3, 4};
doSomething(arr);
System.out.print(arr[1] + " ");
System.out.print(arr[3]);
    ...
public void doSomething(int[] list)
{
    int[] b = list;
    for (int i = 0; i < b.length; i++)
        b[i] = i;
}
```

   (A) 0 0
   (B) 2 4
   (C) 1 3
   (D) 0 2
   (E) 0 3

7. Consider writing a program that reads the lines of any text file into a sequential list of lines. Which of the following is a good reason to implement the list with an ArrayList of String objects rather than an array of String objects?
   (A) The get and set methods of ArrayList are more convenient than the [] notation for arrays.
   (B) The size method of ArrayList provides instant access to the length of the list.
   (C) An ArrayList can contain objects of any type, which leads to greater generality.
   (D) If any particular text file is unexpectedly long, the ArrayList will automatically be resized. The array, by contrast, may go out of bounds.
   (E) The String methods are easier to use with an ArrayList than with an array.

8. Consider writing a program that produces statistics for long lists of numerical data. Which of the following is the best reason to implement each list with an array of `int` (or `double`), rather than an `ArrayList` of `Integer` (or `Double`) objects?

   (A) An array of primitive number types is more efficient to manipulate than an `ArrayList` of wrapper objects that contain numbers.

   (B) Insertion of new elements into a list is easier to code for an array than for an `ArrayList`.

   (C) Removal of elements from a list is easier to code for an array than for an `ArrayList`.

   (D) Accessing individual elements in the middle of a list is easier for an array than for an `ArrayList`.

   (E) Accessing all the elements is more efficient in an array than in an `ArrayList`.

Refer to the following classes for Questions 9–12.

```java
public class Address
{
    private String name;
    private String street;
    private String city;
    private String state;
    private String zip;

    //constructors
        ...

    //accessors
    public String getName()
    { return name; }
    public String getStreet()
    { return street; }
    public String getCity()
    { return city; }
    public String getState()
    { return state; }
    public String getZip()
    { return zip; }
}

public class Student
{
    private int idNum;
    private double gpa;
    private Address address;

    //constructors
        ...

    //accessors
    public Address getAddress()
    { return address; }
    public int getIdNum()
    { return idNum; }
    public double getGpa()
    { return gpa; }
}
```

9. A client method has this declaration, followed by code to initialize the list.

```
Address[] list = new Address[100];
```

Here is a code segment to generate a list of *names only*.

```
for (Address a : list)
    /* line of code */
```

Which is a correct /* *line of code* */?

(A) System.out.println(Address[i].getName());

(B) System.out.println(list[i].getName());

(C) System.out.println(a[i].getName());

(D) System.out.println(a.getName());

(E) System.out.println(list.getName());

10. The following code segment is to print out a list of addresses.

```
for (Address addr : list)
{
    /* more code */
}
```

Which is a correct replacement for /* *more code* */?

```
I. System.out.println(list[i].getName());
   System.out.println(list[i].getStreet());
   System.out.print(list[i].getCity() + ", ");
   System.out.print(list[i].getState() + " ");
   System.out.println(list[i].getZip());
```

```
II. System.out.println(addr.getName());
    System.out.println(addr.getStreet());
    System.out.print(addr.getCity() + ", ");
    System.out.print(addr.getState() + " ");
    System.out.println(addr.getZip());
```

```
III. System.out.println(addr);
```

(A) I only

(B) II only

(C) III only

(D) I and II only

(E) I, II, and III

11. A client method has this declaration.

```
Student[] allStudents = new Student[NUM_STUDS];  //NUM_STUDS is
                                                  //an int constant
```

Here is a code segment to generate a list of Student names only. (You may assume that allStudents has been initialized.)

```
for (Student student : allStudents)
    /* code to print list of names */
```

Which is a correct replacement for /* *code to print list of names* */?

(A) `System.out.println(allStudents.getName());`

(B) `System.out.println(student.getName());`

(C) `System.out.println(student.getAddress().getName());`

(D) `System.out.println(allStudents.getAddress().getName());`

(E) `System.out.println(student[i].getAddress().getName());`

12. Here is a method that locates the Student with the highest idNum.

```
/** Returns Student with highest idNum.
 *  Precondition: Array stuArr of Student is initialized.
 */
public static Student locate(Student[] stuArr)
{
    /* method body */
}
```

Which of the following could replace /* *method body* */ so that the method works as intended?

I.
```
int max = stuArr[0].getIdNum();
for (Student student : stuArr)
    if (student.getIdNum() > max)
    {
        max = student.getIdNum();
        return student;
    }
return stuArr[0];
```

II.
```
Student highestSoFar = stuArr[0];
int max = stuArr[0].getIdNum();
for (Student student : stuArr)
    if(student.getIdNum() > max)
    {
        max = student.getIdNum();
        highestSoFar = student;
    }
return highestSoFar;
```

III.
```
int maxPos = 0;
for(int i = 1; i < stuArr.length; i++)
    if(stuArr[i].getIdNum() > stuArr[maxPos].getIdNum())
        maxPos = i;
return stuArr[maxPos];
```

(A) I only
(B) II only
(C) III only
(D) I and III only
(E) II and III only

Questions 13–15 refer to the Ticket and Transaction classes below.

```java
public class Ticket
{
    private String row;
    private int seat;
    private double price;

    //constructor
    public Ticket(String aRow, int aSeat, double aPrice)
    {
        row = aRow;
        seat = aSeat;
        price = aPrice;
    }

    //accessors getRow(), getSeat(), and getPrice()
        ...

}


public class Transaction
{
    private int numTickets;
    private Ticket[] tickList;

    //constructor
    public Transaction(int numTicks)
    {
        numTickets = numTicks;
        tickList = new Ticket[numTicks];
        String theRow;
        int theSeat;
        double thePrice;
        for (int i = 0; i < numTicks; i++)
        {
            < read user input for theRow, theSeat, and thePrice >
                ...

            /* more code */
        }
    }

    /** Returns total amount paid for this transaction. */
    public double totalPaid()
    {
        double total = 0.0;
        /* code to calculate amount */
        return total;
    }
}
```

13. Which of the following correctly replaces /* *more code* */ in the `Transaction` constructor to initialize the `tickList` array?

    (A) `tickList[i] = new Ticket(getRow(), getSeat(), getPrice());`

    (B) `tickList[i] = new Ticket(theRow, theSeat, thePrice);`

    (C) `tickList[i] = new tickList(getRow(), getSeat(), getPrice());`

    (D) `tickList[i] = new tickList(theRow, theSeat, thePrice);`

    (E) `tickList[i] = new tickList(numTicks);`

14. Which represents correct /* *code to calculate amount* */ in the `totalPaid` method?

    (A)
```
for (Ticket t : tickList)
    total += t.price;
```

    (B)
```
for (Ticket t : tickList)
    total += tickList.getPrice();
```

    (C)
```
for (Ticket t : tickList)
    total += t.getPrice();
```

    (D)
```
Transaction T;
for (Ticket t : T)
    total += t.getPrice();
```

    (E)
```
Transaction T;
for (Ticket t : T)
    total += t.price;
```

15. Suppose it is necessary to keep a list of all ticket transactions. Assuming that there are `NUMSALES` transactions, a suitable declaration would be

    (A) `Transaction[] listOfSales = new Transaction[NUMSALES];`

    (B) `Transaction[] listOfSales = new Ticket[NUMSALES];`

    (C) `Ticket[] listOfSales = new Transaction[NUMSALES];`

    (D) `Ticket[] listOfSales = new Ticket[NUMSALES];`

    (E) `Transaction[] Ticket = new listOfSales[NUMSALES];`

16. The following code fragment is intended to find the smallest value in `arr[0] ... arr[n-1]`, but does not work as intended.

```
/** Precondition:
 *    - arr is an array, arr.length = n.
 *    - arr[0]...arr[n-1] initialized with integers.
 * Postcondition: min = smallest value in arr[0]...arr[n-1].
 */
int min = arr[0];
int i = 1;
while (i < n)
{
    i++;
    if (arr[i] < min)
        min = arr[i];
}
```

For the segment to work as intended, which of the following modifications could be made?

I. Change the line

```
int i = 1;
```

to

```
int i = 0;
```

Make no other changes.

II. Change the body of the `while` loop to

```
{
    if (arr[i] < min)
        min = arr[i];
    i++;
}
```

Make no other changes.

III. Change the test for the `while` loop as follows.

```
while (i <= n)
```

Make no other changes.

(A) I only
(B) II only
(C) III only
(D) I and II only
(E) I, II, and III

17. Refer to method `match` below.

```
/** Returns true if there is an integer k that occurs
 *  in both arrays; otherwise returns false.
 *  Precondition:
 *   - v is an array of int sorted in increasing order
 *   - w is an array of int sorted in increasing order
 *   - N is the number of elements in array v
 *   - M is the number of elements in array w
 *   - v[0]...v[N-1] and w[0]...w[M-1] is initialized with integers.
 *   - v[0] < v[1] < ... < v[N-1] and w[0] < w[1] < ... < w[M-1].
 */
public static boolean match(int[] v, int[] w, int N, int M)
{
    int vIndex = 0, wIndex = 0;
    while (vIndex < N && wIndex < M)
    {
        if (v[vIndex] == w[wIndex])
            return true;
        else if (v[vIndex] < w[wIndex])
            vIndex++;
        else
            wIndex++;
    }
    return false;
}
```

Assuming that the method has not been exited, which assertion is true at the end of every execution of the `while` loop?

(A) `v[0]...v[vIndex-1]` and `w[0]...w[wIndex-1]` contain no common value, `vIndex ≤ N` and `wIndex ≤ M`.

(B) `v[0]...v[vIndex]` and `w[0]...w[wIndex]` contain no common value, `vIndex ≤ N` and `wIndex ≤ M`.

(C) `v[0]...v[vIndex-1]` and `w[0]...w[wIndex-1]` contain no common value, `vIndex ≤ N-1` and `wIndex ≤ M-1`.

(D) `v[0]...v[vIndex]` and `w[0]...w[wIndex]` contain no common value, `vIndex ≤ N-1` and `wIndex ≤ M-1`.

(E) `v[0]...v[N-1]` and `w[0]...w[M-1]` contain no common value, `vIndex ≤ N` and `wIndex ≤ M`.

18. Consider this class.

```java
public class Book
{
    private String title;
    private String author;
    private boolean checkoutStatus;

    public Book(String bookTitle, String bookAuthor)
    {
        title = bookTitle;
        author = bookAuthor;
        checkoutStatus = false;
    }

    /** Change checkout status. */
    public void changeStatus()
    { checkoutStatus = !checkoutStatus; }

    //Other methods are not shown.
}
```

A client program has this declaration.

```java
Book[] bookList = new Book[SOME_NUMBER];
```

Suppose bookList is initialized so that each Book in the list has a title, author, and check-out status. The following piece of code is written, whose intent is to change the checkout status of each book in bookList.

```java
for (Book b : bookList)
    b.changeStatus();
```

Which is true about this code?
- (A) The bookList array will remain unchanged after execution.
- (B) Each book in the bookList array will have its checkout status changed, as intended.
- (C) A NullPointerException may occur.
- (D) A run-time error will occur because it is not possible to modify objects using the enhanced for loop.
- (E) A logic error will occur because it is not possible to modify objects in an array without accessing the indexes of the objects.

Consider this class for Questions 19 and 20.

```
public class BingoCard
{
    private int[] card;

    /** No-argument constructor: Creates BingoCard with
     *  20 random digits in the range 1 - 90.
     */
    public BingoCard()
    { /* implementation not shown */ }

    /* Display BingoCard. */
    public void display()
    { /* implementation not shown */ }
        ...
}
```

A program that simulates a bingo game declares an array of BingoCard. The array has NUMPLAYERS elements, where each element represents the card of a different player. Here is a code segment that creates all the bingo cards in the game.

```
/* declare array of BingoCard */
/* construct each BingoCard */
```

19. Which of the following is a correct replacement for

    /* declare array of BingoCard */?

    (A) int[] BingoCard = new BingoCard[NUMPLAYERS];

    (B) BingoCard[] players = new int[NUMPLAYERS];

    (C) BingoCard[] players = new BingoCard[20];

    (D) BingoCard[] players = new BingoCard[NUMPLAYERS];

    (E) int[] players = new BingoCard[NUMPLAYERS];

20. Assuming that players has been declared as an array of BingoCard, which replacement for /* construct each BingoCard */ is correct?

    ```
    I. for (BingoCard card : players)
            card = new BingoCard();

    II. for (BingoCard card : players)
            players[card] = new BingoCard();

    III. for (int i = 0; i < players.length; i++)
            players[i] = new BingoCard();
    ```

    (A) I only
    (B) II only
    (C) III only
    (D) I and III only
    (E) I, II, and III

Questions 21 and 22 refer to the `Deck` class described below.

A `Deck` class contains an array `cards` with an even number of `Card` values and a `final` variable `NUMCARDS`, which is an odd integer.

21. Here are two possible algorithms for shuffling the deck.

   **Algorithm 1**

   Initialize an array of `Card` called `shuffled` of length `NUMCARDS`.

   Set `k` to 0.

   For `j=0` to `NUMCARDS/2-1`

   - Copy `cards[j]` to `shuffled[k]`

   - Set `k` to `k+2`

   Set `k` to 1.

   For `j=NUMCARDS/2` to `NUMCARDS-1`

   - Copy `cards[j]` to `shuffled[k]`

   - Set `k` to `k+2`

   **Algorithm 2**

   Initialize an array of `Card` called `shuffled` containing `NUMCARDS` slots.

   For `k=0` to `NUMCARDS-1`

   - Repeatedly generate a random integer `j` from 0 to `NUMCARDS-1`,
        until `cards[j]` contains a card not marked as empty

   - Copy `cards[j]` to `shuffled[k]`

   - Set `cards[j]` to empty

   Which is a false statement concerning Algorithms 1 and 2?

   (A) A disadvantage of Algorithm 1 is that it won't generate all possible deck permutations.

   (B) For Algorithm 2, to determine the last element shuffled requires an average of `NUMCARDS` calls to the random number generator.

   (C) Algorithm 2 will lead to more permutations of the deck than Algorithm 1.

   (D) In terms of run time, Algorithm 2 is more efficient than Algorithm 1.

   (E) If Algorithm 1 is repeated several times, it may return the deck to its original state.

22. The following shuffle method is used to shuffle the cards in the Deck class.

```
Line 1: public void shuffle()
Line 2: {
Line 3:     for (int k = NUMCARDS; k > 0; k--)
Line 4:     {
Line 5:         int randPos = (int) (Math.random() * (k + 1));
Line 6:         //swap randomly selected card with card at position k
Line 7:         Card temp = cards[k];
Line 8:         cards[k] = cards[randPos];
Line 9:         cards[randPos] = temp;
Line 10:    }
Line 11: }
```

The method does not work as intended. Which of the following changes should be made to correct the method?

(A) Replace Line 3 with

```
for (int k = NUMCARDS; k >= 0; k--)
```

(B) Replace Line 3 with

```
for (int k = NUMCARDS - 1; k > 0; k--)
```

(C) Replace Line 3 with

```
for (int k = 1; k <= NUMCARDS; k++)
```

(D) Replace Line 5 with

```
int randPos = (int) (Math.random() * k);
```

(E) Replace Lines 7 – 9 with

```
Card temp = cards[randPos];
cards[randPos] = cards[k];
cards[k] = temp;
```

23. Consider these declarations.

```
ArrayList<String> strList = new ArrayList<String>();
String ch = " ";
Integer intOb = new Integer(5);
```

Which statement will cause an error?

(A) strList.add(ch);
(B) strList.add(new String("handy andy"));
(C) strList.add(intOb.toString());
(D) strList.add(ch + 8);
(E) strList.add(intOb + 8);

24. Let `list` be an `ArrayList<Integer>` containing these elements.

    2 5 7 6 0 1

    Which of the following statements would not cause an error to occur? Assume that each statement applies to the given list, independent of the other statements.
    (A) `Object ob = list.get(6);`
    (B) `Integer intOb = list.add(3.4);`
    (C) `list.add(6, 9);`
    (D) `Object x = list.remove(6);`
    (E) `Object y = list.set(6, 8);`

25. Refer to method `insert` below.

```
/** Inserts element in its correct sorted position in list.
 *  Precondition: list contains String values sorted
 *                in decreasing order.
 */
public void insert(ArrayList<String> list, String element)
{
    int index = 0;
    while (element.compareTo(list.get(index)) < 0)
        index++;
    list.add(index, element);
}
```

    Assuming that the type of `element` is compatible with the objects in the list, which is a true statement about the `insert` method?
    (A) It works as intended for all values of `element`.
    (B) It fails for all values of `element`.
    (C) It fails if `element` is greater than the first item in `list` and works in all other cases.
    (D) It fails if `element` is smaller than the last item in `list` and works in all other cases.
    (E) It fails if `element` is either greater than the first item or smaller than the last item in `list` and works in all other cases.

26. Consider the following code segment, applied to `list`, an `ArrayList` of `Integer` values.

```
int len = list.size();
for (int i = 0; i < len; i++)
{
    list.add(i + 1, new Integer(i));
    Object x = list.set(i, new Integer(i + 2));
}
```

    If `list` is initially 6 1 8, what will it be following execution of the code segment?
    (A) 2 3 4 2 1 8
    (B) 2 3 4 6 2 2 0 1 8
    (C) 2 3 4 0 1 2
    (D) 2 3 4 6 1 8
    (E) 2 3 3 2

Questions 27 and 28 are based on the `Coin` and `Purse` classes given below.

```java
/* A simple coin class */
public class Coin
{
    private double value;
    private String name;

    //constructor
    public Coin(double coinValue, String coinName)
    {
        value = coinValue;
        name = coinName;
    }

    /** Returns the value of this coin. */
    public double getValue()
    { return value; }

    /** Returns the name of this coin. */
    public String getName()
    { return name; }

    /** Returns true if this coin equals obj; false otherwise. */
    public boolean equals(Object obj)
    { return name.equals(((Coin) obj).name); }

    //Other methods are not shown.
}


/* A purse holds a collection of coins */
public class Purse
{
    private ArrayList<Coin> coins;

    /** Creates an empty purse. */
    public Purse()
    { coins = new ArrayList<Coin>(); }

    /** Adds aCoin to the purse. */
    public void add(Coin aCoin)
    { coins.add(aCoin); }

    /** Returns the total value of coins in purse. */
    public double getTotal()
    { /* implementation not shown */}

}
```

27. Here is the getTotal method from the Purse class.

```
/** Returns the total value of coins in purse. */
public double getTotal()
{
    double total = 0;
    /* more code */
    return total;
}
```

Which of the following is a correct replacement for /* *more code* */?

(A)
```
for (Coin c : coins)
{
    c = coins.get(i);
    total += c.getValue();
}
```

(B)
```
for (Coin c : coins)
{
    Coin value = c.getValue();
    total += value;
}
```

(C)
```
for (Coin c : coins)
{
    Coin c = coins.get(i);
    total += c.getValue();
}
```

(D)
```
for (Coin c : coins)
{
    total += coins.getValue();
}
```

(E)
```
for (Coin c : coins)
{
    total += c.getValue();
}
```

28. Two coins are said to *match* each other if they have the same name or the same value. You may assume that coins with the same name have the same value and coins with the same value have the same name. A boolean method `find` is added to the `Purse` class.

```
/** Returns true if the purse has a coin that matches aCoin,
 *  false otherwise.
 */
public boolean find(Coin aCoin)
{
    for (Coin c : coins)
    {
        /* code to find match */
    }
    return false;
}
```

Which is a correct replacement for /* *code to find match* */?

```
I.  if (c.equals(aCoin))
        return true;
```

```
II. if ((c.getName()).equals(aCoin.getName()))
        return true;
```

```
III. if ((c.getValue()).equals(aCoin.getValue()))
        return true;
```

(A) I only
(B) II only
(C) III only
(D) I and II only
(E) I, II, and III

29. Which of the following initializes an 8 × 10 matrix with integer values that are perfect squares? (0 is a perfect square.)

```
I.  int[][] mat = new int[8][10];
```

```
II. int[][] mat = new int[8][10];
    for (int r = 0; r < mat.length; r++)
        for (int c = 0; c < mat[r].length; c++)
            mat[r][c] = r * r;
```

```
III. int[][] mat = new int[8][10];
     for (int c = 0; c < mat[r].length; c++)
         for (int r = 0; r < mat.length; r++)
             mat[r][c] = c * c;
```

(A) I only
(B) II only
(C) III only
(D) I and II only
(E) I, II, and III

30. Consider the following code segment.

```
int[][] mat = {{1,3,5},
               {2,4,6},
               {0,7,8},
               {9,10,11}}

for (int col = 0; col < mat[0].length; col++)
    for (int row = mat.length - 1; row > col; row--)
        System.out.println(mat[row][col]);
```

When this code is executed, which will be the fifth element printed?

(A) 3

(B) 4

(C) 5

(D) 6

(E) 7

31. Consider a class that has this private instance variable.

```
private int[][] mat;
```

The class has the following method, alter.

```
public void alter(int c)
{
    for (int i = 0; i < mat.length; i++)
        for (int j = c + 1; j < mat[0].length; j++)
            mat[i][j-1] = mat[i][j];
}
```

If a 3 × 4 matrix mat is

```
1 3 5 7
2 4 6 8
3 5 7 9
```

then alter(1) will change mat to

(A)  1 5 7 7
     2 6 8 8
     3 7 9 9

(B)  1 5 7
     2 6 8
     3 7 9

(C)  1 3 5 7
     3 5 7 9

(D)  1 3 5 7
     3 5 7 9
     3 5 7 9

(E)  1 7 7 7
     2 8 8 8
     3 9 9 9

32. Consider the following method that will alter the matrix `mat`.

```
public static void matStuff(int[][] mat, int row)
{
    int numCols = mat[0].length;
    for (int col = 0; col < numCols; col++)
        mat[row][col] = row;
}
```

Suppose `mat` is originally

```
1  4  9  0
2  7  8  6
5  1  4  3
```

After the method call `matStuff(mat,2)`, matrix `mat` will be

(A)  1  4  9  0
    2  7  8  6
    2  2  2  2

(B)  1  4  9  0
    2  2  2  2
    5  1  4  3

(C)  2  2  2  2
    2  2  2  2
    2  2  2  2

(D)  1  4  2  0
    2  7  2  6
    5  1  2  3

(E)  1  2  9  0
    2  2  8  6
    5  2  4  3

33. Assume that a square matrix mat is defined by

```
int[][] mat = new int[SIZE][SIZE];
//SIZE is an integer constant >= 2
```

What does the following code segment do?

```
for (int i = 0; i < SIZE - 1; i++)
    for (int j = 0; j < SIZE - i - 1; j++)
        swap(mat, i, j, SIZE - j - 1, SIZE - i - 1);
```

You may assume the existence of this swap method.

```
/** Interchange mat[a][b] and mat[c][d]. */
public void swap(int[][] mat, int a, int b, int c, int d)
```

(A) Reflects mat through its major diagonal. For example,

$$
\begin{matrix} 2 & 6 \\ 4 & 3 \end{matrix} \longrightarrow \begin{matrix} 2 & 4 \\ 6 & 3 \end{matrix}
$$

(B) Reflects mat through its minor diagonal. For example,

$$
\begin{matrix} 2 & 6 \\ 4 & 3 \end{matrix} \longrightarrow \begin{matrix} 3 & 6 \\ 4 & 2 \end{matrix}
$$

(C) Reflects mat through a horizontal line of symmetry. For example,

$$
\begin{matrix} 2 & 6 \\ 4 & 3 \end{matrix} \longrightarrow \begin{matrix} 4 & 3 \\ 2 & 6 \end{matrix}
$$

(D) Reflects mat through a vertical line of symmetry. For example,

$$
\begin{matrix} 2 & 6 \\ 4 & 3 \end{matrix} \longrightarrow \begin{matrix} 6 & 2 \\ 3 & 4 \end{matrix}
$$

(E) Leaves mat unchanged.

34. Consider a class `MatrixStuff` that has a private instance variable.

    ```
    private int[][] mat;
    ```

    Refer to method `alter` below that occurs in the `MatrixStuff` class. (The lines are numbered for reference.)

    ```
    Line 1:  /** Precondition:
    Line 2:   *    - the matrix mat is initialized with integers.
    Line 3:   * Postcondition:
    Line 4:   *    - Column c has been removed.
    Line 5:   *    - The last column is filled with zeros.
    Line 6:   */
    Line 7:  public void alter(int[][] mat, int c)
    Line 8:  {
    Line 9:      for (int i = 0; i < mat.length; i++)
    Line 10:         for (int j = c; j < mat[0].length; j++)
    Line 11:             mat[i][j] = mat[i][j+1];
    Line 12:     //code to insert zeros in rightmost column
    Line 13:         ...
    Line 14: }
    ```

    The intent of the method `alter` is to remove column c. Thus, if the input matrix `mat` is

    $$\begin{matrix} 2 & 6 & 8 & 9 \\ 1 & 5 & 4 & 3 \\ 0 & 7 & 3 & 2 \end{matrix}$$

    the method call `alter(mat, 1)` should change `mat` to

    $$\begin{matrix} 2 & 8 & 9 & 0 \\ 1 & 4 & 3 & 0 \\ 0 & 3 & 2 & 0 \end{matrix}$$

    The method does not work as intended. Which of the following changes will correct the problem?

    I.  Change line 10 to

    ```
    for (int j = c; j < mat[0].length - 1; j++)
    ```

    and make no other changes.

    II. Change lines 10 and 11 to

    ```
    for (int j = c + 1; j < mat[0].length; j++)
        mat[i][j-1] = mat[i][j];
    ```

    and make no other changes.

    III. Change lines 10 and 11 to

    ```
    for (int j = mat[0].length - 1; j > c; j--)
        mat[i][j-1] = mat[i][j];
    ```

    and make no other changes.

    (A) I only
    (B) II only
    (C) III only
    (D) I and II only
    (E) I, II, and III

35. This question refers to the following method.

```
public static boolean isThere(String[][] mat, int row, int col,
    String symbol)
{
    boolean yes;
    int i, count = 0;
    for (i = 0; i < SIZE; i++)
        if (mat[i][col].equals(symbol))
            count++;
    yes = (count == SIZE);
    count = 0;
    for (i = 0; i < SIZE; i++)
        if (mat[row][i].equals(symbol))
            count++;
    return (yes || count == SIZE);
}
```

Now consider this code segment.

```
public final int SIZE = 8;
String[][] mat = new String[SIZE][SIZE];
```

Which of the following conditions on a matrix `mat` of the type declared in the code segment will by itself guarantee that

```
isThere(mat, 2, 2, "$")
```

will have the value `true` when evaluated?

   I.  The element in row 2 and column 2 is "$".
  II.  All elements in both diagonals are "$".
 III.  All elements in column 2 are "$".

(A) I only
(B) III only
(C) I and II only
(D) I and III only
(E) II and III only

36. Consider the following method.

```
public static void alterArray(int[] arr)
{
    int mid = arr.length/2;
    for (int i = 0; i < mid; i++)
    {
        int temp = arr[i];
        arr[i] = arr[arr.length - i - 1];
        arr[arr.length - i - 1] = temp;
    }
}
```

If the current state of a matrix mat is

```
2 7 9 5
8 1 4 3
6 5 0 9
```

which matrix will result from the method call `alterArray(mat[2])`?

(A) 2 7 9 5
    3 4 1 8
    6 5 0 9

(B) 2 7 0 5
    8 1 4 3
    6 5 9 9

(C) 5 9 7 2
    3 4 1 8
    9 0 5 6

(D) 2 7 9 5
    8 1 4 3
    9 0 5 6

(E) 5 9 7 2
    8 1 4 3
    6 5 0 9

37. The method `changeNegs` below should replace every occurrence of a negative integer in its matrix parameter with 0.

```
/** Replaces all negative values in mat with 0.
 *  Precondition: mat is initialized with integers.
 */
public static void changeNegs(int[][] mat)
{
    /* code */
}
```

Which is a correct replacement for */* code */*?

```
I. for (int r = 0; r < mat.length; r++)
       for (int c = 0; c < mat[r].length; c++)
           if (mat[r][c] < 0)
               mat[r][c] = 0;
```

```
II. for (int c = 0; c < mat[0].length; c++)
        for (int r = 0; r < mat.length; r++)
            if (mat[r][c] < 0)
                mat[r][c] = 0;
```

```
III. for (int[] row : mat)
         for (int element : row)
             if (element < 0)
                 element = 0;
```

(A) I only

(B) II only

(C) III only

(D) I and II only

(E) I, II, and III

38. A two-dimensional array `rainfall` that contains `double` values will be used to represent the daily rainfall for a given year. In this scheme, `rainfall[month][day]` represents the amount of rain on the given day and month. For example,

    `rainfall[1][15]`    is the amount of rain on Jan. 15
    `rainfall[12][25]`    is the amount of rain on Dec. 25

The array can be declared as follows.

```
double[][] rainfall = new double[13][32];
```

This creates 13 rows indexed from 0 to 12 and 32 columns indexed from 0 to 31, all initialized to 0.0. Row 0 and column 0 will be ignored. Column 31 in row 4 will be ignored, since April 31 is not a valid day. In years that are not leap years, columns 29, 30, and 31 in row 2 will be ignored since Feb. 29, 30, and 31 are not valid days.

Consider the method `averageRainfall` below.

```
/** Precondition:
 *    - rainfall is initialized with values representing amounts
 *       of rain on all valid days.
 *    - Invalid days are initialized to 0.0.
 *    - Feb 29 is not a valid day.
 * Postcondition: Returns average rainfall for the year.
 */
public double averageRainfall(double rainfall[][])
{
    double total = 0.0;
    /* more code */
}
```

Which of the following is a correct replacement for /* *more code* */ so that the postcondition for the method is satisfied?

```
I.  for (int month = 1; month < rainfall.length; month++)
        for (int day = 1; day < rainfall[month].length; day++)
            total += rainfall[month][day];
    return total / (13 * 32);

II. for (int month = 1; month < rainfall.length; month++)
        for (int day = 1; day < rainfall[month].length; day++)
            total += rainfall[month][day];
    return total / 365;

III. for (double[] month : rainfall)
         for (double rainAmt : month)
             total += rainAmt;
     return total / 365;
```

(A) None
(B) I only
(C) II only
(D) III only
(E) II and III only

39. This question is based on the Point class below.

```
public class Point
{
    /** The coordinates. */
    private int x;
    private int y;

    public Point (int xValue, int yValue)
    {
        x = xValue;
        y = yValue;
    }

    /** Returns the x-coordinate of this point. */
    public int getx()
    { return x; }

    /** Returns the y-coordinate of this point. */
    public int gety()
    { return y; }

    /** Sets x and y to new_x and new_y. */
    public void setPoint(int new_x, int new_y)
    {
        x = new_x;
        y = new_y;
    }


    //Other methods are not shown.
}
```

The method changeNegs below takes a matrix of Point objects as parameter and replaces every Point that has at least one negative coordinate with the Point (0,0).

```
/** Replaces every point that has at least one negative coordinate
 *  with Point(0,0).
 *  Precondition:  pointMat is initialized with Point objects.
 */
public static void changeNegs (Point [][] pointMat)
{
    /* code */
}
```

Which is a correct replacement for /* *code* */?

```
 I. for (int r = 0; r < pointMat.length; r++)
        for (int c = 0; c < pointMat[r].length; c++)
            if (pointMat[r][c].getx() < 0
                || pointMat[r][c].gety() < 0)
                    pointMat[r][c].setPoint(0, 0);

II. for (int c = 0; c < pointMat[0].length; c++)
        for (int r = 0; r < pointMat.length; r++)
            if (pointMat[r][c].getx() < 0
                || pointMat[r][c].gety() < 0)
                    pointMat[r][c].setPoint(0, 0);

III. for (Point[] row : pointMat)
        for (Point p : row)
            if (p.getx() < 0 || p.gety() < 0)
                    p.setPoint(0, 0);
```

(A) I only
(B) II only
(C) III only
(D) I and II only
(E) I, II, and III

40. A `Pixel` class has several mutator methods that allow the color of a `Pixel` to be changed. For example,

```
/* Sets amount of red in Pixel to value. */
public void setRed(int value)
{ /* implementation not shown */ }
```

Consider a `Picture` class that has a private instance variable `pixels`, which is a 2D array of `Pixel` objects. There are also `int` variables `rows` and `cols` that contain the number of rows and columns in the `pixels` array.

A method `removeRed` in the `Picture` class sets the red value of every pixel to zero.

```
public void removeRed()
{
    for (int row = 0; row < numRows; row++)
        for (int col = 0; col < numCols; col++)
        {
            /* code to set red value to 0 */
        }
}
```

Which is a correct replacement for /* *code to set red value to 0* */?

I. ```
   Pixel p = pixels[row][col];
   p.setRed(0);
   ```

II. `pixels[row][col].setRed(0);`

III. `pixels[row][col] = 0;`

(A) I only
(B) II only
(C) III only
(D) I and II only
(E) I, II, and III
   ```

41. Consider a class `MatrixStuff` that has a private instance variable `mat`.

    ```
    private int[][] mat;
    ```

The following method uses a vertical mirror down the center of a matrix to reflect the left half of the matrix onto the right. The following two examples show the result of mirroring a two-dimensional array of numbers from left to right vertically. (Another way of saying this is that the right half of the matrix is replaced by a vertical mirror image of the left half.)

**Example 1:**

| mat | | | | | mat after mirroring | | | | |
|---|---|---|---|---|---|---|---|---|---|
| 1 | 2 | 3 | 4 | 5 | 1 | 2 | 3 | 2 | 1 |
| 6 | 7 | 8 | 9 | 10 | 6 | 7 | 8 | 7 | 6 |
| 11 | 12 | 13 | 14 | 15 | 11 | 12 | 13 | 12 | 11 |

**Example 2:**

| mat | | | | mat after mirroring | | | |
|---|---|---|---|---|---|---|---|
| 1 | 2 | 3 | 4 | 1 | 2 | 2 | 1 |
| 5 | 6 | 7 | 8 | 5 | 6 | 6 | 5 |
| 9 | 10 | 11 | 12 | 9 | 10 | 10 | 9 |

```
public static void mirrorVerticalLeftToRight(int[][] mat)
{
    int width = mat[0].length;
    int numRows = mat.length;
    for (int row = 0; row < numRows; row++)
        for (int col = 0; col < width/2; col++)
            /* element assignments */
}
```

Which replacement for */* element assignments */* will make the method work as intended?

(A) `mat[row][col] = mat[row][width - col];`

(B) `mat[row][width - col] = mat[row][col];`

(C) `mat[row][width - 1 - col] = mat[row][col];`

(D) `mat[row][col] = mat[row][width - 1 - col];`

(E) `mat[row][width - 1 - col] = mat[col][row];`

42.  Consider a square matrix in a class that has a private instance variable mat.

```
private int[][] mat;
```

Method alter in the class changes mat.

```
public void alter()
{
    for (int row = 1; row < mat.length; row++)
        for (int col = 0; col < row; col++)
            mat[col][row] = mat[row][col];
}
```

If mat has current value

```
{{1, 2, 3},
 {4, 5, 6},
 {7, 8, 9}}
```

what are the contents of mat after method alter has been executed?

(A)  {{1, 4, 7},
     {4, 5, 8},
     {7, 8, 9}}

(B)  {{1, 4, 7},
     {2, 5, 8},
     {3, 6, 9}}

(C)  {{1, 2, 3},
     {2, 5, 6},
     {3, 6, 9}}

(D)  {{9, 6, 3},
     {8, 5, 6},
     {7, 8, 9}}

(E)  {{1, 2, 3},
     {4, 5, 2},
     {7, 4, 1}}

43. A simple Tic-Tac-Toe board is a 3 × 3 array filled with either X's, O's, or blanks.

    Here is a class for a game of Tic-Tac-Toe.

```
public class TicTacToe
{
    private String[][] board;
    private static final int ROWS = 3;
    private static final int COLS = 3;

    /** Construct an empty board. */
    public TicTacToe()
    {
        board = new String[ROWS][COLS];
        for (int r = 0; r < ROWS; r++)
            for (int c = 0; c < COLS; c++)
                board[r][c] = " ";
    }

    /** Places symbol on board[r][c].
     *  Precondition: The square board[r][c] is empty.
     */
    public void makeMove(int r, int c, String symbol)
    {
        board[r][c] = symbol;
    }

    /** Creates a string representation of the board, e.g.
     *     |o  |
     *     |xx |
     *     |  o|
     * Returns the string representation of board.
     */
    public String toString()
    {
        String s = "";      //empty string
        /* more code */
        return s;
    }
}
```

Which segment represents a correct replacement for /* *more code* */ for the toString method?

(A)
```
for (int r = 0; r < ROWS; r++)
{
    for (int c = 0; c < COLS; c++)
    {
        s = s + "|";
        s = s + board[r][c];
        s = s + "|\n";
    }
}
```

(B)
```
for (int r = 0; r < ROWS; r++)
{
    s = s + "|";
    for (int c = 0; c < COLS; c++)
    {
        s = s + board[r][c];
        s = s + "|\n";
    }
}
```

(C)
```
for (int r = 0; r < ROWS; r++)
{
    s = s + "|";
    for (int c = 0; c < COLS; c++)
        s = s + board[r][c];
}
s = s + "|\n";
```

(D)
```
for (int r = 0; r < ROWS; r++)
    s = s + "|";
for (int c = 0; c < COLS; c++)
{
    s = s + board[r][c];
    s = s + "|\n";
}
```

(E)
```
for (int r = 0; r < ROWS; r++)
{
    s = s + "|";
    for (int c = 0; c < COLS; c++)
        s = s + board[r][c];
    s = s + "|\n";
}
```

## Answer Key

| | | |
|---|---|---|
| 1. **E** | 16. **B** | 31. **A** |
| 2. **C** | 17. **A** | 32. **A** |
| 3. **E** | 18. **B** | 33. **B** |
| 4. **A** | 19. **D** | 34. **D** |
| 5. **C** | 20. **C** | 35. **B** |
| 6. **C** | 21. **D** | 36. **D** |
| 7. **D** | 22. **B** | 37. **D** |
| 8. **A** | 23. **E** | 38. **E** |
| 9. **D** | 24. **C** | 39. **E** |
| 10. **B** | 25. **D** | 40. **D** |
| 11. **C** | 26. **A** | 41. **C** |
| 12. **E** | 27. **E** | 42. **A** |
| 13. **B** | 28. **D** | 43. **E** |
| 14. **C** | 29. **D** | |
| 15. **A** | 30. **E** | |

## Answer Explanations

1. **(E)** Segment I is an initializer list which is equivalent to

```
int[] arr = new int[4];
arr[0] = 0;
arr[1] = 0;
arr[2] = 0;
arr[3] = 0;
```

   Segment II creates four slots for integers, which by default are initialized to 0. The `for` loop in segment III is therefore unnecessary. It is not, however, incorrect.

2. **(C)** If `arr` contains no negative integers, the value of `i` will eventually exceed `N-1`, and `arr[i]` will cause an `ArrayIndexOutOfBoundsException` to be thrown.

3. **(E)** The intent is to sum elements `arr[0]`, `arr[1]`, ..., `arr[arr.length-1]`. Notice, however, that when `i` has the value `arr.length-1`, it is incremented to `arr.length` in the loop, so the statement `sum += arr[i]` uses `arr[arr.length]`, which is out of range.

4. **(A)** The code segment has the effect of removing all occurrences of 0 from array `arr1`. The algorithm copies the nonzero elements to the front of `arr1`. Then it transfers them to array `arr2`.

5. **(C)** If `arr[i]` < `someValue` for all `i` from 2 to `k`, `SMALL` will be printed on each iteration of the `for` loop. Since there are `k - 1` iterations, the maximum number of times that `SMALL` can be printed is `k - 1`.

6. **(C)** Array `arr` is changed by `doSomething`. Here are the memory slots:

Just before `doSomething` is called:

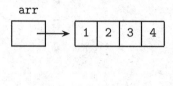

Just after `doSomething` is called, but before the `for` loop is executed:

Just before exiting `doSomething`:

Just after exiting `doSomething`:

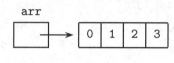

7. **(D)** Arrays are of fixed length and do not shrink or grow if the size of the data set varies. An `ArrayList` automatically resizes the list. Choice A is false: The [] notation is compact and easy to use. Choice B is not a valid reason because an array `arr` also provides instant access to its length with the quantity `arr.length`. Choice C is invalid because an array can also contain objects. Also, generality is beside the point in the given program: The list *must* hold `String` objects. Choice E is false: Whether a `String` object is `arr[i]` or `list.get(i)`, the `String` methods are equally easy to invoke.

8. **(A)** In order for numerical elements to be added to an `ArrayList`, each element must be wrapped in a wrapper class before insertion into the list. Then, to retrieve a numerical value from the `ArrayList`, the element must be unboxed using the `intValue` or `doubleValue` methods. Even though these operations can be taken care of with autoboxing and unboxing, there are efficiency costs. In an array, you simply use the [] notation for assignment (as in `arr[i] = num`) or retrieval (`value = arr[i]`). Note that choices B and C are false statements: Both insertion and deletion for an array involve writing code to shift elements. An `ArrayList` automatically takes care of this through its `add` and `remove` methods. Choice D is a poor reason for choosing an array. While the `get` and `set` methods of `ArrayList` might be slightly more awkward than using the [] notation, both mechanisms work pretty easily. Choice E is false: Efficiency of access is roughly the same.

9. **(D)** For each `Address` object `a` in `list`, access the name of the object with `a.getName()`.

10. **(B)** Since the `Address` class does not have a `toString` method, each data field must explicitly be printed. Segment III would work if there *were* a `toString` method for the class (but there isn't, so it doesn't!). Segment I fails because of incorrect use of the enhanced `for` loop: The array index should not be accessed.

11. **(C)**  Each `Student` name must be accessed via the `getName()` accessor of the `Address` class. The expression `student.getAddress()` accesses the entire address of that student. The `name` field is then accessed using the `getName()` accessor of the `Address` class.

12. **(E)**  Both correct solutions are careful not to lose the student who has the highest `idNum` so far. Segment II does it by storing a reference to the student, `highestSoFar`. Segment III does it by storing the array index of that student. Code segment I is incorrect because it returns the first student whose `idNum` is greater than `max`, not necessarily the student with the highest `idNum` in the list.

13. **(B)**  For each `i`, `tickList[i]` is a new `Ticket` object that must be constructed using the `Ticket` constructor. Therefore eliminate choices C, D, and E. Choice A is wrong because `getRow()`, `getSeat()`, and `getPrice()` are accessors for values *that already exist* for some `Ticket` object. Note also the absence of the dot member construct.

14. **(C)**  To access the price for each `Ticket` in the `tickList` array, the `getPrice()` accessor in the `Ticket` class must be used, since `price` is private to that class. This eliminates choices A and E. Choice B uses the array name incorrectly. Choices D and E incorrectly declare a `Transaction` object. (The method applies to an existing `Transaction` object.)

15. **(A)**  An array of type `Transaction` is required. This eliminates choices C and D. Additionally, choices B and D incorrectly use type `Ticket` on the right-hand side. Choice E puts the identifier `listOfSales` in the wrong place.

16. **(B)**  There are two problems with the segment as given:

    1. `arr[1]` is not tested.
    2. When `i` has a value of `n-1`, incrementing `i` will lead to an out-of-range error for the `if(arr[i] < min)` test.

    Modification II corrects both these errors. The change suggested in III corrects neither of these errors. The change in I corrects (1) but not (2).

17. **(A)**  Notice that either `vIndex` or `wIndex` is incremented at the end of the loop. This means that, when the loop is exited, the current values of `v[vIndex]` and `w[wIndex]` have not been compared. Therefore, you can only make an assertion for values `v[0]..v[vIndex-1]` and `w[0]..w[wIndex-1]`. Also, notice that if there is no common value in the arrays, the exiting condition for the `while` loop will be that the end of one of the arrays has been reached, namely `vIndex` equals `N` or `wIndex` equals `M`.

18. **(B)**  Objects in an array can be changed in an enhanced `for` loop by using mutator methods of the objects' class. The `changeStatus` method, a mutator in the `Book` class, will work as intended in the given code. Choice C would be true if it were not given that each `Book` in `bookList` was initialized. If any given `b` had a value of `null`, then a `NullPointerException` would be thrown.

19. **(D)**  The declaration must start with the type of value in the array, namely `BingoCard`. This eliminates choices A and E. Eliminate choice B: The type on the right of the assignment should be `BingoCard`. Choice C is wrong because the number of slots in the array should be `NUMPLAYERS`, not 20.

20. **(C)**  Segment III is the only segment that works, since the enhanced `for` loop should not be used to replace elements in an array. After the declaration

    ```
    BingoCard[] players = new BingoCard[NUMPLAYERS];
    ```

    each element in the `players` array is `null`. The intent in the given code is to replace each null reference with a newly constructed `BingoCard`.

21. **(D)** The big defect of Algorithm 2 is that it eventually slows down. This is because every time it selects an empty element, it has to loop again. Each of the other choices is true. In choice A, for example, the element `cards[0]` always moves to `shuffled[0]`, eliminating all permutations that have `cards[0]` in a different slot. For choice B, by the time you get to assign the last element, all but two slots of the `cards` array are marked empty. So, on average, you will need to go through `NUMCARDS` tries to find one of those two nonempty slots. For choice C, even though Algorithm 2 is slow, in theory every element in `cards` could land in any given slot in `shuffled`. This is not true for Algorithm 1, where the first element never budges out of the first slot. For choice E, because of the precise ordering of elements in Algorithm 1, the array will always eventually return to its original state, assuming there are sufficient iterations.

22. **(B)** If `k` starts with the value `NUMCARDS`, the method encounters `cards[NUMCARDS]` on Line 7 and throws an `ArrayIndexOutOfBoundsException`.

23. **(E)** All elements added to `strList` must be of type `String`. Each choice satisfies this except choice E. Note that in choice D, the expression `ch + 8` becomes a `String` since `ch` is a `String` (just one of the operands needs to be a `String` to convert the whole expression to a `String`). In choice E, neither `intOb` nor 8 is a `String`.

24. **(C)** The effect of choice C is to adjust the size of the list to 7 and to add the `Integer` 9 to the last slot (i.e., the slot with index 6). Choices A, D, and E will all cause an `IndexOutOfBoundsException` because there is no slot with index 6: the last slot has index 5. Choice B will cause a compile-time error, since it is attempting to add an element of type `Double` to a list of type `Integer`.

25. **(D)** If `element` is smaller than the last item in the list, it will be compared with every item in the list. Eventually `index` will be incremented to a value that is out of bounds. To avoid this error, the test in the `while` loop should be

    ```
    while(index < list.size() && element.compareTo(list.get(index)) < 0)
    ```

    Notice that if `element` is greater than or equal to at least one item in `list`, the test as given in the problem will eventually be false, preventing an out-of-range error.

26. **(A)** Recall that `add(index, obj)` shifts all elements, starting at `index`, one unit to the right, then inserts `obj` at position `index`. The `set(index, obj)` method replaces the element in position `index` with `obj`. So here is the state of `list` after each change:

    ```
    i = 0     6 0 1 8
              2 0 1 8
    i = 1     2 0 1 1 8
              2 3 1 1 8
    i = 2     2 3 1 2 1 8
              2 3 4 2 1 8
    ```

27. **(E)** The value of each `Coin` `c` in `coins` must be accessed with `c.getValue()`. This eliminates choice D. Eliminate choices A and B: The loop accesses each `Coin` in the `coins` `ArrayList`, which means that there should not be any statements attempting to get the next `Coin`. Choice B would be correct if the first statement in the loop body were

    ```
    double value = c.getValue();
    ```

28. **(D)** Code segment III is wrong because the `equals` method is defined for objects only. Since `getValue` returns a `double`, the quantities `c.getValue()` and `aCoin.getValue()` must be compared either using `==`, or as described in the box on p. 70 (better).

29. **(D)**   Segment II is the straightforward solution.  Segment I is correct because it initializes all slots of the matrix to 0, a perfect square.  (By default, all arrays of `int` or `double` are initialized to 0.)  Segment III fails because `r` is undefined in the condition `c < mat[r].length`. In order to do a column-by-column traversal, you need to get the number of columns in each row. The outer `for` loop could be

```
for (int c = 0; c < mat[0].length; c++)
```

Now segment III works.  Note that since the array is rectangular, you can use any index `k` in the conditional `c < mat[k].length`, provided that `k` satisfies the condition $0 \le k < \text{mat.length}$ (the number of rows).

30. **(E)**  When `col` is 0: `row` is 3, then 2, then 1.
    When `col` is 1: `row` is 3, then 2.
    When `col` is 2: `row` is 3.

    Here are the corresponding elements, in order, that are printed:

    ```
    mat[3][0], mat[2][0], mat[1][0],
    mat[3][1], mat[2][1],
    mat[3][2]
    ```

    The fifth element in the list is `mat[2][1]`, which is 7.

31. **(A)**  Method `alter` shifts all the columns, starting at column `c+1`, one column to the left.  Also, it does it in a way that overwrites column `c`.  Here are the replacements for the method call `alter(1)`:

    ```
    mat[0][1] = mat[0][2]
    mat[0][2] = mat[0][3]
    mat[1][1] = mat[1][2]
    mat[1][2] = mat[1][3]
    mat[2][1] = mat[2][2]
    mat[2][2] = mat[2][3]
    ```

32. **(A)**  `matStuff` processes the row selected by the row parameter, 2 in the method call.  The row value, 2, overwrites each element in row 2. Don't make the mistake of selecting choice B—the row labels are 0, 1, 2.

33. **(B)**  Hand execute this for a $2 \times 2$ matrix. `i` goes from 0 to 0 and `j` goes from 0 to 0, so the only interchange is swap `mat[0][0]` with `mat[1][1]`, which suggests choice B. Check with a $3 \times 3$ matrix:

    ```
    i = 0   j = 0   swap mat[0][0] with mat[2][2]
            j = 1   swap mat[0][1] with mat[1][2]
    i = 1   j = 0   swap mat[1][0] with mat[2][1]
    ```

    The elements to be interchanged are shown paired in the following figure.  The result will be a reflection through the minor diagonal.

34. **(D)** The method as given will throw an `ArrayIndexOutOfBoundsException`. For the matrix in the example, `mat[0].length` is 4. The call `mat.alter(1)` gives `c` a value of 1. Thus, in the inner `for` loop, `j` goes from 1 to 3. When `j` is 3, the line `mat[i][j] = mat[i][j+1]` becomes `mat[i][3] = mat[i][4]`. Since columns go from 0 to 3, `mat[i][4]` is out of range. The changes in segments I and II both fix this problem. In each case, the correct replacements are made for each row `i`: `mat[i][1] = mat[i][2]` and `mat[i][2] = mat[i][3]`. Segment III makes the following incorrect replacements as `j` goes from 3 to 2: `mat[i][2] = mat[i][3]` and `mat[i][1] = mat[i][2]`. This will cause both columns 1 and 2 to be overwritten. Before inserting zeros in the last column, `mat` will be

$$
\begin{array}{cccc}
2 & 9 & 9 & 9 \\
1 & 3 & 3 & 3 \\
0 & 2 & 2 & 2
\end{array}
$$

This does not achieve the intended postcondition of the method.

35. **(B)** For the method call `isThere(mat, 2, 2, "$")`, the code counts how many times `"$"` appears in row 2 and how many times in column 2. The method returns `true` only if `count == SIZE` for either the row or column pass (i.e., the whole of row 2 or the whole of column 2 contains the symbol `"$"`). This eliminates choices I and II.

36. **(D)** The matrix `mat` consists of an array of rows, `mat[0]`, `mat[1]`, `mat[2]`, each of which is an array. The method `alterArray` swaps the first and last elements of an array, then the second and second-last elements, and so on, until it reaches the middle of the array. The method call `alterArray(mat[2])` performs this series of swaps on row 2 of the matrix, the bottom row, resulting in the matrix in choice D.

37. **(D)** Segment I is a row-by-row traversal; segment II is a column-by-column traversal. Each achieves the correct postcondition. Segment III traverses the matrix but does not alter it. All that is changed is the local variable `element`. You cannot use this kind of loop to replace elements in an array.

38. **(E)** Since there are 365 valid days in a year, the divisor in calculating the average must be 365. It may appear that segments II and III are incorrect because they include rainfall for invalid days in `total`. Since these values are initialized to `0.0`, however, including them in the total won't affect the final result.

39. **(E)** This is similar to the previous question, but in this case segment I is also correct. This is because instead of *replacing* a matrix element, you are *modifying* it using a mutator method.

40. **(D)** Segment I works because `p` is a reference to the element `pixels[row][col]`. Changing `p` with a mutator method will change the array. Segment II changes the two-dimensional array directly. Segment III fails because `pixels` is not an array of integers.

41. **(C)** Look at Example 2 for this question:

| | mat | | | | mat after mirroring | | |
|---|---|---|---|---|---|---|---|
| 1 | 2 | 3 | 4 | 1 | 2 | 2 | 1 |
| 5 | 6 | 7 | 8 | 5 | 6 | 6 | 5 |
| 9 | 10 | 11 | 12 | 9 | 10 | 10 | 9 |

Now consider one element, 12, say. It must be replaced by its vertical mirror image 9, i.e., mat[2][3]=mat[2][0]. The value of width is 4. See which expression in the answer choices correctly makes this assignment. Eliminate choices A and D right away because col can only have the values 0 and 1 in this algorithm, so mat[2][3] will not be assigned. In choice B, when col has value 1, mat[2][3]=mat[2][1], an incorrect assignment. Choice C works: when row is 2 and col is 0, mat[2][3]=mat[2][0]. In choice E, when row is 2 and col is 0, the assignment mat[2][3]=mat[0][2] is incorrect.

42. **(A)** Method alter places a mirror along the major diagonal and reflects the elements from left to right across this diagonal.

```
1 2 3
4 5 6
7 8 9
```

In this algorithm, when row is 1, col can only be 0, and when row is 2, col takes on the values 0 and 1. Thus, only three elements are altered: mat[0][1], mat[0][2], and mat[1][2]. (Note that the method assigns values to mat[col][row].) These elements are all to the right of the diagonal. Choice A is the only choice that leaves elements to the left of the diagonal unchanged.

43. **(E)** There are three things that must be done in each row:

■ Add an opening boundary line:

```
s = s + "|";
```

■ Add the symbol in each square:

```
for (int c = 0; c < COLS; c++)
    s = s + board[r][c];
```

■ Add a closing boundary line and go to the next line:

```
s = s + "|\n";
```

All of these statements must therefore be enclosed in the outer for loop, that is,

```
for (int r = ...)
```

# 8
# Recursion

## Learning Objectives

In this chapter, you will learn:

→ Recursive methods

→ General form of simple recursive methods

→ Writing recursive methods

→ Analysis of recursive methods

→ Recursive helper methods

→ Recursion in two-dimensional grids

## Recursive Methods

A *recursive method* is a method that calls itself. For example, here is a program that calls a recursive method stackWords:

```
public class WordPlay
{
    public static void stackWords()
    {
        String word = ...;      //read user input
        if (word.equals("."))
            System.out.println();
        else
            stackWords();
        System.out.println(word);
    }

    public static void main(String args[])
    {
        System.out.println("Enter list of words, one per line.");
        System.out.println("Final word should be a period (.)");
        stackWords();
    }
}
```

> In the multiple-choice section of the AP exam, you will be asked to understand and trace recursive methods. You will not, however, be asked to come up with code for recursive methods in the free-response part of the exam.

Here is the output if you enter

```
hold
my
hand
.
```

You get

.
hand
my
hold

The program reads in a list of words terminated with a period, and prints the list in reverse order, starting with the period. How does this happen?

Each time the recursive call to stackWords() is made, execution goes back to the start of a new method call. The computer must remember to complete all the pending calls to the method. It does this by stacking the statements that must still be executed as follows: The first time stackWords() is called, the word "hold" is read and tested for being a period. No, it's not, so stackWords() is called again. The statement to output "hold" (which has not yet been executed) goes on a stack, and execution goes to the start of the method. The word "my" is read. No, it's not a period, so the command to output "my" goes on the stack. And so on. You should picture the stack as looking something like this before the recursive call in which the period is read:

|                                    |
|                                    |
| System.out.println("hand");        |
| System.out.println("my");          |
| System.out.println("hold");        |

Imagine that these statements are stacked like plates. In the final stackWords() call, word has the value ".". Yes, it *is* a period, so the stackWords() line is skipped, the period is printed on the screen, and the method call terminates. The computer now completes each of the previous method calls in turn by "popping" the statements off the top of the stack. It prints "hand", then "my", then "hold", and execution of method stackWords() is complete.[1]

### Note

1. Each time stackWords() is called, a new local variable word is created.
2. The first time the method actually terminates, the program returns to complete the most recently invoked previous call. That's why the words get reversed in this example.

## General Form of Simple Recursive Methods

Every recursive method has two distinct parts:

- A base case or termination condition that causes the method to end.
- A nonbase case whose actions move the algorithm toward the base case and termination.

Here is the framework for a simple recursive method that does not return a value:

---

[1]Actually, the computer stacks the pending statements in a recursive method call more efficiently than the way described. But *conceptually* this is how it is done.

```
public void recursiveMeth( ... )
{
    if (base case)
        < Perform some action >
    else
    {
        < Perform some other action >
        recursiveMeth( ... );     //recursive method call
    }
}
```

The base case typically occurs for the simplest case of the problem, such as when an integer has a value of 0 or 1. Other examples of base cases are when some key is found, or an end-of-file is reached. A recursive algorithm can have more than one base case.

In the `else` or nonbase case of the framework shown, the code fragment < *Perform some other action* > and the method call `recursiveMeth` can sometimes be interchanged without altering the net effect of the algorithm. Be careful though, because what *does* change is the order of executing statements. This can sometimes be disastrous. (See the `eraseBlob` example on p. 318.)

## > Example 1

```
public void drawLine(int n)
{
    if (n == 0)
        System.out.println("That's all, folks!");
    else
    {
        for (int i = 1; i <= n; i++)
            System.out.print("*");
        System.out.println();
        drawLine(n - 1);
    }
}
```

The method call `drawLine(3)` produces this output:

```
***
**
*
That's all, folks!
```

## Note

1. A method that has no pending statements following the recursive call is an example of *tail recursion*. Method `drawLine` is such a case, but `stackWords` is not.
2. The base case in the `drawLine` example is `n == 0`. Notice that each subsequent call, `drawLine(n - 1)`, makes progress toward termination of the method. If your method has no base case, or if you never reach the base case, you will create *infinite recursion*. This is a catastrophic error that will cause your computer eventually to run out of memory and give you heart-stopping messages like `java.lang.StackOverflowError....`

> **Example 2**

```
//Illustrates infinite recursion.
public void catastrophe(int n)
{
    System.out.println(n);
    catastrophe(n);
}
```

> A recursive method must have a base case.

Try running the case `catastrophe(1)` if you have lots of time to waste!

## Writing Recursive Methods

You will not be required to write recursive methods on the AP exam. The sections "Recursive Helper Methods," "Recursion in Two-Dimensional Grids," and "Sample Free-Response Questions 1 and 2" are optional topics. They are included to deepen your understanding of recursion, and to show how recursion is used to solve various coding problems. Recursive algorithms in two-dimensional grids show up often in programming contests, but not on the AP exam. To practice recursion for the exam, you should try all of the multiple-choice questions at the end of this chapter.

> **OPTIONAL TOPIC**

To come up with a recursive algorithm, you have to be able to frame a process *recursively* (i.e., in terms of a simpler case of itself). This is different from framing it *iteratively*, which repeats a process until a final condition is met. A good strategy for writing recursive methods is to first state the algorithm recursively in words.

> **Example 1**

Write a method that returns *n*! (*n* factorial).

| *n*! defined iteratively | *n*! defined recursively |
|---|---|
| 0! = 1 | 0! = 1 |
| 1! = 1 | 1! = (1)(0!) |
| 2! = (2)(1) | 2! = (2)(1!) |
| 3! = (3)(2)(1) | 3! = (3)(2!) |
| … | … |

The general recursive definition for *n*! is

$$n! = \begin{cases} 1 & n = 0 \\ n(n-1)! & n > 0 \end{cases}$$

The definition seems to be circular until you realize that if 0! is defined, all higher factorials are defined. Code for the recursive method follows directly from the recursive definition:

```
/** Compute n! recursively.
 *  Precondition: n is a nonnegative integer.
 */
public static int factorial(int n)
{
    if (n == 0)      //base case
        return 1;
    else
        return n * factorial(n - 1);
}
```

### > Example 2

Write a recursive method `revDigs` that outputs its integer parameter with the digits reversed. For example,

```
revDigs(147)    outputs    741
revDigs(4)      outputs    4
```

First, describe the process recursively: Output the rightmost digit. Then, if there are still digits left in the remaining number n/10, reverse its digits. Repeat this until n/10 is 0. Here is the method:

```
/** Returns n with its digits reversed.
 * Precondition:  n is a nonnegative integer.
 */
public static void revDigs(int n)
{
    System.out.print(n % 10);  //rightmost digit
    if (n / 10 != 0)                //base case
        revDigs(n / 10);
}
```

### Note

On the AP exam, you are expected to "understand and evaluate" recursive methods. This means that you would not be asked to come up with the code for methods such as `factorial` and `revDigs` (as shown above). You could, however, be asked to identify output for any given call to `factorial` or `revDigs`.

## Analysis of Recursive Methods

Recall the Fibonacci sequence 1, 1, 2, 3, 5, 8, 13, …. The $n$th Fibonacci number equals the sum of the previous two numbers if $n \geq 3$. Recursively,

$$\text{Fib}(n) = \begin{cases} 1, & n = 1, 2 \\ \text{Fib}(n-1) + \text{Fib}(n-2), & n \geq 3 \end{cases}$$

Here is the method:

```
/** Returns the nth Fibonacci number.
 * Precondition:  n is a positive integer.
 */
public static int fib(int n)
{
    if (n == 1 || n == 2)
        return 1;
    else
        return fib(n - 1) + fib(n - 2);
}
```

Notice that there are two recursive calls in the last line of the method. So to find Fib(5), for example, takes eight recursive calls to `fib`!

In general, each call to `fib` makes two more calls, which is the tipoff for an exponential algorithm (i.e., one that is *very* inefficient). This is *much* slower than the run time of the corresponding iterative algorithm (see Chapter 6, Question 14).

You may ask: Since every recursive algorithm can be written iteratively, when should programmers use recursion? Bear in mind that recursive algorithms can incur extra run time and memory. Their major plus is elegance and simplicity of code.

---

**General Rules for Recursion**

1. Avoid recursion for algorithms that involve large local arrays—too many recursive calls can cause memory overflow.
2. Use recursion when it significantly simplifies code.
3. Avoid recursion for simple iterative methods like factorial, Fibonacci, and the linear search on p. 316.
4. Recursion is especially useful for
   - Branching processes like traversing trees or directories.
   - Divide-and-conquer algorithms like merge sort and binary search.

---

## Sorting Algorithms That Use Recursion

Merge sort and quicksort are discussed in Chapter 9.

## Recursive Helper Methods

**OPTIONAL TOPIC**

A common technique in designing recursive algorithms is to have a public nonrecursive driver method that calls a private *recursive helper method* to carry out the task. The main reasons for doing this are:

- To hide the implementation details of the recursion from the user.
- To enhance the efficiency of the program.

> **Example 1**

Consider the simple example of recursively finding the sum of the first *n* positive integers.

```
/** Returns 1 + 2 + 3 + ... + n.
 * Precondition: n is a positive integer.
 */
public static int sum(int n)
{
    if (n == 1)
        return 1;
    else
        return n + sum(n - 1);
}
```

Notice that you get infinite recursion if *n* ≤ 0. Suppose you want to include a test for *n* > 0 before you execute the algorithm. Placing this test in the recursive method is inefficient because if *n* is initially positive, it will remain positive in subsequent recursive calls. You can avoid this problem by using a driver method called getSum, which does the test on *n just once*. The recursive method sum becomes a private helper method.

```
public class FindSum
{
    /** Private recursive helper method.
     * Returns 1 + 2 + 3 + ... + n.
     * Precondition: n is a positive integer.
     */
    private static int sum(int n)
    {
        if (n == 1)
            return 1;
        else
            return n + sum(n - 1);
    }

    /* Driver method */
    public static int getSum(int n)
    {
        if (n > 0)
            return sum(n);
        else
        {
            throw new IllegalArgumentException
                    ("Error: n must be positive");
        }
    }
}
```

**Note**

This is a trivial method used to illustrate a private recursive helper method. In practice, you would never use recursion to find a simple sum!

> **Example 2**

Consider a recursive solution to the problem of doing a sequential search for a key in an array of strings. If the key is found, the method returns `true`; otherwise it returns `false`.

The solution can be stated recursively as follows:

- If the key is in `a[0]`, then the key is found.

- If not, recursively search the array starting at `a[1]`.

- If you are past the end of the array, then the key wasn't found.

Here is a straightforward (but inefficient) implementation:

```java
public class Searcher
{
    /** Recursively search array a for key.
     *  Returns true if a[k] equals key for 0 <= k < a.length;
     *  false otherwise.
     */
    public boolean search(String[] a, String key)
    {
        if (a.length == 0)  //base case. key not found
            return false;
        else if (a[0].compareTo(key) == 0) //base case
            return true;                    //key found
        else
        {
            String[] shorter = new String[a.length-1];
            for (int i = 0; i < shorter.length; i++)
                shorter[i] = a[i+1];
            return search(shorter, key);
        }
    }

    public static void main(String[] args)
    {
        String[] list = {"Mary", "Joe", "Lee", "Jake"};
        Searcher s = new Searcher();
        System.out.println("Enter key: Mary, Joe, Lee or Jake.");
        String key = ...;  //read user input
        boolean result = s.search(list, key);
        if (!result)
            System.out.println(key + " was not found.");
        else
            System.out.println(key + " was found.");
    }
}
```

Notice how horribly inefficient the `search` method is: For each recursive call, a new array `shorter` has to be created! It is much better to use a parameter, `startIndex`, to keep track of where you are in the array. Replace the `search` method above with the following one, which calls the private helper method `recurSearch`:

```
/** Driver method. Searches array a for key.
 *  Returns true if a[k] equals key for 0 <= k < a.length;
 *  false otherwise.
 *  Precondition:  a contains at least one element.
 */
public boolean search(String[] a, String key)
{
    return recurSearch(a, 0, key);
}


/** Recursively searches array a for key, starting at startIndex.
 *  Returns true if a[k] equals key for 0 <= k < a.length;
 *  false otherwise.
 *  Precondition:
 *    - a contains at least one element.
 *    - 0 <= startIndex <= a.length.
 */
private boolean recurSearch(String[] a, int startIndex,
    String key)
{
    if(startIndex == a.length)    //base case. key not found
        return false;
    else if(a[startIndex].compareTo(key) == 0) //base case
        return true;                            //key found
    else
        return recurSearch(a, startIndex+1, key);
}
```

### Note

1. Using the parameter `startIndex` avoids having to create a new array object for each recursive call. Making `startIndex` a parameter of a helper method hides implementation details from the user.
2. The helper method is private because it is called only by `search` within the `Searcher` class.
3. It's easy to modify the `search` method to return the index in the array where the key is found: Make the return type `int` and return `startIndex` if the key is found, –1 (say) if it isn't.

Use a recursive helper method to hide private coding details from a client.

## Recursion in Two-Dimensional Grids

Here is a commonly used technique: using recursion to traverse a two-dimensional array. The problem comes in several different guises, for example,

1. A game board from which you must remove pieces.
2. A maze with walls and paths from which you must try to escape.
3. White "containers" enclosed by black "walls" into which you must "pour paint."

In each case, you will be given a starting position (row, col) and instructions on what to do.

**OPTIONAL TOPIC**

The recursive solution typically involves these steps:

*Check that the starting position is not out of range:*
*If (starting position satisfies some requirement)*
*Perform some action to solve problem*
*RecursiveCall(row + 1, col)*
*RecursiveCall(row − 1, col)*
*RecursiveCall(row, col + 1)*
*RecursiveCall(row, col − 1)*

### ⟩ Example

On the right is an image represented as a square grid of black and white cells. Two cells in an image are part of the same "blob" if each is black and there is a sequence of moves from one cell to the other, where each move is either horizontal or vertical to an adjacent black cell. For example, the diagram represents an image that contains two blobs, one of them consisting of a single cell.

Assuming the following Image class declaration, you are to write the body of the eraseBlob method, using a recursive algorithm.

```java
public class Image
{
    private final int BLACK = 1;
    private final int WHITE = 0;
    private int[][] image;    //square grid
    private int size;         //number of rows and columns

    public Image()   //constructor
    { /* implementation not shown */ }

    public void display()    //displays Image
    { /* implementation not shown */ }

    /** If 0 <= row < size, 0 <= col < size, and image[row][col] is
     *  BLACK, sets all cells in the same blob to WHITE.
     *  Otherwise, image is unchanged.
     *  Precondition: Image is defined with either BLACK or WHITE cells.
     */
    public void eraseBlob(int row, int col)
    /* your code goes here */
}
```

✓ **Solution**

```
public void eraseBlob(int row, int col)
{
    if (row >= 0 && row < size && col >= 0 && col < size)
        if (image[row][col] == BLACK)
        {
            image[row][col] = WHITE;
            eraseBlob(row - 1, col);
            eraseBlob(row + 1, col);
            eraseBlob(row, col - 1);
            eraseBlob(row, col + 1);
        }
}
```

**Note**

1.  The ordering of the four recursive calls is irrelevant.
2.  The test

    ```
    if (image[row][col] == BLACK)
    ```

    can be included as the last piece of the test in the first line:

    ```
    if (row >= 0 && ...
    ```

    If `row` or `col` is out of range, the test will short-circuit, avoiding the dreaded `ArrayIndexOutOfBoundsException`.
3.  If you put the statement

    ```
    image[row][col] = WHITE;
    ```

    *after* the four recursive calls, you get infinite recursion if your blob has more than one cell. This is because, when you visit an adjacent cell, one of its recursive calls visits the original cell. If this cell is still `BLACK`, yet more recursive calls are generated, *ad infinitum*.

A final thought: Recursive algorithms can be tricky. Try to state the solution recursively *in words* before you launch into code. Oh, and don't forget the base case!

## Sample Free-Response Question 1

Here is a sample free-response question that uses recursion in a two-dimensional array. See if you can answer it before looking at the solution.

A *color grid* is defined as a two-dimensional array whose elements are character strings having values "b" (blue), "r" (red), "g" (green), or "y" (yellow). The elements are called pixels because they represent pixel locations on a computer screen. For example,

```
                                  y g r
      b b g r                     b y g
      g r g r      r r r r        g r b
                                  b b g
```

A *connected region* for any pixel is the set of all pixels of the same color that can be reached through a direct path along horizontal or vertical moves starting at that pixel. A connected region can consist of just a single pixel or the entire color grid. For example, if the two-dimensional array is called `pixels`, the connected region for `pixels[1][0]` is as shown here for three different arrays.

```
b b g r          y g r b          b b
g r g r          g g y g          b b
                 b g r g
```

The class `ColorGrid`, whose declaration is shown below, is used for storing, displaying, and changing the colors in a color grid.

```java
public class ColorGrid
{
    private String[][] pixels;
    private int rows;
    private int cols;

    /** Creates numRows × numCols ColorGrid from String s. */
    public ColorGrid(String s, int numRows, int numCols)
    { /* to be implemented in part (a) */ }

    /* If 0 <= row < rows and 0 <= col < cols, paints the
     * connected region of pixels[row][col] the newColor.
     * Does nothing if oldColor is the same as newColor.
     *   Precondition:
     *     - pixels[row][col] is oldColor, one of "r","b","g", or "y".
     *     - newColor is one of "r","b","g", or "y".
     */
    public void paintRegion(int row, int col, String newColor,
        String oldColor)
    { /* to be implemented in part (b) */ }

    //Other methods are not shown.
}
```

(a) Write the implementation code for the `ColorGrid` constructor. The constructor should initialize the `pixels` matrix of the `ColorGrid` as follows: The dimensions of `pixels` are numRows × numCols. String s contains numRows × numCols characters, where each character is one of the colors of the grid—"r", "g", "b", or "y". The characters are contained in s row by row from top to bottom and left to right. For example, given that numRows is 3, and numCols is 4, if s is "brrygrggyyyr", pixels should be initialized to be

```
b r r y
g r g g
y y y r
```

Complete the following constructor:

```
/** Creates numRows × numCols ColorGrid from String s. */
public ColorGrid(String s, int numRows, int numCols)
```

(b) Write the implementation of the `paintRegion` method as started below. **Note: You must write a recursive solution.** The `paintRegion` paints the connected region of the given pixel, specified by `row` and `col`, a different color specified by the `newColor` parameter. If `newColor` is the same as `oldColor`, the color of the given pixel, `paintRegion` does nothing. To visualize what `paintRegion` does, imagine that the different colors surrounding the connected region of a given pixel form a boundary. When paint is poured onto the given pixel, the new color will fill the connected region up to the boundary.

For example, the effect of the method call `c.paintRegion(2, 3, "b", "r")` on the `ColorGrid` c is shown here. (The starting pixel is shown in a frame, and its connected region is shaded.)

| before | after |
|--------|-------|
| r r b g y y | r r b g y y |
| b r b y r r | b r b y b b |
| g g r [r] r b | g g b b b b |
| y r r y r b | y b b y b b |

Complete the method `paintRegion` below. **Note: Only a recursive solution will be accepted.**

```
/* If 0 <= row < rows and 0 <= col < cols, paints the
 * connected region of pixels[row][col] the newColor.
 * Does nothing if oldColor is the same as newColor.
 *   Precondition:
 *    - pixels[row][col] is oldColor, one of "r", "b","g", or "y".
 *    - newColor is one of "r","b","g", or "y".
 */
public void paintRegion(int row, int col, String newColor,
    String oldColor)
```

✓ **Solution**

```
(a) public ColorGrid(String s, int numRows, int numCols)
    {
        rows = numRows;
        cols = numCols;
        pixels = new String[numRows][numCols];
        int stringIndex = 0;
        for (int r = 0; r < numRows; r++)
            for (int c = 0; c < numCols; c++)
            {
                pixels[r][c] = s.substring(stringIndex,
                    stringIndex + 1);
                stringIndex++;
            }
    }
```

```
(b) public void paintRegion(int row, int col, String newColor,
        String oldColor)
    {
        if (row >= 0 && row < rows && col >= 0 && col < cols)
            if (!pixels[row][col].equals(newColor) &&
                pixels[row][col].equals(oldColor))
            {
                pixels[row][col] = newColor;
                paintRegion(row + 1, col, newColor, oldColor);
                paintRegion(row - 1, col, newColor, oldColor);
                paintRegion(row, col + 1, newColor, oldColor);
                paintRegion(row, col - 1, newColor, oldColor);
            }
    }
```

**Note**

- In part (a), you don't need to test if `stringIndex` is in range: The precondition states that the number of characters in s is `numRows` × `numCols`.
- In part (b), each recursive call must test whether `row` and `col` are in the correct range for the `pixels` array; otherwise, your algorithm may sail right off the edge!
- Don't forget to test if `newColor` is different from that of the starting pixel. Method `paintRegion` does nothing if the colors are the same.
- Also, don't forget to test if the current pixel is `oldColor`—you don't want to overwrite *all* the colors, just the connected region of `oldColor`!
- The color-change assignment `pixels[row][col]` = `newColor` must precede the recursive calls to avoid infinite recursion.

## Sample Free-Response Question 2

Here is another sample free-response question that uses recursion.

This question refers to the `Sentence` class below. Note: A *word* is a string of consecutive non-blank (and non-whitespace) characters. For example, the sentence

"Hello there!" she said.

consists of the four words

"Hello    there!"    she    said.

```
public class Sentence
{
    private String sentence;
    private int numWords;

    /** Constructor. Creates sentence from String str.
     *            Finds the number of words in sentence.
     * Precondition:  Words in str separated by exactly one blank.
     */
    public Sentence(String str)
    { /* to be implemented in part (a) */ }
```

```
public int getNumWords()
{ return numWords; }

public String getSentence()
{ return sentence; }

/** Returns a copy of String s with all blanks removed. */
private static String removeBlanks(String s)
{ /* implementation not shown */ }

/** Returns a copy of String s with all letters in lowercase.
 *  Postcondition: Number of words in returned string equals
 *                 number of words in s.
 */
private static String lowerCase(String s)
{ /* implementation not shown */ }

/** Returns a copy of String s with all punctuation removed.
 *  Postcondition: Number of words in returned string equals
 *                 number of words in s.
 */
private static String removePunctuation(String s)
{ /* implementation not shown */ }
}
```

(a) Complete the `Sentence` constructor as started below. The constructor assigns `str` to `sentence`. You should write the subsequent code that assigns a value to `numWords`, the number of words in `sentence`.

Complete the constructor below:

```
/** Constructor. Creates sentence from String str.
 *               Finds the number of words in sentence.
 *  Precondition: Words in str separated by exactly one blank.
 */
public Sentence(String str)
{
    sentence = str;
```

(b) Consider the problem of testing whether a string is a palindrome. A *palindrome* reads the same from left to right and right to left, ignoring spaces, punctuation, and capitalization. For example,

A Santa lived as a devil at NASA.
Flo, gin is a sin! I golf.

A public method `isPalindrome` is added to the `Sentence` class. Here is the method and its implementation:

```
/** Returns true if sentence is a palindrome, false otherwise. */
public boolean isPalindrome()
{
    String temp = removeBlanks(sentence);
    temp = removePunctuation(temp);
    temp = lowerCase(temp);
    return isPalindrome(temp, 0, temp.length() - 1);
}
```

The overloaded isPalindrome method contained in the code is a private recursive helper method, also added to the Sentence class. You are to write the implementation of this method. It takes a "purified" string as a parameter—namely, one that has been stripped of blanks and punctuation and is all lowercase letters. It also takes as parameters the first and last indexes of the string. It returns true if this "purified" string is a palindrome, false otherwise.

A recursive algorithm for testing if a string is a palindrome is as follows:

- If the string has length 0 or 1, it's a palindrome.
- Remove the first and last letters.
- If those two letters are the same, and the remaining string is a palindrome, then the original string is a palindrome. Otherwise it's not.

Complete the isPalindrome method below:

```
/** Private recursive helper method that tests whether a substring of
 *  string s, starting at start and ending at end, is a palindrome.
 *  Returns true if the substring is a palindrome, false otherwise.
 *  Precondition: s contains no spaces, punctuation, or capitals.
 */
private static boolean isPalindrome(String s, int start, int end)
```

## ✓ Solution

```
(a) public Sentence(String str)
    {
        sentence = str;
        numWords = 1;
        int k = str.indexOf(" ");
        while (k != -1)    //while there are still blanks in str
        {
            numWords++;
            str = str.substring(k + 1); //substring after blank
            k = str.indexOf(" ");       //get index of next blank
        }
    }
```

```
(b) private static boolean isPalindrome(String s, int start,
            int end)
    {
        if (start >= end)   //substring has length 0 or 1
            return true;
        else
        {
            String first = s.substring(start, start + 1);
            String last = s.substring(end, end + 1);
            if (first.equals(last))
                return isPalindrome(s, start + 1, end - 1);
            else
                return false;
        }
    }
```

### Note

- In part (a), for every occurrence of a blank in `sentence`, `numWords` must be incremented. (Be sure to initialize `numWords` to 1!)
- In part (a), the code locates all the blanks in `sentence` by replacing `str` with the substring that consists of the piece of `str` directly following the most recently located blank.
- Recall that `indexOf` returns -1 if its `String` parameter does not occur as a substring in its `String` calling object.
- In part (b), the `start` and `end` indexes move toward each other with each subsequent recursive call. This shortens the string to be tested in each call. When `start` and `end` meet, the base case has been reached.
- Notice the private static methods in the `Sentence` class, including the helper method you were asked to write. They are static because they are not invoked by a `Sentence` object (no dot member construct). The only use of these methods is to help achieve the postconditions of other methods in the class.

## Chapter Summary

On the AP exam you will be expected to calculate the results of recursive method calls. Recursion becomes second nature when you practice a lot of examples. For the more difficult questions, untangle the statements with either repeated method calls (like that shown in the solution to Question 5 on p. 337), or box diagrams (as shown in the solution to Question 12 on p. 338).

You should understand that recursive algorithms can be *very* inefficient.

# Multiple-Choice Questions on Recursion

1. Which of the following statements about recursion are true?

    I. Every recursive algorithm can be written iteratively.
    II. Tail recursion is always used in "divide-and-conquer" algorithms.
    III. In a recursive definition, a process is defined in terms of a simpler case of itself.

    (A) I only
    (B) III only
    (C) I and II only
    (D) I and III only
    (E) II and III only

2. Which of the following, when used as the /* *body* */ of method sum, will enable that method to compute $1 + 2 + \cdots + n$ correctly for any $n > 0$?

    ```
    /** Returns 1 + 2 + ... + n.
     *  Precondition: n is a positive integer.
     */
    public int sum(int n)
    {
        /* body */
    }
    ```

    I. return n + sum(n - 1);

    II. if (n == 1)
            return 1;
        else
            return n + sum(n - 1);

    III. if (n == 1)
            return 1;
        else
            return sum(n) + sum(n - 1);

    (A) I only
    (B) II only
    (C) III only
    (D) I and II only
    (E) I, II, and III

3. Refer to the method `stringRecur`.

```
public void stringRecur(String s)
{
    if (s.length() < 15)
        System.out.println(s);
    stringRecur(s + "*");
}
```

When will method `stringRecur` terminate without error?
(A) Only when the length of the input string is less than 15
(B) Only when the length of the input string is greater than or equal to 15
(C) Only when an empty string is input
(D) For all string inputs
(E) For no string inputs

4. Refer to method `strRecur`.

```
public void strRecur(String s)
{
    if (s.length() < 15)
    {
        System.out.println(s);
        strRecur(s + "*");
    }
}
```

When will method `strRecur` terminate without error?
(A) Only when the length of the input string is less than 15
(B) Only when the length of the input string is greater than or equal to 15
(C) Only when an empty string is input
(D) For all string inputs
(E) For no string inputs

Questions 5 and 6 refer to method `result`.

```
public int result(int n)
{
    if (n == 1)
        return 2;
    else
        return 2 * result(n - 1);
}
```

5. What value does `result(5)` return?
(A) 64
(B) 32
(C) 16
(D) 8
(E) 2

6. If $n > 0$, how many times will `result` be called to evaluate `result(n)` (including the initial call)?

   (A) 2
   (B) $2^n$
   (C) $n$
   (D) $2n$
   (E) $n^2$

7. Refer to method `mystery`.

```
public int mystery(int n, int a, int d)
{
    if (n == 1)
        return a;
    else
        return d + mystery(n - 1, a, d);
}
```

What value is returned by the call `mystery(3, 2, 6)`?

   (A) 20
   (B) 14
   (C) 10
   (D) 8
   (E) 2

8. Refer to method `f`.

```
public int f(int k, int n)
{
    if (n == k)
        return k;
    else
        if (n > k)
            return f(k, n - k);
        else
            return f(k - n, n);
}
```

What value is returned by the call `f(6, 8)`?

   (A) 8
   (B) 4
   (C) 3
   (D) 2
   (E) 1

9. What does method `recur` do?

```
/** x is an array of n integers.
 * n is a positive integer.
 */
public int recur(int[] x, int n)
{
    int t;
    if (n == 1)
        return x[0];
    else
    {
        t = recur(x, n - 1);
        if (x[n-1] > t)
            return x[n-1];
        else
            return t;
    }
}
```

(A) It finds the largest value in x and leaves x unchanged.

(B) It finds the smallest value in x and leaves x unchanged.

(C) It sorts x in ascending order and returns the largest value in x.

(D) It sorts x in descending order and returns the largest value in x.

(E) It returns x[0] or x[n-1], whichever is larger.

10. Which best describes what the `printString` method below does?

```
public void printString(String s)
{
    if (s.length() > 0)
    {
        printString(s.substring(1));
        System.out.print(s.substring(0, 1));
    }
}
```

(A) It prints string s.

(B) It prints string s in reverse order.

(C) It prints only the first character of string s.

(D) It prints only the first two characters of string s.

(E) It prints only the last character of string s.

11. Refer to the method power.

```
/** Returns base raised to the expo power.
 *  Precondition:
 *    - base is a nonzero real number.
 *     - expo is an integer.
 */
public double power(double base, int expo)
{
    if (expo == 0)
        return 1;
    else if (expo > 0)
        return base * power(base, expo - 1);
    else
        return /* code */;
}
```

Which /* *code* */ correctly completes method power?

(Recall that $a^{-n} = 1/a^n$, $a \neq 0$; for example, $2^{-3} = 1/2^3 = 1/8$.)

(A) (1 / base) * power(base, expo + 1)

(B) (1 / base) * power(base, expo - 1)

(C) base * power(base, expo + 1)

(D) base * power(base, expo - 1)

(E) (1 / base) * power(base, expo)

12. Consider the following method.

```
public void doSomething(int n)
{
    if (n > 0)
    {
        doSomething(n - 1);
        System.out.print(n);
        doSomething(n - 1);
    }
}
```

What would be output following the call doSomething(3)?

(A) 3211211

(B) 1121213

(C) 1213121

(D) 1211213

(E) 1123211

13. A user enters several positive integers at the keyboard and terminates the list with a sentinel (-999). A `writeEven` method reads those integers and outputs the even integers only, in the reverse order that they are read. Thus, if the user enters

```
3 5 14 6 1 8 -999
```

the output for the `writeEven` method will be

```
8 6 14
```

Assume that the user enters at least one positive integer and terminates the list with −999. Here is the method.

```
/** Postcondition: All even integers in the list are output in
 *                 reverse order.
 */
public static void writeEven()
{
    int num = ...;      //read user input
    if (num != -999)
    {
        /* code */
    }
}
```

Which /* *code* */ satisfies the postcondition of method `writeEven`?

```
I.  if (num % 2 == 0)
        System.out.print(num + " ");
    writeEven();
```

```
II. if (num % 2 == 0)
        writeEven();
    System.out.print(num + " ");
```

```
III. writeEven();
     if (num % 2 == 0)
         System.out.print(num + " ");
```

(A) I only
(B) II only
(C) III only
(D) I and II only
(E) I, II, and III

14. Refer to the following recursive method.

```
public int mystery(int n)
{
    if (n < 0)
        return 2;
    else
        return mystery(n - 1) + mystery(n - 3);
}
```

What value is returned by the call mystery(3)?

(A) 12

(B) 10

(C) 8

(D) 6

(E) 4

Questions 15 and 16 refer to method t.

```java
/** Precondition: n is a positive integer. */
public int t(int n)
{
    if (n == 1 || n == 2)
        return 2 * n;
    else
        return t(n - 1) - t(n - 2);
}
```

15. What will be returned by t(5)?

    (A) 4

    (B) 2

    (C) 0

    (D) −2

    (E) −4

16. For the method call t(6), how many calls to t will be made, including the original call?

    (A) 6

    (B) 7

    (C) 11

    (D) 15

    (E) 25

17. This question refers to methods f1 and f2 that are in the same class.

```java
    public int f1(int a, int b)
    {
        if (a == b)
            return b;
        else
            return a + f2(a - 1, b);
    }

    public int f2(int p, int q)
    {
        if (p < q)
            return p + q;
        else
            return p + f1(p - 2, q);
    }
```

    What value will be returned by a call to f1(5, 3)?

    (A) 5

    (B) 6

    (C) 7

    (D) 12

    (E) 15

18. Consider method `foo`.

```
public int foo(int x)
{
    if (x == 1 || x == 3)
        return x;
    else
        return x * foo(x - 1);
}
```

Assuming no possibility of integer overflow, what will be the value of z after execution of the following statement? Note that $n! = (n)(n-1)(n-2)\ldots(2)(1)$.

```
int z = foo(foo(3) + foo(4));
```

(A)  $(15!)/(2!)$

(B)  $3! + 4!$

(C)  $(7!)!$

(D)  $(3! + 4!)!$

(E)  15

Questions 19 and 20 refer to the `IntFormatter` class below.

```
public class IntFormatter
{
    /** Write 3 digits adjacent to each other.
     *  Precondition:  n is a nonnegative integer.
     */
    public static void writeThreeDigits(int n)
    {
        System.out.print(n / 100);
        System.out.print((n / 10) % 10);
        System.out.print(n % 10);
    }


    /** Insert commas in n, every 3 digits starting at the right.
     *  Precondition:  n is a nonnegative integer.
     */
    public static void writeWithCommas(int n)
    {
        if (n < 1000)
            System.out.print(n);
        else
        {
            writeThreeDigits(n % 1000);
            System.out.print(",");
            writeWithCommas(n / 1000);
        }
    }
}
```

19. The method `writeWithCommas` is supposed to print its nonnegative `int` argument with commas properly inserted (every three digits, starting at the right). For example, the integer 27048621 should be printed as 27,048,621. Method `writeWithCommas` does not always work as intended, however. Assuming no integer overflow, which of the following integer arguments will not be printed correctly?

   (A) 896
   (B) 251462251
   (C) 365051
   (D) 278278
   (E) 4

20. Which change in the code of the given methods will cause method `writeWithCommas` to work as intended?

   (A) Interchange the lines `System.out.print(n / 100)` and
       `System.out.print(n % 10)` in method `writeThreeDigits`.
   (B) Interchange the lines `writeThreeDigits(n % 1000)` and
       `writeWithCommas(n / 1000)` in method `writeWithCommas`.
   (C) Change the test in `writeWithCommas` to `if (n > 1000)`.
   (D) In the method `writeWithCommas`, change the line
       `writeThreeDigits(n % 1000)` to `writeThreeDigits(n / 1000)`.
   (E) In the method `writeWithCommas`, change the recursive call
       `writeWithCommas(n / 1000)` to `writeWithCommas(n % 1000)`.

21. Consider the following method.

```
public static void sketch(int x1, int y1, int x2, int y2, int n)
{
    if (n <= 0)
        drawLine(x1, y1, x2, y2);
    else
    {
        int xm = (x1 + x2 + y1 - y2) / 2;
        int ym = (y1 + y2 + x2 - x1) / 2;
        sketch(x1, y1, xm, ym, n - 1);
        sketch(xm, ym, x2, y2, n - 1);
    }
}
```

Assume that the screen looks like a Cartesian coordinate system with the origin at the center, and that drawLine connects (x1,y1) to (x2,y2). Assume also that x1, y1, x2, and y2 are never too large or too small to cause errors. Which picture best represents the sketch drawn by the method call

```
sketch(a, 0, -a, 0, 2)
```

where a is a positive integer?

(A)

(B)

(C)

(D)

(E)
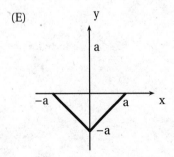

## Answer Key

| | | | | | |
|---|---|---|---|---|---|
| 1. **D** | | 8. **D** | | 15. **E** | |
| 2. **B** | | 9. **A** | | 16. **D** | |
| 3. **E** | | 10. **B** | | 17. **E** | |
| 4. **D** | | 11. **A** | | 18. **A** | |
| 5. **B** | | 12. **C** | | 19. **C** | |
| 6. **C** | | 13. **C** | | 20. **B** | |
| 7. **B** | | 14. **A** | | 21. **B** | |

## Answer Explanations

1. **(D)** Tail recursion is when the recursive call of a method is made as the last executable step of the method. Divide-and-conquer algorithms like those used in merge sort or quicksort have recursive calls *before* the last step. Thus, statement II is false.

2. **(B)** Code segment I is wrong because there is no base case. Code segment III is wrong because, besides anything else, `sum(n)` prevents the method from terminating—the base case `n == 1` will not be reached.

3. **(E)** When `stringRecur` is invoked, it calls itself irrespective of the length of `s`. Since there is no action that leads to termination, the method will not terminate until the computer runs out of memory (run-time error).

4. **(D)** The base case is `s.length()` $\geq 15$. Since `s` gets longer on each method call, the method will eventually terminate. If the original length of `s` is $\geq 15$, the method will terminate without output on the first call.

5. **(B)** Letting $R$ denote the method `result`, we have

$$\begin{aligned} R(5) &= 2 * R(4) \\ &= 2 * (2 * (R(3))) \\ &= \cdots \\ &= 2 * (2 * (2 * (2 * R(1)))) \\ &= 2^5 \\ &= 32 \end{aligned}$$

6. **(C)** For `result(n)` there will be $(n-1)$ recursive calls before `result(1)`, the base case, is reached. Adding the initial call gives a total of $n$ method calls.

7. **(B)** This method returns the $n$th term of an arithmetic sequence with first term `a` and common difference `d`. Letting $M$ denote method `mystery`, we have

$$\begin{aligned} M(3,2,6) &= 6 + M(2,2,6) \\ &= 6 + (6 + M(1,2,6)) \quad \text{(base case)} \\ &= 6 + 6 + 2 \\ &= 14 \end{aligned}$$

8. **(D)** Here are the recursive calls that are made, in order: $f(6,8) \rightarrow f(6,2) \rightarrow f(4,2) \rightarrow f(2,2)$, base case. Thus, 2 is returned.

9. **(A)** If there is only one element in x, then recur returns that element. Having the recursive call at the beginning of the else part of the algorithm causes the if part for each method call to be stacked until t eventually gets assigned to x[0]. The pending if statements are then executed, and t is compared to each element in x. The largest value in x is returned.

10. **(B)** Since the recursive call is made directly following the base case, the System.out.print... statements are stacked up. If printString("cat") is called, here is the sequence of recursive calls and pending statements on the stack:

printString("at")  →  print "c"
printString("t")   →  print "a"
printString("")    →  print "t"

```
                      ┌─────────┐
                      │print "t"│
                      ├─────────┤
                      │print "a"│
                      ├─────────┤
                      │print "c"│
                      └─────────┘
```

Execution stack

When printString(""), the base case, is called, the print statements are then popped off the stack in reverse order, which means that the characters of the string will be printed in reverse order.

11. **(A)** The required code is for a negative expo. For example, power(2, -3) should return $2^{-3} = 1/8$. Notice that

$$2^{-3} = \tfrac{1}{2}\left(2^{-2}\right)$$
$$2^{-2} = \tfrac{1}{2}\left(2^{-1}\right)$$
$$2^{-1} = \tfrac{1}{2}\left(2^{0}\right)$$

In general:

$$2^{n} = \tfrac{1}{2}(2^{n+1}) \quad \text{whenever} \quad n < 0$$

This is equivalent to (1 / base) * power(base, expo + 1).

12. **(C)** Each box in the diagram below represents a recursive call to doSomething. The numbers to the right of the boxes show the order of execution of the statements. Let D denote doSomething.

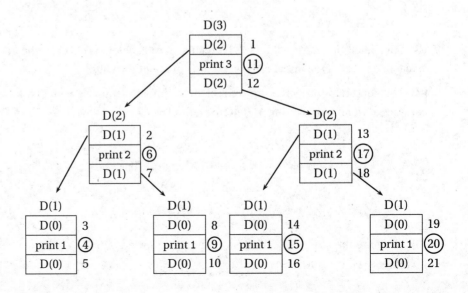

The numbers in each box refer to that method call only. D(0) is the base case, so the statement immediately following it is executed next. When all statements in a given box (method call) have been executed, backtrack along the arrow to find the statement that gets executed next. The circled numbers represent the statements that produce output. Following them in order, statements 4, 6, 9, 11, 15, 17, and 20 produce the output in choice C.

13. **(C)** Since even numbers are printed *before* the recursive call in segment I, they will be printed in the order in which they are read from the keyboard. Contrast this with the correct choice, segment III, in which the recursive call is made before the test for evenness. These tests will be stacked until the last number is read. Recall that the pending statements are removed from the stack in reverse order (most recent recursive call first), which leads to even numbers being printed in reverse order. Segment II is wrong because all numbers entered will be printed, irrespective of whether they are even or not. Note that segment II would work if the input list contained only even numbers.

14. **(A)** Let mystery(3) be denoted $m(3)$. Picture the execution of the method as follows:

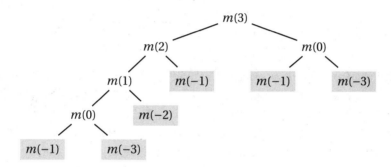

The base cases are shaded. Note that each of the six base case calls returns 2, resulting in a total of 12.

15. **(E)** The method generates a sequence. The first two terms, $t(1)$ and $t(2)$, are 2 and 4. Each subsequent term is generated by subtracting the previous two terms. This is the sequence: 2, 4, 2, −2, −4, −2, 2, 4, .... Thus, $t(5) = -4$. Alternatively,

$$t(5) = t(4) - t(3)$$
$$= [t(3) - t(2)] - t(3)$$
$$= -t(2)$$
$$= -4$$

16. **(D)** Count them! (Note that you stop at $t(2)$ since it's a base case.)

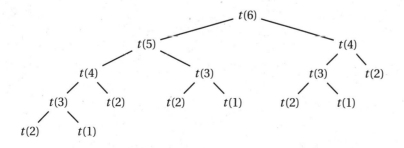

17. **(E)** This is an example of *mutual recursion*, where two methods call each other.

$$f_1(5,3) = 5 + f_2(4,3)$$
$$= 5 + (4 + f_1(2,3))$$
$$= 5 + (4 + (2 + f_2(1,3)))$$
$$= 5 + (4 + (2 + 4))$$
$$= 15$$

Note that $f_2(1,3)$ is a base case.

18. **(A)** foo(3) = 3 (this is a base case). Also, foo(4) = 4 × foo(3) = 12. So you need to find foo(foo(3) + foo(4)) = foo(15).

$$foo(15) = 15 \times foo(14)$$
$$= 15 \times (14 \times foo(13))$$
$$= \cdots$$
$$= 15 \times 14 \times \cdots \times 4 \times foo(3)$$
$$= 15 \times 14 \times \cdots \times 4 \times 3$$
$$= (15)! / (2!)$$

19. **(C)** Suppose that $n = 365051$. The method call writeWithCommas(365051) will write 051 and then execute the call writeWithCommas(365). This is a base case, so 365 will be written out, resulting in 051,365. A number like 278278 (two sets of three identical digits) will be written out correctly, as will a "symmetrical" number like 251462251. Also, any $n < 1000$ is a base case and the number will be written out correctly as is.

20. **(B)** The cause of the problem is that the numbers are being written out with the sets of three digits in the wrong order. The problem is fixed by interchanging writeThreeDigits(n % 1000) and writeWithCommas(n / 1000). For example, here is the order of execution for writeWithCommas(365051).

> writeWithCommas(365) → Base case. Writes 365
> System.out.print(","); → 365,
> writeThreeDigits(051) → 365,051, which is correct

21. **(B)** Here is the "box diagram" for the recursive method calls, showing the order of execution of statements. Notice that the circled statements are the base case calls, the only statements that actually draw a line. Note also that the first time you reach a base case (see circled statement 6), you can get the answer: The picture in choice B is the only one that has a line segment joining (a,0) to (a,-a).

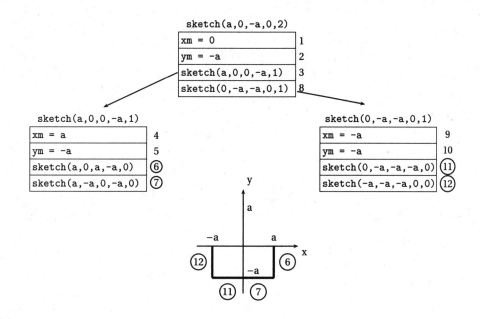

# 9

# Sorting and Searching

*Critics search for ages for the wrong word, which,*
*to give them credit, they eventually find.*
*—Peter Ustinov (1952)*

## Learning Objectives

In this chapter, you will learn:

- → Sorts: selection and insertion sorts
- → Recursive sorts: merge sort and quicksort
- → Sorting algorithms in Java
- → Sequential search
- → Binary search

For each of the following sorting algorithms, assume that an array of $n$ elements, a[0], a[1], ..., a[n-1], is to be sorted in ascending order.

## Sorts: Selection and Insertion Sorts

### Selection Sort

This is a "search-and-swap" algorithm. Here's how it works.

Find the smallest element in the array and exchange it with a[0], the first element. Now find the smallest element in the subarray a[1] ...a[n-1] and swap it with a[1], the second element in the array. Continue this process until just the last two elements remain to be sorted, a[n-2] and a[n-1]. The smaller of these two elements is placed in a[n-2]; the larger, in a[n-1]; and the sort is complete.

Trace these steps with a small array of four elements. The unshaded part is the subarray still to be searched.

```
        8    1    4    6

        1    8    4    6      after first pass

        1    4    8    6      after second pass

        1    4    6    8      after third pass
```

### Note

1. For an array of $n$ elements, the array is sorted after $n-1$ passes.
2. After the $k$th pass, the first $k$ elements are in their final sorted position.

## Insertion Sort

Think of the first element in the array, a[0], as being sorted with respect to itself. The array can now be thought of as consisting of two parts, a sorted list followed by an unsorted list. The idea of insertion sort is to move elements from the unsorted list to the sorted list one at a time; as each item is moved, it is inserted into its correct position in the sorted list. In order to place the new item, some elements may need to be moved to the right to create a slot.

Here is the array of four elements. In each case, the boxed element is "it," the next element to be inserted into the sorted part of the list. The shaded area is the part of the list sorted so far.

| 8 | 1 | 4 | 6 | |
|---|---|---|---|---|
| 1 | 8 | 4 | 6 | after first pass |
| 1 | 4 | 8 | 6 | after second pass |
| 1 | 4 | 6 | 8 | after third pass |

### Note

1. For an array of $n$ elements, the array is sorted after $n-1$ passes.
2. After the $k$th pass, a[0], a[1], ..., a[k] are sorted with respect to each other but not necessarily in their final sorted positions.
3. The worst case for insertion sort occurs if the array is initially sorted in reverse order, since this will lead to the maximum possible number of comparisons and moves.
4. The best case for insertion sort occurs if the array is already sorted in increasing order. In this case, each pass through the array will involve just one comparison, which will indicate that "it" is in its correct position with respect to the sorted list. Therefore, no elements will need to be moved.

> Both insertion and selection sorts are inefficient for large $n$.

## Recursive Sorts: Merge Sort and Quicksort

Selection and insertion sorts are inefficient for large $n$, requiring approximately $n$ passes through a list of $n$ elements. More efficient algorithms can be devised using a "divide-and-conquer" approach, which is used in both the sorting algorithms that follow. Quicksort is not in the AP Java subset.

### Merge Sort

Here is a recursive description of how merge sort works:

If there is more than one element in the array,

    Break the array into two halves.
    Merge sort the left half.
    Merge sort the right half.
    Merge the two subarrays into a sorted array.

> The main disadvantage of merge sort is that it uses a temporary array.

Merge sort uses a merge method to merge two sorted pieces of an array into a single sorted array. For example, suppose array a[0] ... a[n-1] is such that a[0] ... a[k] is sorted and a[k+1] ... a[n-1] is sorted, both parts in increasing order. Example:

```
a[0]   a[1]   a[2]   a[3]   a[4]   a[5]
 2      5      8      9      1      6
```

In this case, a[0] …a[3] and a[4] …a[5] are the two sorted pieces. The method call merge(a,0,3,5) should produce the "merged" array:

```
a[0]   a[1]   a[2]   a[3]   a[4]   a[5]
 1      2      5      6      8      9
```

The middle numerical parameter in merge (the 3 in this case) represents the index of the last element in the first "piece" of the array. The first and third numerical parameters are the lowest and highest indexes, respectively, of array a.

Here's what happens in merge sort:

1. Start with an unsorted list of $n$ elements.
2. The recursive calls break the list into $n$ sublists, each of length 1. Note that these $n$ arrays, each containing just one element, are sorted!
3. Recursively merge adjacent pairs of lists. There are then approximately $n/2$ lists of length 2; then, approximately $n/4$ lists of approximate length 4, and so on, until there is just one list of length $n$.

An example of merge sort follows:

Analysis of merge sort:

1. The major disadvantage of merge sort is that it needs a temporary array that is as large as the original array to be sorted. This could be a problem if space is a factor.
2. Merge sort is not affected by the initial ordering of the elements. Thus, best, worst, and average cases have similar run times.

## Quicksort

**OPTIONAL TOPIC**

For large $n$, quicksort is, on average, the fastest known sorting algorithm. Here is a recursive description of how quicksort works:

If there are at least two elements in the array,
      Partition the array.
      Quicksort the left subarray.
      Quicksort the right subarray.

The `partition` method splits the array into two subarrays as follows: a *pivot* element is chosen at random from the array (often just the first element) and placed so that all items to the left of the pivot are less than or equal to the pivot, whereas those to the right are greater than or equal to it.

For example, if the array is 4, 1, 2, 7, 5, −1, 8, 0, 6, and `a[0]` = 4 is the pivot, the `partition` method produces

$$-1 \quad 1 \quad 2 \quad 0 \quad \boxed{4} \quad 5 \quad 8 \quad 7 \quad 6$$

Here's how the partitioning works: Let `a[0]`, 4 in this case, be the pivot. Markers `up` and `down` are initialized to index values 0 and $n - 1$, as shown. Move the `up` marker until a value less than the pivot is found, or `down` equals `up`. Move the `down` marker until a value greater than the pivot is found, or `down` equals `up`. Swap `a[up]` and `a[down]`. Continue the process until `down` equals `up`. This is the pivot position. Swap `a[0]` and `a[pivotPosition]`.

Notice that the pivot element, 4, is in its final sorted position.

Analysis of quicksort:

1. For the fastest run time, the array should be partitioned into two parts of roughly the same size.

2. If the pivot happens to be the smallest or largest element in the array, the split is not much of a split—one of the subarrays is empty! If this happens repeatedly, quicksort degenerates into a slow, recursive version of selection sort and is very inefficient.

3. The worst case for quicksort occurs when the partitioning algorithm repeatedly divides the array into pieces of size 1 and $n-1$. An example is when the array is initially sorted in either order and the first or last element is chosen as the pivot. Some algorithms avoid this situation by initially shuffling up the given array (!) or selecting the pivot by examining several elements of the array (such as first, middle, and last) and then taking the median.

## Note

For both quicksort and merge sort, when a subarray gets down to some small size $m$, it becomes faster to sort by straight insertion. The optimal value of $m$ is machine-dependent, but it's approximately equal to 7.

## Sorting Algorithms in Java

Unlike the container classes like `ArrayList`, whose elements must be objects, arrays can hold either objects or primitive types like `int` or `double`.

A common way of organizing code for sorting arrays is to create a sorter class with an array private instance variable. The class holds all the methods for a given type of sorting algorithm, and the constructor assigns the user's array to the private array variable.

### > Example

Selection sort for an array of `int`.

```
/* A class that sorts an array of ints from
 * largest to smallest using selection sort. */

public class SelectionSort
{
    private int[] a;

    public SelectionSort(int[] arr)
    { a = arr; }

    /** Swap a[i] and a[j] in array a. */
    private void swap(int i, int j)
    {
        int temp = a[i];
        a[i] = a[j];
        a[j] = temp;
    }
```

```
/** Sort array a from largest to smallest using selection sort.
 *  Precondition: a is an array of ints.
 */
public void selectionSort()
{
    int maxPos, max;

    for (int i = 0; i < a.length - 1; i++)
    {
        //find max element in a[i+1] to a[a.length-1]
        max = a[i];
        maxPos = i;
        for (int j = i + 1; j < a.length; j++)
            if (max < a[j])
            {
                max = a[j];
                maxPos = j;
            }
        swap(i, maxPos); //swap a[i] and a[maxPos]
    }
}
```

## Sequential Search

Assume that you are searching for a key in a list of $n$ elements. A sequential search starts at the first element and compares the key to each element in turn until the key is found or there are no more elements to examine in the list. If the list is sorted, in ascending order, say, stop searching as soon as the key is less than the current list element. (If the key is less than the current element, it will be less than all subsequent elements.)

Analysis:

1. The best case has the key in the first slot.
2. The worst case occurs if the key is in the last slot or not in the list. In the worst case, all $n$ elements must be examined.
3. On average, there will be $n/2$ comparisons.

## Binary Search

**Binary search works only if the array is sorted on the search key.**

If the elements are in a *sorted* array, a divide-and-conquer approach provides a much more efficient searching algorithm. The following recursive pseudocode algorithm shows how the *binary search* works.

Assume that a[low] ... a[high] is sorted in ascending order and that a method binSearch returns the index of key. If key is not in the array, it returns −1.

```
if (low > high)    //Base case. No elements left in array.
    return -1;
else
{
    mid = (low + high)/2;
    if (key is equal to a[mid])   //found the key
        return mid;
    else if (key is less than a[mid]) //key in left half of array
        <binSearch for key in a[low] to a[mid-1]>
    else    //key in right half of array
        <binSearch for key in a[mid+1] to a[high]>
}
```

Note that this algorithm can also be described iteratively. There are no recursive calls, just an adjustment of mid so that the algorithm searches to the left or the right.

Again, assume that a[low]...a[high] is sorted in ascending order and that the method will return the index of key. If key is not in the array, the method will return −1.

```
while (low is less than or equal to high)
{
    int mid = (low + high)/2;
    if (key is equal to a[mid])   //found the key
        return mid;
    else if (key is less than a[mid]) //key in left half of array
        high = mid - 1;
    else  //key in right half of array
        low = mid + 1;
}
//If we get to here, then key is not in array.
return -1;
```

## Note

1. After just one comparison, the binary search algorithm ignores one half of the array elements. This is true for both the iterative and recursive versions.
2. When low and high cross, there are no more elements to examine, and key is not in the array.

For example, suppose 5 is the key to be found in the following array:

```
a[0]   a[1]   a[2]   a[3]   a[4]   a[5]   a[6]   a[7]   a[8]

 1      4      5      7      9      12     15     20      21
```

First pass: low is 0, high is 8.    mid = (0+8)/2 = 4.   Check a[4].
Second pass: low is 0, high is 3.   mid = (0+3)/2 = 1.   Check a[1].
Third pass: low is 2, high is 3.    mid = (2+3)/2 = 2.   Check a[2]. Yes! Key is found.

## Analysis of Binary Search

1. In the best case, the key is found on the first try (i.e., (low + high)/2 is the index of key).

2. In the worst case, the key is not in the array or is at an endpoint of the array. Here, the $n$ elements must be divided by 2 until there is just one element, and then that last element must be compared with the key. An easy way to find the number of comparisons in the worst case is to round $n$ up to the next power of 2 and take the exponent. For example, in the array above, $n$ is 9. Suppose 21 were the key. Round 9 up to 16, which is $2^4$. Thus you would need 4 comparisons with the key to find it. If $n$ is an exact power of 2, the number of comparisons in the worst case equals the exponent plus one. For example, if the number of elements $n = 32 = 2^5$, then the number of comparisons in the worst case is $5 + 1 = 6$. Note that in this discussion, the number of comparisons refers to the number of passes through the search loop of the above algorithm—namely, the outer else piece of code.

3. There's an interesting wrinkle when discussing the worst case of a binary search that uses the above algorithm. The worst case (i.e., the maximum number of comparisons) will either have the key at an endpoint of the array, or be equal to a value that's not in the array. The opposite, however, is not necessarily true: If the key is at an endpoint, or a value not in the array, it is not necessarily a worst case situation.

> The number of comparisons for binary search in the worst case depends on whether $n$ is a power of 2 or not.

As a simple example, consider the array 3, 7, 9, 11, where a[0] is 3 and a[3] is 11. The number of elements $n$ equals 4, which is $2^2$, an exact power of 2. The worst case for searching for a given key will be 3 comparisons, the exponent plus one.

- If the key is 11 (an endpoint of the array), the algorithm will need 3 passes through the search loop to find the key. This is a worst case. Here's how it works:
  1st pass: low = 0 high = 3 mid = 1
  2nd pass: low = 2 high = 3 mid = 2
  3rd pass: low = 3 high = 3 mid = 3
  The key is found during the 3rd pass when you examine a[3]. Thus a key of 11 represents a worst case.

- If the key is 3 (the other endpoint of the array), the algorithm will need 2 passes through the search loop to find the key. Here's how it works:
  1st pass: low = 0 high = 3 mid = 1
  2nd pass: low = 0 high = 0 mid = 0
  The key is found during the 2nd pass when you examine a[0]. Thus a key of 3 is not a worst case situation. The discrepancy is due to the asymmetry of the div operation, which gives values of mid that are closer to the left endpoint than the right.

- If the key is 1 or 20, say (outside the range of array values and not in the array), the algorithm will need 3 passes through the search loop to determine that the key is not in the array, a worst case.

- If the key is 8, say (not in the array but inside the range of array values), the algorithm will need just 2 passes through the search loop to determine that the key is not in the array. This is therefore not a worst case situation.

- If the key is 10, say (not in the array but between a[2] and a[3] in this example), the algorithm will need 3 passes through the search loop to determine that the key is not in the array, a worst case! Here is how it works:

1st pass: `low = 0 high = 3 mid = 1`
2nd pass: `low = 2 high = 3 mid = 2`
3rd pass: `low = 3 high = 3 mid = 3`

When `a[3]` is found to be greater than `key`, the value of `low` becomes 4, while `high` is still 3, which means that the test `if (low > high)` becomes true and is a base case that terminates the algorithm. There are no further comparisons with `key`.

Here is another example, where $n$ is not a power of 2.

Suppose the array is 1, 3, 5, 7, 9. Here $n$ is 5. To find the number of passes in the worst case, round up to the nearest power of 2, which is 8 or $2^3$. In the worst case, the number of passes through the search loop will be 3:

- If the key is 1, there will be 2 passes to find it, which is not a worst case.

- If the key is 9, there will be 3 passes to find it, which is a worst case.

- If the key is 8, there will be 3 passes to find it, which is a worst case.

- If the key is 4, there will be 2 passes to find it, which is not a worst case.

- If the key is any value outside the range of 1 – 9, there will be 3 passes to find it, which is a worst case.

The lessons from these examples is that not every key that is not in the array represents a worst case.

Here are some general rules for calculating the maximum number of loop passes in different binary search situations. In each case it's assumed that the algorithm given in this book is used.

- If $n$, the number of elements, is not a power of 2, round $n$ up to the nearest power of 2. The number of passes in the worst case equals the exponent.

- If $n$ is a power of 2, the number of passes in the worst case equals the exponent plus one.

- Irrespective of $n$, the worst case will always involve a key that is either at the right endpoint or not in the array.

- Irrespective of $n$, any key that is not in the array and is less than `a[0]` or greater than `a[n-1]` will be a worst case situation.

- Irrespective of $n$, any key that is between `a[0]` and `a[n-1]` but is not in the array may or may not be a worst case situation.

## Chapter Summary

You should not memorize any sorting code. You must, however, be familiar with the mechanism used in each of the sorting algorithms. For example, you should be able to explain how the merge method of merge sort works, or how many elements are in their final sorted position after a certain number of passes through the selection sort loop. You should know the best and worst case situations for each of the sorting algorithms.

Be familiar with the sequential and binary search algorithms. You should know that a binary search is more efficient than a sequential search, and that a binary search can only be used for an array that is sorted on the search key.

# Multiple-Choice Questions on Sorting and Searching

1. The decision to choose a particular sorting algorithm should be made based on which of the following?

    I.  Run-time efficiency of the sort
    II.  Size of the array
    III.  Space efficiency of the algorithm

  (A)  I only
  (B)  II only
  (C)  III only
  (D)  I and II only
  (E)  I, II, and III

2. The following code fragment does a sequential search to determine whether a given integer, `value`, is stored in an array `a[0] ... a[n-1]`.

```
int i = 0;
while (/* boolean expression */)
{
    i++;
}
if (i == n)
    return -1;    //value not found
else
    return i;    // value found at location i
```

Which of the following should replace /* *boolean expression* */ so that the algorithm works as intended?
  (A)  `value != a[i]`
  (B)  `i < n && value == a[i]`
  (C)  `value != a[i] && i < n`
  (D)  `i < n && value != a[i]`
  (E)  `i < n || value != a[i]`

3. A feature of data that is used for a binary search but not necessarily used for a sequential search is
  (A)  length of list.
  (B)  type of data.
  (C)  order of data.
  (D)  smallest value in the list.
  (E)  median value of the data.

4. Array `unsortedArr` contains an unsorted list of integers. Array `sortedArr` contains a list of integers sorted in increasing order. Which of the following operations is more efficient for `sortedArr` than `unsortedArr`? Assume the most efficient algorithms are used.

    I. Inserting a new element
    II. Searching for a given element
    III. Computing the mean of the elements

    (A) I only
    (B) II only
    (C) III only
    (D) I and II only
    (E) I, II, and III

5. An algorithm for searching a large sorted array for a specific value $x$ compares every third item in the array to $x$ until it finds one that is greater than or equal to $x$. When a larger value is found, the algorithm compares $x$ to the previous two items. If the array is sorted in increasing order, which of the following describes all cases when this algorithm uses fewer comparisons to find $x$ than would a binary search?
    (A) It will never use fewer comparisons.
    (B) When $x$ is in the middle position of the array
    (C) When $x$ is very close to the beginning of the array
    (D) When $x$ is very close to the end of the array
    (E) When $x$ is not in the array

6. Assume that `a[0]` ... `a[N-1]` is an array of $N$ positive integers and that the following assertion is true.

    $$a[0] > a[k] \text{ for all } k \text{ such that } 0 < k < N$$

    Which of the following *must* be true?
    (A) The array is sorted in ascending order.
    (B) The array is sorted in descending order.
    (C) All values in the array are different.
    (D) `a[0]` holds the smallest value in the array.
    (E) `a[0]` holds the largest value in the array.

7. The following code is designed to set `index` to the location of the first occurrence of `key` in array a and to set `index` to $-1$ if `key` is not in a.

```
index = 0;
while (a[index] != key)
    index++;
if (a[index] != key)
    index = -1;
```

    In which case will this program *definitely* fail to perform the task described?
    (A) When `key` is the first element of the array
    (B) When `key` is the last element of the array
    (C) When `key` is not in the array
    (D) When `key` equals 0
    (E) When `key` equals `a[key]`

8. Consider the following class.

```
/** A class that sorts an array of Integer objects from
 * largest to smallest using a selection sort.
 */
public class Sorter
{
    private Integer[] a;

    public Sorter(Integer[] arr)
    { a = arr; }

    /** Swap a[i] and a[j] in array a. */
    private void swap(int i, int j)
    { /* implementation not shown */ }

    /** Sort array a from largest to smallest using selection sort.
     * Precondition: a is an array of Integer objects.
     */
    public void selectionSort()
    {
        for (int i = 0; i < a.length - 1; i++)
        {
            //find max element in a[i+1] to a[n-1]
            Integer max = a[i];
            int maxPos = i;
            for (int j = i + 1; j < a.length; j++)
                if (max.compareTo(a[j]) < 0) //max less than a[j]
                {
                    max = a[j];
                    maxPos = j;
                }
            swap(i, maxPos);    //swap a[i] and a[maxPos]
        }
    }
}
```

If an array of Integer contains the following elements, what would the array look like after the third pass of selectionSort, sorting from high to low?

$$89 \quad 42 \quad -3 \quad 13 \quad 109 \quad 70 \quad 2$$

| | | | | | | | |
|---|---|---|---|---|---|---|---|
| (A) | 109 | 89 | 70 | 13 | 42 | -3 | 2 |
| (B) | 109 | 89 | 70 | 42 | 13 | 2 | -3 |
| (C) | 109 | 89 | 70 | -3 | 2 | 13 | 42 |
| (D) | 89 | 42 | 13 | -3 | 109 | 70 | 2 |
| (E) | 109 | 89 | 42 | -3 | 13 | 70 | 2 |

9. Refer to method `search`.

```
/** Returns value k such that -1 <= k <= v.length-1.
 * If k >= 0 then v[k] == key.
 * If k == -1, then key != any of the elements in v.
 */
public static int search(int[] v, int key)
{
    int index = 0;
    while (index < v.length && v[index] < key)
        index++;
    if (v[index] == key)
        return index;
    else
        return -1;
}
```

Assuming that the method works as intended, which of the following should be added to the precondition of `search`?

(A) v is sorted smallest to largest.

(B) v is sorted largest to smallest.

(C) v is unsorted.

(D) There is at least one occurrence of key in v.

(E) key occurs no more than once in v.

Questions 10–14 are based on the `binSearch` method and the private instance variable a for some class.

```
private int[] a;

/** Does binary search for key in array a[0]...a[a.length-1],
 *  sorted in ascending order.
 *  Returns index such that a[index]==key.
 *  If key is not in a, returns -1.
 */
public int binSearch(int key)
{
    int low = 0;
    int high = a.length - 1;
    while (low <= high)
    {
        int mid = (low + high) / 2;
        if (a[mid] == key)
            return mid;
        else if (a[mid] < key)
            low = mid + 1;
        else
            high = mid - 1;
    }
    return -1;
}
```

A binary search will be performed on the following list.

| a[0] | a[1] | a[2] | a[3] | a[4] | a[5] | a[6] | a[7] |
|------|------|------|------|------|------|------|------|
| 4    | 7    | 9    | 11   | 20   | 24   | 30   | 41   |

10. To find the key value 27, the search interval *after* the first pass through the `while` loop will be

    (A) a[0]...a[7]
    (B) a[5]...a[6]
    (C) a[4]...a[7]
    (D) a[2]...a[6]
    (E) a[6]...a[7]

11. How many iterations will be required to determine that 27 is not in the list?

    (A) 1
    (B) 3
    (C) 4
    (D) 8
    (E) 16

12. What will be stored in y after executing the following?

    ```
    int y = binSearch(4);
    ```

    (A) 20
    (B) 7
    (C) 4
    (D) 0
    (E) -1

13. If the test for the `while` loop is changed to

    ```
    while (low < high)
    ```

    the `binSearch` method does not work as intended. Which value in the given list will not be found?
    (A) 4
    (B) 7
    (C) 11
    (D) 24
    (E) 30

14. For `binSearch`, which of the following assertions will be true following every iteration of the `while` loop?
    (A) `key = a[mid]` or key is not in a.
    (B) `a[low] ≤ key ≤ a[high]`
    (C) `low ≤ mid ≤ high`
    (D) `key = a[mid]`, or `a[low] ≤ key ≤ a[high]`
    (E) `key = a[mid]`, or `a[low] ≤ key ≤ a[high]`, or key is not in array a.

15. A large sorted array containing about 30,000 elements is to be searched for a value `key` using an iterative binary search algorithm. Assuming that `key` is in the array, which of the following is closest to the smallest number of iterations that will guarantee that `key` is found? Note: $10^3 \approx 2^{10}$.
    (A) 15
    (B) 30
    (C) 100
    (D) 300
    (E) 3000

For Questions 16–19 refer to the `insertionSort` method and the private instance variable a, both in a `Sorter` class.

```
private Integer[] a;

/** Precondition:  a[0],a[1]...a[a.length-1] is an unsorted array
 *                 of Integer objects.
 * Postcondition: Array a is sorted in descending order.
 */
public void insertionSort()
{
    for (int i = 1; i < a.length; i++)
    {
        Integer temp = a[i];
        int j = i - 1;
        while (j >= 0 && temp > a[j])   //temp and a[j] are unboxed
        {
            a[j+1] = a[j];
            j--;
        }
        a[j+1] = temp;
    }
}
```

16. An array of `Integer` is to be sorted biggest to smallest using the `insertionSort` method. If the array originally contains

$$1 \quad 7 \quad 9 \quad 5 \quad 4 \quad 12$$

what will it look like after the third pass of the `for` loop?
   (A) 9 7 1 5 4 12
   (B) 9 7 5 1 4 12
   (C) 12 9 7 1 5 4
   (D) 12 9 7 5 4 1
   (E) 9 7 12 5 4 1

17. When sorted biggest to smallest with `insertionSort`, which list will need the fewest changes of position for individual elements?
   (A) 5, 1, 2, 3, 4, 9
   (B) 9, 5, 1, 4, 3, 2
   (C) 9, 4, 2, 5, 1, 3
   (D) 9, 3, 5, 1, 4, 2
   (E) 3, 2, 1, 9, 5, 4

18. When sorted biggest to smallest with `insertionSort`, which list will need the greatest number of changes in position?
   (A) 5, 1, 2, 3, 4, 7, 6, 9
   (B) 9, 5, 1, 4, 3, 2, 1, 0
   (C) 9, 4, 6, 2, 1, 5, 1, 3
   (D) 9, 6, 9, 5, 6, 7, 2, 0
   (E) 3, 2, 1, 0, 9, 6, 5, 4

19. While typing the `insertionSort` method, a programmer by mistake enters

    ```
    while (temp > a[j])
    ```

    instead of

    ```
    while (j >= 0 && temp > a[j])
    ```

    Despite this mistake, the method works as intended the first time the programmer enters an array to be sorted in descending order. Which of the following could explain this?

        I. The first element in the array was the largest element in the array.
       II. The array was already sorted in descending order.
      III. The first element was less than or equal to all the other elements in the array.

    (A) I only
    (B) II only
    (C) III only
    (D) I and II only
    (E) II and III only

20. The elements in a long list of integers are roughly sorted in decreasing order. No more than 5 percent of the elements are out of order. Which of the following is a valid reason for using an insertion sort rather than a selection sort to sort this list into decreasing order?

        I. There will be fewer comparisons of elements for insertion sort.
       II. There will be fewer changes of position of elements for insertion sort.
      III. There will be less space required for insertion sort.

    (A) I only
    (B) II only
    (C) III only
    (D) I and II only
    (E) I, II, and III

21. Which of the following is a valid reason why merge sort is a better sorting algorithm than insertion sort for sorting long, randomly ordered lists?

        I. Merge sort requires less code than insertion sort.
       II. Merge sort requires less storage space than insertion sort.
      III. Merge sort runs faster than insertion sort.

    (A) I only
    (B) II only
    (C) III only
    (D) I and II only
    (E) II and III only

22. A large array of lowercase characters is to be searched for the pattern "pqrs." The first step in a very efficient searching algorithm is to look at characters with index
    (A) 0, 1, 2, ... until a "p" is encountered.
    (B) 0, 1, 2, ... until any letter in "p" ... "s" is encountered.
    (C) 3, 7, 11, ... until an "s" is encountered.
    (D) 3, 7, 11, ... until any letter in "p" ... "s" is encountered.
    (E) 3, 7, 11, ... until any letter other than "p" ... "s" is encountered.

23. The array names[0], names[1], ..., names[9999] is a list of 10,000 name strings. The list is to be searched to determine the location of some name X in the list. Which of the following preconditions is necessary for a binary search?
    (A) There are no duplicate names in the list.
    (B) The number of names N in the list is large.
    (C) The list is in alphabetical order.
    (D) Name X is definitely in the list.
    (E) Name X occurs near the middle of the list.

24. Consider the following method.

```
/** Precondition:  a[0],a[1]...a[n-1] contain integers. */
public static int someMethod(int[] a, int n, int value)
{
    if (n == 0)
        return -1;
    else
    {
        if (a[n-1] == value)
            return n - 1;
        else
            return someMethod(a, n - 1, value);
    }
}
```

The method shown is an example of
(A) insertion sort.
(B) merge sort.
(C) selection sort.
(D) binary search.
(E) sequential search.

25. The `partition` method for quicksort partitions a list as follows.

    (i) A pivot element is selected from the array.
    (ii) The elements of the list are rearranged such that all elements to the left of the pivot are less than or equal to it; all elements to the right of the pivot are greater than or equal to it.

    **OPTIONAL TOPIC**

    Partitioning the array requires which of the following?
    (A) A recursive algorithm
    (B) A temporary array
    (C) An external file for the array
    (D) A swap algorithm for interchanging array elements
    (E) A merge method for merging two sorted lists

26. Assume that merge sort will be used to sort an array `arr` of n integers into increasing order. What is the purpose of the `merge` method in the merge sort algorithm?
    (A) Partition `arr` into two parts of roughly equal length, then merge these parts.
    (B) Use a recursive algorithm to sort `arr` into increasing order.
    (C) Divide `arr` into n subarrays, each with one element.
    (D) Merge two sorted parts of `arr` into a single sorted array.
    (E) Merge two sorted arrays into a temporary array that is sorted.

27. A binary search is to be performed on an array with 600 elements. In the *worst* case, which of the following best approximates the number of iterations of the algorithm?
    (A) 6
    (B) 10
    (C) 100
    (D) 300
    (E) 600

28. A worst case situation for insertion sort would be

    I. A list in correct sorted order.
    II. A list sorted in reverse order.
    III. A list in random order.

    (A) I only
    (B) II only
    (C) III only
    (D) I and II only
    (E) II and III only

29. Consider a binary search algorithm to search an ordered list of numbers. Which of the following choices is closest to the maximum number of times that such an algorithm will execute its main comparison loop when searching a list of 1 million numbers?
    (A) 6
    (B) 20
    (C) 100
    (D) 120
    (E) 1000

30. Consider these three tasks.

I. A sequential search of an array of $n$ names

II. A binary search of an array of $n$ names in alphabetical order

III. An insertion sort into alphabetical order of an array of $n$ names that are initially in random order

For large $n$, which of the following lists these tasks in order (from least to greatest) of their average case run times?

(A)    II    I    III
(B)    I    II    III
(C)    II    III    I
(D)    III    I    II
(E)    III    II    I

Questions 31–33 refer to the Hi-Lo game described below.

Consider the problem of writing a Hi-Lo game in which a user thinks of an integer from 1 to 100 inclusive and the computer tries to guess that number. Each time the computer makes a guess, the user makes one of three responses.

- "Lower" (i.e., the number is lower than the computer's guess)
- "Higher" (i.e., the number is higher than the computer's guess)
- "You got it in < *however many* > tries!"

31. Suppose the game is programmed so that the computer uses a binary search strategy for making its guesses. What is the maximum number of guesses the computer could make before guessing the user's number?
    (A) 50
    (B) 25
    (C) 10
    (D) 7
    (E) 6

32. Suppose the computer used a *sequential search* strategy for guessing the user's number. What is the maximum number of guesses the computer could make before guessing the user's number?
    (A) 100
    (B) 99
    (C) 50
    (D) 25
    (E) 10

33. Using a sequential search strategy, how many guesses *on average* would the computer need to guess the number?
    (A) 100
    (B) Between 51 and 99
    (C) 50
    (D) 25
    (E) Fewer than 25

## Answer Key

| | | |
|---|---|---|
| 1. **E** | 12. **D** | 23. **C** |
| 2. **D** | 13. **A** | 24. **E** |
| 3. **C** | 14. **E** | 25. **D** |
| 4. **B** | 15. **A** | 26. **D** |
| 5. **C** | 16. **B** | 27. **B** |
| 6. **E** | 17. **B** | 28. **B** |
| 7. **C** | 18. **A** | 29. **B** |
| 8. **A** | 19. **D** | 30. **A** |
| 9. **A** | 20. **A** | 31. **D** |
| 10. **C** | 21. **C** | 32. **B** |
| 11. **B** | 22. **D** | 33. **C** |

## Answer Explanations

1. **(E)** The time and space requirements of sorting algorithms are affected by all three of the given factors, so all must be considered when choosing a particular sorting algorithm.

2. **(D)** Choice B doesn't make sense: The loop will be exited as soon as a value is found that does *not* equal a[i]. Eliminate choice A because, if value is not in the array, a[i] will eventually go out of bounds. You need the i < n part of the boolean expression to avoid this. The test i < n, however, must precede value != a[i] so that if i < n fails, the expression will be evaluated as false, the test will be short-circuited, and an out-of-range error will be avoided. Choice C does not avoid this error. Choice E is wrong because both parts of the expression must be true in order to continue the search.

3. **(C)** The binary search algorithm depends on the array being sorted. Sequential search has no ordering requirement. Both depend on choice A, the length of the list, while the other choices are irrelevant to both algorithms.

4. **(B)** Inserting a new element is quick and easy in an unsorted array—just add it to the end of the list. Computing the mean involves finding the sum of the elements and dividing by $n$, the number of elements. The execution time is the same whether the list is sorted or not. Operation II, searching, is inefficient for an unsorted list, since a sequential search must be used. In sortedArr, the efficient binary search algorithm, which involves fewer comparisons, could be used. In fact, in a sorted list, even a sequential search would be more efficient than for an unsorted list: If the search item were not in the list, the search could stop as soon as the list elements were greater than the search item.

5. **(C)** Suppose the array has 1000 elements and $x$ is somewhere in the first 8 slots. The algorithm described will find $x$ using no more than five comparisons. A binary search, by contrast, will chop the array in half and do a comparison six times before examining elements in the first 15 slots of the array (array size after each chop: 500, 250, 125, 62, 31, 15).

6. **(E)** The assertion states that the first element is greater than all the other elements in the array. This eliminates choices A and D. Choices B and C are incorrect because you have no information about the relative sizes of elements a[1]...a[N-1].

7. **(C)** When key is not in the array, index will eventually be large enough that a[index] will cause an ArrayIndexOutOfBoundsException. In choices A and B, the algorithm will find key without error. Choice D won't fail if 0 is in the array. Choice E will work if a[key] is not out of range.

8. **(A)**

|  | | | | | | | |
|---|---|---|---|---|---|---|---|
| After 1st pass: | 109 | 42 | −3 | 13 | 89 | 70 | 2 |
| After 2nd pass: | 109 | 89 | −3 | 13 | 42 | 70 | 2 |
| After 3rd pass: | 109 | 89 | 70 | 13 | 42 | −3 | 2 |

9. **(A)** The algorithm uses the fact that array v is sorted smallest to largest. The while loop terminates—which means that the search stops—as soon as v[index] >= key.

10. **(C)** The first pass uses the interval a[0]...a[7]. Since mid = (0 + 7)/2 = 3, low gets adjusted to mid + 1 = 4, and the second pass uses the interval a[4]...a[7].

11. **(B)** First pass: Compare 27 with a[3], since low = 0 high = 7 mid = (0 + 7)/2 = 3. Second pass: Compare 27 with a[5], since low = 4 high = 7 mid = (4 + 7)/2 = 5. Third pass: Compare 27 with a[6], since low = 6 high = 7 mid = (6 + 7)/2 = 6. The fourth pass doesn't happen, since low = 6 and high = 5, and therefore the test (low <= high) fails. Using the general rule for finding the number of iterations when key is not in the list: If $n$ is the number of elements, round $n$ up to the nearest power of 2, which is 8 in this case. Note that $8 = 2^3$. Since 27 lies between 4 and 41, there will be 3 iterations of the "divide-and-compare" loop.

12. **(D)** The method returns the index of the key parameter, 4. Since a[0] contains 4, binSearch(4) will return 0.

13. **(A)** Try 4. Here are the values for low, high, and mid when searching for 4:

1st pass:    low = 0,    high = 7,    mid = 3
2nd pass:    low = 0,    high = 2,    mid = 1

After this pass, high gets adjusted to mid −1, which is 0. Now low equals high, and the test for the while loop fails. The method returns −1, indicating that 4 wasn't found.

14. **(E)** When the loop is exited, either key = a[mid] (and mid has been returned) or key has not been found, in which case either a[low] ≤ key ≤ a[high] or key is not in the array. The correct assertion must account for all three possibilities.

15. **(A)** $30,000 = 1000 \times 30 \approx 2^{10} \times 2^5 = 2^{15}$. Since a successful binary search in the worst case requires $\log_2 n$ iterations, 15 iterations will guarantee that key is found. (Note that $30,000 < 2^{10} \times 2^5 = 32,768$.) Shortcut: $30,000 < 2^{15}$. Therefore, the maximum (worst case) number of comparisons that guarantees the key is found is equal to the exponent, 15.

16. **(B)** Start with the second element in the array.

|  | | | | | | |
|---|---|---|---|---|---|---|
| After 1st pass: | 7 | 1 | 9 | 5 | 4 | 12 |
| After 2nd pass: | 9 | 7 | 1 | 5 | 4 | 12 |
| After 3rd pass: | 9 | 7 | 5 | 1 | 4 | 12 |

17. **(B)** An insertion sort compares `a[1]` and `a[0]`. If they are not in the correct order, `a[0]` is moved and `a[1]` is inserted in its correct position. `a[2]` is then inserted in its correct position, and `a[0]` and `a[1]` are moved if necessary, and so on. Since B has only one element out of order, it will require the fewest changes.

18. **(A)** This list is almost sorted in reverse order, which is the worst case for insertion sort, requiring the greatest number of comparisons and moves.

19. **(D)** `j >= 0` is a stopping condition that prevents an element that is larger than all those to the left of it from going off the left end of the array. If no error occurred, it means that the largest element in the array was `a[0]`, which was true in situations I and II. Omitting the `j >= 0` test will cause a run-time (out-of-range) error whenever `temp` is bigger than all elements to the left of it (i.e., the insertion point is 0).

20. **(A)** Look at a small array that is almost sorted:

    10 8 9 6 2

    For <u>insertion sort</u>, you need four passes through this array.
    The first pass compares 8 and 10—one comparison, no moves.
    The second pass compares 9 and 8, then 9 and 10. The array becomes
    10 9 8 6 2—two comparisons, two moves.
    The third and fourth passes compare 6 and 8, and 2 and 6—no moves.
    In summary, there are approximately one or two comparisons per pass and no more than two moves per pass.
    For <u>selection sort</u>, there are four passes too.
    The first pass finds the biggest element in the array and swaps it into the first position. The array is still 10 8 9 6 2—four comparisons. There are two moves if your algorithm makes the swap in this case, otherwise no moves.
    The second pass finds the biggest element from `a[1]` to `a[4]` and swaps it into the second position: 10 9 8 6 2—three comparisons, two moves.
    For the third pass there are two comparisons, and one for the fourth. There are zero or two moves each time.
    Summary: $4 + 3 + 2 + 1$ total comparisons and a possible two moves per pass.
    Notice that reason I is valid. Selection sort makes the same number of comparisons irrespective of the state of the array. Insertion sort does far fewer comparisons if the array is almost sorted. Reason II is invalid. There are roughly the same number of data movements for insertion and selection. Insertion may even have more changes, depending on how far from their insertion points the unsorted elements are. Reason III is wrong because insertion and selection sorts have the same space requirements.

21. **(C)** Reject reason I. Merge sort requires both a `merge` and a `mergeSort` method—*more* code than the relatively short and simple code for insertion sort. Reject reason II. The `merge` algorithm uses a temporary array, which means *more* storage space than insertion sort. Reason III is correct. For long lists, the "divide-and-conquer" approach of merge sort gives it a faster run time than insertion sort.

22. **(D)** Since the search is for a four-letter sequence, the idea in this algorithm is that if you examine every fourth slot, you'll find a letter in the required sequence very quickly. When you find one of these letters, you can then examine adjacent slots to check if you have the required sequence. This method will, on average, result in fewer comparisons than the strictly sequential search algorithm in choice A. Choice B is wrong. If you encounter a "q," "r," or "s" without a "p" first, you can't have found "pqrs." Choice C is wrong because you may miss the sequence completely. Choice E doesn't make sense.

23. **(C)** The main precondition for a binary search is that the list is ordered.

24. **(E)** This algorithm is just a recursive implementation of a sequential search. It starts by testing if the last element in the array, `a[n-1]`, is equal to `value`. If so, it returns the index n - 1. Otherwise, it calls itself with n replaced by n - 1. The net effect is that it examines `a[n-1]`, `a[n-2]`, .... The base case, `if (n == 0)`, occurs when there are no elements left to examine. In this case, the method returns −1, signifying that `value` was not in the array.

25. **(D)** The `partition` algorithm performs a series of swaps until the pivot element is swapped into its final sorted position (see p. 346). No temporary arrays or external files are used, nor is a recursive algorithm invoked. The `merge` method is used for merge sort, not quicksort.

OPTIONAL TOPIC

26. **(D)** Recall the merge sort algorithm:

> Divide `arr` into two parts.
> Merge sort the left side.
> Merge sort the right side.
> Merge the two sides into a single sorted array.

The `merge` method is used for the last step of the algorithm. It does not do any sorting or partitioning of the array, which eliminates choices A, B, and C. Choice E is wrong because `merge` starts with a *single* array that has two sorted parts.

27. **(B)** Round 600 up to the next power of 2, which is $1024 = 2^{10}$. Recall the shortcut: $600 < 2^{10}$, so the worst case equals the exponent, 10.

28. **(B)** If the list is sorted in reverse order, each pass through the array will involve the maximum possible number of comparisons and the maximum possible number of element movements if an insertion sort is used.

29. **(B)** 1 million $= 10^6 = (10^3)^2 \approx (2^{10})^2 = 2^{20}$. Thus, there will be on the order of 20 comparisons.

30. **(A)** A binary search, on average, has a smaller run time than a sequential search. All of the sorting algorithms have greater run times than a sequential search. This is because a sequential search looks at each element once. A sorting algorithm, however, processes *other* elements in the array for each element it looks at.

31. **(D)** The computer should find the number in no more than seven tries. This is because the guessing interval is halved on each successive try:

$$(1) \quad 100 \div 2 = 50 \text{ numbers left to try}$$
$$(2) \quad 50 \div 2 = 25 \text{ numbers left to try}$$
$$(3) \quad 25 \div 2 = 13 \text{ numbers left to try}$$
$$(4) \quad 13 \div 2 = 7 \text{ numbers left to try}$$
$$(5) \quad 7 \div 2 = 4 \text{ numbers left to try}$$
$$(6) \quad 4 \div 2 = 2 \text{ numbers left to try}$$
$$(7) \quad 2 \div 2 = 1 \text{ number left to try}$$

Seven iterations of the loop leaves just 1 number left to try! Don't forget the shortcut. The algorithm is a binary search of 100 possible elements. Rounding 100 up to the next power of 2 gives $128 = 2^7$. The exponent, 7, is the number of guesses in the worst case.

32. **(B)** The maximum number of guesses is 99. A sequential search means that the computer starts at the first possible number—namely, 1—and tries each successive number until it gets to 99. If the user's number is 100, the computer will know that when it tests 99.

33. **(C)** On average the computer will make 50 guesses. The user is equally likely to pick any number between 1 and 100. Half the time it will be less than 50; half the time, greater than 50. So on the average, the distance of the number from 1 is 50.

# Practice Tests

# ANSWER SHEET
## Practice Test 1

**Section I**

1. Ⓐ Ⓑ Ⓒ Ⓓ Ⓔ
2. Ⓐ Ⓑ Ⓒ Ⓓ Ⓔ
3. Ⓐ Ⓑ Ⓒ Ⓓ Ⓔ
4. Ⓐ Ⓑ Ⓒ Ⓓ Ⓔ
5. Ⓐ Ⓑ Ⓒ Ⓓ Ⓔ
6. Ⓐ Ⓑ Ⓒ Ⓓ Ⓔ
7. Ⓐ Ⓑ Ⓒ Ⓓ Ⓔ
8. Ⓐ Ⓑ Ⓒ Ⓓ Ⓔ
9. Ⓐ Ⓑ Ⓒ Ⓓ Ⓔ
10. Ⓐ Ⓑ Ⓒ Ⓓ Ⓔ
11. Ⓐ Ⓑ Ⓒ Ⓓ Ⓔ
12. Ⓐ Ⓑ Ⓒ Ⓓ Ⓔ
13. Ⓐ Ⓑ Ⓒ Ⓓ Ⓔ
14. Ⓐ Ⓑ Ⓒ Ⓓ Ⓔ

15. Ⓐ Ⓑ Ⓒ Ⓓ Ⓔ
16. Ⓐ Ⓑ Ⓒ Ⓓ Ⓔ
17. Ⓐ Ⓑ Ⓒ Ⓓ Ⓔ
18. Ⓐ Ⓑ Ⓒ Ⓓ Ⓔ
19. Ⓐ Ⓑ Ⓒ Ⓓ Ⓔ
20. Ⓐ Ⓑ Ⓒ Ⓓ Ⓔ
21. Ⓐ Ⓑ Ⓒ Ⓓ Ⓔ
22. Ⓐ Ⓑ Ⓒ Ⓓ Ⓔ
23. Ⓐ Ⓑ Ⓒ Ⓓ Ⓔ
24. Ⓐ Ⓑ Ⓒ Ⓓ Ⓔ
25. Ⓐ Ⓑ Ⓒ Ⓓ Ⓔ
26. Ⓐ Ⓑ Ⓒ Ⓓ Ⓔ
27. Ⓐ Ⓑ Ⓒ Ⓓ Ⓔ
28. Ⓐ Ⓑ Ⓒ Ⓓ Ⓔ

29. Ⓐ Ⓑ Ⓒ Ⓓ Ⓔ
30. Ⓐ Ⓑ Ⓒ Ⓓ Ⓔ
31. Ⓐ Ⓑ Ⓒ Ⓓ Ⓔ
32. Ⓐ Ⓑ Ⓒ Ⓓ Ⓔ
33. Ⓐ Ⓑ Ⓒ Ⓓ Ⓔ
34. Ⓐ Ⓑ Ⓒ Ⓓ Ⓔ
35. Ⓐ Ⓑ Ⓒ Ⓓ Ⓔ
36. Ⓐ Ⓑ Ⓒ Ⓓ Ⓔ
37. Ⓐ Ⓑ Ⓒ Ⓓ Ⓔ
38. Ⓐ Ⓑ Ⓒ Ⓓ Ⓔ
39. Ⓐ Ⓑ Ⓒ Ⓓ Ⓔ
40. Ⓐ Ⓑ Ⓒ Ⓓ Ⓔ

# How to Calculate Your (Approximate) AP Computer Science A Score

**Multiple-Choice**

Number correct (out of 40) = _____ ⟸ Multiple-Choice Score

**Free-Response**

Question 1 _____
(out of 9)

Question 2 _____
(out of 9)

Question 3 _____
(out of 9)

Question 4 _____
(out of 9)

Total _____ × 1.11 = _____ ⟸ Free-Response Score
(Do not round.)

**Final Score**

_____ + _____ = _____
Multiple-          Free-          Final Score
Choice          Response          (Round to nearest
Score          Score          whole number.)

### Chart to Convert to AP Grade
### Computer Science A

| Final Score Range | AP Grade[a] |
|---|---|
| 62–80 | 5 |
| 47–61 | 4 |
| 37–46 | 3 |
| 29–36 | 2 |
| 0–28 | 1 |

[a]The score range corresponding to each grade varies from exam to exam and is approximate.

# Practice Test 1

## COMPUTER SCIENCE A
## SECTION I

**Time—1 hour and 30 minutes**
**40 Questions**

**DIRECTIONS:**   Determine the answer to each of the following questions or incomplete statements, using the available space for any necessary scratchwork.  Then decide which is the best of the choices given and fill in the corresponding oval on the answer sheet.  Do not spend too much time on any one problem.

**NOTES:**

- Assume that the classes in the Quick Reference have been imported where needed.
- Assume that variables and methods are declared within the context of an enclosing class.
- Assume that method calls that have no object or class name prefixed, and that are not shown within a complete class definition, appear within the context of an enclosing class.
- Assume that parameters in method calls are not `null` unless otherwise stated.

1. A large Java program was tested extensively, and no errors were found.  What can be concluded?
   (A)  All of the preconditions in the program are correct.
   (B)  All of the postconditions in the program are correct.
   (C)  The program may have bugs.
   (D)  The program has no bugs.
   (E)  Every method in the program may safely be used in other programs.

Questions 2–4 refer to the Worker class below.

```
public class Worker
{
    private String name;
    private double hourlyWage;
    private boolean isUnionMember;

    public Worker()
    { /* implementation not shown */ }

    public Worker(String aName, double anHourlyWage, boolean union)
    { /* implementation not shown */ }

    //Accessors getName, getHourlyWage, getUnionStatus are not shown.

    /** Permanently increase hourly wage by amt.
     *  @param amt the amount of wage increase
     */
    public void incrementWage(double amt)
    { /* implementation of incrementWage */ }

    /** Switch value of isUnionMember from true to false and
     *  vice versa.
     */
    public void changeUnionStatus()
    { /* implementation of changeUnionStatus */ }
}
```

2. Refer to the incrementWage method. Which of the following is a correct
   /* *implementation of* incrementWage */?

   (A) `return hourlyWage + amt;`

   (B) `return getHourlyWage() + amt;`

   (C) `hourlyWage += amt;`

   (D) `getHourlyWage() += amt;`

   (E) `hourlyWage = amt;`

3. Consider the method `changeUnionStatus`. Which is a correct
/* *implementation of* `changeUnionStatus` */?

   I. 
```
if (isUnionMember)
    isUnionMember = false;
else
    isUnionMember = true;
```

  II. `isUnionMember = !isUnionMember;`

 III. 
```
if (isUnionMember)
    isUnionMember = !isUnionMember;
```

(A) I only
(B) II only
(C) III only
(D) I and II only
(E) I, II, and III

4. A client method `computePay` will return a worker's pay based on the number of hours worked.

```
/** Precondition: Worker w has worked the given number of hours.
 *  @param w a Worker
 *  @param hours the number of hours worked
 *  @return amount of pay for Worker w
 */
public static double computePay(Worker w, double hours)
{ /* code */ }
```

Which replacement for /* *code* */ is correct?
(A) `return hourlyWage * hours;`
(B) `return getHourlyWage() * hours;`
(C) `return w.getHourlyWage() * hours;`
(D) `return w.hourlyWage * hours;`
(E) `return w.getHourlyWage() * w.hours;`

5. Consider this program segment. You may assume that `wordList` has been declared as `ArrayList<String>`.

```
for (String s : wordList)
    if (s.length() < 4)
        System.out.println("SHORT WORD");
```

What is the maximum number of times that `SHORT WORD` can be printed?
(A) 3
(B) 4
(C) `s.length()`
(D) `wordList.size() - 1`
(E) `wordList.size()`

6. Refer to the following method.

```
public static int mystery(int n)
{
    if (n == 1)
        return 3;
    else
        return 3 * mystery(n - 1);
}
```

What value does mystery(4) return?

(A) 3

(B) 9

(C) 12

(D) 27

(E) 81

7. Refer to the following declarations.

```
String[] colors = {"red", "green", "black"};
ArrayList<String> colorList = new ArrayList<String>();
```

Which of the following correctly assigns the elements of the colors array to colorList? The final ordering of colors in colorList should be the same as in the colors array.

I.  ```
    for (String col : colors)
        colorList.add(col);
    ```

II. ```
    for (String col : colorList)
        colors.add(col);
    ```

III. ```
     for (int i = colors.length - 1; i >= 0; i--)
         colorList.add(i, colors[i]);
     ```

(A) I only

(B) II only

(C) III only

(D) II and III only

(E) I, II, and III
     ```

8. Often the most efficient computer algorithms use a divide-and-conquer approach, for example, one in which a list is repeatedly split into two pieces until a desired outcome is reached. Which of the following use a divide-and-conquer approach?

    I. Merge sort
    II. Insertion sort
    III. Binary search

    (A) I only
    (B) II only
    (C) III only
    (D) I and III only
    (E) I, II, and III

9. An `Insect` class is to be written, containing the following data fields.

`age`, which will be initialized to `0` when an `Insect` is constructed.

`nextAvailableID`, which will be initialized to `0` outside the constructor and incremented each time an `Insect` is constructed.

`idNum`, which will be initialized to the current value of `nextAvailableID` when an `Insect` is constructed.

`position`, which will be initialized to the location in a garden where the `Insect` is placed when it is constructed.

`direction`, which will be initialized to the direction the `Insect` is facing when placed in the garden.

    Which variable in the `Insect` class should be static?

    (A) `age`
    (B) `nextAvailableID`
    (C) `idNum`
    (D) `position`
    (E) `direction`

**GO ON TO THE NEXT PAGE**

Questions 10 and 11 refer to the classes `Address` and `Customer` given below.

```java
public class Address
{
    private String street;
    private String city;
    private String state;
    private int zipCode;

    public Address(String aStreet, String aCity, String aState,
            int aZipCode)
    { /* implementation not shown */ }

    //Other methods are not shown.
}


public class Customer
{
    private String name;
    private String phone;
    private Address address;
    private int ID;

    public Customer(String aName, String aPhone, Address anAddr,
            int anID)
    { /* implementation not shown */ }

    public Address getAddress()
    { /* implementation not shown */ }

    public String getName()
    { /* implementation not shown */ }

    public String getPhone()
    { /* implementation not shown */ }

    public int getID()
    { /* implementation not shown */ }

    //Other methods are not shown.
}
```

10. Which of the following correctly creates a `Customer` object `c`?

    I. ```
    Address a = new Address("125 Bismark St", "Pleasantville",
        "NY", 14850);
    Customer c = new Customer("Jack Spratt", "747-1674", a, 7008);
    ```

    II. ```
    Customer c = new Customer("Jack Spratt", "747-1674",
        "125 Bismark St, Pleasantville, NY 14850", 7008);
    ```

    III. ```
    Customer c = new Customer("Jack Spratt", "747-1674",
        new Address("125 Bismark St", "Pleasantville", "NY", 14850),
        7008);
    ```

    (A) I only
    (B) II only
    (C) III only
    (D) I and II only
    (E) I and III only

11. Consider an `AllCustomers` class that has the following private instance variable.

    ```
    private Customer[] custList;
    ```

    Given the ID number of a particular customer, a method of the class, `locate`, must find the correct `Customer` record and return the name of that customer. Here is the method `locate`:

    ```
    /** Returns the name of the customer with the specified idNum.
     * Precondition: custList contains a complete list of Customer objects.
     */
    public String locate(int idNum)
    {
        for (Customer c : custList)
            if (c.getID() == idNum)
                return c.getName();
        return null;     //idNum not found
    }
    ```

    A more efficient algorithm for finding the matching `Customer` object could be used if
    (A) `Customer` objects were in alphabetical order by name.
    (B) `Customer` objects were sorted by phone number.
    (C) `Customer` objects were sorted by ID number.
    (D) the `custList` array had fewer elements.
    (E) the `Customer` class did not have an `Address` data member.
    ```

12. The following shuffling method is used to shuffle an array arr of int values. The method assumes the existence of a swap method, where swap(arr,i,j) interchanges the elements arr[i] and arr[j].

```java
public static void shuffle (int[] arr)
{
    for (int k = arr.length - 1; k > 0; k--)
    {
        int randIndex = (int) (Math.random() * (k + 1));
        swap(arr, k, randIndex);
    }
}
```

Suppose the initial state of arr is 1 2 3 4 5, and when the method is executed the values generated for randIndex are 3, 2, 0, and 1, in that order. What will be the final state of arr?

(A) 5 2 1 3 4

(B) 1 2 5 3 4

(C) 5 4 1 3 2

(D) 4 5 1 3 2

(E) 2 5 1 3 4

13. Refer to method `removeWord`.

```
/** Removes all occurrences of word from wordList.
/** Precondition: wordList is an ArrayList of String objects.
 *  Postcondition: All occurrences of word have been removed
 *                 from wordList.
 */
public static void removeWord(ArrayList<String> wordList,
                                                String word)
{
    for (int i = 0; i < wordList.size(); i++)
        if ((wordList.get(i)).equals(word))
            wordList.remove(i);
}
```

The method does not always work as intended. Consider the method call

```
removeWord(wordList, "cat");
```

For which of the following lists will this method call fail?

(A) The cat sat on the mat
(B) The cat cat sat on the mat mat
(C) The cat sat on the cat
(D) cat
(E) The cow sat on the mat

14. A `Clock` class has hours, minutes, and seconds represented by `int` values. It also has each of the following methods: `setTime` to change the time on a `Clock` to the hour, minute, and second specified; `getTime` to access the time; and `toString` to return the time as a `String`. The `Clock` class has a constructor that allows a `Clock` to be created with three `int` parameters for hours, minutes, and seconds. Consider a two-dimensional array of `Clock` values called `allClocks`. A code segment manipulating `allClocks` is as follows.

```
for (Clock[] row : allClocks)
    for (Clock c : row)
        /* more code */
```

Assuming the `Clock` class works as specified, which replacement for /* *more code* */ will cause an error?

I. `System.out.print(c);`

II. `c.setTime(0, 0, 0);`

III. `c = new Clock(0, 0, 0);`

(A) I only
(B) II only
(C) III only
(D) II and III only
(E) I and II only

15. Consider the following method that will access a square matrix mat.

```
/** Precondition: mat is initialized and is a square matrix.
 */
public static void printSomething(int[][] mat)
{
    for (int r = 0; r < mat.length; r++)
    {
        for (int c=0; c<=r; c++)
            System.out.print(mat[r][c] + " ");
        System.out.println();
    }
}
```

Suppose mat is originally

```
0 1 2 3
4 5 6 7
3 2 1 0
7 6 5 4
```

After the method call printSomething(mat) the output will be

(A)  0 1 2 3
     4 5 6 7
     3 2 1 0
     7 6 5 4

(B)  0
     4 5
     3 2 1
     7 6 5 4

(C)  0 1 2 3
     4 5 6
     3 2
     7

(D)  0
     4
     3
     7

(E)  There will be no output. An ArrayIndexOutOfBoundsException will be thrown.

16. Consider two different ways of storing a set of nonnegative integers in which there are no duplicates.

    Method One: Store the integers explicitly in an array in which the number of elements is known. For example, in this method, the set {6, 2, 1, 8, 9, 0} can be represented as follows.

    | 0 | 1 | 2 | 3 | 4 | 5 |
    |---|---|---|---|---|---|
    | 6 | 2 | 1 | 8 | 9 | 0 |

    6 elements

    Method Two: Suppose that the range of the integers is 0 to MAX. Use a boolean array indexed from 0 to MAX. The index values represent the possible values in the set. In other words, each possible integer from 0 to MAX is represented by a different position in the array. A value of true in the array means that the corresponding integer is in the set; a value of false means that the integer is not in the set. For example, using this method for the same set above, {6, 2, 1, 8, 9, 0}, the representation would be as follows (T = true, F = false).

    | 0 | 1 | 2 | 3 | 4 | 5 | 6 | 7 | 8 | 9 | 10 | ... | MAX |
    |---|---|---|---|---|---|---|---|---|---|----|-----|-----|
    | T | T | T | F | F | F | T | F | T | T | F  | ... | F   |

    The following operations are to be performed on the set of integers.

    I. Search for a target value in the set.
    II. Print all the elements of the set.
    III. Return the number of elements in the set.

    Which statement is true?
    (A) Operation I is more efficient if the set is stored using Method One.
    (B) Operation II is more efficient if the set is stored using Method Two.
    (C) Operation III is more efficient if the set is stored using Method One.
    (D) Operation I is equally efficient for Methods One and Two.
    (E) Operation III is equally efficient for Methods One and Two.

17. An algorithm for finding the average of $N$ numbers is

$$\text{average} = \frac{\text{sum}}{N}$$

    where $N$ and sum are both integers. In a program using this algorithm, a programmer forgot to include a test that would check for $N$ equal to zero. If $N$ is zero, when will the error be detected?
    (A) At compile time
    (B) At edit time
    (C) As soon as the value of $N$ is entered
    (D) During run time
    (E) When an incorrect result is output

18. Consider an array arr of 64 distinct int values, which are sorted in increasing order. The first element of the array, arr[0], equals 5, and the last element, arr[63], equals 200. A binary search algorithm will be used to locate various key values. Which of the following is a true statement?

   I. If 5 is the key, it will take exactly 7 iterations of the search loop to locate it.

   II. If 2 is the key, it will take exactly 7 iterations of the search loop to determine that 2 is not in arr.

   III. If 100 is the key, and 100 is equal to arr[62], it will take fewer than 7 iterations of the search loop to locate the key.

   (A) I only
   (B) II only
   (C) III only
   (D) I and II only
   (E) II and III only

19. Consider method getCount below.

```
public static int getCount(String s, String sub)
{
    int count = 0;
    int pos = s.indexOf(sub);
    while (pos >= 0)
    {
        s = s.substring(pos);
        count++;
        pos = s.indexOf(sub);
    }
    return count;
}
```

What will the method call getCount("a carrot and car", "car") return?
   (A) 0
   (B) 1
   (C) 2
   (D) 3
   (E) No value returned. The method is in an infinite loop.

20. Consider a program that deals with various components of different vehicles. Which of the following is a reasonable representation of the relationships among some classes that may comprise the program? Note that an open up-arrow denotes an inheritance relationship and a down-arrow denotes a composition relationship.

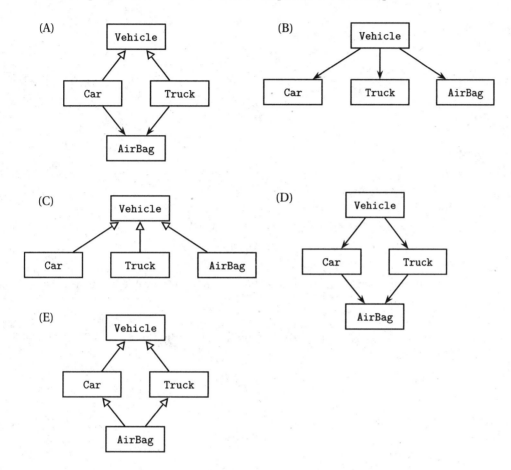

21. Consider the following program segment.

```
/** Precondition: a[0]...a[n-1] is an initialized array of integers,
 *                and 0 < n <= a.length.
 */
    int c = 0;
    for (int i = 0; i < n; i++)
        if (a[i] >= 0)
        {
            a[c] = a[i];
            c++;
        }
    n = c;
```

Which is the best postcondition for the segment? (You may assume that a[0]...a[-1] represents an empty array.)

(A) a[0]...a[n-1] contains no positive integers.

(B) a[0]...a[n-1] contains no negative integers.

(C) a[0]...a[n-1] contains no nonnegative integers.

(D) a[0]...a[n-1] contains no occurrences of zero.

(E) The updated value of n is less than or equal to the value of n before execution of the segment.

22. If a, b, and c are integers, which of the following conditions is sufficient to guarantee that the expression

```
a < c || a < b && !(a == c)
```

evaluates to true?

(A) a < c

(B) a < b

(C) a > b

(D) a == b

(E) a == c

23. Airmail Express charges for shipping small packages by integer values of weight. The charges for a weight $w$ in pounds are as follows.

$$0 < w \le 2 \quad \$4.00$$
$$2 < w \le 5 \quad \$8.00$$
$$5 < w \le 20 \quad \$15.00$$

The company does not accept packages that weigh more than 20 pounds. Which of the following represents the best set of data (weights) to test a program that calculates shipping charges?

(A) 0, 2, 5, 20

(B) 1, 4, 16

(C) −1, 1, 2, 3, 5, 16, 20

(D) −1, 0, 1, 2, 3, 5, 16, 20, 22

(E) All integers from −1 through 22

GO ON TO THE NEXT PAGE

24. Consider the following instance variable and methods in the same class.

```
private int[][] matrix;

/** Precondition: array.length > 0.
  * @return the largest integer in array
  */
private int max(int[] array)
{  /* implementation not shown */  }


/** @return num1 if num1 >= num2; otherwise return num2
  */
public int max(int num1, int num2)
{  /* implementation not shown */  }
```

Suppose `matrix` has a current value of

```
2 1 4 8
6 0 3 9
5 7 7 6
1 2 3 4
```

What will be returned by the following method call in the same class?

```
max(max(matrix[2]), max(matrix[3]))
```

(A) 9

(B) 8

(C) 7

(D) 4

(E) Compile-time error. No value returned.

Questions 25–26 are based on the following class declaration.

```
public class AutoPart
{
    private String description;
    private int partNum;
    private double price;

    public AutoPart(String desc, int pNum, double aPrice)
    { /* implementation not shown */ }

    public String getDescription()
    { return description; }

    public int getPartNum()
    { return partNum; }

    public double getPrice()
    { return price; }

    //Other methods are not shown.
    //There is no compareTo method.
}
```

25. This question refers to the `findCheapest` method below, which occurs in a class that has an array of `AutoPart` as one of its private data fields.

```
private AutoPart[] allParts;
```

The `findCheapest` method examines an array of `AutoPart` and returns the part number of the `AutoPart` with the lowest price whose description matches the `partDescription` parameter. For example, several of the `AutoPart` elements may have "headlight" as their description field. Different headlights will differ in both price and part number. If the `partDescription` parameter is "headlight", then `findCheapest` will return the part number of the cheapest headlight.

```
/** Returns the part number of the cheapest AutoPart
 *  whose description matches partDescription.
 *  Precondition: allParts contains at least one element whose
 *                description matches partDescription.
 */
public int findCheapest(String partDescription)
{
    AutoPart part = null;       //AutoPart with lowest price so far
    double min = LARGE_VALUE;   //larger than any valid price
    for (AutoPart p : allParts)
    {
        /* more code */
    }
    return part.getPartNum();
}
```

Which of the following replacements for /* *more code* */ will find the correct part number?

```
I. if (p.getPrice() < min)
   {
       min = p.getPrice();
       part = p;
   }
```

```
II. if (p.getDescription().equals(partDescription))
        if (p.getPrice() < min)
        {
            min = p.getPrice();
            part = p;
        }
```

```
III. if (p.getDescription().equals(partDescription))
         if (p.getPrice() < min)
             return p.getPartNum();
```

(A) I only
(B) II only
(C) III only
(D) I and II only
(E) I and III only

26. Consider the following method.

```
/** Returns the smaller of st1 and st2.
 * Precondition: st1 and st2 are distinct String objects.
 */
public static String min(String st1, String st2)
{
    if (st1.compareTo(st2) < 0)
        return st1;
    else
        return st2;
}
```

A method in the same class has these declarations.

```
AutoPart p1 = new AutoPart(< suitable values >);
AutoPart p2 = new AutoPart(< suitable values >);
```

Which of the following statements will cause an error?

I. `System.out.println(min(p1.getDescription(), p2.getDescription()));`

II. `System.out.println(min(p1.toString().getDescription(),`
    `p2.toString().getDescription()));`

III. `System.out.println(min(p1, p2));`

(A) I only
(B) II only
(C) III only
(D) I and II only
(E) II and III only

27. This question is based on the following declarations.

```
String strA = "CARROT", strB = "Carrot", strC = "car";
```

Given that all uppercase letters precede all lowercase letters when considering alphabetical order, which is true?

(A) `strA.compareTo(strB) < 0 && strB.compareTo(strC) > 0`

(B) `strC.compareTo(strB) < 0 && strB.compareTo(strA) < 0`

(C) `strB.compareTo(strC) < 0 && strB.compareTo(strA) > 0`

(D) `!(strA.compareTo(strB) == 0) && strB.compareTo(strA) < 0`

(E) `!(strA.compareTo(strB) == 0) && strC.compareTo(strB) < 0`

28. A programmer has a file of names. She is designing a program that sends junk mail letters to everyone on the list. To make the letters sound personal and friendly, she will extract each person's first name from the name string. She plans to create a parallel file of first names only. For example,

| fullName | firstName |
|---|---|
| Ms.  Anjali DeSouza | Anjali |
| Dr.  John Roufaiel | John |
| Mrs.  Mathilda Concia | Mathilda |

Here is a method intended to extract the first name from a full name string.

```
/** Precondition:
 *    - fullName starts with a title followed by a period.
 *    - A single space separates the title, first name, and last name.
 *  @param fullName a string containing a title, period, blank,
 *  and last name
 *  @return the first name only in fullName
 */
public static String getFirstName(String fullName)
{
    final String BLANK = " ";
    String temp, firstName;

    /* code to extract first name */

    return firstName;
}
```

Which represents correct /* *code to extract first name* */?

I.  ```
    int k = fullName.indexOf(BLANK);
    temp = fullName.substring(k + 1);
    k = temp.indexOf(BLANK);
    firstName = temp.substring(0, k);
    ```

II. ```
    int k = fullName.indexOf(BLANK);
    firstName = fullName.substring(k + 1);
    k = firstName.indexOf(BLANK);
    firstName = firstName.substring(0, k);
    ```

III. ```
     int firstBlank = fullName.indexOf(BLANK);
     int secondBlank = fullName.indexOf(BLANK);
     firstName = fullName.substring(firstBlank + 1, secondBlank + 1);
     ```

(A) I only

(B) II only

(C) III only

(D) I and II only

(E) I, II, and III
     ```

Questions 29–31 refer to the ThreeDigitInteger and ThreeDigitCode classes below.

```java
public class ThreeDigitInteger
{
    private int hundredsDigit;
    private int tensDigit;
    private int onesDigit;
    private int value;

    public ThreeDigitInteger(int aValue)
    { /* implementation not shown */ }

    /** Returns the sum of digits for this ThreeDigitInteger. */
    public int digitSum()
    { /* implementation not shown */ }

    /** Returns the sum of the hundreds digit and tens digit. */
    public int twoDigitSum()
    { /* implementation not shown */ }

    //Other methods are not shown.
}

public class ThreeDigitCode extends ThreeDigitInteger
{
    private boolean isValid;

    public ThreeDigitCode(int aValue)
    { /* implementation code */ }

    /** A ThreeDigitCode is valid if and only if the remainder when
     *  the sum of the hundreds and tens digits is divided by 7 equals
     *  the ones digit. Thus 362 is valid while 364 is not.
     *  Returns true if ThreeDigitCode is valid, false otherwise.
     */
    public boolean isValid()
    { /* implementation not shown */ }
}
```

29. Which is a true statement about the classes shown?
    (A) The `ThreeDigitInteger` class inherits the `isValid` method from the class `ThreeDigitCode`.
    (B) The `ThreeDigitCode` class inherits all of the public accessor methods from the `ThreeDigitInteger` class.
    (C) The `ThreeDigitCode` class inherits the constructor from the class `ThreeDigitInteger`.
    (D) The `ThreeDigitCode` class can directly access all the private variables of the `ThreeDigitInteger` class.
    (E) The `ThreeDigitInteger` class can access the `isValid` instance variable of the `ThreeDigitCode` class.

30. Which is correct /* *implementation code* */ for the `ThreeDigitCode` constructor?

    I. `super(aValue);`
       `isValid = isValid();`

    II. `super(value, valid);`

    III. `super(value);`
        `isValid = twoDigitSum() % 7 == onesDigit;`

    (A) I only
    (B) II only
    (C) III only
    (D) I and III only
    (E) I, II, and III

31. Refer to these declarations in a client program.

    ```
    ThreeDigitInteger code = new ThreeDigitCode(127);
    ThreeDigitInteger num = new ThreeDigitInteger(456);
    ThreeDigitCode newCode = new ThreeDigitCode(241);
    ```

    Which of the following subsequent tests will not cause an error?

    I. `if (code.isValid())`

          `...`

    II. `if (num.isValid())`

          `...`

    III. `if (newCode.isValid())`

          `...`

    (A) I only
    (B) II only
    (C) III only
    (D) I and II only
    (E) I and III only

GO ON TO THE NEXT PAGE

32. Consider the following hierarchy of classes.

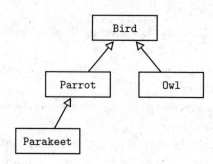

Assuming that each class has a valid no-argument constructor, which of the following declarations in a client program are correct?

I. `Bird b1 = new Parrot();`
   `Bird b2 = new Parakeet();`
   `Bird b3 = new Owl();`

II. `Parakeet p = new Parrot();`
    `Owl o = new Bird();`

III. `Parakeet p = new Bird();`

(A) I only
(B) II only
(C) III only
(D) II and III only
(E) I, II, and III

33. Consider an array `arr` and a list `list` that is an `ArrayList<String>`. Both `arr` and `list` are initialized with string values. Which of the following code segments correctly appends all the strings in `arr` to the end of `list`?

I. `for (String s : arr)`
   `    list.add(s);`

II. `for (String s : arr)`
    `    list.add(list.size(), s);`

III. `for (int i = 0; i < arr.length; i++)`
     `    list.add(arr[i]);`

(A) I only
(B) II only
(C) III only
(D) I and III only
(E) I, II, and III

34. Refer to the nextIntInRange method below.

```
/** Returns a random integer in the range low to high, inclusive. */
public int nextIntInRange(int low, int high)
{
    return /* expression */
}
```

Which /* *expression* */ will always return a value that satisfies the postcondition?

(A) (int) (Math.random() * high) + low;

(B) (int) (Math.random() * (high - low)) + low;

(C) (int) (Math.random() * (high - low + 1)) + low;

(D) (int) (Math.random() * (high + low)) + low;

(E) (int) (Math.random() * (high + low - 1)) + low;

35. Consider the following mergeSort method and the private instance variable a both in the same Sorter class.

```
private int[] a;

/** Sorts a[first] to a[last] in increasing order using merge sort. */
public void mergeSort(int first, int last)
{
    if (first != last)
    {
        int mid = (first + last) / 2;
        mergeSort(first, mid);
        mergeSort(mid + 1, last);
        merge(first, mid, last);
    }
}
```

Method mergeSort calls method merge, which has the following header.

```
/** Merge a[lb] to a[mi] and a[mi+1] to a[ub].
 *  Precondition: a[lb] to a[mi] and a[mi+1] to a[ub] both
 *               sorted in increasing order.
 */
private void merge(int lb, int mi, int ub)
```

If the first call to mergeSort is mergeSort(0,3), how many *further* calls will there be to mergeSort before an array b[0]...b[3] is sorted?

(A) 2

(B) 3

(C) 4

(D) 5

(E) 6

36. A large hospital maintains a list of patients' records in no particular order. To find the record of a given patient, which represents the most efficient method that will work?
  (A) Do a sequential search on the name field of the records.
  (B) Do a binary search on the name field of the records.
  (C) Use insertion sort to sort the records alphabetically by name; then do a sequential search on the name field of the records.
  (D) Use merge sort to sort the records alphabetically by name; then do a sequential search on the name field of the records.
  (E) Use merge sort to sort the records alphabetically by name; then do a binary search on the name field of the records.

Use the following information for Questions 37 and 38.

Here is a diagram that shows the relationship between some of the classes that will be used in a program to draw a banner with block letters.

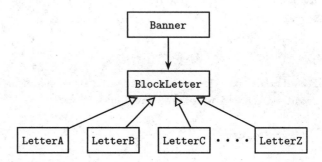

The diagram shows that the `Banner` class uses `BlockLetter` objects, and that the `BlockLetter` class has 26 subclasses, representing block letters from A to Z.

The `BlockLetter` class has a `draw` method

```
public void draw()
```

Each of the subclasses shown implements the `draw` method in a unique way to draw its particular letter. The `Banner` class gets an array of `BlockLetter` and has a method to draw all the letters in this array.

Here is a partial implementation of the `Banner` class.

```
public class Banner
{
    private BlockLetter[] letters;
    private int numLetters;

    /** Constructor. Gets the letters for the Banner. */
    public Banner()
    {
        numLetters = < some integer read from user input >
        letters = getLetters();
    }
}
```

```
/** Returns an array of block letters. */
public BlockLetter[] getLetters()
{
    String letter;
    letters = new BlockLetter[numLetters];
    for (int i = 0; i < numLetters; i++)
    {
        < read in capital letter >

        if (letter.equals("A"))
            letters[i] = new LetterA();
        else if (letter.equals("B"))
            letters[i] = new LetterB();
                ...           //similar code for C through Y
        else
            letters[i] = new LetterZ();
    }
    return letters;
}


/** Draw all the letters in the Banner. */
public void drawLetters()
{
    for (BlockLetter letter : letters)
        letter.draw();
}
}
```

37. You are given the information that `Banner` and `BlockLetter` are two classes used in the program. Which of the following can you conclude about the classes?

   I. `BlockLetter` inherits all the methods of `Banner`.

   II. `Banner` contains at least one `BlockLetter` object.

   III. Each of the subclasses `LetterA`, `LetterB`, `LetterC`, ...`LetterZ` has an overridden `draw` method.

   (A) I only
   (B) II only
   (C) III only
   (D) II and III only
   (E) I, II, and III

38. Which is a true statement about method `drawLetters`?
   (A) It is an overloaded method in the `Banner` class.
   (B) It is an overridden method in the `Banner` class.
   (C) It uses polymorphism to draw the correct letters.
   (D) It will cause a logic error because the `draw` method of the `BlockLetter` class is different from the `draw` methods of its subclasses.
   (E) It will cause a run-time error because there is no `draw` method in the `Banner` class.

39. Consider `method1` and `method2` below, which are identical except for the second to last line of code. Each method returns a new matrix based on the input matrix `mat`.

```
public static int[][] method1(int[][] mat)
{
    int numRows = mat.length;
    int numCols = mat[0].length;
    int[][] newMat = new int[numRows][numCols];
    for (int row = 0; row < numRows; row++)
        for (int col = 0; col < numCols; col++)
            newMat[numRows - row -1][col] = mat[row][col];
    return newMat;
}

public static int[][] method2(int[][] mat)
{
    int numRows = mat.length;
    int numCols = mat[0].length;
    int[][] newMat = new int[numRows][numCols];
    for (int row = 0; row < numRows; row++)
        for (int col = 0; col < numCols; col++)
            newMat[row][col] = mat[numRows - row - 1][col];
    return newMat;
}
```

Suppose the same input matrix is used for `method1` and `method2`, and the output for `method1` is `matrix1` while the output for `method2` is `matrix2`. Which is a true statement about `matrix1` and `matrix2`?

(A) `matrix1` is identical to `matrix2`.

(B) The rows of `matrix1` are the columns of `matrix2`.

(C) `matrix1` is a reflection of `matrix2` across a vertical line on the edge of either matrix.

(D) `matrix1` is a reflection of `matrix2` across a horizontal line on the bottom or top edge of either matrix.

(E) The rows of `matrix1` are the rows of `matrix2` in reverse order.

40. Consider an `ArrayList` cards of `Card` objects that needs to be shuffled. The following algorithm is used for shuffling.

> Create a temporary `ArrayList<Card>`
> Do the following `cards.size()` number of times
>   − Generate a random integer `r` that can index any card in `cards`
>   − Remove the card found at position `r` in `cards` and add it to the end
>     of the temporary `ArrayList`
> Set `cards` to the temporary `ArrayList`

Here is the method that implements this algorithm.

```
Line 1: public void shuffle()
Line 2: {
Line 3:     int size = cards.size();
Line 4:     ArrayList<Card> temp = new ArrayList<Card>();
Line 5:     for (int j = 1; j < size; j++)
Line 6:     {
Line 7:         int index = (int) (Math.random() * size);
Line 8:         temp.add(cards.get(index));
Line 9:     }
Line 10:    cards = temp;
Line 11: }
```

The method does not work as intended. Which of the following changes to `shuffle` would ensure that it works correctly?

I. Replace Line 5 with

```
for (int j = 0; j < size; j++)
```

II. Replace Line 7 with

```
int index = (int) (Math.random() * cards.size());
```

III. Replace Line 8 with

```
temp.add(cards.remove(index));
```

(A) I only
(B) II only
(C) III only
(D) I and III only
(E) I, II, and III

**END OF SECTION I**

# COMPUTER SCIENCE A
# SECTION II

**Time—1 hour and 30 minutes**
**4 Questions**

**DIRECTIONS:** SHOW ALL YOUR WORK. REMEMBER THAT PROGRAM SEGMENTS ARE TO BE WRITTEN IN JAVA.

Write your answers in the separate Free-Response booklet provided.

**NOTES:**

- Assume that the classes in the Quick Reference have been imported where appropriate.

- Unless otherwise noted in the question, assume that parameters in method calls are not `null` and that methods are called only when their preconditions are satisfied.

- In writing solutions for each question, you may use any of the accessible methods that are listed in classes defined in that question. Writing significant amounts of code that can be replaced by a call to one of these methods will not receive full credit.

**GO ON TO THE NEXT PAGE**

1. This question uses a password checker to report whether a given password is weak, medium, or strong. The `PasswordChecker` class is shown below. You will write two methods of the `PasswordChecker` class.

```
public class PasswordChecker
{

    /** Returns the number of digits in s.
     *  Precondition: s contains at least one character.
     */
    public static int numDigits(String s)
    { /* implementation not shown */ }

    /** Returns the number of letters in s.
     *  Precondition: s contains at least one character.
     */
    public static int numLetters(String s)
    { /* implementation not shown */ }

    /** Returns the number of characters in s
     *  that are neither letters nor digits.
     *  Precondition: s contains at least one character.
     */
    public static int numSymbols(String s)
    { /* to be implemented in part (a) */ }

    /** Returns the strength of password p
     *     as described in part (b).
     *  Precondition: p contains at least one character.
     */
    public static String passwordStrength(String p)
    { /* to be implemented in part (b) */ }

    // There may be instance variables, constructors and
    // methods not shown.
}
```

(a) Complete the `numSymbols` method, which finds how many characters in `String s` are neither letters nor digits.

Two helper methods, `numDigits` and `numLetters`, have been provided.

- `numDigits` returns the number of digits in its `String` parameter.
- `numLetters` returns the number of letters in its `String` parameter.

The following are some examples showing the use of `numDigits`, `numLetters`, and `numSymbols`.

| Method Call | Return Value |
| --- | --- |
| numDigits("R2@n49") | 3 |
| numLetters("R2@n49") | 2 |
| numSymbols("R2@n49") | 1 |
| numDigits("!?!?") | 0 |
| numLetters("!?!?") | 0 |
| numSymbols("!?!?") | 4 |

Complete the numSymbols method. You must use numDigits and numLetters appropriately to receive full credit.

```
/** Returns the number of characters in s
 *  that are neither letters nor digits.
 *  Precondition: s contains at least one character.
 */
public static int numSymbols(String s)
```

(b) Write the passwordStrength method. The method returns one of three String values: "strong", "medium", or "weak", depending on the characters of its String parameter p.

Here are the criteria for each type of password. (Assume that the word "symbol" refers to a character that is neither a digit nor a letter.)

■ A strong password is one with at least 8 characters and at least one digit, one letter, and one symbol.

■ A medium password has two possibilities:

  – Between 5 and 8 characters (5 inclusive), at least one of which is a symbol.

  – 8 or more characters, but is missing a digit, letter, or symbol, the second condition for being strong.

■ A weak password has two possibilities:

  – Fewer than 5 characters.

  – Between 5 and 8 characters (5 inclusive), in which none of the characters is a symbol.

Here are some examples.

| Method Call | Return Value |
| --- | --- |
| checkPassword("c@8") | weak |
| checkPassword("c1A2b3") | weak |
| checkPassword("c/A2b3") | medium |
| checkPassword("Two4two?") | strong |
| checkPassword("Hot3dog2019") | medium |

Complete method `passwordStrength`. Assume that `numSymbols` works as specified, regardless of what you wrote in part (a).

```
/** Returns the strength of password p
 *      as described in part (b).
 *   Precondition: p contains at least one character.
 */
public static String passwordStrength(String p)
```

2. In this question, you will write the implementation of a `SnowyOwl` class based on the hierarchy of classes shown below.

The `Owl` class is as follows.

```
public class Owl
{
    private String name;

    public Owl()
    { name = ""; }

    public Owl(String owlName)
    { name = owlName; }

    public String getName()
    { return name; }

    public String getFood()
    { return "furry animals, insects, or small birds"; }
}
```

Here are some features of a `SnowyOwl`.

- It's an `Owl` whose name is always `"Snowy owl"`.
- If the owl is a male, its color is white.
- If it is a female, its color is speckled.
- Food for a `SnowyOwl` depends on what is available. A `SnowyOwl` will randomly eat a hare, a lemming, or a small bird, where each type of food is equally likely.

**GO ON TO THE NEXT PAGE**

The SnowyOwl class should have a private instance variable of type boolean that stores true if the owl is male, false otherwise. It should also have a constructor and a get-Color method that returns a string with the snowy owl's color.

Write the complete SnowyOwl class. Your implementation should meet all specifications for a SnowyOwl.

3. Consider a system for processing names and addresses from a mailing list. A Recipients class will be used as part of this system. The lines in the mailing list are stored in an ArrayList<String>, a private instance variable in the Recipients class. The blank line that separates recipients in the mailing list is stored as the empty string in this list, and the final element in the list is an empty string.

A portion of the mailing list is shown below, with the corresponding part of the ArrayList.

```
Mr. J. Adams
6 Rose St.
Ithaca, NY 14850

Jack S. Smith
12 Posy Way
Suite 201
Glendale, CA 91203

Ms. M.K. Delgado
2 River Dr.
New York, NY 10013

...
```

| 0 | 1 | 2 | 3 | 4 |
|---|---|---|---|---|
| "Mr. J. Adams" | "6 Rose St." | "Ithaca, NY 14850" | "" | "Jack S. Smith" |

| 5 | 6 | 7 | 8 | 9 |
|---|---|---|---|---|
| "12 Posy Way" | "Suite 201" | "Glendale, CA 91203" | "" | "Ms. M.K. Delgado" |

| 10 | 11 | 12 |
|---|---|---|
| "2 River Dr." | "New York, NY 10013" | "" |

...

The `Recipients` class that processes these data is shown below.

```java
public class Recipients
{
    /** The list of lines in the mailing list */
    private ArrayList<String> lines;

    /** Constructor. Fill lines with mailing list data.
     *  Postcondition:
     *    - Each element in lines is one line of the mailing list.
     *    - Lines appear in the list in the same order
     *      that they appear in the mailing list.
     *    - Blank line separators in the mailing list are stored
     *      as empty strings.
     */
    public Recipients()
    { /* implementation not shown */ }

    /** Returns the city contained in the cityZip string of
     *  an address, as described in part (a).
     */
    public String extractCity(String cityZip)
    { /* to be implemented in part (a) */ }

    /** Returns the address of the recipient with the specified
     *  name, as described in part (b).
     */
    public String getAddress(String name)
    {/* to be implemented in part (b) */}

    //Other methods are not shown.
}
```

(a) Write the `extractCity` method of the `Recipients` class. In the `cityZip` parameter the city is followed by a comma, then one blank space, then two capital letters for a state abbreviation, then a space and 5-digit ZIP code. For example, if `cityZip` is `"Ithaca, NY 14850"`, the method call `extractCity(cityZip)` should return `"Ithaca"`.

```
Class information for this question
public class Recipients

private ArrayList<String> lines
public Recipients()
public String extractCity(String cityZip)
public String getAddress(String name)
```

Complete method `extractCity`.

```
/** Returns the city contained in the cityZip string of
 *  an address, as described in part (a).
 */
public String extractCity(String cityZip)
```

(b) Write the `getAddress` method of the `Recipients` class. This method should return a string that contains only the address of the corresponding `name` parameter. For example, if `name` is `"Jack S. Smith"`, a string containing the three subsequent lines of his address should be returned. This string should contain line breaks in appropriate places, including after the last line of the address. This ensures that the address will have the proper address format when printed by a client class. In the given example of name `"Jack S. Smith"`, the printed version of his address string should look like this:

```
Jack S. Smith
12 Posy Way
Suite 201
Glendale, CA 91203
```

Complete method `getAddress`.

```
/** Returns the address of the recipient with the specified
 *  name, as described in part (b).
 */
public String getAddress(String name)
```

4. A puzzle-solving competition is held in a large hall with a two-dimensional arrangement of contestants. Each rectangle below represents one contestant.

A contestant in the contest can be represented by a `Contestant` class, whose partial implementation follows.

```
public class Contestant
{
    private String name;
    private int score;

    /** Returns the name of this contestant. */
    public String getName()
    { return name; }

    /** Returns the score of this contestant. */
    public int getScore()
    { return score; }

    //Constructor and other methods are not shown.
}
```

In parts (a) and (b) you will write two methods of a ContestOrganizer class, whose partial implementation is shown below. A contest organizer keeps track of contestants in a two-dimensional array.

```
public class ContestOrganizer
{
    /** the number of rows of contestants */
    public static final int NUM_ROWS = <some integer>;

    /** the number of columns of contestants */
    public static final int CONTESTANTS_PER_ROW = <some integer>;

    /** The two-dimensional array of contestants */
    private Contestant[][] contestants;

    /** Sorts arr in increasing order by score. */
    private void sort(Contestant[] arr)
    { /* implementation not shown */ }

    /** Sorts each row of contestants into increasing order by score.
     * Postcondition: Contestant with highest score in row[k] is
     *                in the rightmost column of row[k], 0<=k<NUM_ROWS.
     */
    public void sortAllRows()
    { /* to be implemented in part(a) */ }

    /** Returns name of contestant with highest score.
     * Precondition:
     *    - Contestants have not been sorted by score.
     *    - Top score is unique.
     *    - Only one contestant has the highest score.
     */
    public String findWinnerName()
    { /* to be implemented in part(b) */ }
}
```

**GO ON TO THE NEXT PAGE**

(a) Write the ContestOrganizer method sortAllRows. This method should sort the contestants by score in each row, from lowest to highest.

Example: Suppose contestants are as shown below.

Here is what contestants will be after a call to sortAllRows.

In writing sortAllRows, your method *must* use the ContestOrganizer method sort. You may assume that sort works as specified.

Complete method sortAllRows.

```
/** Sorts each row of contestants into increasing order by score.
 *   Postcondition: Contestant with highest score in row[k] is
 *                  in the rightmost column of row[k], 0<=k<NUM_ROWS.
 */
public void sortAllRows()
```

(b) Write the Contestant method findWinnerName, which returns the name of the contestant with the highest score. For example, if the contestants are as shown above, a call to findWinnerName should return "Harry".

When writing findWinnerName, you should assume that the contestants have not yet been sorted by score, and that there is only one contestant with the highest score. In writing your solution, you *must* use method sortAllRows. You may assume that sortAllRows works as specified, regardless of what you wrote in part (a).

Complete method findWinnerName.

```
/** Returns name of contestant with highest score.
 *   Precondition:
 *     - Contestants have not been sorted by score.
 *     - Top score is unique.
 *     - Only one contestant has the highest score.
 */
public String findWinnerName()
```

**STOP**

**END OF EXAM**

# ANSWER KEY
## Practice Test 1

### Section I

| | | | | | |
|---|---|---|---|---|---|
| 1. **C** | | 15. **B** | | 29. **B** | |
| 2. **C** | | 16. **C** | | 30. **A** | |
| 3. **D** | | 17. **D** | | 31. **C** | |
| 4. **C** | | 18. **E** | | 32. **A** | |
| 5. **E** | | 19. **E** | | 33. **E** | |
| 6. **E** | | 20. **A** | | 34. **C** | |
| 7. **A** | | 21. **B** | | 35. **E** | |
| 8. **D** | | 22. **A** | | 36. **A** | |
| 9. **B** | | 23. **D** | | 37. **D** | |
| 10. **E** | | 24. **C** | | 38. **C** | |
| 11. **C** | | 25. **B** | | 39. **A** | |
| 12. **A** | | 26. **E** | | 40. **E** | |
| 13. **B** | | 27. **C** | | | |
| 14. **C** | | 28. **D** | | | |

## Answer Explanations

### Section I

1. **(C)** Testing a program thoroughly does not prove that a program is correct. For a large program, it is generally impossible to test every possible set of input data.

2. **(C)** The private instance variable hourlyWage must be incremented by amt. Eliminate choice E, which doesn't *increment* hourlyWage; it simply *replaces* it by amt. Choice D is wrong because you can't use a method call as the left-hand side of an assignment. Choices A and B are wrong because the incrementWage method is void and should not return a value.

3. **(D)** The value of the boolean instance variable isUnionMember must be changed to the opposite of what it currently is. Segments I and II both achieve this. Note that !true has a value of false and !false a value of true. Segment III fails to do what's required if the current value of isUnionMember is false.

4. **(C)** computePay is a client method and so cannot access the private variables of the class. This eliminates choices A and D. The method getHourlyWage() must be accessed with the dot member construct; thus, choice B is wrong, and choice C is correct. Choice E is way off base—hours is not part of the Worker class, so w.hours is meaningless.

5. **(E)** If s.length() < 4 for all strings in wordList, then SHORT WORD will be printed on each pass through the for loop. Since there are wordList.size() passes through the loop, the maximum number of times that SHORT WORD can be printed is wordList.size().

6. **(E)**

$$\text{mystery}(4) = 3 * \text{mystery}(3)$$
$$= 3 * 3 * \text{mystery}(2)$$
$$= 3 * 3 * 3 * \text{mystery}(1)$$
$$= 3 * 3 * 3 * 3$$
$$= 81$$

7. **(A)** The declaration of the colors array makes the following assignments: colors[0] = "red", colors[1] = "green", and colors[2] = "black". The loop in segment I adds these values to colorList in the correct order. Segment II fails because colors is an array and therefore can't use the get method. The code also confuses the lists. Segment III, in its first pass through the loop, attempts to add colors[2] to index position 2 of colorList. This will cause an IndexOutOfBoundsException to be thrown, since index positions 0 and 1 do not yet exist!

8. **(D)** Merge sort repeatedly splits an array of *n* elements in half until there are *n* arrays containing one element each. Now adjacent arrays are successively merged until there is a single merged, sorted array. A binary search repeatedly splits an array into two, narrowing the region that may contain the key. Insertion sort, however, does no array splitting. It takes elements one at a time and finds their insertion point in the sorted piece of the array. Elements are shifted to allow correct insertion of each element. Even though this algorithm maintains the array in two parts—a sorted part and yet-to-be-sorted part—this is not a divide-and-conquer approach.

9. **(B)** A static variable is shared by all instances of the class. "Static" means that there will be just one memory slot allocated, no matter how many Insects are constructed. All instances of Insect access the same information stored in that slot. When an Insect is created, it will get tagged with the current value of nextAvailableID for that memory slot, which will then be incremented for the next Insect created. All of the other variables—age, idNum, position, direction—are specific to one instance of Insect and should therefore be private instance variables in the class.

10. **(E)** A new Address object must be created, to be used as the Address parameter in the Customer constructor. To do this correctly requires the keyword new preceding the Address constructor. Segment II omits new and does not use the Address constructor correctly. (In fact, it inserts a new String object in the Address slot of the Customer constructor.)

11. **(C)** The algorithm used in method locate is a sequential search, which may have to examine all the objects to find the matching one. A binary search, which repeatedly discards a chunk of the array that does not contain the key, is more efficient. However, it can only be used if the values being examined—in this case customer ID numbers— are sorted. Note that it doesn't help to have the array sorted by name or phone number since the algorithm doesn't look at these values.

12. **(A)** The values of k are consecutively 4, 3, 2, and 1. The values of randIndex are consecutively 3, 2, 0, and 1. Thus, the sequence of swaps and corresponding states of arr will be:

```
swap arr[4] and arr[3]        1 2 3 5 4
swap arr[3] and arr[2]        1 2 5 3 4
swap arr[2] and arr[0]        5 2 1 3 4
swap arr[1] and arr[1]        5 2 1 3 4
```

13. **(B)** The `remove` method of `ArrayList` removes the indicated element, shifts the remaining elements one slot to the left (i.e., it does not leave gaps in the list), and adjusts the size of the list. Consider the list in choice B. The index values are shown:

```
The cat cat sat on the mat mat
 0   1   2   3   4  5   6   7
```

After the first occurrence of `cat` has been removed:

```
The cat sat on the mat mat
 0   1   2  3   4   5   6
```

The value of `i`, which was 1 when `cat` was removed, has now been incremented to 2 in the `for` loop. This means that the word to be considered next is `sat`. The second occurrence of `cat` has been missed. Thus, the given code will fail whenever occurrences of the word to be removed are consecutive. You fix it by not allowing the index to increment when a removal occurs:

```
int i = 0;
while (i < wordList.size())
{
    if ((wordList.get(i)).equals(word))
        wordList.remove(i);
    else
        i++;
}
```

14. **(C)** You should not use an enhanced `for` loop to replace elements, only to access (as in segment I) or modify using a mutator method (as in segment II). Note that segment III will compile and execute, but won't replace the clocks in `allClocks` as intended.

15. **(B)** When `r` is 0, `c` goes from 0 to 0, and just one element, `mat[0][0]`, will be printed. When `r` is 1, `c` goes from 0 to 1, and two elements, `mat[1][0]` and `mat[1][1]`, will be printed, and so on. When `r` is 3, all four elements of row 3 will be printed.

16. **(C)** To return the number of elements in the set for Method One requires no more than returning the number of elements in the array. For Method Two, however, the number of cells that contain true must be counted, which requires a test for each of the MAX values. Note that searching for a target value in the set is more efficient for Method Two. For example, to test whether 2 is in the set, simply check if `a[2] == true`. In Method One, a sequential search must be done, which is less efficient. To print all the elements in Method One, simply loop over the known number of elements and print. Method Two is less efficient because the whole array must be examined: Each cell must be tested for true before printing.

17. **(D)** An `ArithmeticException` will be thrown at run time. Note that if *N* were of type `double`, no exception would be thrown. The variable `sum` would be assigned the value `Infinity`, and the error would only be detected in the output.

18. **(E)** Only statements II and III are true. Note that $n$, the number of elements in the array, is a power of 2: $n = 64 = 2^6$. A worst case takes (exponent + 1) = 7 iterations of the search loop. Statement I is false, since the key is a left endpoint of the array, which does not represent a worst case. The key will be found in 6 iterations. Try it! Statement II, however, is true. It represents a worst case situation, in which the key is not in `arr` and is also outside the range of values of the array. So, there will be 7 passes through the loop. Statement III is true because the key, 100, is an element of `arr` that is not an endpoint. It therefore does not represent a worst case, and the key will be found in fewer than 7 iterations.

19. **(E)** The first value of `pos` is 2, the index of the first occurrence of `"car"` in `"a carrot and car"`. Then `s` gets assigned `"carrot and car"` and `pos` is now 0. Since `pos` is not advanced, it is stuck with a value of 0 and the method has an infinite loop. Notice that you can fix this problem by changing `s=s.substring(pos);` to `s=s.substring(pos+1);`.

20. **(A)** The correct diagram uses two up arrows to show that a `Car` *is-a* `Vehicle` and a `Truck` *is-a* `Vehicle` (inheritance relationship). The two down arrows indicate that a `Car` *has-a* `AirBag` and a `Truck` *has-a* `AirBag` (composition relationship). In each of the incorrect choices, at least one of the relationships does not make sense. For example, in choice B a `Vehicle` *has-a* `Truck`, and in choice E an `AirBag` *is-a* `Car`.

21. **(B)** The postcondition should be a true assertion about the major action of the segment. The segment overwrites the elements of array `a` with the nonnegative elements of `a`. Then `n` is adjusted so that now the array `a[0]...a[n-1]` contains just nonnegative integers. Note that even though choice E is a correct assertion about the program segment, it's not a good postcondition because it doesn't describe the main modification to array `a` (namely, all negative integers have been removed).

22. **(A)** Note the order of precedence for the expressions involved: (1) parentheses, (2) `!`, (3) `<`, (4) `==`, (5) `&&`, (6) `||`. This means that `a < c`, `a < b`, and `!(a == c)` will all be evaluated before `||` and `&&` are considered. The given expression then boils down to `value1 || (value2 && value3)`, since `&&` has higher precedence than `||`. Notice that if `value1` is true, the whole expression is true since (`true || any`) evaluates to true. Thus, `a < c` will guarantee that the expression evaluates to true. None of the other conditions will guarantee an outcome of true. For example, suppose `a < b` (choice B). If `a == c`, then the whole expression will be false because you get `F || F`.

23. **(D)** Test data should always include a value from each range in addition to all boundary values. The given program should also handle the cases in which weights over 20 pounds or any negative weights are entered. Note that choice E contains redundant data. There is no new information to be gained in testing two weights from the same range—both 3 and 4 pounds, for example.

24. **(C)** The `max` methods shown are overloaded methods (same name but different parameter types). In the given statement, `matrix[2]` and `matrix[3]` refer to row 2 and row 3 of the matrix, respectively, each of which is an array of `int`. `max(matrix[2])` is the largest element in row 2, namely 7, and `max(matrix[3])` is the largest element in row 3, namely 4. The given statement is therefore equivalent to `max(7,4)`, which will return 7.

25. **(B)** Segment II correctly checks that the part descriptions match and keeps track of the current part with minimum price. If this is not done, the part whose number must be returned will be lost. Segment I is incorrect because it doesn't check that `partDescription` matches the description of the current part being examined in the array. Thus, it simply finds the `AutoPart` with the lowest price, which is not what was required. Segment III incorrectly returns the part number of the first part it finds with a matching description.

26. **(E)** Statement I is fine: The parameters are `String` objects and can be compared. Statement II shows incorrect usage of the `toString()` method, which returns strings representing the `p1` and `p2` objects. Using the dot operator and `getDescription()` following those strings is meaningless in this context, since `getDescription()` applies to the `AutoPart` class, not the `String` class. Statement III will fail because `p1` and `p2` are not `String` objects and `min` applies to strings. Also, the `AutoPart` class as currently written does not have a `compareTo` method, so `AutoPart` objects cannot be compared.

27. **(C)** Ordering of strings involves a character-by-character comparison starting with the leftmost character of each string. Thus, `strA` precedes `strB` (since `"A"` precedes `"a"`) or `strA.compareTo(strB) < 0`. This eliminates choices B and D. Eliminate choices A and E since `strB` precedes `strC` (because `"C"` precedes `"c"`) and therefore `strB.compareTo(strC) < 0`. Note that `string1.compareTo(string2) == 0` if and only if `string1` and `string2` are equal strings.

28. **(D)** Suppose `fullName` is `Dr. John Roufaiel`. In segment I, the expression `fullName.indexOf(BLANK)` returns 3. Then, `temp` gets assigned the value of `fullName.substring(4)`, which is `John Roufaiel`. Next, `k` gets assigned the value `temp.indexOf(BLANK)`, namely 4, and `firstName` gets assigned `temp.substring(0, 4)`, which is all the characters from 0 to 3 inclusive, namely `John`. Note that segment II works the same way, except `firstName` gets assigned `John Roufaiel` and then reassigned `John`. This is not good style, since a variable name should document its contents as precisely as possible. Still, the code works. Segment III fails because `indexOf` returns the *first* occurrence of its `String` parameter. Thus, `firstBlank` and `secondBlank` will both contain the same value, 3.

29. **(B)** `ThreeDigitCode` is a subclass of `ThreeDigitInteger` and therefore inherits all the public methods of `ThreeDigitInteger` except constructors. All of the statements other than B are false. For choice A, `ThreeDigitInteger` is the superclass and therefore cannot inherit from its subclass. For choice C, constructors are never inherited (see p. 143). For choice D, a subclass can access private variables of the superclass through accessor methods only (see p. 142). For choice E, a superclass cannot access any additional instance variables of its subclass.

30. **(A)** Implementation I works because it correctly calls the superclass constructor by using `super`, with the subclass parameter `aValue`, in its first line. Additionally, it correctly initializes the subclass's `isValid` private instance variable by calling the `isValid` method, which it inherits from the superclass. Implementation II is wrong because the constructor has no boolean validity parameter. Implementation III is wrong because a subclass cannot access a private instance variable of its superclass.

31. **(C)** Test III works because `newCode` is of type `ThreeDigitCode`, which has an `isValid` method. A compile-time error will occur for both tests I and II because at compile time the types of `code` and `num` are both `ThreeDigitInteger`, and the class `ThreeDigitInteger` does not have an `isValid` method. To avoid this error, the `code` object must be cast to `ThreeDigitCode`, its actual type.

32. **(A)** The *is-a* relationship must work from right-to-left: a `Parrot` *is-a* `Bird`, a `Parakeet` *is-a* `Bird`, and an `Owl` *is-a* `Bird`. All are correct. This relationship fails in declarations II and III: a `Parrot` is not necessarily a `Parakeet`, a `Bird` is not necessarily an `Owl`, and a `Bird` is not necessarily a `Parakeet`.

33. **(E)** All three segments traverse the array, accessing one element at a time, and appending it to the end of the `ArrayList`. In segment II, the first parameter of the `add` method is the position in `list` where the next string `s` will be added. Since `list.size()` increases by one after each insertion, this index is correctly updated in each pass through the enhanced `for` loop.

34. **(C)** Suppose you want random integers from 2 to 8, that is, `low` = 2 and `high` = 8. This is 7 possible integers, so you need

    ```
    (int) (Math.random() * 7)
    ```

    which produces 0, 1, 2, ..., or 6. Therefore the quantity

    ```
    (int) (Math.random() * 7) + 2
    ```

    produces 2, 3, 4, ..., or 8. The only expression that yields the right answer with these values is

    ```
    (int) (Math.random() * (high - low + 1)) + low;
    ```

35. **(E)** Here is a "box diagram" for `mergeSort(0,3)`. The boldface numbers 1–6 show the order in which the `mergeSort` calls are made.

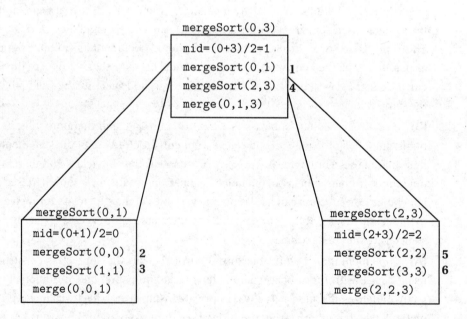

    The `mergeSort` calls in which `first == last` are base case calls, which means that there will be no further method calls.

36. **(A)** Since the records are not sorted, the quickest way to find a given name is to start at the beginning of the list and sequentially search for that name. Choices C, D, and E will all work, but it's inefficient to sort and then search because all sorting algorithms take longer than simply inspecting each element. Choice B won't work: A binary search can only be used for a sorted list.

37. **(D)** Statement I is false because `BlockLetter` is not a subclass of `Banner`. Note that a `BlockLetter` is not a `Banner`. In the UML diagram, the down arrow indicates that a `Banner` *has-a* `BlockLetter`. Statement II is true: The down arrow of the UML diagram shows that one or more `BlockLetter` objects is used in the `Banner` code. Statement III is true: Each of the subclasses overrides the `draw` method of `BlockLetter`, the superclass. Without this feature, the program won't work as intended.

38. **(C)** The `draw` method is polymorphic, which means that it is a superclass (in this case `BlockLetter`) method that is overridden in at least one of its subclasses. During run time, there is dynamic binding between the calling object and the method; that is, the actual instance is bound to its particular overridden method. In the `drawLetters` method, the correct version of `draw` is called during each iteration of the `for` loop, and a banner with the appropriate letters is drawn.

39. **(A)** `method1` creates a mirror image of its parameter `mat` across a horizontal line placed under `mat`. If `mat` is the matrix

    ```
    1 2 3
    4 5 6
    ```

    then the mirror image created below is

    ```
    4 5 6
    1 2 3
    ```

    `method2` also creates a mirror image, this time with the mirror placed *above* its parameter `mat`. Note that the reflection across a horizontal line above

    ```
    1 2 3
    4 5 6
    ```

    is also

    ```
    4 5 6
    1 2 3
    ```

    A good general hint to solve a problem like this is to take a very simple matrix `mat` and generate some elements of `newMat`. It won't take long to see that the two methods produce the same matrix.

40. **(E)** All three changes must be made! In order to move all the `Card` elements to the temporary `ArrayList`, the `for` loop must be executed `size` times. If you start `j` at 1, the loop will be executed `size-1` times. The error in Line 7 is subtle. With each iteration of the loop, the size of the `cards` `ArrayList` is being reduced by 1, so the range of random indexes is getting smaller and smaller. This won't happen if you use `size`, the length of the *original* `cards` list. You must use `cards.size()`, which is the length of the current, shorter list. If you don't make correction III, the random element will not be removed from `cards`. It will (incorrectly) remain there while a copy of it will be added to `temp`. If this error isn't corrected, execution of the method is likely to cause the `temp` list to hold more than one copy of a given card!

**Section II**

1.  (a) 
```java
public static int numSymbols(String s)
{
    return s.length() - (numLetters(s) + numDigits(s));
}
```

(b) 
```java
public static String passwordStrength(String p)
{
    if (p.length() < 5)
        return "weak";
    else if (p.length() >= 5 && p.length() < 8)
    {
        if (numSymbols(p) > 0)
            return "medium";
        else
            return "weak";
    }
    else if (numSymbols(p) > 0 && numLetters(p) > 0 && numDigits(p) > 0)
        return "strong";
    else return "medium";
}
```

**Note**

- For part(b), by the first `else if` test, all passwords with fewer than 5 characters have been taken care of. By the second `else if` test, all passwords with fewer than 8 characters have been taken care of. Therefore, the second `else if` test deals only with passwords that have 8 or more characters, and you don't explicitly need to test for the number of characters.

## Scoring Rubric: Password Checker

| Part (a) | numSymbols | 2 points |
|---|---|---|
| +1 | use `s.length()` | |
| +1 | subtract `(numDigits + numLetters)` | |

| Part (b) | passwordStrength | 7 points |
|---|---|---|
| +1 | test length < 5 | |
| +1 | test length between 5 and 8 | |
| +1 | test `numSymbols > 0` | |
| +1 | else return `"weak"` | |
| +1 | test for digit, letter, and symbol in long password | |
| +1 | return `"strong"` | |
| +1 | return `"medium"` | |

2.

```java
public class SnowyOwl extends Owl
{
    private boolean isMale;

    public SnowyOwl(boolean isAMale)
    {
        super("Snowy Owl");
        isMale = isAMale;
    }

    public String getColor()
    {
        if (isMale)
            return "white";
        else
            return "speckled";
    }

    public String getFood()
    {

        int num = (int) (Math.random() * 3);
        if (num == 0)
            return "hare";
        else if (num == 1)
            return "lemming";
        else
            return "small bird";
    }
}
```

**Note**

- The `Owl` getFood method is overridden to show the specific eating habits of a `SnowyOwl`.
- In the constructor, `super` must be used because there is no direct access to the private instance variables of the `Bird` class. The new variable `isMale` must be initialized in the constructor.
- Note that the noise for `Owl` will always be `"hoot"`. Thus, noise does not need to be provided as a parameter in the `SnowyOwl` constructor.

## Scoring Rubric: Snowy Owl

| | SnowyOwl class | 9 points |
|---|---|---|
| +1 | use of extends in declaration | |
| +1 | constructor declaration | |
| +1 | code using super | |
| +1 | "Snowy owl" parameter | |
| +1 | declaration of getFood | |
| +1 | getColor method | |
| +1 | get random int from 0 to 2 | |
| +1 | if...else statement | |
| +1 | return statements | |

3. (a)
```
public String extractCity(String cityZip)
{
    int commaPos = cityZip.indexOf(",");
    return cityZip.substring(0, commaPos);
}
```

(b)
```
public String getAddress(String name)
{
    int index = 0;
    while(index < lines.size() && !name.equals(lines.get(index)))
        index++;
    index++;
    String s = "";
    while (!(lines.get(index).equals("")))
    {
        s += lines.get(index) + "\n";
        index++;
    }
    return s;
}
```

**Note**

- Part (b) first finds the name that matches the parameter, and then builds a string out of the next two or three lines that comprise the address. Again, the empty string signals that the end of the address has been reached.
- The escape character string, "\n", inserts a line break into the string.

## Scoring Rubric: Mailing List

| Part (a) | extractCity | 3 points |
|---|---|---|
| +1 | locate comma in ZIP code | |
| +1 | return substring that contains the city | |
| +1 | substring parameters | |

| Part (b) | getAddress | 6 points |
|---|---|---|
| +1 | loop to search for name | |
| +1 | loop to traverse lines until end of address is reached | |
| +1 | check range of index | |
| +1 | concatenate lines of address | |
| +1 | newline characters | |
| +1 | return string containing address | |

4.  (a)
```java
public void sortAllRows()
{
    for(Contestant[] row: contestants)
        sort(row);
}
```

   (b)
```java
public String findWinnerName()
{
    sortAllRows();
    int max = contestants[0][0].getScore();
    String winner = contestants[0][0].getName();
    for(int k = 0; k < NUM_ROWS; k++)
    {
        Contestant c = contestants[k][CONTESTANTS_PER_ROW - 1];
        if (c.getScore() > max)
        {
            winner = c.getName();
            max = c.getScore();
        }
    }
    return winner;
}
```

**Note**

- Part (a) uses the Java feature that a two-dimensional array is an array of arrays. Thus, each row, which is an array of Contestant, can be sorted using the helper method sort.
- Part (b) uses the fact that after you sort all the rows of contestants, the winning contestant will be in the last column of the matrix of contestants. When you go through the loop, searching for a score that's higher than the current max, be sure to store the name that goes with that score!

# Scoring Rubric: Two-Dimensional Contest Organizer

| Part (a) | sortAllRows | 2 points |
|---|---|---|
| +1 | loop over the rows of Contestants | |
| +1 | sort each row | |

| Part (b) | findWinnerName | 7 points |
|---|---|---|
| +1 | call sortAllRows | |
| +1 | get score of top scorer in first row | |
| +1 | get name of top scorer in first row | |
| +1 | loop over all rows | |
| +1 | accessing contestant in last column | |
| +1 | test for score higher than max | |
| +1 | adjust winner and max if higher score found | |

# ANSWER SHEET
## Practice Test 2

**Section I**

1. Ⓐ Ⓑ Ⓒ Ⓓ Ⓔ
2. Ⓐ Ⓑ Ⓒ Ⓓ Ⓔ
3. Ⓐ Ⓑ Ⓒ Ⓓ Ⓔ
4. Ⓐ Ⓑ Ⓒ Ⓓ Ⓔ
5. Ⓐ Ⓑ Ⓒ Ⓓ Ⓔ
6. Ⓐ Ⓑ Ⓒ Ⓓ Ⓔ
7. Ⓐ Ⓑ Ⓒ Ⓓ Ⓔ
8. Ⓐ Ⓑ Ⓒ Ⓓ Ⓔ
9. Ⓐ Ⓑ Ⓒ Ⓓ Ⓔ
10. Ⓐ Ⓑ Ⓒ Ⓓ Ⓔ
11. Ⓐ Ⓑ Ⓒ Ⓓ Ⓔ
12. Ⓐ Ⓑ Ⓒ Ⓓ Ⓔ
13. Ⓐ Ⓑ Ⓒ Ⓓ Ⓔ
14. Ⓐ Ⓑ Ⓒ Ⓓ Ⓔ

15. Ⓐ Ⓑ Ⓒ Ⓓ Ⓔ
16. Ⓐ Ⓑ Ⓒ Ⓓ Ⓔ
17. Ⓐ Ⓑ Ⓒ Ⓓ Ⓔ
18. Ⓐ Ⓑ Ⓒ Ⓓ Ⓔ
19. Ⓐ Ⓑ Ⓒ Ⓓ Ⓔ
20. Ⓐ Ⓑ Ⓒ Ⓓ Ⓔ
21. Ⓐ Ⓑ Ⓒ Ⓓ Ⓔ
22. Ⓐ Ⓑ Ⓒ Ⓓ Ⓔ
23. Ⓐ Ⓑ Ⓒ Ⓓ Ⓔ
24. Ⓐ Ⓑ Ⓒ Ⓓ Ⓔ
25. Ⓐ Ⓑ Ⓒ Ⓓ Ⓔ
26. Ⓐ Ⓑ Ⓒ Ⓓ Ⓔ
27. Ⓐ Ⓑ Ⓒ Ⓓ Ⓔ
28. Ⓐ Ⓑ Ⓒ Ⓓ Ⓔ

29. Ⓐ Ⓑ Ⓒ Ⓓ Ⓔ
30. Ⓐ Ⓑ Ⓒ Ⓓ Ⓔ
31. Ⓐ Ⓑ Ⓒ Ⓓ Ⓔ
32. Ⓐ Ⓑ Ⓒ Ⓓ Ⓔ
33. Ⓐ Ⓑ Ⓒ Ⓓ Ⓔ
34. Ⓐ Ⓑ Ⓒ Ⓓ Ⓔ
35. Ⓐ Ⓑ Ⓒ Ⓓ Ⓔ
36. Ⓐ Ⓑ Ⓒ Ⓓ Ⓔ
37. Ⓐ Ⓑ Ⓒ Ⓓ Ⓔ
38. Ⓐ Ⓑ Ⓒ Ⓓ Ⓔ
39. Ⓐ Ⓑ Ⓒ Ⓓ Ⓔ
40. Ⓐ Ⓑ Ⓒ Ⓓ Ⓔ

## How to Calculate Your (Approximate) AP Computer Science A Score

**Multiple-Choice**

Number correct (out of 40)   =   _____   ⟸   Multiple-Choice Score

**Free-Response**

Question 1   _____
(out of 9)

Question 2   _____
(out of 9)

Question 3   _____
(out of 9)

Question 4   _____
(out of 9)

Total   _____   ×   1.11   =   _____   ⟸   Free-Response Score
(Do not round.)

**Final Score**

_____   +   _____   =   _____
Multiple-         Free-            Final Score
Choice           Response         (Round to nearest
Score            Score            whole number.)

### Chart to Convert to AP Grade
### Computer Science A

| Final Score Range | AP Grade[a] |
|---|---|
| 62–80 | 5 |
| 47–61 | 4 |
| 37–46 | 3 |
| 29–36 | 2 |
| 0–28 | 1 |

[a]The score range corresponding to each grade varies from exam to exam and is approximate.

# Practice Test 2
## COMPUTER SCIENCE A
## SECTION I

**Time—1 hour and 30 minutes**
**40 Questions**

**DIRECTIONS:** Determine the answer to each of the following questions or incomplete statements, using the available space for any necessary scratchwork. Then decide which is the best of the choices given and fill in the corresponding oval on the answer sheet. Do not spend too much time on any one problem.

**NOTES:**

- Assume that the classes in the Quick Reference have been imported where needed.
- Assume that variables and methods are declared within the context of an enclosing class.
- Assume that method calls that have no object or class name prefixed, and that are not shown within a complete class definition, appear within the context of an enclosing class.
- Assume that parameters in method calls are not `null` unless otherwise stated.

1. What output is produced by the following line of code?

```
System.out.println("\"This is\n very strange\"");
```

(A) \This is\n very strange\

(B) "This is very strange"

(C) This is
    very strange

(D) \"This is
     very strange\"

(E) "This is
     very strange"

2. A certain class, `SomeClass`, contains a method with the following header.

```
public int getValue(int n)
```

Suppose that methods with the following headers are now added to `SomeClass`.

   I. `public int getValue()`

  II. `public double getValue(int n)`

 III. `public int getValue(double n)`

Which of the above headers will cause an error?

(A) I only

(B) II only

(C) III only

(D) I and II only

(E) I and III only

3. Consider the following statement.

```
int num = /* expression */;
```

Which of the following replacements for `/* expression */` creates in `num` a random integer from 2 to 50, including 2 and 50?

(A) `(int)(Math.random() * 50) - 2`

(B) `(int)(Math.random() * 49) - 2`

(C) `(int)(Math.random() * 49) + 2`

(D) `(int)(Math.random() * 50) + 2`

(E) `(int)(Math.random() * 48) + 2`

4. Consider the following code segment.

```
int num = 0, score = 10;
if (num != 0 && score / num > SOME_CONSTANT)
    statement1;
else
    statement2;
```

What is the result of executing this statement?

(A) An `ArithmeticException` will be thrown.

(B) A syntax error will occur.

(C) *statement1*, but not *statement2*, will be executed.

(D) *statement2*, but not *statement1*, will be executed.

(E) Neither *statement1* nor *statement2* will be executed; control will pass to the first statement following the `if` statement.

5. The following shuffle algorithm is used to shuffle an array of `int` values, `nums`.

```
public void shuffle ()
{
    for (int k = nums.length - 1; k > 0; k--)
    {
        int randPos = (int) (Math.random() * (k + 1));
        int temp = nums[k];
        nums[k] = nums[randPos];
        nums[randPos] = temp;
    }
}
```

Suppose the initial state of `nums` is 8, 7, 6, 5, 4, and when the method is executed the values generated for `randPos` are 3, 2, 0, 0, in that order. What element will be contained in `nums[2]` after execution?

(A) 8

(B) 7

(C) 6

(D) 5

(E) 4

6. Consider the following instance variables and method `assignValues` in the same class.

```
private int numRows;
private int numCols;
private int[][] mat;

/** arr has numCols elements */
private void assignValues(int[] arr, int value)
{
    for (int k = 0; k < arr.length; k++)
        arr[k] = value;
}
```

Which of the following code segments will correctly assign `mat` to have the value 100 in each slot? You may assume that the instance variables have all been correctly initialized.

```
I.   for (int row = 0; row < numRows; row++)
         assignValues(mat[row], 100);

II.  for (int col = 0; col < numCols; col++)
         assignValues(mat[col], 100);

III. for (int[] row: mat)
         for (int num: row)
             num = 100;
```

(A) I only

(B) II only

(C) III only

(D) I and II only

(E) I and III only

7. Consider the following inheritance hierarchy.

Which of the following declarations will not cause an error? You may assume that each of the classes above has a no-argument constructor.

    I. `WheatCereal w = new Cereal();`

   II. `Cereal c1 = new Cereal();`

  III. `Cereal c2 = new RiceCereal();`

(A) I only
(B) II only
(C) III only
(D) II and III only
(E) I, II, and III

Questions 8 and 9 refer to the following class definitions.

```
public Class1
{
    public void method1()
    { /* implementation not shown */ }
}


public class Class2 extends Class1
{
    public void method2()
    { /* implementation not shown */ }

    //Private instance variables and other methods are not shown.
}


public class Class3 extends Class2
{
    public void method3(Class3 other)
    { /* implementation not shown */ }

    //Private instance variables and other methods are not shown.
}
```

8. Assuming that `Class1`, `Class2`, and `Class3` have no-argument constructors, which is (are) valid in a client class?

   I. `Class1 c1 = new Class2();`

  II. `Class2 c2 = new Class3();`

 III. `Class1 c3 = new Class3();`

  (A) I only
  (B) II only
  (C) III only
  (D) I and II only
  (E) I, II, and III

9. Consider the following declarations in a client class.

```
Class3 ob3 = new Class3();
Class2 ob2 = new Class2();
```

Which method calls would be legal?

   I. `ob3.method1();`

  II. `ob2.method3(ob3);`

 III. `ob3.method3(ob2);`

  (A) I only
  (B) II only
  (C) III only
  (D) II and III only
  (E) I, II, and III

10. Refer to the following program segment.

```
for (int n = 50; n > 0; n = n / 2)
    System.out.println(n);
```

How many lines of output will this segment produce?

(A) 50

(B) 49

(C) 7

(D) 6

(E) 5

11. Let list be an ArrayList<String> containing only these elements.

```
"John", "Mary", "Harry", "Luis"
```

Which of the following statements will cause an error to occur?

I. list.set(2, "6");

II. list.add(4, "Pat");

III. String s = list.get(4);

(A) I only

(B) II only

(C) III only

(D) II and III only

(E) I, II, and III

12. Consider the following static method.

```
public static int compute(int n)
{
    for (int i = 1; i < 4; i++)
        n *= n;
    return n;
}
```

Which of the following could replace the body of compute, so that the new version returns the identical result as the original for all n?

(A) return 4 * n;

(B) return 8 * n;

(C) return 64 * n;

(D) return (int) Math.pow(n, 4);

(E) return (int) Math.pow(n, 8);

13. Consider the following instance variable and method.

```
private int[] nums;

/** Precondition: nums contains int values in no particular order.
 */
public int getValue()
{
    for (int k = 0; k < nums.length; k++)
    {
        if (nums[k] % 2 != 0)
            return k;
    }
    return -1;
}
```

Suppose the following statement is executed.

```
int j = getValue();
```

If the value returned in j is a positive integer, which of the following best describes the contents of nums?

(A) The only odd int in nums is at position j.

(B) All values in positions 0 through j-1 are odd.

(C) All values in positions 0 through j-1 are even.

(D) All values in positions nums.length-1 down to j+1 are odd.

(E) All values in positions nums.length-1 down to j+1 are even.

14. Consider the following method.

```
public int mystery (int n)
{
    if (n == 0)
        return 0;
    else if (n % 2 == 1)
        return n;
    else
        return n + mystery(n - 1);
}
```

What will be returned by a call to mystery(6)?

(A) 6

(B) 11

(C) 12

(D) 27

(E) 30

15. Consider the following code segment.

```
int num1 = value1, num2 = value2, num3 = value3;
while (num1 > num2 || num1 > num3)
{
    /* body of loop */
}
```

You may assume that `value1`, `value2`, and `value3` are `int` values. Which of the following is sufficient to guarantee that /* *body of loop* */ will never be executed?

(A) There is no statement in /* *body of loop* */ that leads to termination.

(B) `num1 < num2`

(C) `num1 < num3`

(D) `num1 > num2 && num1 > num3`

(E) `num1 < num2 && num1 < num3`

16. Consider the following two classes.

```
public class Performer
{
    public void act()
    {
        System.out.print(" bow");
        perform();
    }

    public void perform()
    {
        System.out.print(" act");
    }
}

public class Singer extends Performer
{
    public void act()
    {
        System.out.print(" rise");
        super.act();
        System.out.print(" encore");
    }

    public void perform()
    {
        System.out.print(" aria");
    }
}
```

Suppose the following declaration appears in a class other than `Performer` or `Singer`.

```
Performer p = new Singer();
```

What is printed as a result of the call `p.act();`?

(A) rise bow aria encore
(B) rise bow act encore
(C) rise bow act
(D) bow act aria
(E) bow aria encore

Use the program description below for Questions 17–19.

A car dealer needs a program that will maintain an inventory of cars on his lot. There are four types of cars: sedans, station wagons, electric cars, and SUVs. The model, year, color, and price need to be recorded for each car, plus any additional features for the different types of cars. The program must allow the dealer to

- Add a new car to the lot.
- Remove a car from the lot.
- Correct any data that have been entered.
- Display information for any car.

17. The programmer decides to have these classes: Car, Inventory, Sedan, SUV, ElectricCar, and StationWagon. Which statement is true about the relationships between these classes and their attributes?

    I. There are no inheritance relationships between these classes.
    II. The Inventory class *has-a* list of Car objects.
    III. The Sedan, SUV, ElectricCar, and StationWagon classes are independent of each other.

    (A) I only
    (B) II only
    (C) III only
    (D) I and II only
    (E) II and III only

18. Suppose that the programmer decides to have a Car class and an Inventory class. The Inventory class will maintain a list of all the cars on the lot. Here are some of the methods in the program.

```
addCar          //adds a car to the lot
removeCar       //removes a car from the lot
displayCar      //displays all the features of a given car
setColor        //sets the color of a car to a given color
                //   (may be used to correct data)
getPrice        //returns the price of a car
displayAllCars  //displays features for every car on the lot
```

In each of the following, a class and a method are given. Which is the least suitable choice of class to be responsible for the given method?
    (A) Car, setColor
    (B) Car, removeCar
    (C) Car, getPrice
    (D) Car, displayCar
    (E) Inventory, displayAllCars

19. Suppose `Car` is a superclass and `Sedan`, `StationWagon`, `ElectricCar`, and `SUV` are sub-classes of `Car`. Which of the following is the most likely method of the `Car` class to be overridden by at least one of the subclasses (`Sedan`, `StationWagon`, `ElectricCar`, or `SUV`)?

    (A) `setColor(newColor)`    `//sets color of Car to newColor`
    (B) `getModel()`            `//returns model of Car`
    (C) `displayCar()`          `//displays all features of Car`
    (D) `setPrice(newPrice)`    `//sets price of Car to newPrice`
    (E) `getYear()`             `//returns year of Car`

20. Consider the following segment of code.

    ```
    String word = "conflagration";
    int x = word.indexOf("flag");
    String s = word.substring(0, x);
    ```

    What will be the result of executing the above segment?
    (A) A syntax error will occur.
    (B) String `s` will be the empty string.
    (C) String `s` will contain `"flag"`.
    (D) String `s` will contain `"conf"`.
    (E) String `s` will contain `"con"`.

21. A two-dimensional matrix `mat` with at least one row is initialized and will be traversed using a row-major (row-by-row, left-to-right) traversal. Which represents the last element accessed?

    (A) `mat[mat.length][mat[0].length]`
    (B) `mat[mat[0].length][mat.length]`
    (C) `mat[mat.length - 1][mat[0].length - 1]`
    (D) `mat[mat[0].length - 1][mat.length - 1]`
    (E) `mat[mat.length - 1][mat.length - 1]`

22. A class of 30 students rated their computer science teacher on a scale of 1 to 10 (1 means awful and 10 means outstanding). The `responses` array is a 30-element integer array of the student responses. An 11-element array `freq` will count the number of occurrences of each response. For example, `freq[6]` will count the number of students who responded 6. The quantity `freq[0]` will not be used.

Here is a program that counts the students' responses and outputs the results.

```java
public class StudentEvaluations
{
    public static void main(String args[])
    {
        int[] responses = {6,6,7,8,10,1,5,4,6,7,
                           5,4,3,4,4,9,8,6,7,10,
                           6,7,8,8,9,6,7,8,9,2};
        int[] freq = new int[11];
        for (int i = 0; i < responses.length; i++)
            freq[responses[i]]++;
        //output results
        System.out.print("rating" + "   " + "frequency\n");
        for (int rating = 1; rating < freq.length; rating++)
            System.out.print(rating + "   " +
                freq[rating] + "\n");
    }
}
```

Suppose the last entry in the initializer list for the `responses` array was incorrectly typed as 12 instead of 2. What would be the result of running the program?

(A) A rating of 12 would be listed with a frequency of 1 in the output table.

(B) A rating of 1 would be listed with a frequency of 12 in the output table.

(C) An `ArrayIndexOutOfBoundsException` would be thrown.

(D) A `StringIndexOutOfBoundsException` would be thrown.

(E) A `NullPointerException` would be thrown.

Questions 23–25 are based on the three classes below.

```java
public class Employee
{
    private String name;
    private int employeeNum;
    private double salary, taxWithheld;

    public Employee(String aName, int empNum, double aSalary,
        double aTax)
    { /* implementation not shown */ }

    /** @return pre-tax salary */
    public double getSalary()
    { return salary; }

    public String getName()
    { return name; }

    public int getEmployeeNum()
    { return employeeNum; }

    public double getTax()
    { return taxWithheld; }

    public double computePay()
    { return salary - taxWithheld; }
}

public class PartTimeEmployee extends Employee
{
    private double payFraction;

    public PartTimeEmployee(String aName, int empNum, double aSalary,
        double aTax, double aPayFraction)
    { /* implementation not shown */ }

    public double getPayFraction()
    { return payFraction; }

    public double computePay()
    { return getSalary() * payFraction - getTax();}
}

public class Consultant extends Employee
{
    private static final double BONUS = 5000;

    public Consultant(String aName, int empNum, double aSalary,
        double aTax)
    { /* implementation not shown */ }

    public double computePay()
    { /* implementation code */ }
}
```

23. The `computePay` method in the `Consultant` class redefines the `computePay` method of the `Employee` class to add a bonus to the salary after subtracting the tax withheld. Which represents correct /* ***implementation code*** */ of `computePay` for `Consultant`?

  I. `return super.computePay() + BONUS;`

  II. `super.computePay();`
     `return getSalary() + BONUS;`

  III. `return getSalary() - getTax() + BONUS;`

  (A) I only
  (B) II only
  (C) III only
  (D) I and III only
  (E) I and II only

24. Consider these valid declarations in a client program.

```
Employee e = new Employee("Noreen Rizvi", 304, 65000, 10000);
Employee p = new PartTimeEmployee("Rafael Frongillo", 287, 40000,
     7000, 0.8);
Employee c = new Consultant("Dan Lepage", 694, 55000, 8500);
```

Which of the following method calls will cause an error?
  (A) `double x = e.computePay();`
  (B) `double y = p.computePay();`
  (C) `String n = c.getName();`
  (D) `int num = p.getEmployeeNum();`
  (E) `double g = p.getPayFraction();`

25. Consider the `writePayInfo` method.

```
/** Writes Employee name and pay on one line. */
public static void writePayInfo(Employee e)
{ System.out.println(e.getName() + " " + e.computePay()); }
```

The following piece of code invokes this method.

```
Employee[] empList = new Employee[3];
empList[0] = new Employee("Lila Fontes", 1, 10000, 850);
empList[1] = new Consultant("Momo Liu", 2, 50000, 8000);
empList[2] = new PartTimeEmployee("Moses Wilks", 3, 25000, 3750,
    0.6);
for (Employee e : empList)
    writePayInfo(e);
```

What will happen when this code is executed?

(A) A `NullPointerException` will be thrown.

(B) An `ArrayIndexOutOfBoundsException` will be thrown.

(C) A compile-time error will occur, with the message that the `getName` method is not in the `Consultant` class.

(D) A compile-time error will occur, with the message that an instance of an `Employee` object cannot be created.

(E) A list of employees' names and corresponding pay will be written to the screen.

GO ON TO THE NEXT PAGE

26. Consider an array `arr` that is initialized with `int` values. The following code segment stores in `count` the number of positive values in `arr`.

```
int count = 0, index = 0;
while (index < arr.length)
{
    if (arr[index] > 0)
        count++;
    index++;
}
```

Which of the following is equivalent to the above segment?

```
I. int count = 0;
   for (int num : arr)
   {
       if (arr[num] > 0)
           count++;
   }
```

```
II. int count = 0;
    for (int num : arr)
    {
        if (num > 0)
            count++;
    }
```

```
III. int count = 0;
     for (int i = 0; i < arr.length; i++)
     {
         if (arr[i] > 0)
             count++;
     }
```

(A) I only
(B) II only
(C) III only
(D) II and III only
(E) I and III only

27. A square matrix is declared as

```
int[][] mat = new int[SIZE][SIZE];
```

where SIZE is an appropriate integer constant. Consider the following method.

```
public static void mystery(int[][] mat, int value, int top, int left,
    int bottom, int right)
{
    for (int i = left; i <= right; i++)
    {
        mat[top][i] = value;
        mat[bottom][i] = value;
    }
    for (int i = top + 1; i <= bottom - 1; i++)
    {
        mat[i][left] = value;
        mat[i][right] = value;
    }
}
```

Assuming that there are no out-of-range errors, which best describes what method mystery does?

(A) Places value in corners of the rectangle with corners (top, left) and (bottom, right)
(B) Places value in the diagonals of the square with corners (top, left) and (bottom, right)
(C) Places value in each element of the rectangle with corners (top, left) and (bottom, right)
(D) Places value in each element of the border of the rectangle with corners (top, left) and (bottom, right)
(E) Places value in the topmost and bottommost rows of the rectangle with corners (top, left) and (bottom, right)

28. Consider the following declaration.

```
ArrayList<Integer> list = new ArrayList<Integer>();
```

Which of the following code segments will place the integers 1 to 10, in any order, in the empty list?

```
I. for (int i = 0; i < 10; i++)
       list.add(i + 1);

II. for (int i = 0; i < 10; i++)
        list.add(i, i + 1);

III. for (int i = 9; i >= 0; i--)
         list.add(i, i + 1);
```

(A) I only
(B) II only
(C) III only
(D) I and II only
(E) I, II, and III

GO ON TO THE NEXT PAGE

29. Assume that a Book class has a compareTo method in which, if b1 and b2 are Book objects, b1.compareTo(b2) is a negative integer if b1 is less than b2, a positive integer if b1 is greater than b2, and 0 if b1 equals b2. The following method is intended to return the index of the "smallest" book—namely, the book that would appear first in a sorted list of Book objects.

```
/** Precondition:
 *   - books is initialized with Book objects.
 *   - books.length > 0.
 */
public static int findMin(Book[] books)
{
    int minPos = 0;
    for (int index = 1; index < books.length; index++)
    {
        if ( /* condition */ )
        {
            minPos = index;
        }
    }
    return minPos;
}
```

Which of the following should be used to replace /* *condition* */ so that findMin works as intended?

(A) books[index] < books[minPos]

(B) books[index] > books[minPos]

(C) books[index].compareTo(books[minPos]) > 0

(D) books[index].compareTo(books[minPos]) >= 0

(E) books[index].compareTo(books[minPos]) < 0

30. Refer to the static method removeNegs shown below.

```
/** Precondition:  list is an ArrayList<Integer>.
 *  Postcondition: All negative values have been removed from list.
 */
public static void removeNegs(ArrayList<Integer> list)
{
    int index = 0;
    while (index < list.size())
    {
        if (list.get(index).intValue() < 0)
        {
            list.remove(index);
        }
        index++;
    }
}
```

For which of the following lists will the method not work as intended?

(A) 6 -1 -2 5
(B) -1 2 -3 4
(C) 2 4 6 8
(D) -3
(E) 1 2 3 -8

31. A sorted list of 120 integers is to be searched to determine whether the value 100 is in the list. Assuming that the most efficient searching algorithm is used, what is the maximum number of elements that must be examined?

    (A) 7
    (B) 8
    (C) 20
    (D) 100
    (E) 120

32. Consider a sorted array `arr` of $n$ elements, where $n$ is large and $n$ is even. Under which conditions will a sequential search of `arr` be faster than a binary search?

    I.  The target is not in the list.

    II. The target is in the first position of the list.

    III. The target is in `arr[1 + n/2]`.

    (A) I only
    (B) II only
    (C) III only
    (D) I and III only
    (E) II and III only

33. Refer to the following data field and method.

```java
private int[] arr;

/** Precondition: arr.length > 0 and index < arr.length. */
public void remove(int index)
{
    int[] b = new int[arr.length - 1];
    int count = 0;
    for (int i = 0; i < arr.length; i++)
    {
        if (i != index)
        {
            b[count] = arr[i];
            count++;
        }
    }
    /* assertion */
    arr = b;
}
```

Which of the following assertions is true when the /* *assertion* */ line is reached during execution of remove?

(A) b[k] == arr[k] for 0 <= k < arr.length.

(B) b[k] == arr[k + 1] for 0 <= k < arr.length.

(C) b[k] == arr[k] for 0 <= k <= index, and
b[k] == arr[k + 1] for index < k < arr.length - 1.

(D) b[k] == arr[k] for 0 <= k < index, and
b[k] == arr[k + 1] for index <= k < arr.length - 1.

(E) b[k] == arr[k] for 0 <= k < index, and
b[k] == arr[k + 1] for index <= k < arr.length.

34. Consider the following code segment.

```java
for (int n = 25; n >= 0; n /= 2)
    System.out.println(n);
```

When the segment is executed, how many passes through the for loop will there be?

(A) Fewer than 5

(B) Between 5 and 12, inclusive

(C) Between 13 and 25, inclusive

(D) Between 26 and 100, inclusive

(E) More than 100

Questions 35–37 refer to the `TennisPlayer`, `GoodPlayer`, and `WeakPlayer` classes below. These classes are to be used in a program to simulate a game of tennis.

```
public class TennisPlayer
{
    private String name;

    public TennisPlayer(String aName)
    { name = aName; }

    public boolean serve()
    { /* implementation not shown */ }
}

public class GoodPlayer extends TennisPlayer
{
    public GoodPlayer(String aName)
    { /* implementation not shown */ }

    public boolean serve()
    { /* implementation not shown */ }
}

public class WeakPlayer extends TennisPlayer
{
    public WeakPlayer(String aName)
    { /* implementation not shown */ }

    /** Returns true if serve is in (45% probability),
     *  false if serve is out (55% probability).
     */
    public boolean serve()
    { /* implementation not shown */ }
}
```

35. Which of the following declarations will cause an error? You may assume all the constructors are correctly implemented.

    (A) `WeakPlayer t = new TennisPlayer("Smith");`

    (B) `TennisPlayer g = new GoodPlayer("Jones");`

    (C) `TennisPlayer w = new WeakPlayer("Henry");`

    (D) `TennisPlayer p = null;`

    (E) `WeakPlayer q = new WeakPlayer("Grady");`

36. Refer to the `serve` method in the `WeakPlayer` class.

```
/** Returns true if serve is in (45% probability),
 *  false if serve is out (55% probability).
 */
public boolean serve()
{ /* implementation */ }
```

Which of the following replacements for /* *implementation* */ satisfy the postcondition of the serve method?

    I. 
```
double value = Math.random();
return value >= 0 || value < 0.45;
```

    II. 
```
double value = Math.random();
return value < 0.45;
```

    III. 
```
int val = (int) (Math.random() * 100);
return val < 45;
```

    (A) I only

    (B) II only

    (C) III only

    (D) II and III only

    (E) I, II, and III

37. Consider the following class definition.

```
public class Beginner extends WeakPlayer
{
    private double costOfLessons;

    //methods of Beginner class
        ...
}
```

Refer to the following declarations and method in a client program.

```
TennisPlayer w = new WeakPlayer("Harry");
TennisPlayer b = new Beginner("Dick");
Beginner bp = new Beginner("Ted");

public void giveEncouragement(WeakPlayer t)
{ /* implementation not shown */ }
```

Which of the following method calls will cause an error?

I.   `giveEncouragement(w);`

II.  `giveEncouragement(b);`

III. `giveEncouragement(bp);`

(A) I only
(B) II only
(C) III only
(D) I and II only
(E) I, II, and III

38. A matrix class that manipulates matrices contains the following declaration.

```
private int[][] mat = new int[numRows][numCols];
```

Consider the following method that alters matrix mat.

```
public void doSomething()
{
    int width = mat[0].length;
    int numRows = mat.length;
    for (int row = 0; row < numRows; row++)
        for (int col = 0; col < width/2; col++)
            mat[row][col] = mat[row][width - 1 - col];
}
```

If mat has current value

```
1 2 3 4 5 6
1 3 5 7 9 11
```

what will the value of mat be after a call to doSomething?

(A) 1 2 3 3 2 1
    1 3 5 5 3 1

(B)  6 5 4 4 5 6
    11 9 7 7 9 11

(C)  6 5 4 3 2 1
    11 9 7 5 3 1

(D) 1 2 3 4 5 6
    1 2 3 4 5 6

(E) 1 3 5 7 9 11
    1 3 5 7 9 11

Questions 39 and 40 refer to the following information.

Consider an array `arr` that is sorted in increasing order, and method `findMost` given below. Method `findMost` is intended to find the value in the array that occurs most often. If every value occurs exactly once, `findMost` should return -1. If there is more than one value that occurs the most, `findMost` should return any one of those. For example, if `arr` contains the values [1,5,7,7,10], `findMost` should return 7. If `arr` contains [2,2,2,7,8,8,9,9,9], `findMost` should return 2 or 9. If `arr` contains [1,2,7,8], `findMost` should return -1.

```
Line 1:  /** Precondition:  arr sorted in increasing order.
Line 2:   */
Line 3:  public static int findMost(int[] arr)
Line 4:  {
Line 5:      int index = 0;
Line 6:      int count = 1;
Line 7:      int maxCountSoFar = 1;
Line 8:      int mostSoFar = arr[0];
Line 9:      while (index < arr.length - 1)
Line 10:     {
Line 11:         while (index < arr.length - 1 &&
Line 12:                 arr[index] == arr[index + 1])
Line 13:         {
Line 14:             count++;
Line 15:             index++;
Line 16:         }
Line 17:         if (count > maxCountSoFar)
Line 18:         {
Line 19:             maxCountSoFar = count;
Line 20:             mostSoFar = arr[index];
Line 21:         }
Line 22:         index++;
Line 23:     }
Line 24:     if (maxCountSoFar == 1)
Line 25:         return -1;
Line 26:     else
Line 27:         return mostSoFar;
Line 28: }
```

39. The method `findMost` does not always work as intended. An *incorrect* result will be returned if `arr` contains the values

    (A) [1,2,3,4,5]

    (B) [6,6,6,6]

    (C) [1,2,2,3,4,5]

    (D) [1,1,3,4,5,5,5,7]

    (E) [2,2,2,4,5,5]

40. Which of the following changes should be made so that method `findMost` will work as intended?

    (A) Insert the statement `count = 1;` between Lines 20 and 21.

    (B) Insert the statement `count = 1;` between Lines 21 and 22.

    (C) Insert the statement `count = 1;` between Lines 16 and 17.

    (D) Insert the statement `count = 0;` between Lines 23 and 24.

    (E) Insert the statement `count = 1;` between Lines 23 and 24.

**END OF SECTION I**

# COMPUTER SCIENCE A
# SECTION II

**Time—1 hour and 30 minutes**
**4 Questions**

**DIRECTIONS:** SHOW ALL YOUR WORK. REMEMBER THAT PROGRAM
SEGMENTS ARE TO BE WRITTEN IN JAVA.

Write your answers in the separate Free-Response booklet provided.

**NOTES:**

- Assume that the classes in the Quick Reference have been imported where appropriate.

- Unless otherwise noted in the question, assume that parameters in method calls are not `null` and that methods are called only when their preconditions are satisfied.

- In writing solutions for each question, you may use any of the accessible methods that are listed in classes defined in that question. Writing significant amounts of code that can be replaced by a call to one of these methods will not receive full credit.

1. A WordSet, whose partial implementation is shown in the class declaration below, stores a set of String objects in no particular order and contains no duplicates. Each word is a sequence of capital letters only.

```java
public class WordSet
{
    /** Constructor initializes set to empty. */
    public WordSet()
    { /* implementation not shown */ }

    /** Returns the number of words in set. */
    public int size()
    { /* implementation not shown */ }

    /** Adds word to set.
     */
    public void insert(String word)
    { /* implementation not shown */ }

    /** Removes word from set if present, else does nothing.
     */
    public void remove(String word)
    { /* implementation not shown */ }

    /** Returns kth word in alphabetical order, where 1 <= k <= size().
     */
    public String findkth(int k)
    { /* implementation not shown */ }

    /** Returns true if set contains word, false otherwise. */
    public boolean contains(String word)
    { /* implementation not shown */ }

    //Other instance variables, constructors, and methods are not shown.
}
```

The findkth method returns the $k$th word in alphabetical order in the set, even though the implementation of WordSet may not be sorted. The number $k$ ranges from 1 (corresponding to first in alphabetical order) to $N$, where $N$ is the number of words in the set. For example, if WordSet s stores the words {"GRAPE", "PEAR", "FIG", "APPLE"}, here are the values when s.findkth(k) is called.

| k | values of s.findkth(k) |
|---|---|
| 1 | APPLE |
| 2 | FIG |
| 3 | GRAPE |
| 4 | PEAR |

GO ON TO THE NEXT PAGE

Class information for this question

```
public class WordSet

public WordSet()
public int size()
public void insert(String word)
public void remove(String word)
public String findkth(int k)
public boolean contains(String word)
```

(a) Write a client method `countA` that returns the number of words in `WordSet` s that begin with the letter "A." In writing `countA`, you may call any of the methods of the `WordSet` class. Assume that the methods work as specified.

Complete method `countA`.

```
/** Returns the number of words in s that begin with "A".
 */
public static int countA(WordSet s)
```

(b) Write a client method `removeA` that removes all words that begin with "A" from a non-null `WordSet`. If there are no such words in s, then `removeA` does nothing. In writing `removeA`, you may call method `countA` specified in part (a). Assume that `countA` works as specified, regardless of what you wrote in part (a).

Complete method `removeA`.

```
/** Removes from WordSet s all words that begin with the letter "A".
 *  Precondition:  WordSet is not null.
 *  Postcondition: WordSet s contains no words that begin with
 *                 "A", but is otherwise unchanged.
 */
public static void removeA(WordSet s)
```

2. A clothing store sells shoes, pants, and tops. The store also allows a customer to buy an "outfit," which consists of three items: one pair of shoes, one pair of pants, and one top.

Each clothing item has a description and a price. The four types of clothing items are represented by the four classes `Shoes`, `Pants`, `Top`, and `Outfit`. All four classes are subclasses of a `ClothingItem` class, shown below.

```java
public class ClothingItem
{
    private String description;
    private double price;

    public ClothingItem()
    {
        description = "";
        price = 0;
    }

    public ClothingItem(String descr, double aPrice)
    {
        description = descr;
        price = aPrice;
    }

    public String getDescription()
    { return description; }

    public double getPrice()
    { return price; }
}
```

The following diagram shows the relationship between the `ClothingItem` class and the `Shoes`, `Pants`, `Top`, and `Outfit` classes.

The store allows customers to create `Outfit` clothing items, each of which includes a pair of shoes, pants, and a top. The description of the outfit consists of the description of the shoes, pants, and top, in that order, separated by `"/"` and followed by a space and `"outfit"`. The price of an outfit is calculated as follows. If the sum of the prices of any two items equals or exceeds $100, there is a 25% discount on the sum of the prices of all three items. Otherwise there is a 10% discount.

For example, an outfit consisting of sneakers ($40), blue jeans ($50), and a T-shirt ($10) would have the name `"sneakers/blue jeans/T-shirt outfit"` and a price of $0.90(40 + 50 + 10) = \$90.00$. An outfit consisting of loafers ($50), cutoffs ($20), and dress-shirt ($60) would have the description "loafers/cutoffs/dress-shirt outfit" and price 0.75(50 + 20 + 60) = $97.50.

Write the `Outfit` subclass of `ClothingItem`. Your implementation must have just one constructor that takes three parameters representing a pair of shoes, pants, and a top, in that order.

A client class that uses the `Outfit` class should be able to create an outfit, get its description, and get its price. Your implementation should be such that the client code has the following behavior:

```
Shoes shoes;
Pants pants;
Top top;
/* Code to initialize shoes, pants, and top */

ClothingItem outfit =
    new Outfit (shoes, pants, top); //Compiles without error
ClothingItem outfit =
    new Outfit (pants, shoes, top); //Compile-time error
ClothingItem outfit =
    new Outfit (shoes, top, pants); //Compile-time error
```

3. Consider a note keeper object that is designed to store and manipulate a list of short notes. Here are some typical notes:

```
pick up drycleaning
special dog chow
car registration
dentist Monday
dog license
```

A note is represented by the following class.

```
public class Note
{
    /** Returns a one-line note. */
    public String getNote()
    { /* implementation not shown */ }

    //There may be instance variables, constructors, and methods
    //that are not shown.
}
```

A note keeper is represented by the NoteKeeper class shown below.

```
public class NoteKeeper
{
    /** The list of notes */
    private ArrayList<Note> noteList;

    /** Prints all notes in noteList, as described in part(a).
     */
    public void printNotes()
    { /* to be implemented in part (a) */}

    /** Removes all notes with specified string from noteList,
     *  as described in part (b).
     *  If none of the notes in noteList contains the given string,
     *  the list remains unchanged.
     */
    public void removeNotes(String str)
    { /* to be implemented in part (b) */ }

    //There may be instance variables, constructors, and methods
    //that are not shown.
}
```

PRACTICE TEST 2

(a) Write the NoteKeeper method printNotes. This method prints all of the notes in noteList, one per line, and numbers the notes, starting at 1. The output should look like this.

```
1. pick up drycleaning
2. special dog chow
3. car registration
4. dentist Monday
5. dog license
```

Complete method printNotes.

```
/** Prints all notes in noteList, as described in part(a).
 */
public void printNotes()
```

(b) Write the `NoteKeeper` method `removeNotes`. Method `removeNotes` removes all notes from `noteList` that contain the string specified by the parameter. The ordering of the remaining notes should be left unchanged. For example, suppose that a `NoteKeeper` variable, `notes`, has a `noteList` containing the following.

```
[pick up drycleaning, special dog chow, car registration,
  dentist Monday, dog license]
```

The method call `notes.removeNotes("dog")` should modify the `noteList` of `notes` to be

```
[pick up drycleaning, car registration, dentist Monday]
```

The method call `notes.removeNotes("cow")` should leave the list shown above unchanged.

Here's another example. If `noteList` contains

```
[pick up car, buy carrots, dog license, carpet cleaning]
```

the method call `notes.removeNotes("car")` should modify the `noteList` of notes to be

```
[dog license]
```

Complete method `removeNotes`.

```
/** Removes all notes with specified string from noteList,
 *  as described in part (b).
 *  If none of the notes in noteList contains the given string,
 *  the list remains unchanged.
 */
public void removeNotes(String str)
```

4.  Consider the problem of keeping track of the available seats in a theater. Theater seats can be represented with a two-dimensional array of integers, where a value of 0 shows a seat is available, while a value of 1 indicates that the seat is occupied. For example, the array below shows the current seat availability for a show in a small theater.

|       | [0] | [1] | [2] | [3] | [4] | [5] |
|-------|-----|-----|-----|-----|-----|-----|
| [0]   | 0   | 0   | 1   | 1   | 0   | 1   |
| [1]   | 0   | 1   | 0   | 1   | 0   | 1   |
| [2]   | 1   | 0   | 0   | 0   | 0   | 0   |

The seat at slot [1][3] is taken, but seat [0][4] is still available.

A show can be represented by the Show class shown below.

```java
public class Show
{
    /** The seats for this show */
    private int[][] seats;

    private final int SEATS_PER_ROW = <some integer value>;
    private final int NUM_ROWS = <some integer value>;

    /** Reserve two adjacent seats and return true if this was
     *  successfully done, false otherwise, as described in part (a).
     */
    public boolean twoTogether()
    { /* to be implemented in part (a) */ }

    /** Return the lowest seat number in the specified row for a
     *  block of seatsNeeded empty adjacent seats, as described in part (b).
     */
    public int findAdjacent(int row, int seatsNeeded)
    { /* to be implemented in part (b) */ }

    //There may be instance variables, constructors, and methods
    //that are not shown.
}
```

(a) Write the `Show` method `twoTogether`, which reserves two adjacent seats and returns `true` if this was successfully done. If it is not possible to find two adjacent seats that are unoccupied, the method should leave the show unchanged and return `false`. For example, suppose this is the state of a show.

|      | [0] | [1] | [2] | [3] | [4] | [5] |
|------|-----|-----|-----|-----|-----|-----|
| [0]  | 0   | 0   | 1   | 1   | 0   | 1   |
| [1]  | 0   | 1   | 0   | 1   | 0   | 1   |
| [2]  | 1   | 0   | 0   | 0   | 1   | 1   |

A call to `twoTogether` should return `true`, and the final state of the show could be any one of the following three configurations.

|      | [0] | [1] | [2] | [3] | [4] | [5] |
|------|-----|-----|-----|-----|-----|-----|
| [0]  | 1   | 1   | 1   | 1   | 0   | 1   |
| [1]  | 0   | 1   | 0   | 1   | 0   | 1   |
| [2]  | 1   | 0   | 0   | 0   | 1   | 1   |

OR

|      | [0] | [1] | [2] | [3] | [4] | [5] |
|------|-----|-----|-----|-----|-----|-----|
| [0]  | 0   | 0   | 1   | 1   | 0   | 1   |
| [1]  | 0   | 1   | 0   | 1   | 0   | 1   |
| [2]  | 1   | 1   | 1   | 0   | 1   | 1   |

OR

|      | [0] | [1] | [2] | [3] | [4] | [5] |
|------|-----|-----|-----|-----|-----|-----|
| [0]  | 0   | 0   | 1   | 1   | 0   | 1   |
| [1]  | 0   | 1   | 0   | 1   | 0   | 1   |
| [2]  | 1   | 0   | 1   | 1   | 1   | 1   |

For the following state of a show, a call to `twoTogether` should return `false` and leave the two-dimensional array as shown.

|      | [0] | [1] | [2] | [3] | [4] | [5] |
|------|-----|-----|-----|-----|-----|-----|
| [0]  | 0   | 1   | 0   | 1   | 1   | 0   |
| [1]  | 1   | 1   | 0   | 1   | 0   | 1   |
| [2]  | 0   | 1   | 1   | 1   | 1   | 1   |

**GO ON TO THE NEXT PAGE**

---

Class information for this question
```
public class Show

private int[][] seats
private final int SEATS_PER_ROW
private final int NUM_ROWS
public boolean twoTogether()
public int findAdjacent(int row, int seatsNeeded)
```

---

Complete method twoTogether.

```
/** Reserve two adjacent seats and return true if this was
 *  successfully done, false otherwise, as described in part (a).
 */
public boolean twoTogether()
```

(b)  Write the Show method findAdjacent, which finds the lowest seat number in the specified row for a specified number of empty adjacent seats. If no such block of empty seats exists, the findAdjacent method should return -1. No changes should be made to the state of the show, irrespective of the value returned.

For example, suppose the diagram of seats is as shown.

|      | [0] | [1] | [2] | [3] | [4] | [5] |
|------|-----|-----|-----|-----|-----|-----|
| [0]  | 0   | 1   | 1   | 0   | 0   | 0   |
| [1]  | 0   | 0   | 0   | 0   | 1   | 1   |
| [2]  | 1   | 0   | 0   | 1   | 0   | 0   |

The following table shows some examples of calling findAdjacent for show.

| Method call            | Return value |
|------------------------|--------------|
| show.findAdjacent(0,3) | 3            |
| show.findAdjacent(1,3) | 0 or 1       |
| show.findAdjacent(2,2) | 1 or 4       |
| show.findAdjacent(1,5) | -1           |

Complete method findAdjacent.

```
/** Return the lowest seat number in the specified row for a
 *  block of seatsNeeded empty adjacent seats, as described in part (b).
 */
public int findAdjacent(int row, int seatsNeeded)
```

## STOP

## END OF EXAM

# ANSWER KEY
## Practice Test 2

### Section I

| | | | | | |
|---|---|---|---|---|---|
| 1. **E** | | 15. **E** | | 29. **E** | |
| 2. **B** | | 16. **A** | | 30. **A** | |
| 3. **C** | | 17. **E** | | 31. **A** | |
| 4. **D** | | 18. **B** | | 32. **B** | |
| 5. **A** | | 19. **C** | | 33. **D** | |
| 6. **A** | | 20. **E** | | 34. **E** | |
| 7. **D** | | 21. **C** | | 35. **A** | |
| 8. **E** | | 22. **C** | | 36. **D** | |
| 9. **A** | | 23. **D** | | 37. **D** | |
| 10. **D** | | 24. **E** | | 38. **B** | |
| 11. **C** | | 25. **E** | | 39. **E** | |
| 12. **E** | | 26. **D** | | 40. **B** | |
| 13. **C** | | 27. **D** | | | |
| 14. **B** | | 28. **D** | | | |

## Answer Explanations

### Section I

1. **(E)** The string parameter in the line of code uses two escape characters:
   \", which means print a double quote.
   \n, which means print a newline character (i.e., go to the next line).

2. **(B)** The intent of the programmer is to have overloaded `getValue` methods in `SomeClass`. Overloaded methods have different signatures, where the signature of a method includes the name and parameter types only. Thus, the signature of the original method is `getValue(int)`. The signature in header I is `getValue()`. The signature in header II is `getValue(int)`. The signature in header III is `getValue(double)`. Since the signature in header II is the same as that of the given method, the compiler will flag it and say that the method already exists in `SomeClass`. Note: The return type of a method is not included in its signature.

3. **(C)** The expression `(int)(Math.random() * 49)` produces a random integer from 0 through 48. (Note that 49 is the number of possibilities for `num`.) To shift this range from 2 to 50, add 2 to the expression.

4. **(D)** Short-circuit evaluation of the boolean expression will occur. The expression (num != 0) will evaluate to false, which makes the entire boolean expression false. Therefore the expression (score/num > SOME_CONSTANT) will not be evaluated. Hence no division by zero will occur, and there will be no ArithmeticException thrown. When the boolean expression has a value of false, only the else part of the statement, *statement2*, will be executed.

5. **(A)** The values of k are, consecutively, 4, 3, 2, and 1. The values of randPos are, consecutively, 3, 2, 0, and 0. Thus, the sequence of swaps and corresponding states of nums will be:

| | |
|---|---|
| swap nums[4] and nums[3] | 8 7 6 4 5 |
| swap nums[3] and nums[2] | 8 7 4 6 5 |
| swap nums[2] and nums[0] | 4 7 8 6 5 |
| swap nums[1] and nums[0] | 7 4 8 6 5 |

Thus, the element in nums[2] is 8.

6. **(A)** A matrix is stored as an array of arrays; that is, each row is an array. Therefore it is correct to call a method with an array parameter for each row, as is done in segment I. Segment II fails because mat is not an array of columns. The segment would cause an error, since mat[col] refers to a *row*, not a column. (If the number of rows were less than the number of columns, the method would throw an ArrayIndexOutOfBoundsException. If the number of rows were greater than the number of columns, the method would correctly assign the value 100 to the first n rows, where n is the number of columns. The rest of the rows would retain the values before execution of the method.) Segment III fails because this is incorrect usage of an enhanced for loop, which should not be used to assign new elements in the matrix. The matrix remains unchanged.

7. **(D)** Declaration I fails because it fails this test: Cereal *is-a* WheatCereal? No. Notice that declarations II and III pass this test: Cereal *is-a* Cereal? Yes. RiceCereal *is-a* Cereal? Yes.

8. **(E)** All satisfy the *is-a* test! Class2 *is-a* Class1. Class3 *is-a* Class2. Class3 *is-a* Class1. Note: Since Class3 is a subclass of Class2, it automatically implements any interfaces implemented by Class2, its superclass.

9. **(A)** Method call I works because Class3 inherits all the methods of Class1 and Class2. Method call II fails because Class2 does not inherit the methods of Class3, its subclass. Method call III uses a parameter that fails the *is-a* test: ob2 is *not* a Class3, which the parameter requires.

10. **(D)** After each execution of the loop body, n is divided by 2. Thus, the loop will produce output when n is 50, 25, 12, 6, 3, and 1. The final value of n will be 1 / 2, which is 0, and the test will fail.

11. **(C)** Statement III will cause an IndexOutOfBoundsException because there is no slot 4. The final element, "Luis", is in slot 3. Statement I is correct: It replaces the string "Harry" with the string "6". It may look peculiar in the list, but the syntax is correct. Statement II looks like it may be out of range because there is no slot 4. It is correct, however, because you must be allowed to add an element to the end of the list.

12. **(E)** The effect of the given algorithm is to raise n to the 8th power.
When $i = 1$, the result is $n * n = n^2$.
When $i = 2$, the result is $n^2 * n^2 = n^4$.
When $i = 3$, the result is $n^4 * n^4 = n^8$.

13. **(C)** The method traverses `nums`, starting at position 0, and returns the current position the first time it finds an odd value. This implies that all values in positions 0 through the current index – 1 contained even numbers.

14. **(B)** Since `n == 6` fails the two base case tests, the method call `mystery(6)` returns `6 + mystery(5)`. Since 5 satisfies the second base case test, `mystery(5)` returns 5, and there are no more recursive calls. Thus, `mystery(6)` = 6 + 5 = 11.

15. **(E)** In order for /* *body of loop* */ not to be executed, the test must be false the first time it is evaluated. A compound OR test will be false if and only if both pieces of the test are false. Thus, choices B and C are insufficient. Choice D fails because it guarantees that both pieces of the test will be *true*. Choice A is wrong because /* *body of loop* */ may be executed many times, until the computer runs out of memory (an infinite loop!).

16. **(A)** When `p.act()` is called, the `act` method of `Singer` is executed. This is an example of polymorphism. The first line prints `rise`. Then `super.act()` goes to the `act` method of `Performer`, the superclass. This prints `bow` and then calls `perform()`. Again, using polymorphism, the `perform` method in `Singer` is called, which prints `aria`. Now, completing the `act` method of `Singer`, `encore` is printed. The result?

    ```
    rise bow aria encore
    ```

17. **(E)** Statement I is false: The `Sedan`, `StationWagon`, and `SUV` classes should all be subclasses of `Car`. Each one satisfies the *is-a* `Car` relationship. Statement II is true: The main task of the `Inventory` class should be to keep an updated list of `Car` objects. Statement III is true: A class is independent of another class if it does not require that class to implement its methods.

18. **(B)** The `Inventory` class is responsible for maintaining the list of all cars on the lot. Therefore methods like `addCar`, `removeCar`, and `displayAllCars` must be the responsibility of this class. The `Car` class should contain the `setColor`, `getPrice`, and `displayCar` methods, since all these pertain to the attributes of a given `Car`.

19. **(C)** Each subclass may contain additional attributes for the particular type of car that are not in the `Car` superclass. Since `displayCar` displays all features of a given car, this method should be overridden to display the original plus additional features.

20. **(E)** The expression `word.indexOf("flag")` returns the index of the first occurrence of `"flag"` in the calling string, `word`. Thus, x has value 3. (Recall that the first character in `word` is at index 0.) The method call `word.substring(0, x)` is equivalent to `word.substring(0, 3)`, which returns the substring in `word` from 0 to 2—namely, `"con"`. The character at index 3 is not included.

21. **(C)** The number of rows in `mat` is given by `mat.length`. The indexes of the rows range from 0 to `mat.length - 1`. The number of columns in `mat` is given by `mat[0].length`. You can think of this as the length of the array represented by `mat[0]`, the first row. (Note that all the rows have the same length, but it is wise to use `mat[0]`, since you know that the matrix has at least one row. For example, `mat[1]` may be out of bounds.) The indexes of the columns range from 0 to `mat[0].length - 1`. The last element to be accessed in a row-by-row (or column-by-column) traversal is in the bottom right corner—namely, `mat[mat.length - 1][mat[0].length - 1]`.

22. **(C)** If the `responses` array contained an invalid value like 12, the program would attempt to add 1 to `freq[12]`. This is out of bounds for the `freq` array.

23. **(D)** Implementation I calls `super.computePay()`, which is equivalent to the `computePay` method in the `Employee` superclass. The method returns the quantity (`salary - taxWithheld`). The `BONUS` is then correctly added to this expression, as required. Implementation III correctly uses the public accessor methods `getSalary` and `getTax` that the `Consultant` class has inherited. Note that the `Consultant` class does not have direct access to the private instance variables `salary` and `taxWithheld`. Implementation II incorrectly returns the salary plus `BONUS`—there is no tax withheld. The expression `super.computePay()` returns a value equal to salary minus tax. But this is neither stored nor included in the `return` statement.

24. **(E)** Note that `p` is declared to be of type `Employee`, and the `Employee` class does not have a `getPayFraction` method. To avoid the error, `p` must be cast to `PartTimeEmployee` as follows:

    ```
    double g = ((PartTimeEmployee) p).getPayFraction();
    ```

25. **(E)** The code does exactly what it looks like it should. The `writePayInfo` parameter is of type `Employee` and each element of the `empList` array *is-a* `Employee` and therefore does not need to be cast to its actual instance type. This is an example of polymorphism, in which the appropriate `computePay` method is chosen during run time. There is no `ArrayIndexOutOfBoundsException` (choice B) since the array is accessed using an enhanced `for` loop. None of the array elements is null; therefore, there is no `NullPointerException` (choice A). Choice C won't happen because the `getName` method is inherited by both the `Consultant` and `PartTimeEmployee` classes. Choice D would occur if the `Employee` superclass were abstract, but it's not.

26. **(D)** Segment I is incorrect because `num` is not an index in the loop: It is a value in the array. Thus, the correct test is `if (num > 0)`, which is correctly used in segment II. Segment III is a regular `for` loop, exactly equivalent to the given `while` loop.

27. **(D)** The first `for` loop places `value` in the top and bottom rows of the defined rectangle. The second `for` loop fills in the remaining border elements on the sides. Note that the `top + 1` and `bottom - 1` initializer and terminating conditions avoid filling in the corner elements twice.

28. **(D)** Segment I works because each int value, `i + 1`, is autoboxed in an `Integer`. Segment II works similarly using an overloaded version of the `add` method. The first parameter is the index and the second parameter is the element to be added. Segment III fails because an attempt to add an element to an empty list at a position other than 0 will cause an `IndexOutOfBoundsException` to be thrown.

29. **(E)** Eliminate choices A and B: When comparing `Book` objects, you cannot use simple inequality operators; you *must* use `compareTo`. For the calling object to be *less than* the parameter object, use the *less than* 0 test (a good way to remember this!).

30. **(A)** Method `removeNegs` will not work whenever there are consecutive negative values in the list. This is because removal of an element from an `ArrayList` causes the elements to the right of it to be shifted left to fill the "hole." The index in the given algorithm, however, always moves one slot to the right. Therefore in choice A, when -1 is removed, -2 will be passed over, and the final list will be `6 -2 5`.

31. **(A)** If the list is sorted, a binary search is the most efficient algorithm to use. Binary search chops the current part of the array being examined in half, until you have found the element you are searching for, or there are no elements left to look at. In the worst case, you will need to divide by 2 seven times:

$$120/2 \rightarrow 60$$
$$60/2 \rightarrow 30$$
$$30/2 \rightarrow 15$$
$$15/2 \rightarrow 7$$
$$7/2 \rightarrow 3$$
$$3/2 \rightarrow 1$$
$$1/2 \rightarrow 0$$

Shortcut: Round 120 to the nearest power of 2, 128. Since $128 = 2^7$, the number of comparisons in the worst case equals the exponent, 7.

32. **(B)** For a sequential search, all $n$ elements will need to be examined. For a binary search, the array will be chopped in half a maximum of $\log_2 n$ times. When the target is in the first position of the list, a sequential search will find it in the first comparison. The binary search, which examines a middle element first, will not. Condition I is a worst case situation for the sequential search. It will require far more comparisons than a binary search. Condition III is approximately the middle of the list, but it won't be found on the first try of the binary search. (The first try examines `arr[n/2]`.) Still, the target *will* be located within fewer than $\log n$ tries, whereas the sequential search will need more than $n/2$ tries.

33. **(D)** The `remove` method removes from `arr` the element `arr[index]`. It does this by copying all elements from `arr[0]` up to but not including `arr[index]` into array `b`. Thus, `b[k] == arr[k]` for `0 <= k < index` is true. Then it copies all elements from `arr[index + 1]` up to and including `arr[arr.length - 1]` into `b`. Since no gaps are left in `b`, `b[k] == arr[k + 1]` for `index <= k < arr.length - 1`. The best way to see this is with a small example. If `arr` is 2, 6, 4, 8, 1, 7, and the element at `index` 2 (namely, the 4) is to be removed, here is the picture:

```
         0   1  [2]  3   4   5
arr  →  | 2 | 6 | 4 | 8 | 1 | 7 |

         0   1  [2]  3   4
b    →  | 2 | 6 | 8 | 1 | 7 |
```

```
b[0] == arr[0]
b[1] == arr[1]
b[2] == arr[3]
b[3] == arr[4]
b[4] == arr[5]
```

Notice that `arr.length` is 6, but `k` ends at 4.

34. **(E)** The segment is an example of an infinite loop. Here are successive values of n, which is updated with successive divisions by two using the div operator:

```
25, 12, 6, 3, 1, 0, 0, 0, ...
```

Note that 0/2 equals 0, which never fails the n >= 0 test.

35. **(A)** Choice A is illegal because it fails this test: TennisPlayer *is-a* WeakPlayer? The answer is no, not necessarily.

36. **(D)** The statement

```
double value = Math.random();
```

generates a random double in the range $0 \le$ value $< 1$. Since random doubles are uniformly distributed in this interval, 45 percent of the time you can expect value to be in the range $0 \le$ value $< 0.45$. Therefore, a test for value in this range can be a test for whether the serve of a WeakPlayer went in. Since Math.random() never returns a negative number, the test in implementation II, value < 0.45, is sufficient. The test in implementation I would be correct if || were changed to && ("or" changed to "and"—both parts must be true). Implementation III also works. The expression

```
(int) (Math.random() * 100)
```

returns a random integer from 0 to 99, each equally likely. Thus, 45 percent of the time, the integer val will be in the range $0 \le$ val $\le 44$. Therefore, a test for val in this range can be used to test whether the serve was in.

37. **(D)** Method calls I and II will each cause a compile-time error: The parameter must be of type WeakPlayer, but w and b are declared to be of type TennisPlayer. Each of these choices can be corrected by casting the parameter to WeakPlayer. Method call III works because bp *is-a* WeakPlayer.

38. **(B)** The method copies the elements from columns 3, 4, and 5 into columns 2, 1, and 0, respectively, as if there were a vertical mirror down the middle of the matrix. To see this, here are the values for the given matrix: width = 6, width/2 = 3, numRows = 2. The variable row goes from 0 to 1 and column goes from 0 to 2. The element assignments are

```
mat[0][0] = mat[0][5]
mat[0][1] = mat[0][4]
mat[0][2] = mat[0][3]
mat[1][0] = mat[1][5]
mat[1][1] = mat[1][4]
mat[1][2] = mat[1][3]
```

39. **(E)** In choice E, findMost returns the value 5. This is because count has not been reset to 1, so that when 5 is encountered, the test count>maxCountSoFar is true, causing mostSoFar to be incorrectly reassigned to 5. In choices A, B, and C, the outer while loop is not entered again, since a second run of equal values doesn't exist in the array. So mostSoFar comes out with the correct value. In choice D, when the outer loop is entered again, the test count>maxCountSoFar just happens to be true anyway and the correct value is returned. The algorithm fails whenever a new string of equal values is found whose length is shorter than a previous string of equal values.

40. **(B)** The count variable must be reset to 1 as soon as index is incremented in the outer while loop, so that when a new run of equal values is found, count starts out as 1.

## Section II

1. (a)
```
public static int countA(WordSet s)
{
    int count = 0;
    while (count < s.size() &&
            s.findkth(count + 1).substring(0, 1).equals("A"))
        count++;
    return count;
}
```

Alternatively,

```
public static int countA(WordSet s)
{
    boolean done = false;
    int count = 0;
    while (count < s.size() && !done)
    {
        String nextWord = s.findkth(count + 1);
        if (nextWord.substring(0,1).equals("A"))
            count++;
        else
            done = true;
    }
    return count;
}
```

(b)
```
public static void removeA(WordSet s)
{
    int numA = countA(s);
    for (int i = 1; i <= numA; i++)
        s.remove(s.findkth(1));
}
```

Alternatively,

```
public static void removeA(WordSet s)
{
    while (s.size() != 0 &&
            s.findkth(1).substring(0, 1).equals("A"))
        s.remove(s.findkth(1));
}
```

## Note

- In part (a), to test whether a word starts with "A", you must compare the first letter of word, that is, word.substring(0,1), with "A".
- In part (a), you must check that your solution works if s is empty. For the given algorithm, count < s.size() will fail and short-circuit the test, which is desirable since s.findkth(1) will violate the precondition of findkth(k)—namely, that k cannot be greater than size().

- The parameter for s.findkth must be greater than 0, hence the use of s.findkth(count+1) in part (a).
- For the first solution in part (b), you get a subtle intent error if your last step is s.remove(s.findkth(i)). Suppose that s is initially {"FLY", "ASK", "ANT"}. After the method call s.remove(s.findkth(1)), s will be {"FLY", "ASK"}. After the statement s.remove(s.findkth(2)), s will be {"ASK"}!! The point is that s is adjusted after each call to s.remove. The algorithm that works is this: If *N* is the number of words that start with "A", simply remove the first element in the list *N* times. Note that the alternative solution avoids the pitfall described by simply repeatedly removing the first element if it starts with "A." The alternative solution, however, has its own pitfall: The algorithm can fail if a test for s being empty isn't done for each iteration of the while loop.

## Scoring Rubric: Word Set

| Part (a) | countA | 6 points |
| --- | --- | --- |
| +1 | use a count variable (declare, initialize, return) | |
| +1 | loop over the word set using findkth | |
| +1 | findkth(count + 1) | |
| +1 | substring(0, 1) | |
| +1 | equals("A") | |
| +1 | update count | |

| Part (b) | removeA | 3 points |
| --- | --- | --- |
| +1 | call to countA | |
| +1 | for loop | |
| +1 | remove each word that starts with "A" | |

```
2.   public class Outfit extends ClothingItem
     {
         private Shoes shoes;
         private Pants pants;
         private Top top;

         public Outfit (Shoes aShoes, Pants aPants, Top aTop)
         {
             shoes = aShoes;
             pants = aPants;
             top = aTop;
         }

         public String getDescription()
         {
             return shoes.getDescription() + "/" + pants.getDescription()
                     + "/" + top.getDescription() + " outfit";
         }
     }
```

```
    public double getPrice()
    {
        if (shoes.getPrice() + pants.getPrice() >= 100
                ||shoes.getPrice() + top.getPrice() >= 100
                ||top.getPrice() + pants.getPrice() >= 100)
            return 0.75 * (shoes.getPrice() + pants.getPrice() +
                    top.getPrice());
        else
            return 0.90 * (shoes.getPrice() + pants.getPrice() +
                    top.getPrice());
    }
}
```

### Note

- To access the price and descriptions of items that make up an outfit, your class needs to have variables of type Shoes, Pants, and Top.
- The private instance variables in the Outfit class should not be of type String! Note that in that case, the ordering of the parameters—shoes, pants, and top—becomes irrelevant, and your solution violates the specification that a compile-time error occurs with different ordering of the parameters.

## Scoring Rubric: Clothing Item

|  | Outfit class | 9 points |
|---|---|---|
| +1 | class header with keyword extends | |
| +1 | private instance variables of types Shoes, Pants, and Top | |
| +1 | Outfit constructor with parameters of types Shoes, Pants, and Top | |
| +1 | assignment of instance variables in constructor | |
| +1 | getDescription header | |
| +1 | return concatenated string of outfit descriptions | |
| +1 | getPrice header | |
| +1 | test for amount of discount | |
| +1 | return corresponding price with correct discount | |

3.  (a) 
```
public void printNotes()
{
    int count = 1;
    for (Note note: noteList)
    {
        System.out.println(count + ". " + note.getNote());
        count++;
    }
}
```

Alternative solution for part (a):

```
public void printNotes()
{
    for (int index = 0; index < noteList.size(); index++)
        System.out.println(index + 1 + ". "
            + noteList.get(index).getNote());
}
```

(b)
```
public void removeNotes(String str)
{
    int index = 0;
    while (index < noteList.size())
    {
        String note = noteList. get(index).getNote();
        if (note.indexOf(str) == -1)
            index++;
        else
            noteList.remove(index);
    }
}
```

**Note**

- In part (b), you should increment the index only if you don't remove a note. This is because removing an element causes all notes following the removed item to shift one slot to the left. If, at the same time, the index moves to the right, you may miss elements that need to be removed.

## Scoring Rubric: Note Keeper

| Part (a) | printNotes | 4 points |
|---|---|---|
| +1 | initialize count of notes | |
| +1 | loop over notes in noteList | |
| +1 | print current number and corresponding note | |
| +1 | increment count | |

| Part (b) | removeNotes | 5 points |
|---|---|---|
| +1 | loop over notes in noteList | |
| +1 | get Note that corresponds to current index | |
| +1 | use getNote to access current note as string | |
| +1 | test whether parameter str is contained in current note | |
| +1 | remove note containing str | |

4. (a)
```
public boolean twoTogether()
{
    for (int r = 0; r < NUM_ROWS; r++)
        for (int c = 0; c < SEATS_PER_ROW-1; c++)
            if (seats[r][c] == 0 && seats[r][c+1] == 0)
            {
                seats[r][c] = 1;
                seats[r][c+1] = 1;
                return true;
            }
    return false;
}
```

```
(b) public int findAdjacent(int row, int seatsNeeded)
    {
        int index = 0, count = 0, lowIndex = 0;
        while (index < SEATS_PER_ROW)
        {
            while (index < SEATS_PER_ROW && seats[row][index] == 0)
            {
                count++;
                index++;
                if (count == seatsNeeded)
                    return lowIndex;
            }
            count = 0;
            index++;
            lowIndex = index;
        }
        return -1;
    }
```

**Note**

- In part (a), you need the test c < SEATS_PER_ROW-1, because when you refer to seats[r][c+1], you must worry about going off the end of the row and causing an ArrayIndexOutOfBounds exception.
- In part (b), every time you increment index, you need to test that it is in range. This is why you need this test twice: index < SEATS_PER_ROW.
- In part (b), every time you reset the count, you need to reset the lowIndex, because this is the value you're asked to return.
- In parts (a) and (b), the final return statements are executed only if all rows in the show have been examined unsuccessfully.

## Scoring Rubric: Theater Seats

| Part (a) | twoTogether | 4 points |
|---|---|---|
| +1 | traverse all seats | |
| +1 | test for two adjacent empty seats | |
| +1 | assign seats as taken | |
| +1 | return false if two together not found | |

| Part (b) | findAdjacent | 5 points |
|---|---|---|
| +1 | nested loop to search for seats together | |
| +1 | range check for seats[row][index] | |
| +1 | update counts for inner and outer loops | |
| +1 | update indexes for inner and outer loops | |
| +1 | test count to see if number of seats needed has been found | |

# Appendix: Glossary of Useful Computer Terms

*I hate definitions.*
*—Benjamin Disraeli*, Vivian Grey *(1826)*

**API library:** Applications Program Interface library. A library of classes for use in other programs. The library provides standard interfaces that hide the details of the implementations.

**Applet:** A graphical Java program that runs in a web browser or applet viewer.

**Application:** A stand-alone Java program stored in and executed on the user's local computer.

**Binary number system:** Base 2.

**Bit:** From "binary digit." Smallest unit of computer memory, taking on only two values, 0 or 1.

**Buffer:** A temporary storage location of limited size. Holds values waiting to be used.

**Byte:** Eight bits. Similarly, megabyte (MB, $10^6$ bytes) and gigabyte (GB, $10^9$ bytes).

**Bytecode:** Portable (machine-independent) code, intermediate between source code and machine language. It is produced by the Java compiler and interpreted (executed) by the Java Virtual Machine.

**Cache:** A small amount of "fast" memory for the storage of data. Typically, the most recently accessed data from disk storage or "slow" memory is saved in the main memory cache to save time if it's retrieved again.

**Cloud computing:** A new form of Internet-based computing that shares data and computer processing resources on demand.

**Compiler:** A program that translates source code into object code (machine language).

**CPU:** The central processing unit (computer's brain). It controls the interpretation and execution of instructions. It consists of the arithmetic/logic unit, the control unit, and some memory, usually called "on-board memory" or cache memory. Physically, the CPU consists of millions of microscopic transistors on a chip.

**Cyberspace:** An abstract environment in which any communication with the Internet occurs.

**Debugger:** A program that helps find errors by tracing the values of variables in a program.

**Decimal number system:** Base 10.

**GUI:** Graphical user interface.

**Hardware:** The physical components of computers. These are the ones you can touch, for example, the keyboard, monitor, printer, CPU chip.

**Hertz (Hz):**  One cycle per second.  It refers to the speed of the computer's internal clock and gives a measure of the CPU speed.  Similarly, megahertz (MHz, $10^6$ Hz) and gigahertz (GHz, $10^9$ Hz).

**Hexadecimal number system:**  Base 16.

**High-level language:**  A human-readable programming language that enables instructions that require many machine steps to be coded concisely, for example, Java, C++, Pascal, BASIC, FORTRAN.

**HTML:**  Hypertext Markup Language.  The instructions read by web browsers to format web pages, link to other websites, and so on.

**IDE:**  Integrated Development Environment.  Provides tools such as an editor, compiler, and debugger that work together, usually with a graphical interface.  Used for creating software in a high-level language.

**Interpreter:**  A program that reads instructions that are not in machine language and executes them one at a time.

**Javadoc:**  A program that extracts comments from Java source files and produces documentation files in HTML. These files can then be viewed with a web browser.

**JavaScript:**  (Not to be confused with Java, the programming language.)  A dynamic programming language most commonly used as part of web browsers.

**JVM (Java Virtual Machine):**  An interpreter that reads and executes Java bytecode on any local machine.

**Linker:**  A program that links together the different modules of a program into a single executable program after they have been compiled into object code.

**Low-level language:**  Assembly language.  This is a human-readable version of machine language, where each machine instruction is coded as one statement.  It is translated into machine language by a program called an assembler.  Each different kind of CPU has its own assembly language.

**Mainframe computer:**  A large computer, typically used by large institutions, such as government agencies and big businesses.

**Malware:**  (Short for malicious software.) Any software designed to disrupt computer operation or gain access to private computer systems. For example, viruses, spyware, ransomware, etc.

**Microcomputer:**  Personal computer.

**Minicomputer:**  Small mainframe.

**Mobile app:**  Software designed to run on smartphones and other mobile devices.

**Modem:**  A device that connects a computer to a phone line or TV cable.

**Network:**  Several computers linked together so that they can communicate with each other and share resources.

**Object code:**  Machine language. Produced by compiling source code.

**Octal number system:**  Base 8.

**Operating system:** A program that controls access to and manipulation of the various files and programs on the computer. It also provides the interface for user interaction with the computer. Some examples: Windows, MacOS, and Linux.

**Primary memory:** RAM. This gets erased when you turn off your computer.

**RAM:** Random Access Memory. This stores the current program and the software to run it.

**ROM:** Read Only Memory. This is permanent and nonerasable. It contains, for example, programs that boot up the operating system and check various components of the hardware. In particular, ROM contains the BIOS (Basic Input Output System)—a program that handles low-level communication with the keyboard, disk drives, and so on.

**SDK:** Sun's Java Software Development Kit. A set of tools for developing Java software.

**Secondary memory:** Hard drive, disk, magnetic tapes, CD-ROM, and so on.

**Server:** The hub of a network of computers. Stores application programs, data, mail messages, and so on, and makes them available to all computers on the network.

**Software:** Computer programs written in some computer language and executed on the hardware after conversion to machine language. If you can install it on your hard drive, it's software (e.g., programs, spreadsheets, word processors).

**Source code:** A program in a high-level language like Java, C++, Pascal, or FORTRAN.

**Swing:** A Java toolkit for implementing graphical user interfaces.

**Transistor:** Microscopic semiconductor device that can serve as an on-off switch.

**URL:** Uniform Resource Locator. An address of a web page.

**USB flash drive:** A removable and rewritable device that fits into a USB port of a computer.

**Virus:** A computer program that can replicate itself and spread from one computer to another. A form of malware.

**Web app:** Software designed to run inside a web browser.

**Web browser:** A software application for finding and presenting information on the web.

**Workstation:** Desktop computer that is faster and more powerful than a microcomputer.

# Index